Perspectives and Strategies of Family Business Resiliency in Unprecedented Times

Hotniar Siringoringo
Gunadarma University, Indonesia

Ravindra Hewa Kuruppuge
University of Peradeniya, Sri Lanka

A volume in the Advances in Logistics, Operations, and Management Science (ALOMS) Book Series

IGI Global
PUBLISHER of TIMELY KNOWLEDGE

Published in the United States of America by
IGI Global
Business Science Reference (an imprint of IGI Global)
701 E. Chocolate Avenue
Hershey PA, USA 17033
Tel: 717-533-8845
Fax: 717-533-8661
E-mail: cust@igi-global.com
Web site: http://www.igi-global.com

Library of Congress Cataloging-in-Publication Data

Names: Siringoringo, Hotniar, 1965- editor. | Kuruppuge, Ravindra Hewa, 1975- editor.
Title: Perspectives and strategies of family business resiliency in unprecedented times / edited by Hotniar Siringoringo, Ravindra Hewa Kuruppuge.
Description: Hershey, PA : Business Science Reference, [2023] | Includes bibliographical references and index. | Summary: "This book is intended to provide relevant evidence and a theoretical framework of how a family business survives in difficult times such as an economic recession or a pandemic across countries. It will be written for researchers who want to improve their understanding of how a family business survives in difficult times across countries and for professionals as insightful information to run the business"-- Provided by publisher.
Identifiers: LCCN 2022046933 (print) | LCCN 2022046934 (ebook) | ISBN 9781668473948 (hardcover) | ISBN 9781668473955 (paperback) | ISBN 9781668473962 (ebook)
Subjects: LCSH: Family-owned business enterprises. | Family-owned business enterprises--Management. | Crisis management.
Classification: LCC HD62.25 .P47 2023 (print) | LCC HD62.25 (ebook) | DDC 338.7--dc23/eng/20220929
LC record available at https://lccn.loc.gov/2022046933
LC ebook record available at https://lccn.loc.gov/2022046934

This book is published in the IGI Global book series Advances in Logistics, Operations, and Management Science (ALOMS) (ISSN: 2327-350X; eISSN: 2327-3518)

British Cataloguing in Publication Data
A Cataloguing in Publication record for this book is available from the British Library.

For electronic access to this publication, please contact: eresources@igi-global.com.

Advances in Logistics, Operations, and Management Science (ALOMS) Book Series

John Wang
Montclair State University, USA

ISSN:2327-350X
EISSN:2327-3518

MISSION

Operations research and management science continue to influence business processes, administration, and management information systems, particularly in covering the application methods for decision-making processes. New case studies and applications on management science, operations management, social sciences, and other behavioral sciences have been incorporated into business and organizations real-world objectives.

The **Advances in Logistics, Operations, and Management Science** (ALOMS) Book Series provides a collection of reference publications on the current trends, applications, theories, and practices in the management science field. Providing relevant and current research, this series and its individual publications would be useful for academics, researchers, scholars, and practitioners interested in improving decision making models and business functions.

COVERAGE

- Networks
- Decision analysis and decision support
- Production Management
- Computing and information technologies
- Risk Management
- Political Science
- Organizational Behavior
- Marketing engineering
- Finance
- Information Management

The Advances in Logistics, Operations, and Management Science (ALOMS) Book Series (ISSN 2327-350X) is published by IGI Global, 701 E. Chocolate Avenue, Hershey, PA 17033-1240, USA, www.igi-global.com. This series is composed of titles available for purchase individually; each title is edited to be contextually exclusive from any other title within the series. For pricing and ordering information please visit http://www.igi-global.com/book-series/advances-logistics-operations-management-science/37170. Postmaster: Send all address changes to above address.

Titles in this Series

For a list of additional titles in this series, please visit: http://www.igi-global.com/book-series/

Futuristic Technology Perspectives on Entrepreneurship and Sustainable Innovation
Sanjay Misra (Ostfold University, Norway) Amit Jain (Amity University, India) Manju Kaushik (Amity University, India) and Chitreshh Banerjee (Amity University, India)
Business Science Reference • © 2023 • 300pp • H/C (ISBN: 9781668458716) • US $250.00

Cases on Managing Dairy Productive Chains
Eduardo Guilherme Satolo (São Paulo State University, Brazil) and Priscilla Ayllen Bustos Mac-Lean (São Paulo State University, Brazil)
Engineering Science Reference • © 2023 • 320pp • H/C (ISBN: 9781668454725) • US $235.00

Moving From R&D Development to Production and Sales in Start-Up Companies
Amiram Porath (APC, Israel)
Business Science Reference • © 2023 • 181pp • H/C (ISBN: 9781799856856) • US $195.00

Advanced Research and Real-World Applications of Industry 5.0
Mahmoud Numan Bakkar (Abu Dhabi Vocational Education and Training Institute (ADVETI), Institute of Applied Technology (IAT), UAE) and Elspeth McKay (Cogniware.com.au, Australia)
Business Science Reference • © 2023 • 315pp • H/C (ISBN: 9781799888055) • US $250.00

Cases on International Business Logistics in the Middle East
Islam Abdelbary (Arab Academy for Science, Technology, and Maritime Transport, Egypt & University of Plymouth, UK) Sandra Haddad (Arab Academy for Science, Technology, and Maritime Transport, Egypt) and Ghada Elkady (Arab Academy for Science, Technology, and Maritime Transport, Egypt)
Business Science Reference • © 2023 • 342pp • H/C (ISBN: 9781668446867) • US $240.00

Examining the Vital Financial Role of SMEs in Achieving the Sustainable Development Goals
Dalila Taleb (University of Abou Bakr Belkaïd, Algeria) Mohammed El Amine Abdelli (University of Brest, France) Afef Khalil (University of Tunis, Carthage, Tunisia) and Asma Sghaier (University of Sousse, Tunisia)
Business Science Reference • © 2023 • 275pp • H/C (ISBN: 9781668448342) • US $250.00

IGI Global
PUBLISHER of TIMELY KNOWLEDGE

701 East Chocolate Avenue, Hershey, PA 17033, USA
Tel: 717-533-8845 x100 • Fax: 717-533-8661
E-Mail: cust@igi-global.com • www.igi-global.com

Table of Contents

Detailed Table of Contents

A family business is a venture which is possessed and controlled by family members. Many family businesses were started from small scales and grow to become multinational companies, such as Walmart, Berkshire Hathaway, Ford Motor Company, etc. Family businesses have been proven play important roles in driving the global economy. This kind of business creates an average of 60% of jobs and contributes to global gross domestic product an average of 67%. During this economic crisis that is happening globally, family businesses have proven their resilience to the crisis.

The pandemic has had a very serious influence on the businesses, organizations, and on the everyday life of the population, though the impact may vary from region to region. In general, the pandemic brought unfavourable situations, though there are businesses that could take benefit from this "new normal" situation. The extent of the impact surely depends on the specific economic and social conditions of the region that determine the adaptability to the new tendencies. Regardless of the sector, or the size of the businesses, there is one thing in common: all the businesses had to be creative, innovative, and had to have a strategy for the short and middle term. In this chapter, the authors would like to provide a national-level overview of the

The Covid-19 pandemic has influenced the economy over the world. In Vietnam, Covid-19 emerged on January 23, 2020, and has encountered several outbreaks across the country, which has caused negative impacts on the economy. The Covid-19 has influenced all aspects of socio-economic life, creating difficulties for all businesses, especially small and medium family businesses (SMEs family businesses). SMEs account for most of Vietnam's firms and have important roles in the economy. Based on the current situation, the chapter explores the potential impacts of the Covid-19 pandemic outbreak on SME family businesses. Moreover, we discussed the strategies of SME family businesses and the government's policies during this period.

The Covid-19 pandemic brought about a major economic breakdown throughout the world due to the shutting down of businesses and organizations. Covid –19 took a toll on India also, the second-most populous country. In India, family-run businesses are the deep-rooted, oldest, and most widespread form of business ownership. Most family businesses, while keeping the welfare of their customers, employees, and communities in mind, have resorted to remote work and halting non-essential work. The government of India took measures mainly consisting of an increased moratorium period, corporate tax cuts, lower interest on delayed tax payments, extension in return filing deadline, and other policy decisions. This study discusses the impact of Covid-19 on family businesses and how family businesses cope with the shock to the system. In addition, it covers innovative and strategic solutions adopted by the family businesses as a shield to their business against the impact of the crisis and to grow progressively overcoming the pandemic situation.

The emergence of the novel Coronavirus disease (Covid-19) has changed our norms and lifestyles. In facing this crisis, businesses in general are often struggling to sustain their livelihood and legacy. For Chinese family dynasties that are in their third generations, i.e. YTL Corporation Berhad in Malaysia and Lippo Group in Indonesia, they are able to apply Christian ethics and xinyong "信用" virtues that enable longevity and fostering workplace innovation during the Covid-19 crisis. Christianity business ethics and xinyong practices can be connected through routine applications of Christ-centered decision-makings that are evident in business environments and social impacts. Nevertheless, integrating cultural norms and Chinese confucion virtues such as xinyong in family businesses can be challenging in ensuring the CFBs sustainability. Hence, this chapter sheds light on the journey of the two families' Chinese dynasties, as they apply Christian faith and xinyong along with impactful actions to develop new solutions leading to longevity.

The textile business is an excellent example for permanent transformations of the lifestyle of consumers. The first cycle in the Darwinism of the European textile sector was dominated by traders' knowledge about the sources of the product-materials and opportunities for processing. In a second phase covering the start of industrial mass-production and professional mass-distribution, outlets for textiles were established with benchmarks at high frequency spots in down-towns of acclomerations like Berlin, Cologne, London, or Paris. Department stores became the anchor of cities and for life-style driven citizens. In the third phasis the outlet-dominance is attacked by IT-driven businesses by the development of tools like the European article numbering-system, chips and QR-codes, clouds for big data and data mining, artificial intelligence, and virtual reality. For the textile traders it is an improvement of the efficiency by the ability to control the total supply chain electronically. Of course, this is resulting in big changes for the supply patterns.

The business succession is the most critical event in the life of a family business, and represents a challenging scenario for the decisions that must be made. It therefore becomes a strategic objective to avoid factors that can negatively influence the assessment of the situation by the actors involved. This chapter explores the cognitive mechanisms (biases) that influence the decision-making process at the basis of the business transmission. Although already known and empirically supported in many fields of business and management, these cognitive factors have systematically been overlooked by previous family business literature. By exploring how these biases play a role in affecting business succession planning, and by putting emphasis on the human nature of the decision process of the incumbent, this study adds new insights to recent succession literature that highlights the central role of the cognitive processes during family firm succession.

The COVID-19 pandemic affects all aspects of life for everyone in this world. In Indonesia, micro, small, and medium enterprises (MSMEs), which are mostly family businesses, are among the worst hit, since they do not have the stable capital backup as is the case in big enterprises. Since MSMEs contribute significantly to Indonesia's GDP, this problem needs government assistance for its recovery. Policies at several levels are put to practice and to be implemented. Digitalization of businesses has started even before the pandemic, and is more widely utilized in this condition. Therefore, the policies emphasize regulating the digitalization of MSMEs from the provision of the internet to accommodating their transactions.

The sudden spread of Covid-19 around the world is causing significant damages to the corporate sector. Family businesses are not an exception to the crisis. During a pandemic, one of the most distinctive traits of a family business may be to react effectively to keep the business afloat. Family firms have been exposed to be better equipped to survive periods of political uncertainty and natural disasters with the courses of a mix of long-term horizon, and social and political capital. Conceptually, little is still acknowledged about how they survive and sustain during the COVID-19 pandemic, and the implications of family control on the ability of firms to overcome a pandemic are unclear. The authors explore how family businesses in the floriculture sector in Sri Lanka react and cope with this unexpected crisis, COVID-19. This study reveals how institutional theory links with macro, micro, and meso levels of interactions, and the model offers a richer understanding of the survival, resilience, and renewal process of floriculture family businesses in Sri Lanka.

This chapter explores family business conditions during the COVID-19 pandemic. To fulfill this goal, data from Biro Pusat Statistik (Statistics Indonesia) and national/international mass media were used. More than 95% of business in Indonesia are family business. Family businesses based on scale vary from home industry, micro, small, medium, to the big corporations. Family businesses play an essential role in driving Indonesia's economy. Statistically, 80% of Indonesia's GNP is contributed by family businesses. In 2019 family businesses contributed to a GDP of 53.28%.

Preface

We give thanks to Almighty Lord for the abundant blessings upon us in completing this edited book. Unprecedented times, such as Coronavirus-19 (COVID-19) greatly impacted the economy since it has been set as pandemic by the WHO. In the present context even, mostly government policies around the world are addressing the COVID-19 pandemic by limiting economic activities. Closing the entrance from abroad even movements among cities in the same country disrupted the supply chain. Product and raw material distribution as the important part in the economic activities was hampered. In the same way, the movement of consumers was also hampered either because of the physical distancing policy or because consumers were afraid to go out of the house to shop. A similar problem was experienced by production entities in the world. Due to mobility restriction, non-vital manufactures had to close or producing in a small capacity.

These conditions certainly affect all companies either it is big corporation or home industry. The family business is the forerunner of most companies, including a big corporation, such as Kentucky Fried Chicken. Family business is an important economic driver over the world. So thus, the objective of this book was to provide comprehensive information of how family business survives and thrives during the COVID-19 pandemic. Accordingly, the book was titled as "Perspectives and Strategies of Family Business Resiliency in Unprecedented Times

This book refers to family businesses which represent more than 80% of all businesses in the world. Theoretically, it is proved that these businesses all over the world are suffering from survival issues. However, practically, evidence supports that family businesses do outperform other businesses. This book provides comprehensive information about family business from various countries such as Indonesia, Sri Lanka, Malaysia, India, Vietnam, Oman, Italy, Hungary, and Europe. To cover all the information, this edited book consists of 12 chapters.

The first chapter is the introduction contains the concept of family business, the role of family business in driving the economy, and un-precedented times and economy. We can find the information of how the Hungarian family businesses sustain during the COVID-19. One chapter from Oman discuss paradigm shift from traditional to communication and technology acceptance model for survival of family business. Reader also can find a discussion of family business survival strategy in COVID 19 pandemic in Malaysia. From context of Vietnam, the authors provide evidence the impact of COVID-19 pandemic on the small and medium family businesses which is another chapter of this book.

A chapter from India discuss how the family business cope with the crisis. One chapter discusses Christian Ethics and Xinyong practices leading to longevity post COVID-19 pandemic among Chinese family businesses in Indonesia and Malaysia. Another chapter discuss the long-term cycles of innovation in Europe's textile business. Reader also can find the discussion of cognitive biases affecting business transmission planning in family firms from a theoretical framework. The chapters from Indonesia discuss the digitalization as a part of policy implementation in overcoming COVID-19 pandemic, and the condition of family business during a pandemic. The chapters from Sri Lanka provides evidence how the floriculture sector turns covid-19 challenges into opportunities.

Chapter 1 talks about how a family business is a venture which is possessed and controlled by "family members". Many family businesses were started from small scale and grow to become multinational company, such as Walmart, Berkshire Hathaway, Ford Motor Company, etc. Family businesses have been proven play important role in driving economy globally. This kind of business creates an average of 60% of jobs and contributes to global gross domestic product an average of 67%. The family businesses have shown their resilience to crises. During the economic crisis that happens globally, family businesses have proven their resilience to the crisis. Similarly, during the covid-19 pandemic many family businesses still survive.

The pandemic has had a very serious influence on the businesses, organizations as well as on everyday life of the population, though the impact may vary from region to region. In general, the pandemic brought unfavourable situations, though there are businesses that could take benefit from this "new normal" situation. The extent of the impact surely depends on the specific economic and social conditions of the region that determine the adaptability to the new tendencies. Regardless of the sector, or the size of the businesses, there is one thing in common: all the businesses had to be creative, innovative and had to have a strategy for the short and middle term. In Chapter 2, we would like to provide a national-level overview of the economic and social impacts of the pandemic, the measures are taken to boost the economy. Secondly, we intend to provide a more targeted picture about the Hungarian family businesses, how they managed to survive and offset the unexpected impacts of the pandemic - based on primary research.

The deadly outbreak of different variants of COVID-19 has not only created havoc on millions of lives and public health but has severely impacted the global market and shattered many countries' economies. A general phenomenon of shortage in public income, rise in unemployment, and breakdown in manufacturing and service industries have been noticed worldwide. Transportation, tourism, and accommodation industries have been badly affected. Oman has not been exempted from COVID-19 mitigation measures. Through case studies, the authors explain the traditional resources of Omani family businesses and their adaptive approach to new media technology, resilience, and strategic communication to respond to the crisis created by the pandemic. Chapter 3 will contribute as a reference document for the researchers to conduct a comparative study.

The authors in Chapter 4 thoroughly discussed the financial mapping and strategies of family-owned businesses in Malaysia to tackle economic downturn brought by the COVID-19 pandemic. As most of the organizations in this nation are family-claimed, the financial execution of the privately-run companies in Malaysia draws a more prominent impact on its entire economy. Close by the financial hardships brought by consecutive lockdowns, Malaysian family-owned businesses were fighting with computerized upskilling as the interest in web-based business soar since the time individuals were locked inside their homes. Subsequently, that was something the older generations of the organization attempted to oversee since their customary technique for coordinating business had no hint of advanced innovations. Regardless, the youthful age of those families grasped the meaning of advancement and digitalization. They are presently more confident that their economic condition will improve in the event that they can figure out how to adjust to the ongoing industry climate.

The COVID-19 pandemic has influenced the economy over the world. In Vietnam, the COVID-19 emerged on January 23, 2020, and has encountered several outbreaks across the country, which has caused negative impacts on the economy. The COVID -19 has influenced all aspects of socio-economic life, creating difficulties for all businesses, especially small and medium family businesses (SMEs family businesses). SMEs account for most of Vietnam's firms and have important roles in the economy. Based on the current situation, Chapter 5 explores the potential impacts of the COVID-19 pandemic outbreak on SME family businesses. Moreover, we discussed the strategies of SME family businesses and the government's policies during this period.

Chapter 6 focuses on how the COVID-19 pandemic brought about a major economic breakdown throughout the world due to the shutting down of businesses and organizations. COVID-19 took a toll on India, the second-most populous country, also. In India, family-run businesses are the deep-rooted, oldest, and most widespread form of business ownership. Most family businesses, while keeping the welfare of their customers, employees, and communities in mind have resorted to remote work and halting non-essential work. The government of India took measures mainly consisting of an increased moratorium period, corporate tax cuts, lower interest on delayed tax payments, extension in return filing deadline, and other policy decisions. This study discusses the impact of COVID-19 on family businesses and how family businesses cope with the shock to the system. In addition, it covers innovative and strategic solutions adopted by the family businesses as a shield to their business against the impact of the crisis and to grow progressively overcoming the pandemic situation.

Chapter 7 speaks on how the emergence of the novel Coronavirus disease (COVID-19) has changed our norms and lifestyles. In facing this crisis, businesses in general are often struggling to sustain their livelihood and legacy. For Chinese family dynasties that are in their third generations, i.e., YTL Corporation Berhad in Malaysia and Lippo Group in Indonesia, they are able to apply Christian ethics and xinyong "信用" virtues that enable longevity and fostering workplace innovation during the COVID-19 crisis. Christianity business ethics and xinyong practices can be connected through routine applications of Christ-centered decision-makings that are evident in business environments and social impacts. Nevertheless, integrating cultural norms and Chinese Confucian virtues such as Xinyong in family businesses can be challenging in ensuring the CFBs sustainability. Hence, this chapter sheds light on the journey of the two families' Chinese dynasties, as they apply Christian faith and Xinyong along with impactful actions to develop new solutions leading to longevity.

Chapter 8 is about how the textile business is an excellent example for permanent transformations of the life-style of consumers. The first cycle in the Darwinism of the European textile sector was dominated by traders' knowledge about the sources of the product-materials and opportunities for processing. In a second phase covering the start of industrial mass-production and professional mass-distribution outlets for textiles were established with benchmarks at high frequency spots in down-towns of agglomerations like Berlin, Cologne, London, or Paris. Department stores became the anchor of cities and for life-style driven citizens. In the third phasis the outlet-dominance is attacked by IT-driven businesses by the development of tools like the European Article Numbering-system, chips and QR-codes, clouds for big data and data mining, artificial intelligence and virtual reality. For the textile traders it is an improvement of the efficiency by the ability to control the total supply chain electronically. Of course, this is resulting in big changes for the supply patterns.

The business succession is the most critical event in the life of a family business and represents a challenging scenario for the decisions that must be made. It therefore becomes a strategic objective to avoid factors that can negatively influence the assessment of the situation by the actors involved. Chapter 9 explores the cognitive mechanisms (biases) that influence the decision-making process at the basis of the business transmission. Although already known and empirically supported in many fields of business and management, these cognitive factors have systematically been overlooked by previous family business literature. By exploring how these biases play a role in affecting business succession planning, and by putting emphasis on the human nature of the decision process of the incumbent, this study adds new insights to recent succession literature that highlights the central role of the cognitive processes during family firm succession.

The COVID-19 pandemic affected all aspects of life of everyone in this world. In Indonesia, micro, small, and medium enterprises (MSMEs), which are mostly family businesses, are among the worst hit, since they do not have the stable capital backup as the case in big enterprises. Since MSMEs contribute significantly to Indonesia's GDP, this problem needs government assistance for its recovery. Policies at several levels are put to practice and to be implemented. Chapter 10 looks at how digitalization of businesses has started even before the pandemic and is more widely utilized in this condition. Therefore, the policies emphasize on regulating the digitalization of MSMEs from the provision of the Internet to accommodating their transactions.

In Chapter 11, we know that the sudden spread of COVID-19 around the world is causing significant damages to the corporate sector. Family businesses are not an exception to the crisis. During a pandemic, one of the most distinctive traits of a family business may be to react effectively to keep the business afloat. Family firms have been exposed to be better equipped to survive periods of political uncertainty and natural disasters with the courses of a mix of long-term horizon, and social and political capital. Conceptually, little is still acknowledged about how they survive and sustain during the COVID-19 pandemic and the implications of family control on the ability of firms to overcome a pandemic are unclear. We explore how family businesses in the floriculture sector in Sri Lanka react and cope with this unexpected crisis, COVID-19. Our study reveals how institutional theory links with macro, micro, and meso levels of interactions and the model offers a richer understanding of the survival, resilience, and renewal process of floriculture family businesses in Sri Lanka.

Chapter 12 contributes to providing family business conditions during the COVID-19 pandemic. To fulfill this goal, data from Biro Pusat Statistik (Statistics Indonesia) and national/international mass media. More than 95% of business in Indonesia is family business. These family businesses vary from the home industry to big corporations. Family businesses based on scale vary from home industry, micro, small, medium to the big corporation. Family businesses play an essential role in driving Indonesia's economy. Statistically, 80% of Indonesia's GNP is contributed by family businesses. In 2019 family businesses contributed to a GDP of 53.28%.

This book comprises the thoughts of many experts from different countries. For that please allow us to express our deepest gratitude to the contributors of the chapter, Dr. Misdiyono and Dr. Sri Murtiasih from Indonesia, Prof. Henrietta

Nagy and Izabella Oláh from Hungray, Dr. Tripathi Sangeeta and Dr. Al Shahri Muna from Oman, Mr. Md Tanvir Alam Tonmoy and Dr. Narentheren Kaliappen from Malaysia, Dr. Nhan Thi Thanh Do, Dr. suu Duy Nguyen, Dr. Oanh Kieu Le Dao, and Ms. Trang Ngoc Thuy Le from Vietnam, Dr. Garima Madan Dua, Dr. Gaurva Gupta, Divya Jain, and Kanhiya Garg from India, Dr. Dr Lee Kean Yew from Malaysia, Dr. Jacob Donald Tan from Indonesia, Prof. Bernd Hallier from Germany, Dr. Violena Hubenova Nencheva from Mexico, Dr. Filippo Ferrari from Italy, Yuhilza Hanum from Indonesia, Dr. Kanchana Wijayawardena, Dr. Chandra Padmini, and Dr. Vilani Sachitra from Sri Lanka, Prof. Dr. E.S. Margianti and Dr. Sudaryanto from Indonesia. Our deepest gratitude is also addressed to Elizabeth Barrantes, Assistant Development Editor of IGI who continuously support us in whole processes. Without her advice and support it will be impossible to complete this edited book. Lastly but not the least, we express our deepest gratitude to the IGI Global publisher for giving us an opportunity to collaborate in publishing this edited book.

Hotniar Siringoringo
Gunadarma University, Indonesia

Ravindra Hewa Kuruppuge
University of Peradeniya, Sri Lanka

Chapter 1
Introduction

Hotniar Siringoringo
Gunadarma University, Indonesia

Ravindra H. Kuruppuge
Peradeniya University, Sri Lanka

Misdiyono Misdiyono
Gunadarma University, Indonesia

Sri Murtiasih
Gunadarma University, Indonesia

ABSTRACT

A family business is a venture which is possessed and controlled by family members. Many family businesses were started from small scales and grow to become multinational companies, such as Walmart, Berkshire Hathaway, Ford Motor Company, etc. Family businesses have been proven play important roles in driving the global economy. This kind of business creates an average of 60% of jobs and contributes to global gross domestic product an average of 67%. During this economic crisis that is happening globally, family businesses have proven their resilience to the crisis.

DOI: 10.4018/978-1-6684-7394-8.ch001

INTRODUCTION

The Concept of Family Business

Scholars most likely will be agree when someone state that the "family businesses" contribute to the economy and community significantly around the world. Evidently, many scholars showed the family businesses as nation gross domestic product (GDP) driver. This fact motivates scholars (both practitioners and researchers) and policymakers to study FB. According to Chua et al. (1999) "family business" is a venture which is possessed and controlled by "family members". Similar to this, a family business (FB) can be described as a company (from home industry to big corporation) which its capital majority own by a family member (Rosenblatt et al., 1985; Dede & Ayranci, 2014) and key decision makers are family members (Rosenblatt et al., 1985). Further, scholars described that a business can be categorized as FB if there are multi-generation and dominant family elements that guarantee distinctive dynamics and sustainable relationships in FB (Chaudhary & Batra, 2018; Hussain & Ismail, 2015).

We can also view an FB as "a company where the voting majority is in the hands of the controlling family; including the founder(s) who intend to pass the business on to their descendants" (International Finance Corporation (IFC), 2018, p. 13). FB is a profit-seeking business. The character of a "family" business will remain attached to a business even though the business may have been managed by a CEO who is not a family member, but majority of the stock are still possessed by members of the company's founding family. Although the CEO is not a family member but as the main shareholder, they play a role in the decision-making process as well as in forming and formulating the vision and mission of the business (Lee et al., 2017; Mukarram et al., 2018; Panicker, 2017; Ye et al., 2019). Based on the above definition, we may argue an FB is not always managed by family members, but they possess most of its capital.

THE ROLE OF FAMILY BUSINESS IN DRIVING THE ECONOMY

Family businesses play a significant role in the national economies around the world (Sharma et al., 2001; Astrachan & Shanker, 2003; Siakas et al., 2014; Mathews & Blumentritt, 2015; Sarbah & Xiao, 2015; Pipatanantakurn & Ractham, 2016; De Massis et al., 2018; Andrews, 2020; Miroshnychenko et al., 2020) by creating jobs and generating wealth (Songini & Gnan, 2015; Randerson et al., 2015). The family businesses absorb a large number of workers and produce output for economic growth (Collins & O'Regan, 2011; Liñán et al., 2019; Paul, 2020).

Aside from its contribution, FB shows better growth than non-FB. For instance, Miroshnychenko et al. (2021) performed a study across 43 countries during a 10-year period. They showed that family business has higher growth on average compared to non-family business. According to IFC (2018) more than 70% of business in the world is in the form of family businesses, creates an average of 60% of jobs, and contributes to global gross domestic product an average of 67%.

Fromthepointofviewofjobscreation,basedonWikipediadata,Walmarthas2.3million employees, Berkshire Hathaway has 360,000 employees, and The Ford Motor company has 186,000 employees (https://en.wikipedia.org/wiki/List_of_the_largest_family_bus inesses - access 7th January 2022). According to McKenzie data, measured using the gross domestic product (GDP), a family business generates revenue of approximately 1 billion USD on average. This figure place family business as 80 percent contributor to the world's GDP. Along with it, Rivo-López et al (2021) stated family business contributes to human welfare and happiness by providing job stability. Being able to survive in a crisis means providing job stability for its employees.

The role of a family business in driving the national economy and the world economy is evident from the evolution of business size. Many largest corporations start from a family business and still manage until the second generation of the family. Fifty largest family businesses around the world based on revenue (https://en.wikipedia.org/wiki/List_of_the_largest_family_bus inesses - access 7th January 2022), sequentially starting from the highest revenue to the lowest is shown in Table 1. Among them, 14 companies in the USA, 7 in Germany, 6 in France, 4 in South Korea, three in India, two in China, two in Switzerland, two in Canada, one in Luxembourg, one in Brazil, one in Mexico, one in Belgium, one in Japan, one in Denmark, one in Hongkong, one in the Netherlands, and one in Spain. The first 10 biggest are located in The USA (rank no 1, 2, 5, 7, 8, 9, and 10), Italy (rank no 3), and Germany (rank no. 4 and 6).

Of those fifty largest family businesses, three of them are listed in the 50 largest companies in the world based on revenue. They are Walmart, Berkshire Hathaway, and Ford Motor Company (https://en.wikipedia.org/wiki/List_of_largest_companies_by_r evenue). Walmart is the largest family business as well as the largest company in the world based on revenue.

Table 1. Fifty largest family business based on revenue

Rank	Name	Rank	Name	Rank	Name	Rank	Name
1	The Walmart	14	Country Garden	27	Midea Group	40	C.K. Hutchison Holdings
2	Berkshire Hathaway	15	Schaeffler Group	28	Tyson Foods	41	L'Oréal
3	Exor	16	Roche Holding	29	Idemitsu Kōsan	42	Louis Dreyfus Company
4	Schwarz Group	17	LG Corporation	30	Groupe Casino	43	Phoenix Pharmahandel
5	Ford Motor Company	18	LVMH	31	A. P. Møller-Mærsk	44	Penske Corporation
6	BMW	19	George Weston Limited	32	Power Corporation of Canada	45	CMA CGM
7	Koch Industries	20	Aditya Birla Group	33	Auchan	46	HE Butt Grocery
8	Cargill	21	ArcelorMittal	34	Nike	47	Mercadona
9	Comcast	22	JBS S.A.	35	Mars Incorporated	48	Bolloré
10	Dell Technologies	23	América Móvil	36	Aldi	49	Pilot Flying J.
11	Robert Bosch GmbH	24	Gunvor	37	Reyes Holdings	50	CJ Group
12	Reliance Industries	25	Anheuser-Busch InBev	38	Tata Motors		
13	SK Group	26	Hanwha Group	39	Porsche		

UNPRECEDENTED TIME AND THE ECONOMY

Humans have repeatedly experienced unprecedented times. Many factors gave rise to an unprecedented time, such as war, disease, politics, and others. Large-scale wars have occurred twice in this world, that were world war 1 and world war 2. The impact of world wars 1 and 2 on humanity and the economy has been widely conveyed in written form, missing family members, hunger, poverty, etc.

The war that recently occurred between Russia and Ukraine did not only have an impact on humanity and the economy in the two countries, but also had an economic impact on other countries, especially countries in Europe. The war started on 24 February 2022 and the end is yet to be seen. Astrov et al. (2022) assessed the impact of Russia-Ukraine war on humanitarian, economic, and financial in the short and medium term. They showed both Russia and Ukraine experience continuous bad economic growth in short and medium term. For Russia due to economic isolation and for Ukraine due to people migration and infrastructure destruction. For the EU, the Russian invasion causing high inflation especially in Central and Eastern Europe (Turkey, Czech Republic, Slovakia, Hungary, Poland, and Slovenia).

Wars don't just happen between countries. The world has also experienced terrorist attacks that have had an impact on humanity and the economy. Terrorist attacks occur in various countries. There are several terrorist attacks that are considered the most violent because they killed many people. The most difficult terrorist attacks to be forgotten by humans is probably the September 11, 2001 in New York City, United States of America, which destroyed the Twin Towers of the World Trade Center within 2 hours with around 3,000 deaths.

The four incidents in Iraq in 2007, 2013, 2014 and 2016 are also hard to forget because people suffered heavy casualties. The four incidents are included in the 10 terrorist attacks in the world with the most victims. The first attack kills the second most (after the world trade center twin tower). August 14, 2007, was the Yazidi settlement bombing that killed 2,996 people. The second attack in July 2013 killed 389 people. The third attack occurred May 15-21, 2014, killing 500 people. The fourth attack that occurred in Baghdad July 3, 2016, killed 341 people.

In Indonesia terrorist attacks have occurred frequently since the 1980s. The darkest was the incident in Bali, October 12, 2002. This attack killed 203 people. This incident is included in the 10 terrorist attacks in the world with the most victims. The terrorist attack on August 19, 1978 in Iran is ranked 4th based on the death toll. The attack occurred when hundreds of people were watching in a cinema and resulted in the death of 422 people. The terrorist attacks in Trujillo, Colombia in 1988 and 1994 killed 400 people. Russia is also not free from terrorist attacks. A total of 385 people died on September 1, 2004 due to a terrorist attack causing the incident to be the 7th highest based on the death toll. In Nigeria on 5-6 May 2014 terrorist killed 336 people putting this attack into 9th position based on the number of victims. The 10th mass murder due to terrorists occurred on Air India 1985 which killed 329 passengers.

These terrorist attacks not only result in deaths but also affect the economy. The significance of the influence of terrorist attacks on the world economy is still being debated. Some claim that although there is an effect, it is small enough to be insignificant (such as Becker & Murphy, 2001). But other scholars show that terrorist attacks have a significant impact on the economy, at least in countries that are victims of terrorists (such as Abadie & Gardeazabal, 2003; Chen & Siems, 2004; Enders & Sandler, 1996; Pshisva & Suarez, 2006; Abadie & Gardeazabal, 2008; Bardwell & Iqbal, 2020).

Over two decades of terrorist attacks in Basque country, Abadie and Gardeazabal (2003) found the decrease of gross domestic product per capita to a 10%. This statistic shows the massive impact of terrorist attacks on country economic. Enders and Sandler (1996) as well as Abadie and Gardeazabal (2008) showed the impact of terrorist attacks on economy through the decreasing of foreign direct investment. Enders and Sandler (1996) showed the evidence in Spain (during the period of 1976-1991) and in Greece (during the period of 1975-1991). Whilst Abadie and Gardeazabal (2008) showed the evidence in 196 countries.

Bardwell and Iqbal (2020) studied the effect of terrorism on economic during 2000 until 2018. As many as eight of the biggest terrorist attacks were recorded during the period 2000-2018 as mentioned above. According to Bardwell and Iqbal (2020) massive economic impact occurred until 2014 worth of $US 111 billion. More than 36% ($US 40.6 billion) of this economic lost due to the September 11, 2001, terrorist attacks in the USA; whilst around 4% ($US 4.3 billion) of this economic lost due to August 14, 2007 terrorist attacks in Iraq.

Surprisingly, Shahbaz (2013) found that good economic growth enhances terrorism maneuvers in Pakistan. It shows that economic growth and terrorist activities is bi-directional relationship. Terrorist can take advantage from good economy growth to support procurement their equipment and other resources. Conversely, low economy growth and poverty may trigger the emergence of terrorism. Poor people will be easily recruited to becomes terrorist.

Pandemic (epidemic) also affects humanity and economic globally. Pandemic has occurred a few times in the world. Based on literature (Perry & Fetherston, 1997; Riedel, 2005; Glatter & Finkelman, 2021), before the coronavirus 19 (covid-19) outbreak, there have been three pandemic periods caused by viruses or bacteria. There is no exact figure for the number of deaths worldwide during the three pandemic periods, but it is estimated that more than 200 million died during the three pandemic periods. The first epidemic that is called as "Justinian plague" happen in year of 541-542 was suspected originates from India (Glatter & Finkelman, 2021) or Egypt (Riedel, 2005) and reaches Constantinople. The second epidemic that is known as "the black death" happen around 1346-1353 (Benedictow, 2004) and recorded as the most fatal pandemic in human history, engender the mortality of 25 million people only in Europe (Glatter & Finkelman, 2021). The black death lasted more than 130 years (Riedel, 2005).

The Yunnan Province in southeast China is the origin of the third pandemic that happen around the year of 1855 although the outbreaks had started since 1772 (Riedel, 2005). Probably this pandemic is the longest ever until now since it lasted up to the year of 1950. Total death due to this pandemic in India during 1898 until 1918 is recorded 12 million deaths. The current pandemic that started end of 2019 in Wuhan China is considered as the worst post World War II (Huynh, 2020). The current pandemic is known as coronavirus disease of 2019 (covid-19) that caused by the spread of virus variants of SARS-COV-2. Its spread is very fast due to high mobility of people globally. Even in 2021, the world is shocked by the latest variants that are easier to infect and even more deadly.

Since the first wave at the end of 2019, various predictions regarding the end of the spread of Covid-19 have been debunked. The promising hope appears at the end of 2022 that this pandemic will soon end as endemic. During these three years pandemic, 6,826,716 deaths accounted and 683,287,033 cases globally (https://www.worldometers.info/coronavirus, accessed on 26th March 2023). Based on death statistics, the covid-19 pandemic is categorized as milder than three previous pandemics.

The covid-19 pandemic has influenced almost all activities in all countries over the world. The impact of the pandemic on the social and economic activities of countries has been reported from all over the world. The impact on the economic globally not only due to cessation of many economic activities in implementing lockdown or social distancing but also the need for expenditure to handle the covid-19 patients. The implementation of lockdown or social distancing for months has caused many productive activities to be closed. Economic turnover does not occur. Shopping centers, restaurants, hotels, cinemas, tourist attractions, travel, and other productive businesses were forced to close. The closure was not only due to the government's lockdown or social distancing policy but also because of the huge cost to keep doing activities.

The closure of various activities for months led to the loss of consumers. Declining consumer purchasing power has pushed many economic activities to close. Even though the company remains open during the social distancing or lockdown period, operational costs are very expensive which causes the company to become un-competitive. Additional operational costs are needed to prevent employees from contracting the Covid-19 virus by changing the work environment and providing medical equipment such as room sprays, masks, vitamins, and others.

Economic condition during the unprecedented times can be figured out from different aspects. Abadie and Gardeazabal (2008) described terrorist risks is related with net foreign direct investment (FDI). When the terrorist risk is high the net FDI will decrease. Many scholars studied the impact of the latest global financial crisis and the covid-19 pandemic on economic. Cheema et al. (2022) described the economic situation during the financial crisis and the covid-19 pandemic using stock market "the safe heaven". "The safe heaven" in this term is "precious metals, currencies, US treasures, and corporate bonds". Precious metal analyzed is gold and silver. Only two currencies analyzed, those are US dollar and Swiss franc.

The observed US Treasuries capital markets are T-bills and T-bonds. Meanwhile, the corporate bonds being analyzed are AAA-grade. Cheema et al. (2022) concluded that during global financial crisis in the year 2008, the US dollar, the Swiss franc and T-bonds (gold, silver and T-bills) serve as an weak intermediaries. During the covid-19 pandemic, Cheema et al. (2022) found gold becomes a very risky asset in stock market, especially in China and Japan. Meanwhile silver is becoming riskier in all countries. They found that gold, silver, US dollar, and T-bonds get weaker during the covid-19 pandemic compared to global financial crisis.

Shibata (2021) compared the effect of global financial crisis and the covid-19 pandemic on economy of the USA. The indicators deployed are 1). "worker characteristics", 2). "job characteristics–social", "tele-workable", and "essential" jobs, and 3) "wage distributions". Their results show the different between the global financial crisis and covid-19 pandemic impact in terms of age, education, gender, and ethnic group. In global financial crisis, youth and low education employees are affected more. Meanwhile in the covid-19 pandemic, "women" and "Hispanics" are influenced more severely. Surprisingly, "teleworkable", social and essential jobs have been historically less cyclical. This historical a-cyclicality of "teleworkable" occupations is attributable to its higher share of skilled workers. Unlike during the global financial crisis, however, employment in social industries fell more whereas employment in "teleworkable" and essential jobs fell less during the pandemic crisis. During both recessions, workers at low-income earnings have suffered more than top-income earners, suggesting a significant distributional impact of the two recessions. Lastly, a large share of unemployed persons was on temporary layoff during the covid-19 recession, unlike the global financial crisis.

Whilst Shibata (2021) compared the USA economic on global financial crisis and the covid-19 pandemic, Yousaf et al. (2022) analyzed the GCC (Saudi Arabia, UAE, Qatar, Kuwait, Oman, and Bahrain) economics post global financial crisis and the covid-19 pandemic. The stock market was the object of their analysis. They use return and volatility spill overs indicators in analyzing the stock market condition. They provided evidence that return and volatility spill overs significantly increase on global financial crisis and the covid-19 pandemic.

Wahidin et al. (2021) studied the economic situation before and after the global financial crisis using the bond market's. They showed the "bond market's" influence "economic growth" positively before the crisis. The key financial-growth sources through which carry on from the "bond market" are ultimately distributed to the most prolific investments emerge to be disconnected after the crisis.

The condition of a family business during a crisis is complicated to describe. During a pandemic, some family business can be very resilient and socially responsible which are successful both for themselves and for other stakeholders. The ability to survive in difficult times is also possible because family businesses develop "human", "financial", "reputational", and "relational capital" as a long-term orientation and desire for family continuity in business (Le Breton-Miller & Miller, 2022). Whilst Conz et al. (2020) stated the ability of the family businesses to survive can be happen because of "proactive development", "predictive control", "adaptive consolidation", and "stable perpetuation".

Family businesses as the driver of most of the country's economy over the world (Andrews, 2020) are also not spared from the impact of the coronavirus pandemic. Siringoringo and Kuruppuge (2021) for instance showed the covid-19 pandemic affects country economic growth. Although the density of covid-19 transmission is not the same in the two countries and the policies adopted to overcome the situation are also different, both countries experience a very sharp decline in economic growth. Sri Lanka experienced sharp decline in economic growth in the first quarter of 2020 while Indonesia experience negative economic growth in the second quarter of 2020.

The family businesses have shown their resilience to crises. During the economic crisis that happens globally, family businesses have proven their resilience to the crisis. What are the factors that support the family business to survive the storm of crisis? Extensive research has been performed in studying the key factors of success of a family business not only its survival in the crisis but also its growth in a competitive environment. The factors identified as playing an important role in the resilience of family businesses to crises and grow in a competitive environment ranging from internal to external factors.

To successfully survive and grow, family businesses should receive and keep up with a competitive advantage that directs to superior performance. This competitive advantage is formed by various conditions and factors, such as "national institution environment" and "family control" (Miroshnychenko et al., 2021), family governance mechanism (Cicek et al, 2020), the involvement and the interaction of family members (Andrews, 2020; Habbershon & Williams, 1999; Habbershon et al., 2003), technology adoption (Wielsma and Brunninge, 2019; Rashid & Ratten, 2020), etc. Miroshnychenko et al. (2021) showed that the good governance of the national government plays an important role in supporting the growth and competitiveness of family businesses. National environments such as "less corruption", "more democratic", "more subject to rule of law", and "effective government policies" support the success of a family business.

Related to family control, Miroshnychenko et al. (2021) showed that "family control has an economically significant impact on growth rates and important implications for both family firm theory and practice". Cicek et al. (2021) stated that the achievement of "family business" is influenced by "family governance mechanisms". They showed that family meetings enact a key role in the success of a family business. The most important of family meetings indicators are soft relational and qualitative issues.

Corporate entrepreneurship is an indicator of family business success. When corporate entrepreneurship is going well, the performance of the family business will certainly increase. Corporate entrepreneurship at another side is affected by various factors such as socioemotional wealth, family identity, and social ties (Saleem et al., 2020).

Accordingly, Andrews (2020) stated that majority of family business employees are members of the family in 62% of family businesses. Family business competitive advantage can be achieved because it has picturesque assets and capability, which is derived from the interaction between the family and the business (Habbershon and Williams, 1999; Habbershon et al., 2003). The interaction of family and management is important in family business sustainability. Another big challenge in a family business is the succession of family businesses between generations and the transfer of core business values.

Technology also plays an important role in the survival of a family business, especially in the era of the covid-19 pandemic. Micro and small businesses which are the most common form of early family business struggle to overcome the barriers to using technology, either because of not having competent resources or because of the costs of procuring technology (Rashid and Rattern, 2020). Especially in the era of digitation (Wielsma and Brunninge, 2019) and the covid-19 pandemic, mastery and use of digital technology are absolute.

The family businesses experienced ups and downs as happen with other businesses type. The ups and downs of FB are not only happened during unprecedented times but also in regular period. Cho et al. (2018) provides an overview of the relationship between ownership and business continuity in the context of SME family businesses. The continuity of a family business in the form of an SME has an "inverted U-shape curve linear" relationship with family ownership. If the SME CEO comes from a family, then there is an inverted U-shaped relationship between family ownership and SME survival. Positive effects will increase at low levels of family ownership while negative effects will increase at high levels of family ownership. In the case of the CEO being the next generation of family members, the negative effects of high levels of family ownership will be very strong.

REFERENCES

Abadiea, A., & Gardeazabal, J. (2008). Terrorism and the world economy. *European Economic Review*, *52*(1), 1–27. doi:10.1016/j.euroecorev.2007.08.005

Andrews, P. (2020). Globally Most Businesses Are Family Owned. *Family Business United.* https://familybusinessunited.com/2020/10/27/globally-most-businesses-are-family-owned/

Astrov, V., Ghodsi, M., Grieveson, R., Holzner, M., Kochnev, A., Landesmann, M., Pindyuk, O., Stehrer, R., Tverdostup, M., & Bykova, A. (2022). Russia's invasion of Ukraine: Assessment of the humanitarian, economic, and financial impact in the short and medium term. *International Economics and Economic Policy*, *19*(2), 331–381. doi:10.100710368-022-00546-5

Bardwell, H., & Iqbal, M. (2020). The Economic Impact of Terrorism from 2000 to 2018. *Peace Economics, Peace. Science & Public Policy*, *27*(2), 227–261.

Benedictow, O. J. (2004). The Black Death 1346-1353: The Complete History. Boydell Press.

Campopiano, G., De Massis, A. V., & Kotlar, J. (2019). Environmental jolts, family-centered non-economic goals and innovation: Toward a framework of family firm resilience. In E. Memili & C. Dibrell (Eds.), *The palgrave handbook of heterogeneity among family firms* (pp. 773–789). Palgrave Macmilan.

Cheema, M. A., Faff, F., & Szulczyk, K. R. (2022). The 2008 global financial crisis and COVID-19 pandemic: How safe are the safe haven assets? *International Review of Financial Analysis*, *83*, 102316. doi:10.1016/j.irfa.2022.102316 PMID:36536650

Cho, J., Miller, D., & Lee, J. (2018). Too much of a good thing: Family involvement and the survival of listed Korean firms. *Journal of Family Business Strategy*, *9*(4), 223–237. doi:10.1016/j.jfbs.2018.10.001

Chua, J. H., Chrisman, J. J., & Sharma, P. (1999). Defining the family business by behavior. *Entrepreneurship Theory and Practice*, *23*(4), 19–39. doi:10.1177/104225879902300402

Cicek, A., Kelleci, R., & Vandekerkhof, P. (2021). Determinants of family meetings in private family businesses. *Journal of Family Business Management*. . doi:10.1108/JFBM-11-2020-0110

Conza, E., Lamb, P. W., & De Massis, A. (2020). Practicing resilience in family firms: An investigation through T phenomenography. *Journal of Family Business Strategy*, *11*(2), 100355. doi:10.1016/j.jfbs.2020.100355

De Massis, A., Frattini, F., Majocchi, A., & Piscitello, L. (2018). Family firms in the global economy: Toward a deeper understanding of internationalization determinants, processes, and outcomes. *Global Strategy Journal*, *8*(1), 3–21. doi:10.1002/gsj.1199

Dede, N. P., & Ayranci, E. (2014). Exploring the connections among spiritual leadership, altruism, and trust in family businesses. *Quality & Quantity*, *48*(6), 3373–3400. doi:10.100711135-013-9962-x

Glatter, K. A., & Finkelman, P. (2021). History of the Plague: An Ancient Pandemic for the Age of COVID-19. *The American Journal of Medicine*, *134*(2), 176–181. doi:10.1016/j.amjmed.2020.08.019 PMID:32979306

Habbershon, T. G., Williams, M., & MacMillan, I. C. (2003). A unified system perspective of family firm performance. *Journal of Business Venturing*, *18*(4), 451–465. doi:10.1016/S0883-9026(03)00053-3

Habbershon, T. G., & Williams, M. L. (1999). A resource-based framework for assessing the strategic advantages of family firms. *Family Business Review*, *12*(1), 1–25. doi:10.1111/j.1741-6248.1999.00001.x

Huynh, T. L. D. (2020). The COVID-19 risk perception: A survey on socio-economics and media attention. *Economic Bulletin*, *40*(1), 758–764.

International Finance Corporation. (2018). *Family business governance handbook*. IFC. https://www.ifc.org/wps/wcm/connect/2c93b2cb-dec6-4819-9ffb60335069cbac/Family_Business_Governance_Handbook.pdf?MOD=AJPERES&CVID=mskqtDE.

Lawton, G. (2022). Plague: Black death bacteria persists and could cause a pandemic. Wilson, E. (ed.). New Scientist. London.

Le Bretton-Miller, I., & Miller, D. (2022). Family businesses under COVID-19: Inspiring models – Sometimes. *Journal of Family Business Strategy*, *13*(100452), 100452. doi:10.1016/j.jfbs.2021.100452

Mathews, T., & Blumentritt, T. (2015). A sequential choice model of family business succession. *Small Business Economics*, *45*(1), 15–37. doi:10.100711187-015-9628-2

Miroshnychenko, I., De Massis, A., Miller, D., & Barontini, R. (2021). Family Business Growth Around the World. *Entrepreneurship Theory and Practice*, *45*(4), 682–708. doi:10.1177/1042258720913028

Perry, R. D., & Fetherston, J. D. (1997, January). Perry, Robert d. and Fetherston, Jacqueline D. Yersinia pestis—Etiologic Agent of Plague. *Clinical Microbiology Reviews*, *10*(1), 35–66. doi:10.1128/CMR.10.1.35

Pipatanantakurn, K., & Ractham, V. V. (2016). Knowledge creation aiding family business succession plan. *International Journal of Business and Management Science*, *6*(1), 63–84.

Randerson, K., Bettinelli, C., Fayolle, A., & Anderson, A. (2015). Family entrepreneurship as a field of research: Exploring its contours and contents. *Journal of Family Business Strategy*, *6*(3), 143–154. doi:10.1016/j.jfbs.2015.08.002

Rashid, S., & Ratten, V. (2020). A dynamic capabilities approach for the survival of Pakistani family-owned business in the digital world. *Journal of Family Business Management*, *10*(4), 373–387. doi:10.1108/JFBM-12-2019-0082

Riedel, S. (2005). Plague: From natural disease to bioterrorism. *Proceedings - Baylor University. Medical Center*, *18*(2), 116–124. doi:10.1080/08998280.2005.11928049 PMID:16200159

Rivo-López, E., Villanueva-Villar, M., Vaquero-García, A., & Lago-Peñas, S. (2021). Do family firms contribute to job stability? Evidence from the great recession. *Journal of Family Business Management*, *12*(1), 152–169. doi:10.1108/JFBM-06-2020-0055

Rosenblatt, P., de Mik, L., Anderson, R., & Johnson, P. (1985). *The family in business: Understanding and dealing with the challenges entrepreneurial families face*. Jossey-Bass.

Saleem, I., Siddique, I., & Ahmed, A. (2020). An extension of the socioemotional wealth perspective Insights from an Asian sample. *Journal of Family Business Management*, *10*(4), 293–312. doi:10.1108/JFBM-04-2019-0022

Sarbah, A., & Xiao, W. (2015). Good corporate governance structures: A must for family businesses. *Journal of Business and Management*, *3*, 40–57.

Shahbaz, M. (2013). Linkages between inflation, economic growth and terrorism in Pakistan. *Economic Modelling*, *32*, 496–506. doi:10.1016/j.econmod.2013.02.014

Sharma, P., Chrisman, J. J., Pablo, A. L., & Chua, J. H. (2001). Determinants of initial satisfaction with the succession process in family firms: A conceptual model. *Entrepreneurship Theory and Practice*, *25*(3), 17–35. doi:10.1177/104225870102500302

Shibata, I. (2021). The distributional impact of recessions: The global financial crisis and the COVID-19 pandemic recession. *Journal of Economics and Business*, *115*, 105971. doi:10.1016/j.jeconbus.2020.105971 PMID:35702646

Siakas, K., Naaranoja, M., Vlachakis, S., & Siakas, E. (2014). Family businesses in the new economy: How to survive and develops in times of financial crisis. *Procedia Economics and Finance*, *9*, 331–341. doi:10.1016/S2212-5671(14)00034-3

Siringoringo, H., & Kuruppuge, R. H. (2021). Government Policies During Pandemic: Indonesian vs Sri Lankan Perspective. In V. Kumar & G. Gupta (Eds.), *Strategic Management during a Pandemic*. Routledge. doi:10.4324/9781003125648-8

Songini, L., & Gnan, L. (2015). Family involvement and agency cost control mechanisms in family small and medium-sized enterprises. *Journal of Small Business Management, 53*(3), 748–779. doi:10.1111/jsbm.12085

van der Merwe, P., Saayman, A., & Jacobs, C. (2021). Assessing the economic impact of COVID-19 on the private wildlife industry of South Africa. *Global Ecology and Conservation, 28*, e01633. doi:10.1016/j.gecco.2021.e01633 PMID:34541259

Wahidin, D., Akimov, A., & Roca, E. (2021). The impact of bond market development on economic growth before and after the global financial crisis: Evidence from developed and developing countries. *International Review of Financial Analysis, 77*, 101865. doi:10.1016/j.irfa.2021.101865

Wielsma, A. J., & Brunninge, O. (2019). 'Who am I? Who are we?' Understanding the impact of family business identity on the development of individual and family identity in business families. *Journal of Family Business Strategy, 10*(1), 38–48. doi:10.1016/j.jfbs.2019.01.006

Yousaf, I., Beljid, M., Chaibi, A., & Ajlouni, A. A. L. (2022). Do volatility spillover and hedging among GCC stock markets and global factors vary from normal to turbulent periods? Evidence from the global financial crisis and Covid-19 pandemic crisis. *Pacific-Basin Finance Journal, 73*, 101764. doi:10.1016/j.pacfin.2022.101764

Chapter 2
COVID-19 Pandemic and Hungarian Family Businesses

Henrietta Nagy
Milton Friedman University, Hungary

Izabella Oláh
Hungarian University of Agriculture and Life Sciences, Hungary

ABSTRACT

The pandemic has had a very serious influence on the businesses, organizations, and on the everyday life of the population, though the impact may vary from region to region. In general, the pandemic brought unfavourable situations, though there are businesses that could take benefit from this "new normal" situation. The extent of the impact surely depends on the specific economic and social conditions of the region that determine the adaptability to the new tendencies. Regardless of the sector, or the size of the businesses, there is one thing in common: all the businesses had to be creative, innovative, and had to have a strategy for the short and middle term. In this chapter, the authors would like to provide a national-level overview of the economic and social impacts of the pandemic,and the measures are taken to boost the economy. Secondly, the authors intend to provide a more targeted picture about the Hungarian family businesses, and how they managed to survive and offset the unexpected impacts of the pandemic, based on primary research.

DOI: 10.4018/978-1-6684-7394-8.ch002

1. INTRODUCTION

The first coronavirus 19 (covid-19) cases were detected at the end of February 2020. Two Iranian students studying in Hungary were proved to be infected. Both came back to Hungary from their home country. The third was an elderly man coming home from Italy. So, the pandemic in Hungary started in the last days of February and the restrictions came into effect 2 weeks after, in the middle of March. Until now (9 July 2021) 808,437 people (8.26%) are reported to have been infected, 741,293 (7.58%) recovered from the illness, and 30,004 died (3.71% of those infected).

Figure 1 shows the distribution of infected citizens, while the colour of the counties on the map of the country differs based on the rate of infected people in the total population of each county. We can see that regarding the absolute numbers, Budapest the capital city was the first in the rank, reporting 17.8% of those who have been infected, however, due to the high population density, the colour of the capital is not the darkest. If we add the agglomeration, Pest County data to that of the capital, they represent 31.7% of the infected people in the country. It means a huge concentration of the pandemic in the middle of Hungary, which is the economic core of the country.

While Nógrád county, reporting the 3rd worst data is with the darkest colouring. Since that county has a huge number of commuters to the capital, a lot of people have been infected at their workplace and on public transport vehicles. Since the population size is a lot lower than in the agglomeration, the share of infected in the total population was the highest in the country. We need to mention that Nógrád county is among the least developed counties of Hungary, despite its proximity to the center. We can also see on the map that the Transdanubian counties (West-Hungary), representing the most developed group in the country, were also hit hard, making the catch-up and recharging of the economy more difficult.

The average age of those who died is in 74 years, which means that mainly the elderly people were/are at risk, especially those who suffer from other illnesses as well. According to Hungarian statistics, covid-19-caused deaths are those which happened after a positive covid test. Other countries only count those deaths which happened obviously due to the virus; therefore, the death statistics may differ and be incomparable with each other.

Vaccination in Hungary started on 18 January 2021. Until 7 July 2021, 5,523,878 people (56.5% of the population) got at least the first dose, while 5,072,024 people are fully vaccinated (52,5% of the population). Since the middle of June 2021, young people between 12-15 years of age can also be vaccinated. Hungary is the only country in the European Union where there is an oversupply from vaccines, meaning that there are far more vaccines available than the number of those not vaccinated yet. It means that it is only the decision of the citizens to get the vaccine.

Figure 1. The territorial distribution of covid-19 infected citizens in Hungary (09/07/2021)
Source: Cabinet of the Prime Minister of Hungary 2021, https://koronavirus.gov.hu/terkepek/fertozottek

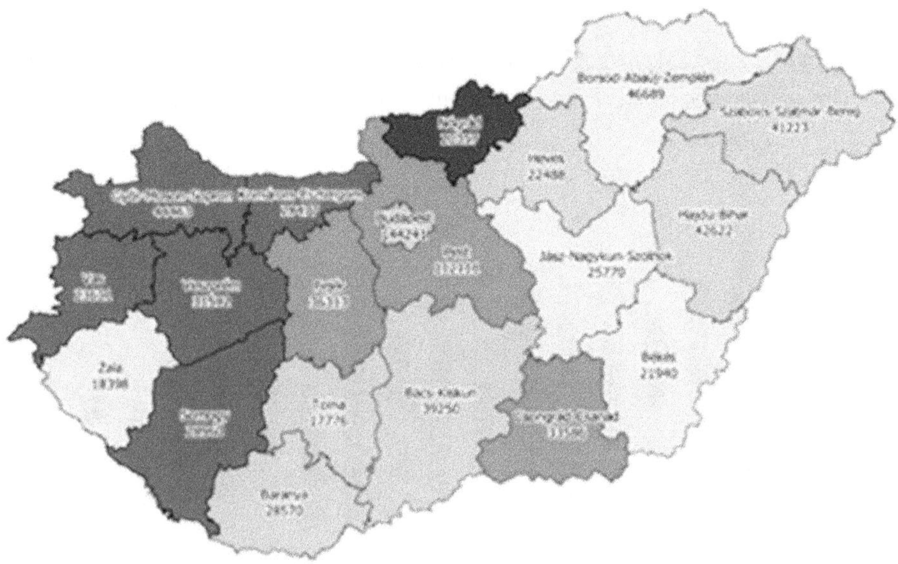

1.1. Economic and Social Indicators during the Pandemic

Based on the results so far, the pandemic caused by covid-19 has put all actors in the economy to the test. In addition to their previous roles, businesses had to prove themselves in new areas. In addition to ensuring financial and economic stability, the protection of the physical and mental health of workers and partners has also received a great deal of attention. Of course, this role was valid for all economic actors, regardless of size, sector, and form of operation. Crisis management for businesses has drawn attention not only to the challenges but also to the opportunities that, in addition to being a way out of the situation, offer stability and growth potential.

Regarding the country-level statistics, as Figure 2 shows, the employment rate fluctuated during the pandemic and reached its lowest point by April 2021. It is also interesting that the employment rate reached its peak in October 2020.

As Figure 3 shows, the largest shrink in employment can be seen in social care, accommodation services, catering, agriculture, healthcare, and social work. On one hand, it dramatically made the battle with the pandemic very difficult, since, in the healthcare and social care sectors, 60,000 fewer people were employed in 2021 spring than 1 year before. On the other hand, the decreasing employment in agriculture, accommodation, and catering is somehow understandable, since small family farms tried to reduce the job-related costs while due to the lockdown, people were not allowed to visit restaurants or hotels.

Figure 2. The employment rate in Hungary (%)
Source: own computation based on data from Central Statistical Office, 2021.

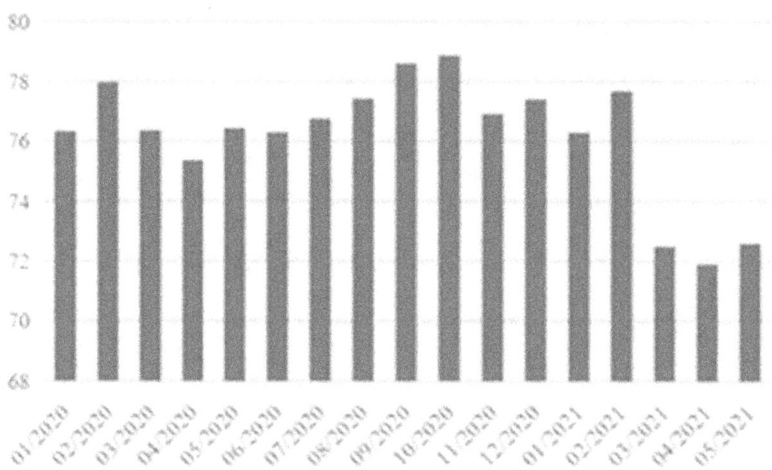

At the same time, the following sectors increased their employment during the pandemic: public administration, education, scientific activity, construction industry, information, and communication as well as financial services. Parallel with employment, we need to analyze the unemployment tendency as well. As Figure 4 shows, the unemployment rate in Hungary also fluctuated and was the highest in May, August 2020, and January 2021.

If we look at the European situation, Figure 5 reflects that the change in the unemployment rate in the EU member states ranged from -2.5 to 2.7 percent. The worst is the case in Ireland, where the unemployment in May 2021 was 2.5% higher than 1 year before. At the EU level, the change was -0.4, meaning that on average, the European community was able to reduce the unemployment rate. Hungary is coloured in green in Figure 5, showing that the country managed to decrease the unemployment rate by 0.6% compared to one year before. It is also the result of the pro-active approach of the Government of Hungary to the economic and social challenges, caused by the pandemic.

Figure 3. Sectoral employment in Hungary based on the average March-May 2020 and that of 2021
Source: own computation based on data from Central Statistical Office, 2021.

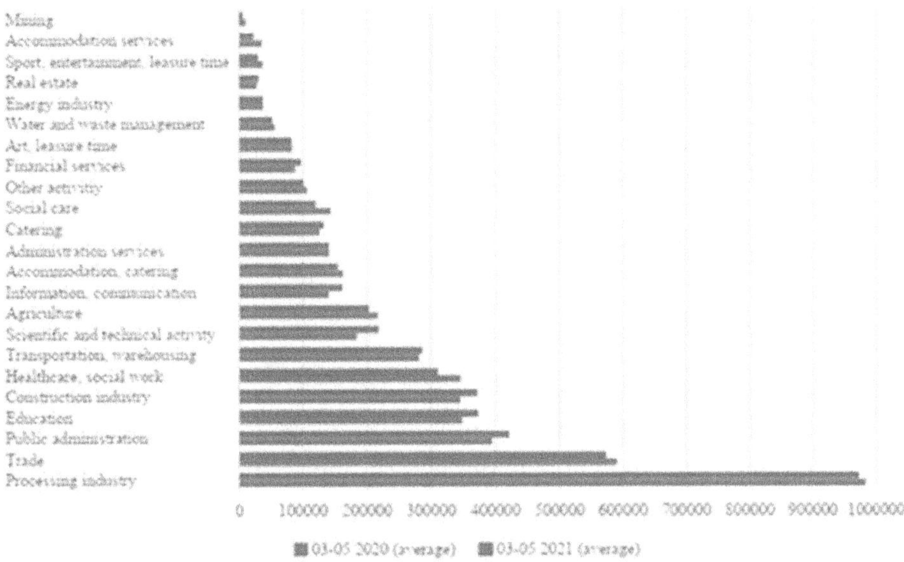

Figure 4. The unemployment rate in Hungary (%)
Source: own computation based on data from Central Statistical Office, 2021.

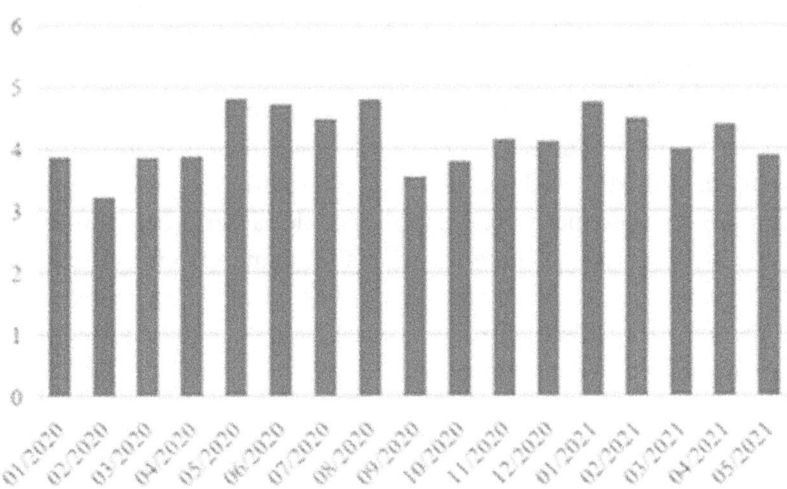

Figure 5. The change in the unemployment rate compared to May 2020 in the EU27 (%)
Source: own computation based on Eurostat data, 2021.

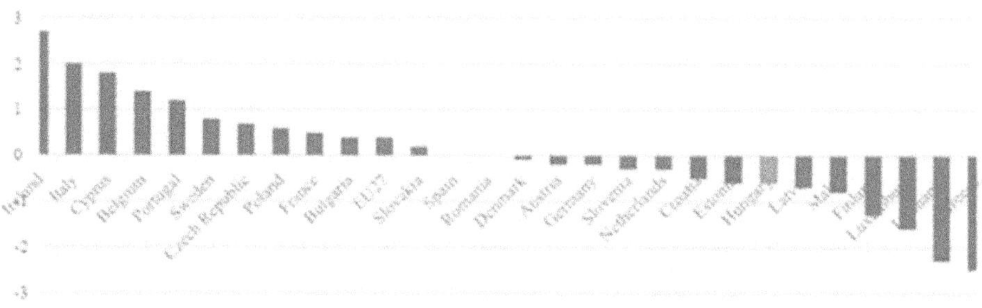

We also need to mention alternative ways to mitigate the shock caused by the pandemic, namely working from home. In Figure 6 we can see the share of those among the total employed who worked from home in home office during the period of the pandemic. It is clear that the share of people in the home office fluctuated during the examined period but is in close relationship with the waves of the pandemic. An increased number of people worked in-home offices just after the outbreak (March-June 2020) and showed a significant increase at the beginning of 2021 when the 3rd wave came. Since most of the companies had to revise their employment strategies, and they realized that it may be more cost-effective, the share of the home office is expected to stagnate at around 2-3% in the future.

As the figures above show, people faced various challenges over the examined period, they had to adapt to the new, unprecedented situation. Many lost their jobs or had to reduce working hours, resulting in lower income for the families. As Figure 7 shows, compared to 1 year before data, the package of products/services people purchased during the pandemic changed a lot. We can see that the purchase of food even decreased, while the package-delivery, internet-based purchases jumped and stayed high. We can see that as prevention, people rather ordered products on the internet with home-delivery. There was also a jump in the purchase of medicine in March 2020 when the lockdown started, but later it rather stagnated. In terms of non-food products, considered luxury products in a pandemic period, the volume of purchase decreased in the country.

Figure 6. The share of those working in home office among the total employed in Hungary (%)
Source: own computation based on data from Central Statistical Office, 2021.

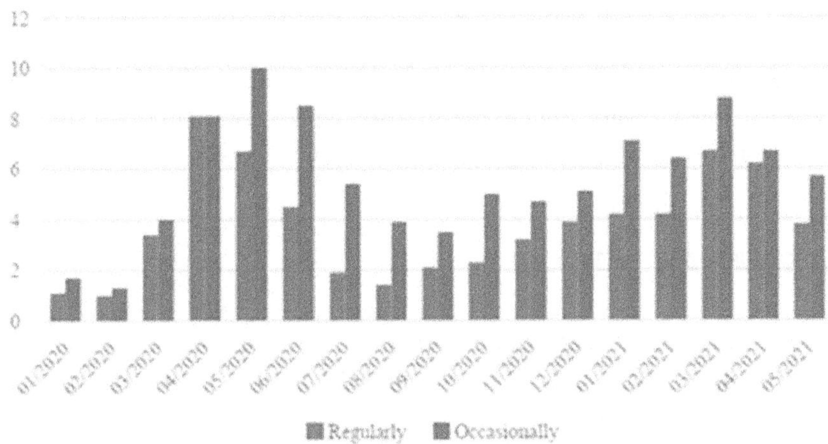

Figure 7. The change in the volume of purchases in Hungary (100=the same month the previous year, %)
Source: own computation based on data from Central Statistical Office, 2021.

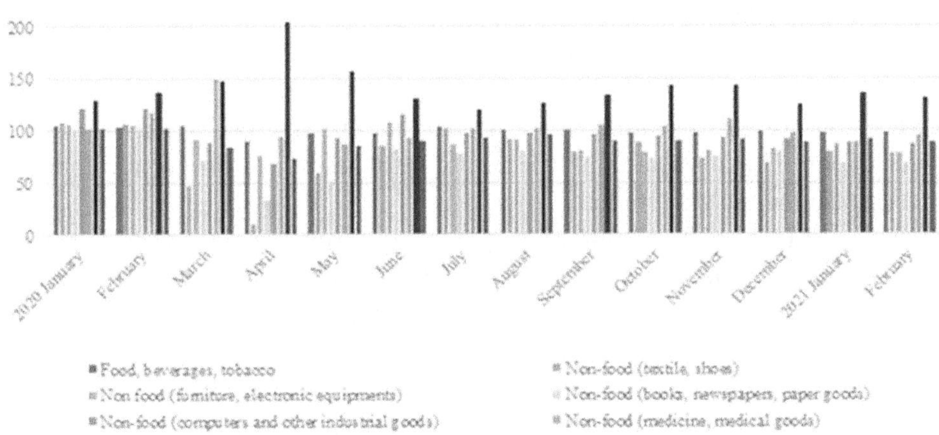

Based on a survey carried out among the Hungarian SMEs in 2020, we can state that the pandemic influenced SMEs with a well-defined strategy less than other businesses. The Hungarian case reflects that the pandemic had a less negative impact on the agriculture and construction industry compared to other sectors – probably due to the open-air activities. However, tourism and catering suffered the most, since over 90% of the businesses were pending their activities. We must also mention that transportation, warehousing, home-delivery, and e-commerce were those which benefited from the unfavourable global and national economic situation.

2. MATERIAL AND METHOD

This chapter is based on secondary statistical data and primary research results from structured in-depth interviews among Hungarian family businesses. The statistical data were obtained from the Central Statistical Office, and the data and analytical information necessary for corporate decision-making concerning specific companies were obtained from the partner control interface of Bisnode Hungary Ltd. (A member of the Dun & Bradstreet group of companies). We reached the family businesses involved in the research in several ways. We contacted some of them based on the database of the Business Community of Hungarian Business Leaders (MVÜK), which has been operating in Hungary for 11 years and offers a membership-based business community to its members. We contacted several of them through the National Association of Family Businesses. The aim of the association is to represent the values and interests of the family businesses, which form a significant basis of Hungary's economic potential. In order to ensure the long-term successful operation of the Hungarian enterprises, in addition to the representation of interests, the knowledge, contact capital and expertise accumulated in the association are also shared.

Szinergia Ltd. (which is itself a family business) working in the field of project management and leadership development has also helped to find family businesses as widely as possible. In addition, there are family businesses in the network of personal relationships.

After analysing and processing the documents already prepared on the topic, in addition to the general characteristics, we examine the factors that may affect the survival and adaptation strategy of the interviewed enterprises. Structured in-depth interviews with business leaders, in addition to getting to know the general mapping of the business, allowed us to explore in detail the specific strategies they implemented. This is how the concrete examples became visible. In addition to economic and management issues, we would like to add a new aspect to the study, including the Philip Zimbardo model of time perspective. In a sense, the method is about experiencing a problem-solving mechanism. We assume that the leadership characteristics of firms with resilience and good adaptability are future-oriented.

As a result of previous studies, it can be observed that more than half of the micro and SMEs operating in Hungary can be defined as family businesses. Pandemic-induced reactions can be seen in several areas. For example, most of the smaller companies have greeted the digital revolution, as their suddenly changed position has moved the majority of businesses towards the digital space. In times of uncertainty, the need to maintain continuity naturally increases – so, in several cases, the issue of generational change has come to the forefront. With the increase of social responsibility, it has become possible to credibly represent family values, so the consolidation of social esteem and the resulting long-term benefits can be interpreted as a positive return for the businesses involved. The increase in the value of trust capital and its retaining power can also be experienced which can also provide a stable basis for long-term company operations.

In addition to the abovementioned effects, the pandemic has outlined many characteristics such as decision-making ability, reaction time, willingness to innovate, and strategic thinking that can be developed to create more resilient businesses and entrepreneurial environments.

In several EU countries, including Malta or the Czech Republic, the legal framework determines which businesses are considered family businesses. However, in Hungary, it is not clear yet what can be called a family business-due to the lack of a proper legal background. Delimitation would be an important step for several reasons. On the one hand, it would allow us to determine more precisely how many family businesses exist and operate in the country. This would be an initial step toward a uniform basis for public administration and statistical data. After that, it would be possible to create a unified and coordinated supporting environment that effectively helps the operation of family businesses (Piac és profit. 2019.). However, creating a definition is not an easy task at all. It is necessary to keep in mind the peculiarities of domestic entrepreneurship and international practice, while, at the same time, incorporating the ownership structure and operating mechanism expected from family businesses must be a task while creating a unique definition.

Due to the lack of concrete legislative background, in our research, we have examined various international and domestic definitions for the delimitation in the area under study. Finally, we came to the conclusion that in the present study the delimitation established by the Budapest University of Economics is used as a basis (Kása et al 2019, 152). According to that concept, we consider companies, having a registered office in Hungary, to be family businesses*:

A – which consider themselves to be a family business, or
B – where at least 51% of the enterprise is owned by a family, and

C – the family is involved in the management of the business, or
D – family members are involved in the business as employees in the operation of, or
E – the transfer of management and ownership takes place in part or in full within the family.

* The basis of the family relationship is the marriage or the parent-child, sibling relationship/sister-brother relationship, which can be based on the blood relationship or adoption.

With this delimitation, it is possible to outline the mental map of the image (identity) formed of ourselves, and in the case of {B + CDE}, the undertakings concerned are delimited on the basis of factual data.

In our primary study 50 Hungarian family businesses were involved. In the vast majority of cases, we conducted a structured in-depth interview with the head of the family business (96%), and in the other cases with a family member also working in the business (4%). In terms of sectors of the national economy, agriculture, construction, logistics, accommodation services, information and communication, real estate, human and health care, as well as arts, entertainment and leisure activities were also represented in the research. We also involved businesses in education, trade, and consultancy. The group of entrepreneurs in the survey shows a mixed picture. Thus, the information obtained during the survey provides a more nuanced picture of the reactions and views of Hungarian family businesses.

The structured in-depth interview consisted of four main parts. The first section included rather general questions about the business and also outlined whether the respondent (regardless of the statistics) defined the business as a family business or not. In addition to the basic data of the company (name, registered office, year of establishment, main profile), the general questions included the target market (foreign and/or domestic) and the generation of the company.

In the second phase of the interview, we explored the period before the covid-19 pandemic. We mainly targeted what plans and prospects the businesses had before the pandemic or when it was recognized that it would affect much of the market (either directly or indirectly). In the third stage, we examined the period of the pandemic with a strong emphasis on changes in the life and environment of the business, their mechanism of impact, and the responses and management strategies provided by the businesses. We assessed how the pandemic affected their preliminary plans and what specific impact it had on employee's turnover. Whether their markets narrowed or expanded, and what change could be observed by suppliers, partners, and customers.

We also asked companies what (new) challenges they faced and according to which strategy they responded. As the decision-makers have great influence on the existence of the business, we also asked the representatives of the family businesses what they had experienced most in the situation caused by covid-19. Or what was the thought or guideline that helped them to get through these difficult times. Also in this section, we were wondering if they had asked for help with the crisis management of the company and, if so, "where/from" and "whom/in what" topic.

In the fourth part of the structured in-depth interview, we summarized the experiences caused by covid-19 situation (both for the business and the individuals). Here are the insights and experiences and long-term effects that, in retrospect, really defined this period and can help during the next wave. Following the structured in-depth interview, respondents who were open (22%) to examine their time perspective, completed Philip Zimbardo's time perspective test (Zimbardo and Sword, 2017). Our time perspective, without knowing it, has a decisive impact on our privacy, work, careers, behaviours, and relationships.

Data and information revealed during the study were presented anonymously. In presenting the results, our main goal was to present the important insights, experiences, and strategies presented in the in-depth interviews, building on each other so that both differences and similarities would emerge. Finally, based on these, we summarized the conclusions that were drawn for family businesses (regardless of size and activity).

3. RESULTS AND DISCUSSION

3.1 General Overview of the Family Businesses in Hungary

According to the survey carried out and published by Opten (business providing services related to company registry), there are over 204,000 familiar businesses which are 40% of the associated companies in Hungary. Family relations are the most determinant in businesses operated by more than one family member since family members are linked not only because of family relations but because of the joint work, too (Opten, 2020). Among such businesses, there are 42,000 businesses where exclusively family members own and work in the business. In the modern Hungarian economy, family-related businesses started to operate only recently, though tens of thousands of families make attempts to synchronize the business and family life. Thus, it is important to see clearly how efficiently those over 200,000 businesses work.

The familiar character has a positive effect on the operation in general. Statistics prove that 64% of the family businesses are trustworthy above the average level. It can be considered as the success of family businesses that the annual income of 1,100 businesses exceeds 1 billion HUF. In 50% of the family businesses sibling relations can be identified, in 38% father-child relationship, while in 33% mother-child one. In the last few years, the share of father-child relations decreased, while the sibling-relations increased, referring to the fact that in my family businesses the older generations already passed the management of the businesses to the children.

If we look at the distribution of the family businesses in Hungary, we can see that there is a high concentration in the capital and the agglomeration (Pest county). In the capital, Budapest, the number of family businesses per 1,000 inhabitants is the highest, exceeding 10. It can be considered a very high concentration, if we look at the population in the capital (approx. 20% of the total population). Altogether, the capital and its agglomeration (the county around the capital) represent almost half of the total number of multi-membered family businesses operating in the country. The lowest numbers can be identified in the least-developed counties of Hungary in the eastern region, along the borders of Ukraine and Romania.

Table 1. The number of multi-membered family businesses in the counties of Hungary, 2020

County	Number of family businesses (excluding the one-man businesses)	Number of family businesses per 1000 inhabitants
Capital (Budapest)	**19833**	**11.32**
Pest	10016	7.83
Baranya	2307	6.4
Komárom-Esztergom	1724	5.76
Zala	1542	5.74
Csongrád	2287	5.73
Győr-Moson-Sopron	2665	5.7
Bács-Kiskun	2858	5.67
Tolna	1196	5.5
Hajdú-Bihar	2852	5.4
Veszprém	1840	5.39
Somogy	1579	5.24
Fejér	2186	5.23
Vas	1269	5
Heves	1323	4.49
Borsod-Abaúj-Zemplén	2693	4.19
Jász-Nagykun-Szolnok	1522	4.11
Békés	1373	4.11
Szabolcs-Szatmár-Bereg	2156	3.9
Nógrád	578	3.05

Source: Opten, 2020.06.02 https://www.opten.hu/kozlemenyek/a-hazai-cegek-40-szazaleka-csaladi-jellegu-vallalkozas

3.2 The Family Businesses Surveyed in the Research

During our research we have read about family businesses, the thoughts associated with micro and SMEs include resilience as a characteristic of many of us (article published in Világgazdaság (17 May 2021). However, in the situation caused by the pandemic, all businesses (regardless of industry, size, and structural/ownership structure) found themselves in a difficult and new situation. The economic recession has affected all market participants, directly or indirectly. Following the ever-changing regulations during the pandemic, employers had to ensure the health and safety of workers (both physically, mentally, and financially). At the same time, businesses had to become crisis-resilient in all areas of their operations-taking into account anomalies in organizational operations, the relative establishment of financial stability and the ever-changing external and internal environment.

Let's review a professional summary on the topic based on an interview with Szinergia Ltd. which business is involved in the examination of family businesses from several approaches. On one hand, as a company with a history of almost 30 years, it has supported the generational change of many family companies, on the other hand, it is also a family-owned company itself. Their experience can be read below (István Havrancsik, Dóra Havrancsik, Email to Izabella Oláh, September 06. 2021.):

"The outbreak of the covid-19 pandemic put extra pressure on family businesses—along with many other companies—in 2020. Family businesses could respond resiliently to these challenges, especially where 2nd generation already took part in the management of the company. As we saw, the families held a special assembly—governing board of the family business and finances—focusing on strategic changes. Most of our clients deliberately decided not to do layoffs, thus providing security for the employees even on the cost of decreased profit for the owners. They sooner postponed cost payments and investments to avoid cash flow problems and applied for governmental funds to keep their staff.

These transgenerational companies made cost-optimization instead of cost-cutting. The ever-postponed IT infrastructure improvements and online marketing efforts took place—mainly due to the agility and tech-savvy attitude of the young generation who could rely on the experience and stability of the older generation. The economic environment put pressure on the companies to deploy synergy in the management between the different co-operation styles of the different generations. Having done so, they were able to improve-despite the mounting uncertainties and difficulties.

The pandemic called for the emphasized introduction of home-based working in the most positions applicable. Our experience shows that trust grew significantly even in companies with strict employee systems and procedures in place. Working from home had a favourable effect on home-work balance, making more companies flexible, regarding the social and family stance of crew members. Organizations lacking trust towards online working were slow to fight the crisis, compared to those where managers believed their team—including younger generation members—were doing their job unseen.

Summarizing the success factors of well-performing family businesses during the pandemic, we can mention the followings:

- cooperation of generations and finding synergies;
- pre-emptive approach to corporate strategy modification;
- cooperation based on trust.

This experience meant family businesses did not only survive but thrive, and were able to pass on the valuable experience and knowledge to their successors."

Regarding the size of the family businesses involved in the research, it can be said that the survey was very widespread (Table 2.). Based on the net sales revenue in 2020, we categorized the companies into groups. Those with annual net sales of less than HUF 50 million accounted for 18% of the surveyed enterprises. They are typically family businesses with 2-3 employees, mainly engaged in agricultural production, tourism, and other ancillary services. Enterprises with annual net sales of between HUF 50 and 99 million were 28% represented. This group also had a significant presence of companies interested in agriculture and the food industry, but also companies dealing with real estate and health-related services, horticulture, and IT. There are larger differences in terms of employment, these companies employ 3-10 people depending on the type of activity.

Thirty percent of the enterprises included in the study were family businesses with annual sales between HUF 100 and 399 million. For companies with a lower turnover, companies specialized in the retail and wholesale of automotive parts and construction and other goods already appear here. There are several restaurants and catering units as well as a gas station and a tobacco shop. Family businesses in the field of education and counseling are also included in this income category. The more heterogeneous a group is, the greater differences can be observed. This is also the case here since from this size category upwards, a larger variance can be observed for employees. Although some relatively small enterprises (3-4 people) can be observed even above 100 million, their number is much lower than in the case of enterprises with less turnover. Most of these family businesses are characterized by more than 10 employees.

Table 2. Family businesses surveyed by size class

Category		Percent
> 50 HUF million		18
50< > 99 HUF million		28
100 < > 399 HUF million		30
400 < > 999 HUF million		8
1 < > 5 HUF billion		16

Source: own computation based on data from own survey, 2021.

The next group includes those enterprises which already generate annual net sales of over HUF 400 million, but do not yet reach HUF 1 billion. Companies from construction, IT developments and related consulting, healthcare and culture and entertainment sectors were represented, with a total of 8 percent of the companies surveyed. The number of employees shows relatively large differences. There are companies with 10 people or even with 25 employees. As mentioned above, it greatly depends on the activity and resource need of the company, how much/what kind of workforce it employs.

The last category includes 16 percent of enterprises, with annual net sales exceeding HUF 1 billion (but not reaching HUF 5 billion). This group includes family businesses operating in construction, transportation, logistics, agricultural market services, tourism, and hospitality. A member of the group surveyed is also a family business trading with household appliances and parts and providing related services, as well as in the wholesale of fashion goods or household goods. In terms of employment data, in several cases, these family businesses have more than 50 employees and in some cases even more than 90 employees.

3.3 Overview of the Impact of the Pandemic on the Sectors of Hungary

In the followings, we try to reflect which sector suffered from the covid-19 pandemic's direct and indirect impacts, and how these have become felt and managed by family businesses.

3.3.1 Primary Sector-Agriculture

In the light of the results of other branches of the national economy, agriculture was less directly affected by the negative effects of the covid-19 pandemic. Uncertainty and intermittent supply and sales difficulties have affected this area and other sectors of the economy. However, as the demand for food (primarily for basic food) did not decrease during the crisis, we cannot talk about a significant loss of income in the field of agriculture that would be related to the pandemic situation. Revenues from stable demand increased reliability in terms of lending-which is of great value in uncertain times, not just for investors. The primary difficulties in the agricultural sector were caused by stagnant transport and procurement conditions, as well as by the increase in the purchase prices of input materials and components. At the same time, however, the market price of the products produced also increased. So, most of the higher expenses could be realized in the market with rising purchase prices (According to the article published by Portfolio.hu on November 17, 2020).

Based on the results of in-depth interviews conducted in the field of agriculture, it can be stated that the respondents do not feel that this sector has been greatly affected by the covid-19 pandemic. There were no major disruptions to work in compliance with current pandemic regulations. **Regarding their business strategy, there has not been much change over this period.** It was not common to postpone the investments planned before the pandemic, only their implementation (construction, planning) took a short time. In these cases, the main reasons similarly were **the precarious situation and the time spent waiting**, which increased the duration of investments and developments. Digitization, as in all areas of our lives (e.g. in education, home office, communication, shopping, etc.), has received a lot of emphases here as well. Although the digitalization of agriculture has been a decisive development and strategic direction for several years (decades) by both the sectoral policy and the economy, the benefits of digitalization and its impact on business have now been highlighted from a new perspective.

Confirming this, the majority of interviewees see the opportunity to further develop their business and enhance digitalization. This strategy was born not only of stable professional convictions but also of the currently announced tenders that have a significant influence on this decision. One of the key tender options is the ongoing tender "VP2-4.1.8-21 Support for precision developments related to the digital transition to agriculture".

In the case of family businesses operating in agriculture (as it is mentioned below in the case of family businesses of other sectors), the deepening of intergenerational cooperation during the viral situation was formulated. According to the survey data, digitization can also be considered a lobby for generational change, as, unlike the older age group, it is an integral part of the life of the newer generation. Thus, the sharing of knowledge and tasks between the generations, as well as the building on and complementarity of knowledge, has become tangible.

3.3.2 Secondary Sector-Construction

Interviews with several smaller and larger players in the construction sector revealed that this sector and industry faced different challenges and were affected differently during the pandemic period compared to businesses of other sectors.

Their preliminary plans did not change fundamentally, they just had to rethink their schedule. **The constantly changing environment** (health, regulatory) in this sector also required continuous **redesign, and thus allowed more room for developmental, "changing" and innovative ideas**. In addition, the reports provided an opportunity to discover and exploit the opportunities and needs offered by the new situation. The correctness of the business policy and strategic directions taken in previous periods has been confirmed (due to the market experience so far, the accumulation of cargo stocks in the weaker period; opening up to larger and more stable customer demands while maintaining the high quality usual for small projects). The pandemic has opened up opportunities for businesses to absorb and integrate highly skilled and experienced workers returning from international markets in the long term.

Both online work and the home office have also partially appeared in the construction industry (in areas where this is feasible). This has made many businesses aware that there are workflows that work with high-sometimes even higher-efficiency online (online meetings have replaced face-to-face meetings, often supplemented by several hours of driving). In many cases, some kind of online communication channel has been set up to replace the personal communication that has taken place so far. This ensures the flow of information and proper interaction between employees.

The regulations also encouraged other process improvements that have become integral components of efficiency gains and process optimization. For example, a development could be created that arranges the materials to be delivered in groupage, thus reducing the cost of transportation on both the business and user sides. Businesses have emphasized the importance of **creating reserves, even if it slows down the growth rate of the business.** It can be said that "slower but more secure" growth and development results in a more stable business in the long run.

3.3.3 Tertiary Sector – Services

The majority (66%) of companies surveyed in this sector operate in the fields of logistics, healthcare, tourism and hospitality, education, trade, and other services.

In the area of shipping, there was a resurgence following the initial precarious situation. People avoided personal contact and changingtheir daily services, much of the shopping was online. At the same time, the demand for delivery/home delivery has increased. These increased and changed demands (contactless takeover, payment) have **created development and optimization demands** on businesses. In addition, it required more self-discipline and focus. It was observed that during the pandemic, many workers from other sectors shifted to the logistics companies. It did not only create difficulties but also provided an **opportunity for incorporating new and creative ideas, thus for renewal**.

In the health care sector (we examined it not from the point of view of those operating in primary care, but from the point of view of private practices and private clinics), the work was as continuous as possible, with maximum compliance. Moreover, in many cases, congestion and the resulting overtime were typical and common. Due to the explosively increased demand for medical masks, gloves, and disinfectants, the price of these products has multiplied and in some cases were available only in limited amounts-which has also made it difficult for healthcare professionals to work daily.

We have also seen explosive changes in education and counseling. The family businesses operating in these sectors have largely switched to the development of online and hybrid training and counseling processes and their practical application. Businesses that have already begun to build online systems in the background have been able to respond well and quickly but have not received so much emphasis earlier. They also have the competencies to make them quickly usable in practice.

In the strategy used by businesses, the online presence has received more emphasis than before. In the case of some companies, the focus shifted from training to consulting. Accordingly, they have already prepared for this portfolio expansion, so the changing demands did not affect them completely unexpectedly. The situations that generated change required flexibility for all actors. There were some doubts about the effectiveness of online counseling and training, but these were dispelled on the fly.

They managed to identify the elements and techniques that can be used effectively in online training as well. Moreover, the benefits of online methods have been articulated on both sides (trainers and clients). Such benefits are, for example, the reduction of travel time, the possibility of "non-stationary" work. These experiences have remained with us and have been integral to the post-deregulation period (regardless of industry). Therefore, these experiences have encouraged businesses in the **field of education to optimize and streamline their other processes as well.**

For example, several people have started making changes to the office building to meet new and built-in needs. Thus, in the case of several companies, it was possible to create an office instead of the previously fixed workstations, which allows flexible individual and group work (both online and offline) and helps creative and creative work. With the sudden change in the communication channel, the marketing tools that can be connected to it have also changed. **Online communication and related conscious online marketing** have opened up new markets for those who realized it.

Businesses in the **tourism and hospitality** sector stated that they "**had to focus on survival**". A large percentage of family businesses surveyed retained their employees (there was a fluctuation and dropout that would have been expected even with general operation). In the first wave, they got into the work with great enthusiasm, trying to open towards the **food delivery and takeaway system**. Some businesses have also used innovative trends, starting to deliver "covid safe", one by one vacuum-packed, easily regenerated foods, almost among the first in the country.

All this was done with the aim of extracting enough income to be at least enough to pay wages. However, this has rarely succeeded. These restaurants have served and are keeping in mind the needs of the local population, so it is not the tourists who come to them that account for a significant part of their traffic. This is partly due to the fact that they were in a relatively better position than their competitors built on tourists at the time of the restrictions and were able to survive. (According to the experience of businesses, restaurants that build on tourists still have serious problems.) It is also thanks to this retaining and loyal attitude that these restaurants were able to open their doors to their guests immediately after opening, with the usual team in the usual quality.

With regard to suppliers and transport difficulties, I state that most of the difficulties that arise here can be eliminated if the **procurement of raw materials is solved through Hungarian producers with Hungarian suppliers.** Specific difficulties can also be observed in the **trade and services sector**. In international trade, there is a tendency for transport prices to rise sharply (by up to 600 percent) and, in parallel, high transport demands to increase transport times-so the movement of goods has slowed down. For example, an **innovative company** has redesigned the product it manufactures and markets to be flat packable-**optimizing costs for** both itself and customers. A significant number of businesses mentioned that there was a high degree of uncertainty on the part of the customer, both economically and socially. This also has direct effects on the market, with some products and services lagging behind (products related to offices and companies, while others rising) (security, basic food, health services, and products).

Another company highlighted that it is due to the fact that the **needs of the partners** can be met quickly by having a personal, **close relationship** with them. So, they are watching all their needs so that they can deliver the solution. This is how it happened during the epidemic period, the needs generated by the market were quickly recognized and the goods were procured in front of others. From the **point of view of procurement, the presence of working capital is essential,** since whoever pays in advance has priority in such situations. Online shopping and administration have also reshaped this area. Although webshops were already widespread and used by many, the epidemic situation has now given every business a big boost to actively appear online. Several also pointed out that **warehouse and package preparation colleagues can work immediately from an order placed on the online interface,** while in the case of the more traditional order, it must first be converted into a manageable order. So, **process optimization** in this area can also be achieved through online solutions.

3.4 What did the Covid-19 Situation Trigger from Family Businesses and What Lessons did it Provide?

In-depth interviews, in addition to the company's strategies and lines of action, sometimes revealed personal experiences of the covid-19 pandemic, where human relationships and fears also became visible. These clearly had an impact on the internal and external processes of the company, as well as on the solutions used. Although some of these have been addressed above, in the following we present this topic along the main issues covered by the structured in-depth interviews.

At the beginning of the study, we asked the family business leaders when they recognized the pressure for change, what new challenges they faced, and how they responded to those challenges? Based on the responses, it can be said that the majority of family businesses participating in the research recognized the time for change relatively early and made the necessary decisions quickly and decisively. Among the respondents, in addition to making quick decisions, reducing and rationalizing costs, collecting receivables and stabilizing their situation, it was also important to inform the workforce quickly and credibly. **In uncertain times,** when it changes from day to day and it is necessary to do the increased work in the usual quality and with great care, it can only be done with a **cohesive and supportive team behind us.** In addition to all this, it has proved important in this situation that, in addition to sharing the burden, ideas can also come to the surface.

In one of the larger companies, for example, **the manager called the employees together and informed them of the situation.** He told the employees that he was aware that he would be expected to find a solution and support in the precarious situation, but unfortunately, he could tell nothing but the truth. And the truth is that in this precarious situation, it may happen that salaries and headcount need to be reduced, and the biggest risk is that although the work has been done, they are not being paid by the partners.

After informing the employees about the real risks and outcomes, the manager stated that he was committed to keeping the company and therefore doing his best. He asked the employees to think through the situation and make suggestions. **So, in**

addition to authentic and clear communication, he involved them in the process. This proved to be a very good idea because the **reaction of the workers was that in order for everyone to keep their jobs, they give up part of their pay collectively.** He sought the help of a communications consultant for this crisis management, consistently leading the jointly developed process throughout the organization.

Several business leaders put it that **this was the time when they could do things they did not do in "peaceful times"**. Plans so far (even if with re-tuning) need to be implemented now. They are the ones who have experienced this situation as a challenge and have set a mix of creation and fleeing forward on their flag. One of them summarized as follows:

"Those who love challenges are lubricated during this period. Now there was an opportunity for continuous innovation and things that might have just been in the drawer so far-someone who feels good in construction, and governance-he cannot just complete in management".

The importance of creating reserves and liquid capital has already been addressed. There was an entrepreneur who, by reclaiming his private wealth, kept his companies at high risk and put him on a path of development.

More than half of the businesses mentioned **family reunification and working side by side** as extra ammunition. Not only is the harmony of the different forms of knowledge and knowledge represented by generations valued in a precarious situation, but so is cohesion and retention. This attitude also has an impact on employees and partners.

At the end of the interview, we asked managers **what insights the pandemic brought and what are strategies and important elements they will keep in mind if the next wave comes.**

The answers were mixed, but the essence was in common.

Most businesses have drawn attention to the creation of reserves and to the fact that creating stability is always more important than unlimited development. In addition to stability, great emphasis was placed on building financial independence and creating liquid funds.

For several companies, it was a great advantage that the cargo holds were filled up when the pandemic broke out so that they could serve their customers unhindered despite the loss of production or supply disruptions.

As a result of the pandemic, many people were able to experience the benefits of online work, discussions, and training. Moreover, for many, running their business online has even resulted in market growth with cost savings. However, in addition to the beneficial effects of online opportunities, many have recognized that working online can go unnoticed by the new "self-exploitation". (Because we save time and put it to work and leave the necessary rest periods).

The situation created by covid-19 also drew attention to the transience and power of the present moment. Most businesses stressed the need to keep a good team because it has value and retention (including family value). However, it has also been stated that they need to be independent of any factors that may hinder their effective operation either being an unsuitable employee, supplier, or partner. It can also be described as a kind of cost optimization process.

The next recognition and heartfelt idea are that even in trouble, the values of the business must be authentically represented and communicated transparently. In terms of communication, efficiency, and speed, as well as the involvement of employees, were also formulated. There should also be an opportunity to think and come up with ideas and to build consensus.

In addition to the additional burdens, crisis management has projected directions that offer opportunities for survival and strengthening. However, this requires a quick response, the ability to change as well as a team. Generational change did not intensify in these times, in fact, it was more a matter of generating and helping each other. Human relationships have become more valuable. The emphasis was not on differences, but on how they can help each other at work and in life.

Following the structured in-depth interview, only 22% of respondents completed the **Zimbardo time perspective test**. Based on the results, no clear demands can be drawn, however, it seems that there are positive expectations about the future among the respondents. Therefore, the authors intend to investigate the method further in future research on a similar topic.

4. CONCLUSION

The network of the family businesses is woven through the economy. Their significance is not only manifested in the main sectors of the economy, but they also function as an invisible glue. Retention, solidarity and closeness, the ability to innovate and the willingness to believe are the qualities that distinguish them from all other forms of enterprises. The family businesses also incorporate the features hidden in their structure into their operations. Entrepreneurship is not only a means of generating income, but also a heritage and identity, as well as a retaining community not only for family members but also for employees. Hungarian businesses, regardless of industry, recognized this period as an opportunity for change. Managers of family businesses agree that the pandemic caused unexpected problems, urged them to make important decisions regarding the future of the businesses, including ones about innovation and renewal.

ACKNOWLEDGMENTS

This research was carried out with the participation of several Hungarian companies. Thanks to Bisnode Hungary Ltd. (member of Dun & Bradstreet Group) for research access. We would like to thank the Business Community of Hungarian Business Leaders (MVÜK), the National Association of Family Enterprises and the Szinegria Ltd. for achieving family businesses.

We would also like to thank the family businesses who participated in the research and helped us with their responses, professional and managerial experiences, and network of contacts.

REFERENCES

Cabinet of the Hungarian Prime Minister. (2021). *Részt Veszünk Az Uniós Lőszerbeszerzésben, De Csakis A Magyar Katonák Kapnak Belőle Lőszert.* Hungarian Prime Minister. https://koronavirus.gov.hu/terkepek/fertozottek

Havrancsik, I., & Havrancsik, D. (2021). Summary on the answers of family-owned business to the challenges of the pandemic by Szinergia Ltd. *Europea.* https://ec.europa.eu/eurostat https://www.ksh.hu/?lang=hu

Kása, R., Radácsi, L., and Csákné, F.J. (2019). Családi vállalkozások definíciós operacionalizálása és hazai arányuk becslése a kkv-szektoron belül. [Definitional operationalization of family businesses and estimation of their domestic share within the SME sector.] *Statisztikai szemle, 97*, 146-174 doi:10.20311/stat2019.2.hu0146

Opten. (2020). *A hazai cégek 40 százaléka családi jellegű vállalkozás.* [40 percent of domestic companies are family businesses.] Opten. https://www.opten.hu/kozlemenyek/a-hazai-cegek-40-szazaleka-csaladi-jellegu-vallalkozas

Piac és profit. (2019). Nem mindegy, mit nevezünk családi vállalkozásnak. *Piac és profit.* https://piacesprofit.hu/kkv_cegblog/nem-mindegy-mit-nevezunk-csaladi-vallalkozasnak/3/

Portfolio. (2020). There is a sector that has not been harmed by the coronavirus - Modernization of agriculture can accelerate. *Portfolio.* https://www.portfolio.hu/bank/20201117/van-olyan-szektor-aminek-nem-artott-a-koronavirus-felgyorsulhat-a-mezogazdasag-modernizacioja-457322

Világgazdaság. (2021). A családi vállalkozások lehetnek a járvány nagy nyertesei. [Family businesses can be the big winners of the epidemic.] *Világgazdaság*. https://www.vg.hu/cegvilag/2021/05/a-csaladi-vallalkozasok-lehetnek-a-jarvany-nagy-nyertesei

Zimbardo, P., & Sword, R. K. M. (2017). Living and Loving Better with Time Perspective Therapy: Healing from the Past, Embracing the Present, Creating an Ideal Future. MCFarland & Company, Inc.

Chapter 3
Paradigm Shift From Traditional to Communicaiton and Technology Acceptance Models for the Survival of Family Businesses in Oman

Sangeeta Tripathi
University of Technology and Applied Sciences, Salalah, Oman

Muna Al Shahri
University of Technology and Applied Sciences, Salalah, Oman

ABSTRACT

The deadly outbreak of different variants of covid-19 has not only created havoc on millions of lives and public health but has severely impacted the global market and shattered many countries' economies. A general phenomenon of shortage in public income, rise in unemployment, and breakdown in manufacturing and service industries have been noticed worldwide. Transportation, tourism, and accommodation industries have been badly affected. Oman has not been exempted from covid-19 mitigation measures. Through case studies, the authors explain the traditional resources of Omani family businesses and their adaptive approach to new media technology, resilience, and strategic communication to respond to the crisis created by the pandemic. This chapter will contribute as a reference document for the researchers to conduct a comparative study.

DOI: 10.4018/978-1-6684-7394-8.ch003

INTRODUCTION

Oman is a beautiful country situated in the Arabian Peninsula (Tripathi & Al Shahri, 2016). It has an absolute monarchy governing system, where the Sultan is the supreme head of the Majlis Al Dawla (State Council) and Majlis Ashura. The 86 members of the State Council get appointed by His Majesty. In contrast, A'shura Council members get elected by Omani citizens democratically to represent them to discuss public issues and concerns for solutions (Sultanate of Oman, State Council. (n.d.). Oman shares its geographic borders with Yemen, Saudi Arabia, and the UAE.

Along with rich culture and tradition, Oman has an enthralling story of building from an old conservative nation to a prosperous modern state. Late Sultan Qaboos Bin Said's vision was clear and focused on comprehensive modernization policies. When the Late His Majesty ascended to the throne in 1970, he formulated his plans and balanced them with regional tribal cultural and country-ethnic values. His sole aim was to improve the living standards of the Omani people and establish Oman as a peaceful and safe country for everyone.

Women were granted their voting rights in 1994 and could contest as candidates in 2000 (Räisänen, J. 2018). This revolutionary decision made Oman the first nation in the Gulf Cooperation Council (GCC) to give women voting rights. In the 2015 election, women secured 7 seats out of 84 seats in the Al-Shura Council. Currently, 18 percent of the State Council members are women (Räisänen, J. 2018). The country's well-formulated foreign policies laid the foundation in this regard and made Oman a favorite place for business and work.

Oman's economy is mainly reliant on crude oil and natural gas. Oman's government encourages SMEs and family businesses to promote self-employment in the private and public sectors (ALkiyumi, 2017). "Fund for Development of Youth Projects" under Royal decree 76/98 (8th Nov.1998 and "Al – Raffd" program under Royal decree 6/2013 (Jan.2013)) aims to enhance SMEs and family businesses in the Sultanate. Under the 9th five-year program, the stress was laid on the diversification of the economy, Omanization, and the privatization process to boost and support the country's economy in the past five years.

Some potential economic drivers such as tourism, fisheries, manufacturing, logistics, and mining have been identified to grow (Oman focuses on diversification and infrastructure investment, 2018). After the desire of the Late Sultan Qaboos Bin aid, His Majesty Sultan Haitham Bin Tariq assumed the reins in 2020. He emphasized foreign investment and Omanization policy that underpin Oman Vision 2040 to facilitate more jobs for Omani youth. A new royal decree 107/2020 (August 18, 2020) has merged two governments programs Riyada (Royal decree 36/2013) and Al Rafdd (Royal decree 6/2013) (Jobel, 2021; SMEs in Oman come to the fore during the covid-19 pandemic, 2021) to encourage SMEs and family business in Oman.

The authority for Small and Medium Enterprises (SMEs) works as arms to develop small and medium enterprises to contribute to the country's economy. This body provides support, business advisory, SMEs toolkit mentoring, and training programs. SMEs' toolkit supports local entrepreneurs by providing international partners and expert guidance (Dave, 2021). Oman Development Bank (ODB) is also working to promote local business. Despite the economic difficulties created by the pandemic, the bank played a significant role in stimulating the country's economy. The bank applied Oman government directives to deal with the pandemic's economic impact. For example, averting loan installments for six months from April 2020 was one of the best decisions to relieve the SMEs and family businesses starting up in the Sultanate.

ODB has achieved an encouraging result despite the pandemic-created challenges, in line with Oman's vision for 2040. The summary of ODB credit performance for 2020 proves this fact. In 2020, 11,812 approved loan was recorded. It was an increase of 83 percent compared to 2019. The total amount was 68.8 million Rials. In addition, the support from the Oman government has created a breath-taking atmosphere for already-established SMEs and family businesses (Oman Development Bank - Annual Report 2020).

The Ministry of Social Development, Department of service of family development, signed a cooperation agreement with Zubair Small Enterprises Centre on September 14, 2021, to develop support programs to help social security families (Zubair SEC signed an agreement with the Ministry of Social Development, 2021). A specialized training program has been included under this agreement to enhance and develop entrepreneurial and management skills. Oman's family business is integral to the country's Gross Domestic Product (GDP). Oman's government understands this very well. That is why they keep pushing and promoting family businesses during this unprecedented time.

According to June 2021 data issued by the National Centre for Statistics and Information, the registration of SMEs reached 54,726 compared to 44,448 in June 2020, shortly after the pandemic started in Oman. These small enterprises became a helping hand to the people of Oman and lessened the impact of the covid-19 pandemic on the economy and community. However, the Oman News Agency statement announced an increase of SMEs by 23.1 percent in June 2021. Around 50,000 small, micro, and medium enterprises have been registered with the Authority for Small and Medium Enterprises Development (ONA, Oman registered over 20 percent increase in SMEs, 2021).

HISTORY AND PRESENT STATUS OF THE FAMILY BUSINESS IN OMAN

The family business is a concept that has been introduced previously in Oman. Though the country mainly relied on crude oil and gas, some prominent clans used to be involved in the family business before the Renaissance (Oman's Leading Business Clans, 2020), such as Suhail Bahwan (established in 1965) and Zubair Corporation LLC. (Established in 1967), Shanfari Group of Companies (established in 1960), etc.

After ascending to the throne, Late His Majesty Sultan Qaboos started a new development era. In 1970, Late Sultan Qaboos Bin Said united the Sultanate, and massive development programs began under his leadership. In this development drive, the family business had included education, health care, a housing scheme for the nationals, promoting foreign investment, and encouraging SME entrepreneurs. Saud Bahwan Group (established in 1977) and Mohsin Haidar Darwish Group of companies (established in 1987) have been considered the most significant family group business after the beginning of the Renaissance. These family businesses groups are extensively involved in infrastructure development, marketing customer care, automotive, allied business, heavy vehicle trading, construction, equipment, turnkey projects, municipal and civic services, manufacturing property and real estate, travel, and tourism business, marine, defense, oilfield, drilling, engineering, etc. Now, these groups are dealing internationally (Mohsin Haider Darwish 2020, n.d.).

To encourage local entrepreneurs, SMEs, and family businesses in the Sultanate, the Oman government took several initiatives, such as the "Sanad" Fund in 2001 (Yasin & Khansari, 2022), the "Al Raffd" Fund in 2013, and the SMEs fund in 2014, etc. Sultan Qaboos University has become another vehicle to promote SMEs. They often organize several events to bridge the gap between educational institutions, markets, and SMEs. In May 2017, they organized an event linking Oman's Higher Education Institutions with the public and private sectors. The Sas program to promote ICT-based business also helps build a robust ICT sector in Oman. Oman's government vision and efforts escalated different business establishments at local and national levels (Shukaili et al., 2020).

Oman's government's plans, programs, and policies have embodied Omani women's participation in all fields alongside men. This enhances their national role in various sectors. As a result, they could prove themselves as significant players in the country's sustainable economic growth process.

Due to the government's efforts and women empowerment drives, families' engagement and interest in opening family businesses have been noticed. The family business is considered an integral part of Oman's economy as it contributes to the national GDP that sustains diversified economic growth. Women entrepreneurs and families are mainly involved in designing cosmetics, perfumes, natural soap, abaya, and tailoring projects, pickles making and its preservation, canning, and packaging catering, banquet, Omani craft, frankincense, and oil for natural beauty use (Tripathi & Al Shahri, 2016; Ashok, 2021).

To support families engaged in business, the Oman Ministry of Social Development organized a campaign in 2021. Its name is: "You are creative, you are productive." It was held in Barka to help display their products in a campaign that included different activities to improve the social security of Omani families through supportive material awareness workshops and others. From time to time, some other campaigns have been conducted. For example, to eradicate the pandemic impact, OMRAN Group launched a program in September 2021. It aims to support and encourage aspiring entrepreneurs and artists to showcase their talents, skills, and capabilities (Paul, 2021). Table 1 shows how Oman SMEs have grown yearly (National Centre for Statistics, Riyada annual report, 2019, Oman, I. Islamic Banking Growth and SMEs Development).

Table 1. Yearly growth of SMEs in Oman

Year	Registered Number of SMEs	Percentage of Increase
2016	25,692	46 percent
2017	31,836	23.91 percent
2018	37,289	17.12 percent
2019	42,698	14.05 percent
2020	48,669	14 percent

Fresh data released in August 2021 by NCSI Oman displayed that the total registration for SMEs reached 56,687. It is 24 percent more than last year. The surge in SME registration can be seen region-wise as well. The Governorate of Al Dakhiliyah received a 20.1 percent increase, Dhofar 23.8 percent, North Sharqiyah 21.2 percent, South Sharqiya 27.5 percent, South Batinah 28.1 percent, Al Dhahira 17.4 percent, Al Buraimi 23.9 percent, AL Wusta 37.5 percent, and Musandam 44.9 percent. The registered SMEs in Muscat were the highest of all governorates. It has 17,927 SMEs (Shukaili, et al. 2020).

By December 2020, the SMEs Fund funded 142 small and medium enterprises with 13 million Omani Rials. The Al Raffd Fund has also approved 22,563 loans by the end of April 2020. More than 99 million Omani Rials have been given to flourishing entrepreneurs and SMEs until April. Due to this, 4,229 direct employments have been generated for Omani youth, with 64.77 percent male and 35.3 percent females. Repayment of loans 83.9 percent displays the growth of opened and established SMEs. It has been noticed that most of these SMEs are being handled like a family business. It means family members are involved or associated with the firm as owners and managers.

Due to its collective nature, Oman's culture and the cooperative nature-society are highly ancillary to the family-based business (Nasseri, 2020). Despite the significant role of family businesses in Oman's sustainable economic growth, minimal studies are available on family businesses. This is a big reason national data related to SMEs is available, but the exact percentage of families engaged in business is yet to be available. According to Oman Global Entrepreneurship Monitor National Report, 2019-2020, all the Middle East Countries benefit from the proliferation of family business traditions. In 2019, 26.6 percent of Omani entrepreneurs set up their early-stage startups to continue a family tradition business. This percentage is noticeable but lower than in GCC countries (Shukaili et al., 2020). Figure 1 depicts Omani motivation to continue the family businesses compared to other countries.

Figure 1. Oman's Global position on motivation to continue a family tradition at early-stage entrepreneurship[1]

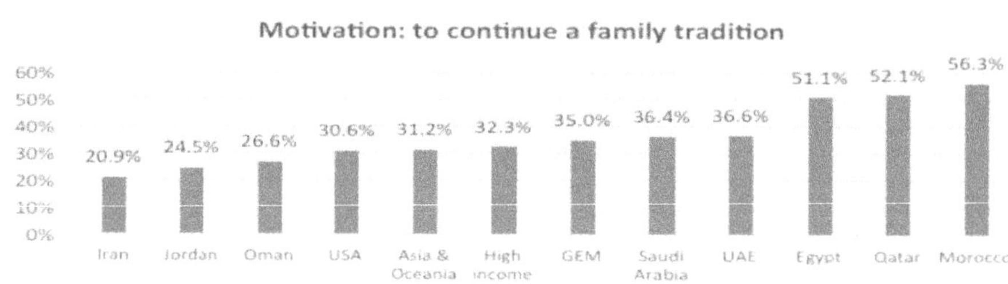

After ascending to the throne, His Majesty Sultan Haitham Bin Tareq focuses on Oman Vision 2040. Omanization processes and national framework conditions help SMEs and family businesses in Oman. The national framework conditions include finance availability, government policies to promote SMEs and entrepreneurship, taxes, training of professional skills at different levels of education, legal and commercial infrastructure, market dynamics and regulations, and social and cultural contexts. The covid-19 crisis has given the opportunity in disguise to avail maximum use of the digital platform. Therefore, it can be considered a new horizon for SMEs and family businesses. Increasing numbers of SMEs can be seen as job scarcity, desire to create great wealth, aspiration, and continued family business tradition work as prevalent motivators for early-stage entrepreneurship in Oman. Figure 2 shows the different motivators at different levels of business stages.

Figure 2. Different motivations for entrepreneurs at different entrepreneurial stages[2]

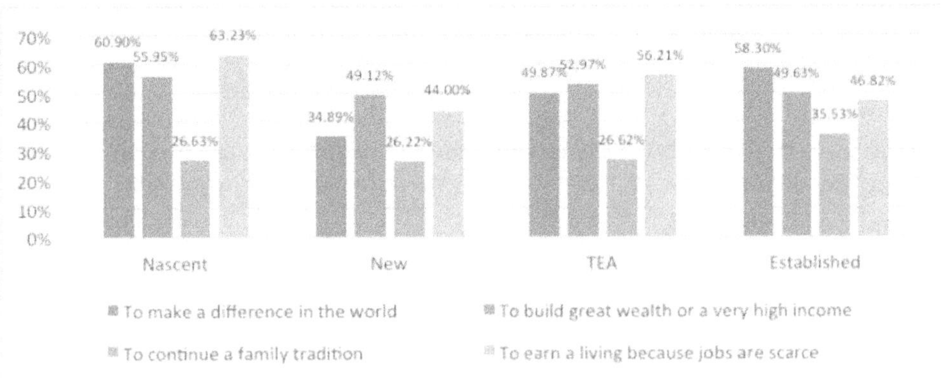

Due to pandemics, economic pressure has been experienced worldwide. Oman is not unimpaired of its impact. However, the increasing registration number of Oman SMEs during 2020 and 2021 shows a positive sign for the country's economic growth. Increasing SMEs and most such firms owned and controlled by family members are an encouraging phenomenon for Oman Vision 2040. Therefore, it has become essential to investigate family business growth and scope in the Sultanate. Due to the long pandemic lockdown, the normal functioning of businesses was directly connected with the business houses' sale-purchase and cash flow circle. Therefore, it created financial challenges to running the business smoothly.

Other issues, such as human resource management, retention, and marketing management, were more experienced by entrepreneurs and family business owners. The sudden closure of economic activities gave a big jolt to the country's business. It took time to create survival strategies to overbear the pandemic obstacles. This chapter discusses the survival strategies of SMEs and family businesses. It also examines how communication and digitalization innovation has changed traditional business. That indicates a paradigm shift from traditional business practices to communication technology accepted models and diffusion of the innovative framework.

TRADITIONAL BUSINESS MODEL

Before covid-19, Oman's businesses were more based traditional model (as shown in Figure 1). In the era of digital technology, these companies have been using social media as a communication tool to approach customers directly since 2012. However, it has yet to be intensely enforced. Like any other country's business model, Omani companies and manufacturers connected with distributors and retailers' networks to reach out to their customers. Print advertising was mainly used to communicate to the masses.

It has been observed that some traditional and small family businesses used to reach out to their customers directly through their retail outlet networks, as shown in Figure 2. However, in some cases, they do not have retail outlets. Instead, they use a direct-to-customer business model, manufacturing their product and running their business from home. For communication, they use world-to-mouth publicity. It is displayed in Figure 3.

Figure 3. Traditional business model
(Designed by Authors)

Figure 4. Reaching Customers through their Retail Outlet Networks[3]

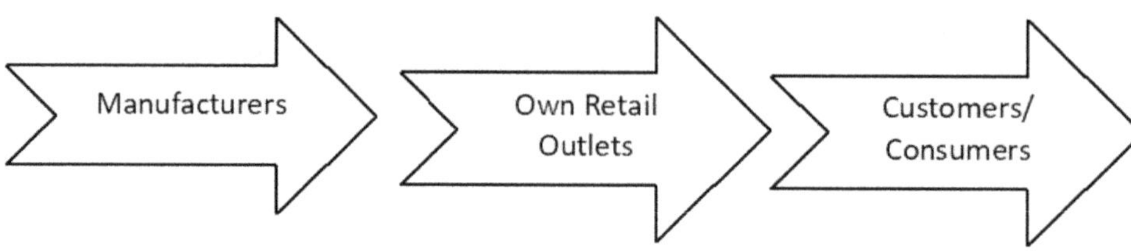

Figure 5. Direct-to-Customer Business Model[4]

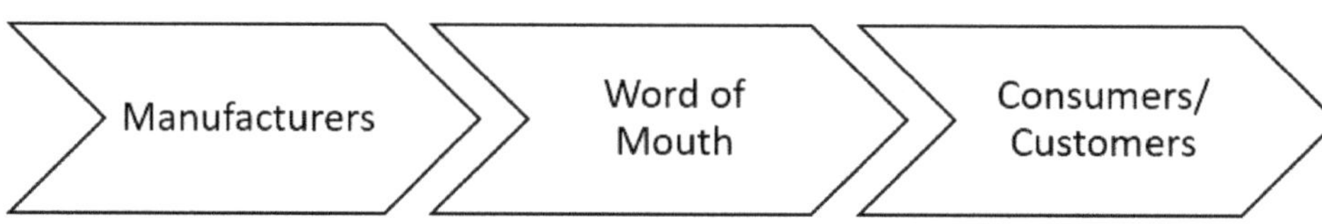

EMERGING TRENDS IN BUSINESS IN RECENT YEARS:

According to research in 2015 (Tripathi & Al Shahri, 2016), Omani women use social media channels to empower themselves and aspire to create a difference. Their businesses are getting done with family support. The homemakers turned entrepreneurs involved in Oman's traditional business of frankincense, perfume, skincare oil, hand-made soap, and well-being products. Their selection of frankincense for their family business is related to Oman's culture and heritage.

During the 12th century, the trading of frankincense and maritime was the main strength of Oman's business. Since then, frankincense has been an integral part of Omani culture and is considered a symbol of life for the Dhofar people. It is used as incense in prayers and other occasions. In addition, Luban has restorative and healing properties. Some Omani women make oil and perfume from frankincense in Salalah, Dhofar. They also produce skin care products, soap, and other well-being products.

They do not rely on the distributor or retailers' networks to reach out to their target consumers, but they sell their products through Instagram, Facebook, Snapchat, and WhatsApp networks. They rarely use print and electronic media advertising. Instead, they use social media and other new media portals to showcase the features of their products to their followers. This trend in business was steadily getting popular.

Covid-19 has accelerated communication technology adoption as an accepted model among buyers and sellers (Modgil, Dwivedi, Rana, Gupta, & Kamble, 2021). However, due to the covid-19 pandemic, millions of lives are stuck at home worldwide. Countries had imposed lockdowns to control covid-19 infection, which halted normal business activities. As a result, reverse growth in worldwide economies has been recorded. Oman has also experienced the same. This situation forced doctors, teachers, psychologists, and businesspeople to accept available technology-driven platforms such as zoom, google meet, and other social media applications to perform their work. It could be called a desperate period when confined people in their homes wanted to connect to the outside world without any training. Due to this reason, it cannot be called a smooth transition.

Shifting to online platforms was a new arrangement comprised of different digital technology elements. This emerged rapidly with some more addition and facilitation. However, it took time to start work online by adopting technology business models and diffusion of innovative framework models for SMEs and family businesses. In addition, it requires a specific collaboration between customers and buyers, an effective communication strategy, a support mechanism to facilitate customers, and a system to attend to grievances and feedback. With initial struggle and several grievances, Oman SMEs and family businesses have adopted technology-driven platforms to connect to their customers.

DIFFERENT MODELS AND THEIR RELEVANCE TO SURVIVAL STRATEGIES OF FAMILY BUSINESS

In the era of communication technology, our approaches have already been replaced due to different needs. Before covid-19, we used new media applications for many reasons, but they needed to be thoroughly followed. After the deadly outbreak of covid-19, everyone has been forced to think beyond the boundaries, whether they intend to use it. Like academics and other professions, businesspeople started looking at different models and theories to develop survival strategies. The high magnitude of infection and the long pandemic lockdown stressed the financial front of SMEs and family businesses. These circumstances forced business people to adopt technology-accepted models and innovative framework models. Many family businesses that run as a home industry have adopted technology models into their business. However, some of them have very little interest in its use. That is why they are resistant to adopting innovation and technology acceptance models.

THEORETICAL FRAMEWORK

Technology Acceptance Model (TAM) was developed by Fred Davis and Richard Bagozzi in 1985. TAM works on four core variables, as shown in Figure 4.

Figure 6. Technology acceptance model

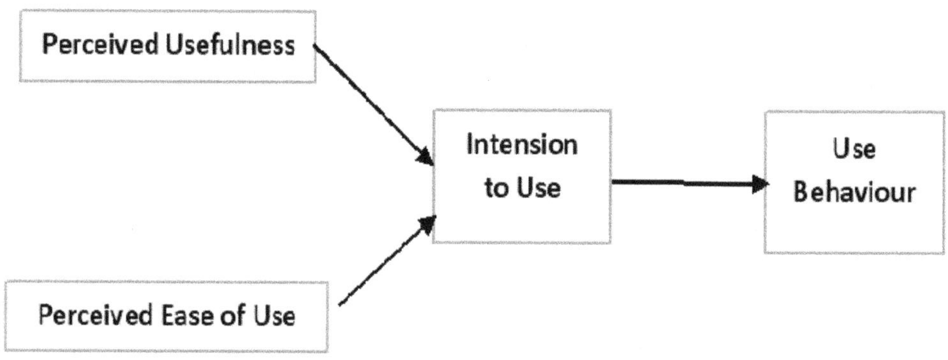

This model received several changes from different scholars. It was adjusted in 1989 first time with the word-external variable. Davis, Fred, Richard Bagozzi, and P. Warsaw believed that some external variables affect core variables (Davis,

Bagozzi, and Warshaw 1989). More factors were added in 2000 by V. Venkatesh and F.D. Davis. This enhanced model is called the TAM 2 model, which explains perceived usefulness (P.U.) as the string variable. Several factors can influence P.U. Figure 5 illustrates these factors. Perceived usefulness is the first step toward selecting a technology to use. The second variable, 'ease of use,' motivates users to accept software and different digital applications (Venkatesh & Davis, 2000). These mentioned TAM models indicate that different variables have affected the intention and use behavior. This finally affects the approach of businessmen to their customers and consumers.

Figure 7. TAM2 model
(Adapted from Venkatesh and Davis, 2000)

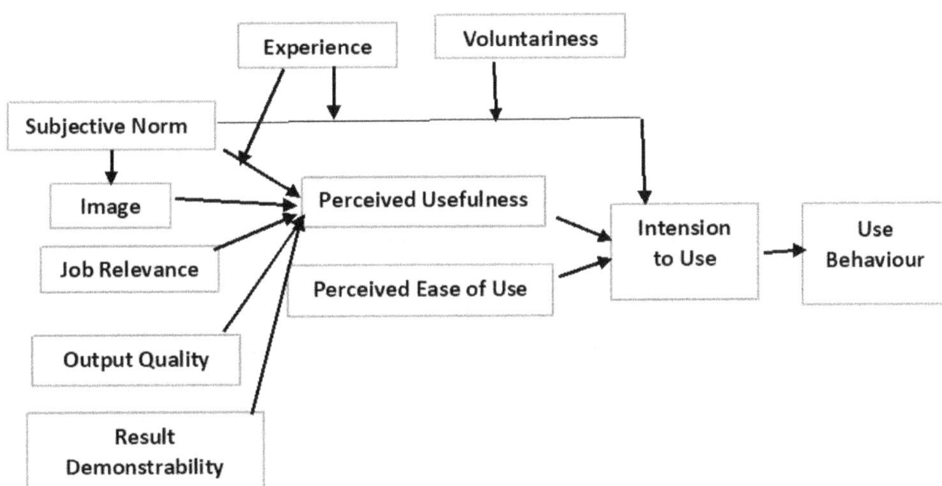

In 2008, some more factors were added to TAM 2 by V. Venkatesh and H. Bala. For example, computer self-efficacy, external control perception, computer anxiety, playfulness, perceived enjoyment, and objective usability can influence the second core variable- perceived ease of use (Venkatesh & Bala, 2008).

DIFFERENT DIFFUSION OF INNOVATIVE FRAMEWORK

E. M. Rogers developed an innovative framework model in 1962. This model talks about the importance of awareness that can be done through strategic communication via different channels (Kosała and Wach 2014, Aleke, Ojiako and Wainwright 2011).

Figure 8. Diffusion of the innovative framework model

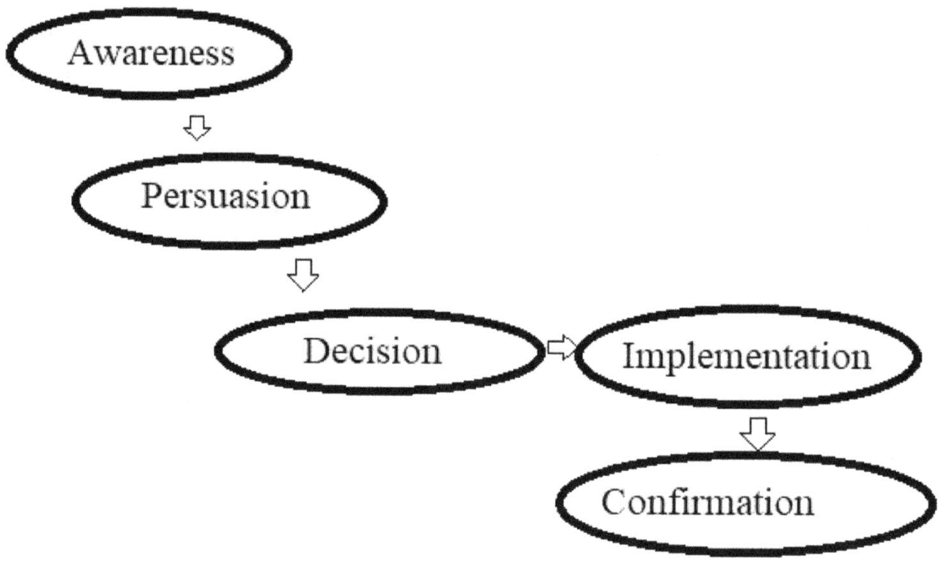

The authors discuss these three models to facilitate an understanding of how technology and communication are accomplishing each other in the present time. Communication plays a significant role when we want to create awareness regarding anything. At the same time, technology is used to impart information. The diffusion of innovation model indicates that awareness is the first step for persuading the target public to call for action and make decisions. This decision may be a rejection or adoption. Awareness, interest, evaluation, and trial play a significant role in adopting emerging technology. In the present scenario of covid-19, family businesses and SMEs have gone through all these stages to adopt relevant technology and other innovative ways to approach their customers. They opted for these models to develop their survival strategies.

CONCEPTUAL FRAMEWORK

The authors have adopted the extended TAM model, adding value to communication and awareness. According to the present pandemic scenario, there is a strong need to add communication elements. Communication is essential in creating awareness about the usefulness of different software and digital applications. In addition, the communication brings awareness about accessing the product through online portals. Figure 7 shows how communication can influence perceived usefulness, and perceived ease of use can further impact the intention to use the product or services and influence future behavior. Digital literacy helps them at this stage, and they generate interest in behavioral intention. Stage four – actual system use differs from person to person.

Figure 9. Adopted TAM model[5]

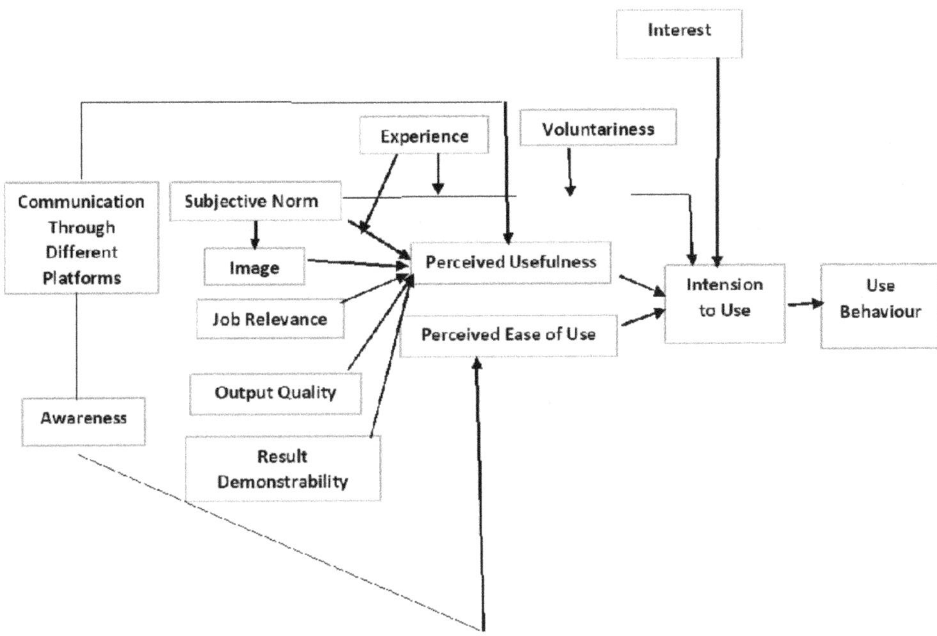

METHODOLOGY

The study is exploratory research. Therefore, a purposive sampling technique has been applied. Twenty-nine in-depth interviews have been conducted from Salalah, Dhofar region. During sample selection, the authors noticed that many SMEs work as family businesses in Oman. They control and manage company functions, sales, and marketing with their family members. That is why the intended respondents are mainly from SMEs such as perfume manufacturers, frankincense, incense, Luban, Skincare, haircare, home décor, fashion, clothing, abaya, and well-being.

The criteria for selecting these SMEs/ family businesses is the range of their employees, which was 2 to 300. A well-structured open-ended set of questions was prepared in Arabic and English languages. The in-depth interviews were conducted in October 2021. Important criterion has been devised to address the research questions, aiming to understand the prevalent challenges experienced by SMEs/ family business during the pandemic period, their strategies to manage the venue and human resources, marketing communication, and the paradox of accepting technology to approach their target buyers. How different communication platforms have helped them to overbear the crisis.

RESULT AND DISCUSSION

Case Study

The four cases have been discussed in this chapter from Omani SMEs and family businesses of frankincense, perfume, hair care, Skincare, and cosmetic products during the pandemic crisis. These case studies are designed around five criteria to address research questions and compare followed strategies vs. no strategies, as shown in Table 2.

Table 2. Research questions criteria

No	Criteria	The coding is based on interviewees' responses
1.	Prevalent challenges experienced	1. Financial aspects 2. Human resource 3. Suppliers and distributions difficulties 4. Sale purchase 5. Marketing issues
2.	Strategies based on human resource and venue management	1. Salary cutting 2. Employee termination 3. Sending them for a particular leave without pay 4. Shifting offices to home for cost-cutting
3.	Strategies related to communication and technology for marketing	1. Traditional communication approach 2. Fully shifted to new media for marketing and sale 3. Using new technology to reach out to old customers' networks
4.	Any paradox while accepting diffusion of Innovative framework or communication technology accepted model	1. No paradox with techno-savvy customers 2. Not feasible like field selling
5.	Digital communication channels help in crisis-overbearing strategies	1. Elements of new media worked well 2. Supported fully

Shoaa Al Shams perfume, Ajmal Perfume, Belle ame Shop for perfume, and cosmetics have been included in the case study. These three family businesses followed strategies by adopting a communication technology accepted model and diffusion of innovative framework model to overbear the pandemic challenges. On the other hand, the Maski perfume brand did not follow any strategy even though it had a social media account. Instead, they waited to get the crisis over. Table 3 shows the activity of 11 SMEs and family businesses on social media during the pandemic.

Table 3. Details some SMEs and family businesses active on social media during the pandemic

Name of SMEs and Family Businesses available on Instagram	Posts of the products	Followers	Following
BINSHEKHAN	148	54.6k	03
Al Maqam Perfume	1286	19.8k	5840
Shoes Alshams	101	51.3k	24
Al Annabi Perfume	33	70k	03
Junaid Perfume	1390	106k	0
Al Misak	91	5883	457
Oud Elite	242	7347	2
Loris Perfume	130	261k	0
Ajmal Perfume Oman	1106	24.5k	16
Furat La Perfume	20.5k	148k	68
Belle ame Oman	817	2350	571

CASE STUDY ONE

Shoaa Al Shams company started as SME in 2010, but seven family members later managed the company function. Amaima Mohammed Ahmed Alhamiary, the owner of Shoaa Al Shams, started her business on a small scale and opted for a direct customer business model. This model is described in figure three. First, she promoted and advertised her products through word of mouth without using communication tools. Later, with WhatsApp's advent, she used it to reach prospective customers. As a result, her brand of perfume, cosmetics, Skincare, and haircare became already established. She was not following the traditional way of approaching customers, but even then, the pandemic crisis has impacted her business a lot.

Like other businesses, she also experienced lockdown difficulties such as a dropdown in demand, supplier limitations, delivery products, and marketing issues. To sustain her business, she shifted her way of reaching customers by opening an Instagram account in January 2021. She used rigorous sales promotion and offered customers incentives and gifts to attract more customers. Now she has a barcode and a website for her products. Through these means, she is expanding her business to all GCC countries. She found herself an adapter to the diffusion of the innovative framework model. Now she is using all elements of social media to attract more customers.

Her strong communication relations with the Omani community and the quality of her products became ancillary to her survival during the pandemic crisis. Social media elements such as pictures, videos, and word-of-mouth information about the products' experience have worked great. It influences prospective customers. Technology-mediated communication helped the customers to perceive the usefulness of their products, and its easy-use nature evoked intention among the customers to adopt the product for future use. She found that communication channels and social media drivers significantly reduced the impact of the covid-19 crisis. No paradox was found while dealing with techno-savvy customers in the digital era.

CASE STUDY TWO

Ajmal Perfume started their family business in 1951. The owner's wife and two children have managed this brand with 24 showrooms in Oman. Among 24, four showrooms in Salalah. The manufacturing of this perfume is taking place in Dubai. This year the brand is celebrating its 70-year success glory. Last year, they could not escape of covid-19 effect on their business.

They adopted a communication and technology acceptance model to vanquish the pandemic impact. They have had their social media accounts since 2013, but during the pandemic, they accelerated all elements to promote sales through these networking sites. They strongly believe in the people's quality and trust, which is why they never offered any discount on their showroom's product. However, they are now offering discounts on online purchases on special occasions. Incense and perfume are integral to Omani culture, so the online strategy worked well.

Due to the lockdown, delivery was limited. So, the company shifted its delivery timing to relaxing hours and offered a free delivery option on bulk purchases. Their strong community relations, the quality of the products, and pricing helped them sustain themselves during the crisis. No paradox was experienced while dealing with techno-savvy customers in the digital era.

CASE STUDY THREE

Belle ame Shop for perfumes and cosmetics is a family business. To curtail the impact of covid-19 on their business, they cut 50 percent of the salary of their employees. They managed their delivery timing according to lockdown relaxation. To sustain their business, they completely shifted to social media platforms.

The Salalah community is very cooperative. They supported this manufacturer by communicating their experience to their network through social media, helping prospective customers perceive the usefulness of perfumes and cosmetics. It invokes customers' intention to buy their product and repeat the action in the future. Social media retrenched physical distance by bringing customers virtually during social distancing. It has become easy to deal with modern techno-savvy customers without any paradox.

CASE STUDY FOUR

Maski brand perfume did not follow any strategy though the pandemic lockdown has impacted their business. Dropdown sales and purchases have created immense financial difficulty for the owner. Even though he believed that the traditional business model is more relevant and honest, it does not involve manipulating facts. A lack of technical knowledge may cause many threats. Community relations worked more than anything else.

The landlord of the showroom has waived almost six months' rent which has become an excellent relief for different businesses in Salalah. That is why the Maski perfume owner emphasized community relations, quality, and innovative products and shared customers' experiences through word of mouth for his business survival. He trusted third-party endorsement more than advertising. Maski brand perfume and skincare products are known for their luxury, quality, and presentation.

It has particular demand among young Omani girls and brides for wedding gifts. In addition, its excellent packaging attracts its buyers; that is why the owner of the Maski brand has been assured that his brand will revive once the pandemic gets over. He admits that communication is a prerequisite for a business's success in the era of digital technology. First, pictures and videos significantly generate demand for the product; quality sustains the demand. Though he does not use social media, he believes it is the need of the hour. It has undoubtedly reduced the severe impact of the pandemic on people's businesses.

DISCUSSION

The Discussion is based on the interviewees' responses. The conclusion is drawn based on the frequency of responses from the interviewees.

Figure 10. Types of Business Projects

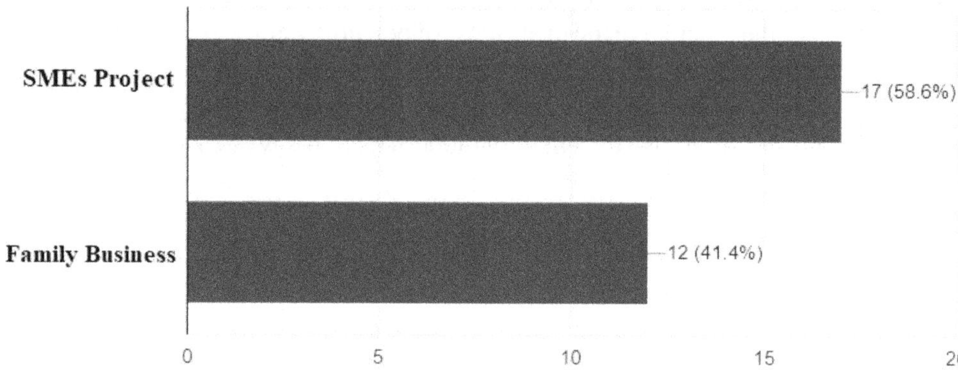

Figure 8 displays that 41.1 percent of SMEs work as a family business in Salalah. 79.3 percent of interviewees had experienced pandemic impact. They said that the pandemic hit their business severely. However, this impact was dissimilar for different business houses. Drop down in demand, lockdown difficulties, supplier limitation, marketing, and delivery issues were significant challenges experienced by 48.3 percent of respondents. In comparison, 41.4 percent said it was mainly lockdown difficulties that limited the customers.

Figure 11. Strategies to overbear the challenges during the pandemic

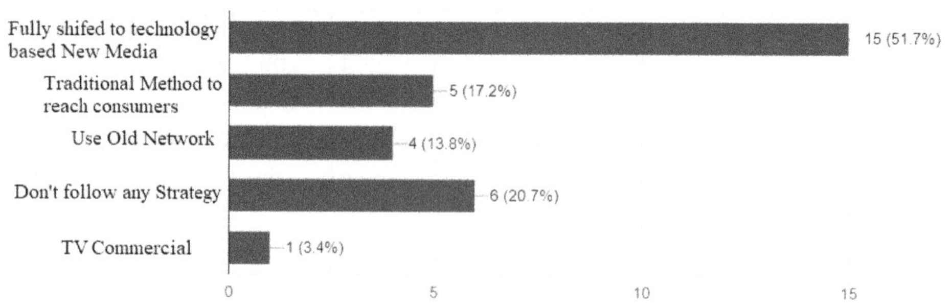

To smite the challenges, 13.8 percent of respondents said they had reduced the number of employees, while 26.16 percent said they had shifted their showrooms and retail outlets to a smaller place. Some of them were working from home as well. In addition, 34.5 percent of interviewees said they offered free delivery options for bulk purchases. In comparison, 20.4 percent of interviewees applied mixed strategies like 50 percent salary cutting, sales- promotions, and time management according to government orders.

As shown in Figure 9, 51.7 percent of interviewees said they have shifted to social networking sites for survival. In comparison, 31 percent said they used phones and other traditional communication tools to reach out to their customer's network. 20.7 percent of interviewees needed to follow a strategy. They just waited to get over the pandemic and open the economic activities in the country. Another 51.7 percent of interviewees mentioned that the quality of their product worked as the main element that helped them survive their business during the pandemic. In comparison, 39.7 percent stated that quality, trust, brand loyalty, fair pricing, and product usefulness generated demand during the pandemic crisis.

Figure 12. Significance of communication and new media in survival strategy

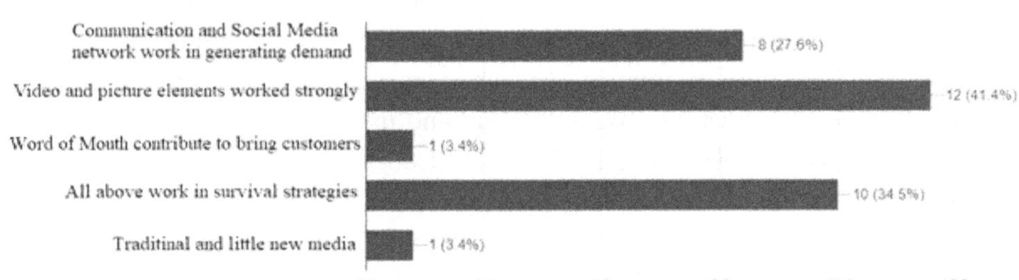

Figure 10 shows the communication and technology accepted model and diffusion of the innovative framework model. Among respondents, 27.6 percent of interviewees said it helped create awareness about the product's availability online. As a result, it persuades the customers to make their purchase decision. Another 41.4 percent of interviewees mentioned that video and picture elements on social media contributed to generating product demand. In comparison, 34.5 percent stated that it had made customers about the availability of the different products in the local surrounding that is easy to reach. Finally, 82.8 percent of interviewees said communication technology had become a great savior during the pandemic. The pandemic and extended lockdown would have killed the SMEs and family businesses if social media had not been available.

The pilot study in this book chapter displays the impact of the pandemic on Oman SMEs and family businesses. The Oman government took several measures to improve framework conditions to mitigate the pandemic impact, particularly policies supporting relevant SMEs and family businesses. As a result, these framework conditions are better than in 2019 and can be considered a robust assessment of the government's response to the pandemic.

1. SMEs and family businesses develop strategies to alleviate the pandemic's influence on the business. It took months to design and work on new platforms. Because it also needs consumer contributions, some family businesses have started online dealing only after January 2021.
2. Of 29 participants, 15 have adopted communication, technology-accepted, and innovative framework models. This indicates a reasonable degree of shifting traditional SMEs and family businesses to technology-accepted future trading.
3. Six participants perceived the usefulness of new media and its ease of use, but they did not apply its use in any survival strategy. This shows their resisting intention to use and use behavior.
4. External variables fully influence perceived usefulness and ease of use, contributing to variance in intention and usage behavior. For example, financial fraud, quality manipulations, and breach of trust are external variables that can cause variance in 'want to use and 'rigid and inflexible to use or interact.'
5. It has also been observed that the most used applications were Instagram, Snapchat, Facebook, and WhatsApp, like social media applications. At the same time, business apps were not used by SMEs and family businesses.
6. Strategies related to human resource management, salary cutting, and shifting of the showrooms have also been adopted for the businesses' survival.
7. The delivery of the product was also an issue during the pandemic. So, to deal with this difficulty, SMEs and family businesses have changed the timing according to relaxation hours and offered free delivery options on bulk purchases.
8. A 24 percent surge in SME registration until August 2021 is positive news for Oman, which creates a strong hope for a balanced recovery from the pandemic.

LIMITATIONS AND IMPLICATIONS OF THE STUDY

This book chapter is based on data collected through interviews. While conducting interviews, the authors faced difficulties as tropical cyclone Shaheen hit the northern part of Oman on October 03, 2021. The ferocious speedy wind and heavy rain created havoc, flooding streets and badly interrupting electricity and internet facilities. The raging cyclone turned cities and towns into lakes and rivers. It disturbed the living of Muscat, Al Musannah, Suwaiq, Saham, Khabourah, and Sohar people. In such circumstances, it becomes difficult to conduct interviews from north Oman. Therefore, the authors have included SMEs and family businesses from Dhofar, Salalah, the southern part of Oman.

The present study is qualitative and based on 29 interview responses. This study is conducted to understand the pandemic's immediate impact on SMEs/ family businesses and survival strategies. Therefore, GCC countries must be addressed when assessing the impact of Covid-19 on the world economy. Furthermore, a quantitative study can be conducted in Muscat and other GCC countries to facilitate a comprehensive understanding of the pandemic's impact on family businesses/ SMEs and their survival strategies.

The present study can be considered a reference document to investigate the impact of online interaction on goodwill and trust for SMEs and family business during the pandemic crisis. The study has raised questions related to cultural and traditional values that played a role in SMEs/ family businesses' survival. The present study indicates that Dhofar's culture, shared traditional values, different relationships among community members and old customer relations played a significant role in shifting online business. Different social media platforms play a vital role in approaching these prior known buyers. During the world health crisis, the Dhofar family business used online communication to make local people aware of their localized value chain, which has become a great advantage point.

CONCLUSION

This book chapter has broadly attempted to extend an understanding of SMEs and family businesses' challenges and survival strategies during the covid-19 pandemic crisis in Oman. Their survival strategies displayed a paradigm shift from traditional business practices to a communication technology acceptance model for future trading. There is no paradox found as another contributing party, 'New Consumers' are techno-savvy and aware of the usefulness of new media networks. They are already using different social media applications and are familiar with them.

Some variances have been noticed in SMEs and family business owners' intentions of use and their actual user behavior that some external factors have influenced. Frankincense, perfume, and incense are integral parts of Omani culture. This was the biggest reason that its demand remained relatively high. SMEs and the family businesses involved in its trading could sustain themselves even though people were confined in their houses during the pandemic. Haircare, Skincare, cosmetics, and well-being products have a routine demand that helps survive. After the lockdown, these products' business returns to normal without difficulties. Demand is improving steadily. Like their retail trading, SMEs and family businesses give equal importance to their online platform, which they have run under pandemic circumstances. Better offers and reasonable pricing are still available for online customers.

REFERENCES

Aleke, B., Ojiako, U., & Wainwright, D. (2011). ICT adoption in developing countries: Perspectives from small-scale agribusinesses. *Journal of Enterprise Information Management*, *24*(1), 68–84. doi:10.1108/17410391111097438

ALkiyumi. B. (2017, July 18). Economic Impact of Family Business. *Oman Observer*. https://www.omanobserver.om/article/77433/Opinion/economic-impact-of-family-businesses

Ashok, R. (2021, July 04). Omani Women empowered to run family business. *Gulf News*. https://gulfnews.com/world/gulf/oman/omani-women-empowered-to-run-family-business-1.80424959

Authority of Small and Medium Enterprises Development. (n.d.). Omanportal. https://omanportal.gov.om/wps/wcm/connect/en/site/home/gov/gov1/gov5governmentorganizations/raffd/raffd_1

Back to the Future: The SBGH Story. (n.d.). Suhail Bahwan Group. https://www.suhailbahwangroup.com/corporate-profile/back-to-the-future

Dave, S. (2021). *Oman government's support to SMEs*. Ooredoo. https://www.ooredoo.om/Showcasepage/OmanSupportSmes.aspx

Davis, F. D., Bagozzi, R. P., & Warshaw, P. R. (1989). User Acceptance of Computer Technology: A Comparison of Two Theoretical Models. *Management Science*, *35*(8), 982–1003. Retrieved 2021, from https://www.jstor.org/stable/2632151v. doi:10.1287/mnsc.35.8.982

Al Roya Press and Publishing House. (2019). *Entrepreneurship Research & Case Studies from Oman*. Al Roya Press and Publishing House. https://www.ibrict.edu.om/ieu/resources/Ent_resources/Entrepreneurship%20Research%20&%20Case%20Studies%20from%20Oman.pdf

United Nations. (2015). *Fund for Development of Youth Projects*. United Nations: Economic and Social Commission for Western Asia. https://archive.unescwa.org/fund-development-youth-projects

Jobel, K. (2021). *Reduced Inequalities-The Start of SMEs in Oman.* Sustainable Oman. https://sustainableoman.com/reduced-inequalities-the-start-of-smes-in-oman/

Kosała, M., & Wach, K. (2014). Linking Regional Knowledge Laboratory and Growth of SMEs – Empirical Investigation in Southern Region of Poland. *Research Gate.* https://www.researchgate.net/publication/274374372_Linking_Regional_Knowledge_Laboratory_and_Growth_of_smes_-_Empirical_Investigation_in_Southern_Region_of_Poland

Lai, P. (2017). The Literature Review of Technology Adoption Models and Theories for the Novelty Technology. *JISTEM -. Journal of Information Systems and Technology Management, 14*(1). doi:10.4301/S1807-17752017000100002

Leaders in Drilling & Oilfield Services. (2021). MB Holding Co. http://www.mbholdingco.com

Mohsin Haider Darwish. (2020). NH Doman. https://www.mhdoman.com/

Monitor, G. E. (2020). *National Report 2019 -2020.* Unizwa. https://www.unizwa.edu.om/Final%20Oman%20GEM%20National%20report2019_2020_Oct%2020.pdf

Nasseri, Z. A. (2020, June 14). Al Raffd Funds R.O. 99m among 2,563 SMEs. *Oman Observer.* https://www.omanobserver.om/article/12628/Main/al-raffd-funds-ro-99m-among-2563-smes

Oman Budget. (2021). Ministry of Finance. https://mof.gov.om/Portals/1/documents/Financial-reports/The-state-budget/2021/2021(Eng).pdf

Oman Development Bank - Annual Report (2020). Oman Development Bank. https://odb.om/public/uploads/docs/ODB_AR20_eng.pdf

Oman focuses on diversification and infrastructure investment. (2018). Oxford Business Group. https://oxfordbusinessgroup.com/overview/strong-and-stable-sultanate-continues-evolve-focus-diversification-and-infrastructure-investment

Business Gateways. (2021). *Oman registers 14% increase in the number of SMEs in 2020.* Business Gateways. https://businessgateways.com/news/2021/02/09/Oman-registers-14-per-cent-number-SMEs-2020

Oman's Leading Business Clans. (2020). Muscat Daily. https://www.muscatdaily.com/2020/06/29/omans-leading-business-clans/

ONA. (2021). Oman registers over 20% increase in SMEs. *Times of Oman.* https://timesofoman.com/article/103300-oman-registers-over-20-increase-in-smes

ONA. (2021). Over 56,000 SMEs registered in Oman till August 2021. *Times of Oman*https://timesofoman.com/article/108177-over-56000-smes-registered-in-oman-till-august-2021

ONA.(2021). Over 50,000 SMEs registered in Oman till June 2021. *Times of Oman*. https://timesofoman.com/article/105418-over-50000-smes-registered-in-oman-till-june-2021

Paul, M. (2021). Oman unveils new tourism campaign to promote art and culture. *Travel Daily Media*. https://www.traveldailymedia.com/oman-unveils-new-tourism-campaign-to-promote-art-and-culture/

Saud Bahwan Group. (2021). *About*. Saud Bahwan Group. https://saudbahwangroup.com/

Shanfari Group of Companies. (2016). *About*. Shanfari Group of Companies. https://www.shanfari.com/about.php

Shukaili, A. A., Kassim, N. M., Al Suleimani, B., Ahmed, Z., Mondal, S., & Kausar, Y. (2020). *Global Entrepreneurship Monitor: Oman National Report 2019*. Authority for Small and Medium Enterprise Development. Global Entrepreneurship. https://www.unizwa.edu.om/Final%20Oman%20GEM%20National%20report2019_2020_Oct%2020.pdf

ONA. (2021, June 08). SMEs in Oman come to the fore during the COVID pandemic. *Times of Oman*. https://timesofoman.com/article/102336-smes-in-oman-come-to-the-fore-during-covid-pandemic

The Zubair Corporation. (2021). *About*. The Zubair Corporation. https://zubaircorp.com/en/about/the-zubair-story

Forbes. (n.d.). Top 100 Arab Family Businesses In The Middle East 2020. *Forbes Middle East*. https://www.forbesmiddleeast.com/list/top-100-arab-family-businesses-in-the-middle-east-2020-1

Tripathi, S., & Al Shahri, M. (2016). Omani Community in Digital Age: A Study of Omani Women Using Back Channel Media to Empower Themselves for Frontline Entrepreneurship. *International Journal of Information and Communication Engineering*, *10*(6).

Venkatesh, V., & Bala, H. (2008). Technology Acceptance Model 3 and a Research Agenda on Interventions. Decision Science. *Decision Sciences*, *39*(2), 273–315. doi:10.1111/j.1540-5915.2008.00192.x

Venkatesh, V., & Davis, F. D. (2000). A Theoretical Extension of the Technology Acceptance Model: Four Longitudinal Field Studies. *Management Science*, *46*(2), 186–204. doi:10.1287/mnsc.46.2.186.11926

Yasin, N., & Khansari, Z. (2022). The Context for Business in Oman. In L.-P. Dana, A. Salamzadeh, V. Ramadani, & R. Palalić, Understanding Contexts of Business in Western Asia (pp. 43–58). World Scientific Publishing Company. doi:10.1142/9789811229695_0003

Zawawi Group. (2021). *Leading Business Group in the Sultanate of Oman*. Zawawi Group. https://www.zawawigroup.com/

Times of Oman. (2021). Zubair SEC signed an agreement with the Ministry of Social Development. *Times of Oman*. https://timesofoman.com/article/106693-zubair-sec-signs-agreement-with-the-ministry-of-social-development

ENDNOTES

1 Source: Oman Global Entrepreneurship Monitor Report 2019-2020

2 **Source:** Oman Global Entrepreneurship Monitor Report, 2019-2020

3 Source: Self-design by authors based on present business practiced

4 Source: Self-design by authors based on present business practiced

5 Source. Designed by authors based on the present scenario and TAM model

Chapter 4
Family Business Survival Strategy in the COVID-19 Pandemic:
Evidence From Malaysia

Md Tanvir Alam Tonmoy
Universiti Utara Malaysia, Malaysia

Narentheren Kaliappen
Universiti Utara Malaysia, Malaysia

ABSTRACT

The authors thoroughly discussed the financial mapping and strategies of family-owned businesses in Malaysia to tackle economic downturn brought by the COVID-10 pandemic. As most of the organizations in this nation are family-claimed, the financial execution of the privately-run companies in Malaysia draws a more prominent impact on its entire economy. Close by the financial hardships brought by consecutive lockdowns, Malaysian family-owned businesses were fighting with computerized upskilling as the interest in web-based business soar since the time individuals were locked inside their homes. Subsequently, that was something the older generations of the organization attempted to oversee since their customary technique for coordinating business had no hint of advanced innovations. Regardless, the youthful age of those families grasped the meaning of advancement and digitalization. They are presently more confident that their economic condition will improve in the event that they can figure out how to adjust to the ongoing industry climate.

DOI: 10.4018/978-1-6684-7394-8.ch004

INTRODUCTION

Like the rest of the world's family businesses, Malaysian family-owned companies have also suffered from covid-19 economically. Family-owned businesses make a fundamental piece of the Malaysian economy. Approximately 70% of the businesses in the country are family-owned (Amran & Ahmad, 2011). Most of the family businesses in Malaysia advanced from customary family-owned organizations. Most Malaysian family firms are small businesses, and the business's founders deal with the daily work with assistance from the family's young members and close relatives. Various noticeable firms are family-controlled, and the quantity of Malaysian firms is expanding yearly. Even though covid-19 has hit these family businesses hard, many are still ambitious that in the future, they will push back and rise in sales (PricewaterhouseCoopers, 2021).

BACKGROUND

Family-owned Businesses in Malaysia

According to Cheng & Co, family businesses in Malaysia contribute over 67% towards the country's GDP (Cheng & Co, 2019). This means that Malaysia's economic growth heavily depends on these family-owned organizations' financial performance. These organizations come in all sizes, from small businesses to large corporations. The large corporations that control the majority of the country's GDP are Robert Kuok's Kerry Group, Tan Sri Lim Kok Thay's Genting Group, Tan Sri Lee Shin Cheng's IOI Group, Tan Sri Quek Leng Chan's Hong Leong Group and Tan Sri Yeoh Tiong Lay's YTL Group which are from the sugar, real estate, shipping, palm oil, finance to utilities and tourism sectors of Malaysia (Yap). The majority, however, are small-size family-owned businesses, mostly owned by Chinese families (Amran & Ahmad, 2011). From a management perspective, these family firms have grown from traditional family-controlled businesses and choose to trail less of the founder's business culture and embrace western business styles.

Family businesses are still trying to balance the impacts of covid-19 and, struggling with more apparent demands and responsibilities, are confronting new scopes and threats that could elevate or crush their business. In a 2021 survey run by PWC, it was reported that in Malaysia, family businesses could grow in 2022 compared to 2021; since the people of the country are yet to be fully vaccinated, they are still required to abide by the lockdown rules (PricewaterhouseCoopers, 2021).

Table 1. Pre-Covid-19 family business performance 2020 (PricewaterhouseCoopers, 2021)

Sales (Growth)	47%
Sales (Reduction)	29%

Table 2. Expected growth for 2021 & 2022 (PricewaterhouseCoopers, 2021)

	2021	2022
Aggressive	18%	33%
Steady	43%	59%

Indeed, even before the pandemic, just 47% of the respondents from Malaysia were anticipating growth in sales for 2020. All around the world, somewhat 55% anticipated sales growth for 2020.

Figure 1. Growth in last financial year (Pre- Covid 19), %

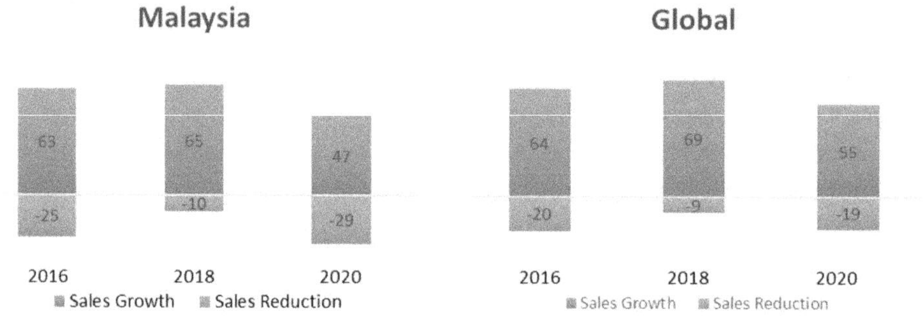

METHODOLOGY

The authors wrote this chapter via document analysis and literature review. Document analysis is a method of social research and a robust research instrument in its own right; it is also an indispensable component of most triangulation schemes, the combination of methods used to explore the same topic (Bowen, 2009). In order to seek convergence and corroboration, qualitative researchers typically utilise at least two distinct data sources and methodologies to access at least two different resources. Triangulation aims to assemble credible evidence from multiple sources (Bowen, 2009). This document analysis allowed the writers to collect data from journal publications, newspapers, magazines, government policy papers, and company annual reports.

MAIN FOCUS OF THE CHAPTER

Challenges

Understanding the lockdown procedures declared by the Malaysian government

In order to look into the challenges that the family businesses in Malaysia are facing due to the pandemic, it is crucial to study Malaysia's all lockdown phases. So, we covered the lockdown guidelines provided by the Malaysian government from March 2020 till October 2021. The types of restrictions implemented by the Malaysian government are as follows,

Table 3. Lockdown chronology in Malaysia (Yusof, 2021))

Phase	Date
MCO effective from 18 Mar 2020 to 3 May 2020	
1	18 Mar – 31 Mar 2020
2	1 Apr – 14 Apr 2020
3	15 Apr – 28 Apr 2020
4	29 Apr – 3 May 2020
CMCO effective from 4 May 2020 to 9 Jun 2020	
1	4 May – 12 May 2020
2	3 May – 9 Jun 2020
RMCO effective from 10 Jun 2020 to 31 Mar 2021	
1	10 Jun – 31 Aug 2020
2	1 Sep – 31 Dec 2020
3	1 Jan – 31 Mar 2021
MCO from 11 Jan to 31 Mar 2021	
Every state switched between MCO, CMCO, RMCO, EMCO, and semi-EMCO relying upon the covid-19 condition in each state.	
Total Lockdown from 1 Jun to 28 Jun 2021	

1. Enhanced Movement Control Order (EMCO or Enhanced MCO)
2. Semi Enhanced Movement Control Order (SEMCO)
3. Conditional Movement Control Order (CMCO)
4. Recovery Movement Control Order (RMCO)

The lockdowns have impacted significant business sectors in Malaysia. These are mostly tourism, aviation, logistics, energy, and agriculture industries. Malaysia's strict lockdown announcement, Movement Control Order, MCO led to the shutdown of all tourist attractions across the country, which negatively impacted hundreds if not thousands of local businesses such as hotels, restaurants, entertainment facilities, travel agencies and so on. Even though we experienced lower gas prices, the sudden drop in travel demands heavily affected the aviation and logistics industries. However, a significant increase in online consumption helped numerous supply chain service providers stay in business. However, because of the MCO, those businesses eventually slowed down and could not reach their whole productivity level. When China and Europe started dropping their demands for unrefined palm oil and other organic products, Malaysia's feeble food security condition triggered the fear of sustainability.

Figure 2. Degree of impact in specific sectors in Malaysia
(Ernst & Young, 2020)

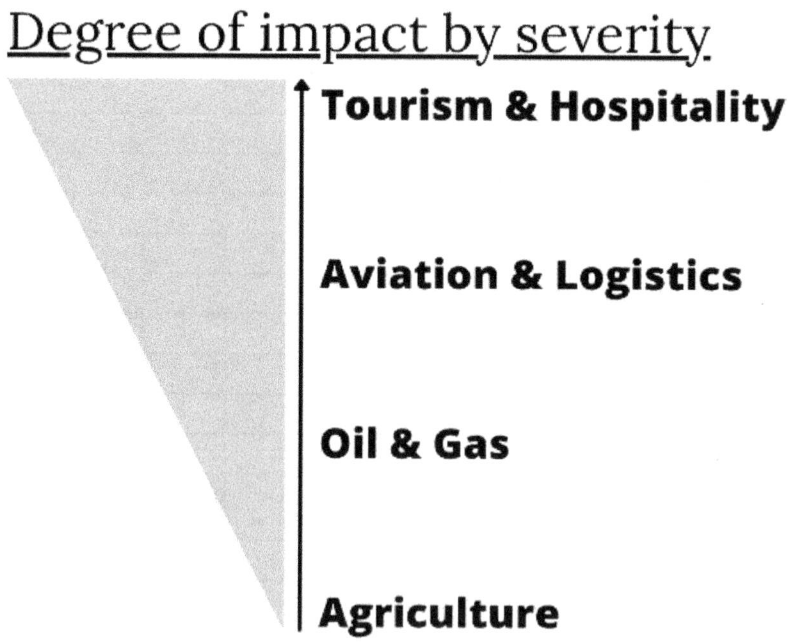

Handing Responsibilities to the Next Generation and Digital Integration

In Western nations, we can see a long-formed habit of professionalism where the third or even fourth generations are already handling the family business and tend to seek external professional assistance when necessary. However, in the case of Malaysia, the majority of family-owned businesses are yet to complete their second-generation cycle. When PWC did a "NextGen" survey in 2019, we learned that the 2nd generation of the family manages around two-thirds of family business affairs in Malaysia. The survey also reported that about 88% of NextGen are already involved in their business activities, and 70% have earned leadership roles for specific initiatives. However, 30% of the respondents lacked self-confidence and constantly sensed that they needed to be proven worthy of their position before allocating their thoughts and knowledge to improve the business style, which is why only 40% of the respondents showed ambitious signs of leadership in developing their way of running the family business. Loke Shu Kew, who leads NexGen club, says that the first generation that has been running the business for 40 to 50 years lacks trust in the second generation because they are comparably inexperienced. It is also not relatively easy to learn the whole business framework in a short time. Loke added that since the Malaysian family businesses are relatively young, they must nurture NexGen and hand them responsibilities gradually instead of hiring professionals as the Western family business owners do.

Table 4. PwC's NextGen Survey 2019- Malaysia Report (PricewaterhouseCoopers, 2020)

88% involved in family business affairs	67% believing in digitalization to compete	47% claim to own businesses that are indistinguishable	30% lacking confidence

Most respondents between 25 and 40 expressed high interest in digitizing their family businesses. However, first-generation business owners are not enthusiastic about such a proposal since their traditional way of doing business has been somewhat smooth for decades. Therefore, when the second generations show more interest in digitally transforming the business rather than embracing the conventional method, they trust the young leaders less with their investments (PricewaterhouseCoopers, 2020).

While the existing management may not sense a genuine requirement for change, NextGens have recognized a few key drivers that will cause the privately-owned businesses to remain alert. A large part of NextGen has seen aggressive rivalry from other industry players and changes in consumer demands in a quickly advancing commercial place (Lim, 2020). NextGen's first concern is to set up the business for the digital world. Around 66% of respondents needed to execute a computerized business system, with about 60% focusing on advancing the worker's skills and putting resources into new business designs. To execute these progressions and accumulate the certainty of the current age of business pioneers, Malaysian NextGens are taking a gander at working inside their domain of skill and zeroing in on spaces of progress. Roughly 67% of the respondents accepted they were profoundly capable of critical thinking and strategic reasoning, while 47% evaluated themselves exceptionally regarding understanding the business and economic drifts (PricewaterhouseCoopers, 2020).

Figure 3. Future priorities of Malaysian family business (PricewaterhouseCoopers, 2021)

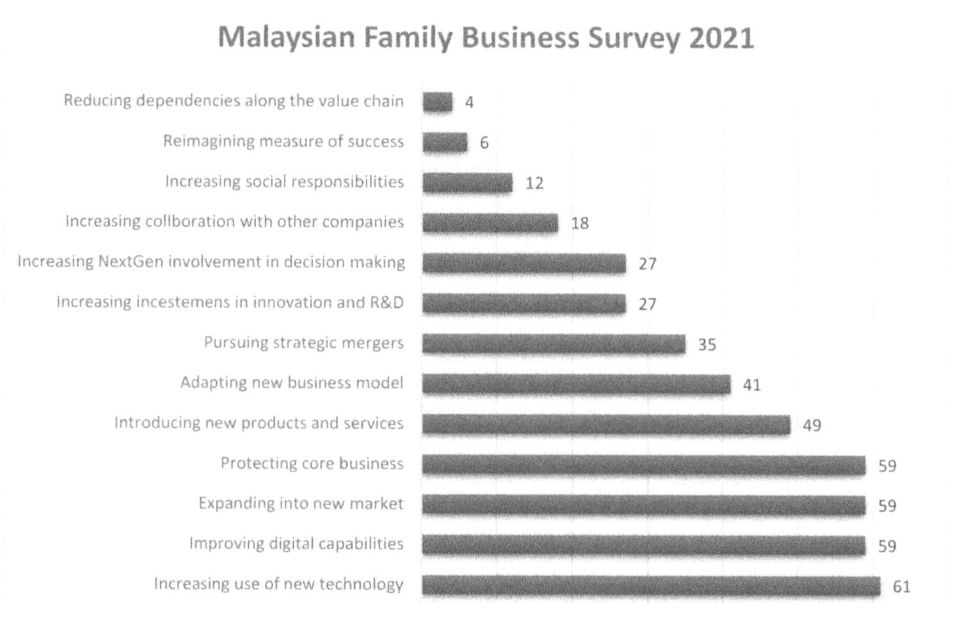

Trust and Communication

A most recent 2021 overview showed that in 61% of family-run companies in Malaysia where the individuals from that family would impart about the business consistently, and just 57% expressed that a specific straightforwardness stayed in the family as far as sharing the critical data. Ultimately, 45% of family-owned companies shared that the entire family has a shared objective about working on the business overall (PricewaterhouseCoopers, 2021).

Financial Struggle

While the Malaysian government focused on reducing the number of cases with constant changes in the lockdown regulations, the country's family businesses kept suffering financially. According to PwC, over 70% of the family businesses in Malaysia suffered economically, with a continuous decline in profit (PricewaterhouseCoopers, 2021). When the manufacturing industries were ordered to halt their work for two months during the MCO 1.0, its growth shrank by 8.3% in 2020, causing many workers to lose their jobs immediately. Pre-covid, when Malaysia had a persistent trade surplus for about 14 years, during MCO 1.0 in April 2020, it stated a deficit of RM3.5 billion. When MCO 2.0 was implemented, the impacts appeared less extreme due to fewer restrictions. MCO 2.0 mainly focused on restarting the country's economy. So, it allowed SMEs and manufacturers to reopen their businesses. However, many SMEs were still suffering financially as the hit they took during MCO 1.0 was quite extreme.

Additionally, consumers' spending tendency has changed rapidly since the first lockdown. People started saving more and spending less as they became more pessimistic towards Malaysia's economic growth, and therefore the overall sales and profits plummeted significantly. MCO 3.0 brought a total economic disaster for SMEs in Malaysia. When there was a spike in positive cases in May 2021, the government declared an emergency lockdown which will only be lifted when daily cases are below 4000. Datuk Michael Kang, President of the Small Medium Enterprise Association (SME Association) in Malaysia, fears that under MCO 3.0, 37.7% of total SMEs will shut down if there is no drastic improvement. According to his prediction, such a scenario would cause 2 million Malaysians to lose their livelihood, and the country would lose 1% of its total GDP because of halting its export production (Arfa, 2021).

Table 5. Economic situation in Malaysia during MCO 1.0 & 2.0 (Arfa, 2021)

MCO Phases	Economic Situations
MCO 1.0	Economic dip: -17.2%, Total loss of RM 2.4billion a day
MCO 2.0	GDP contracted by 0.5%, Total recorded loss of RM 600million daily

SOLUTIONS AND RECOMMENDATIONS

Business Survival Strategies

Many business leaders are taking a step back and rethinking and redesigning their family business structure due to several challenges brought on by covid-19. However, with a positive mindset, these leaders consider the current situation an opportunity to question their work model and succession planning.

Performance and Priorities

Although covid-19 has hit these family businesses hard, many are aspiring they will push back and ascend in sales later on. 92% of those overviewed by PWC expect a re-visitation of the pre-pandemic development rate by 2022. This is because they hope to develop rapidly and forcefully with a consistent increase rate. This appeared shockingly hopeful as the survey was conducted even before the country's government had supported any immunization. The latest overview of the expected growth rates of family businesses in Malaysia lines up with the rate of the 2018's study (PricewaterhouseCoopers, 2021).

Figure 4. Growth ambitions comparison %

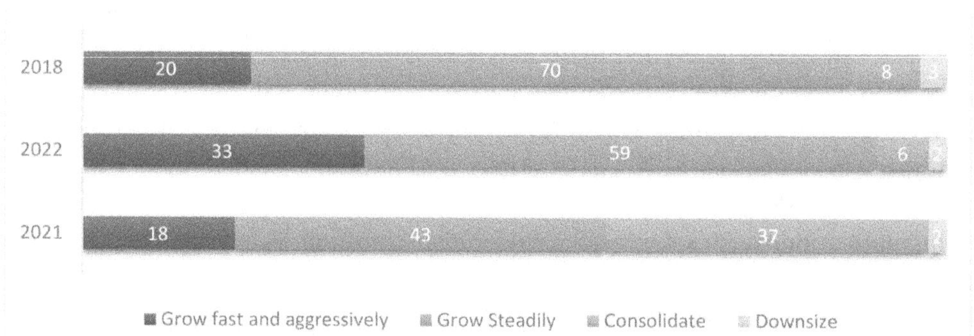

Embracing New Technologies and Digital Transformation

The NextGen business leaders already understand the importance of bringing current technologies into their family business. They now know that it is no longer an option but an absolute necessity for the survival of their business (PricewaterhouseCoopers, 2021). However, a survey shows that even though 59% of Malaysian family businesses are trying to work on their digital capabilities and 61% are prioritizing the growing use of the latest machinery. They are still way behind compared to the businesses in the Asia Pacific region, America and Europe, which means the digital productivity level is comparably low. Since the current pandemic was a direct catalyst in increasing online consumption, businesses should adapt and take action fast to remain competitive in the marketplace. PwC Malaysia stated that technology would rapidly affect most Malaysian family businesses' work culture in the next five years (PricewaterhouseCoopers, 2021). While the rest of the world is becoming increasingly competitive through the use of the latest technologies, Malaysian companies are facing the threat of being left behind in the digital world. Therefore, the new generation leaders are heavily prioritizing upskilling their workforce and bringing in people that are experts in adapting to the new workstyle. While 24% of the family businesses have already penetrated the so-called digital space, 76% stated they still need more time to adapt (PricewaterhouseCoopers, 2021).

Figure 5. Priority rate in use of latest technologies and embracing digitalization (PricewaterhouseCoopers, 2021)

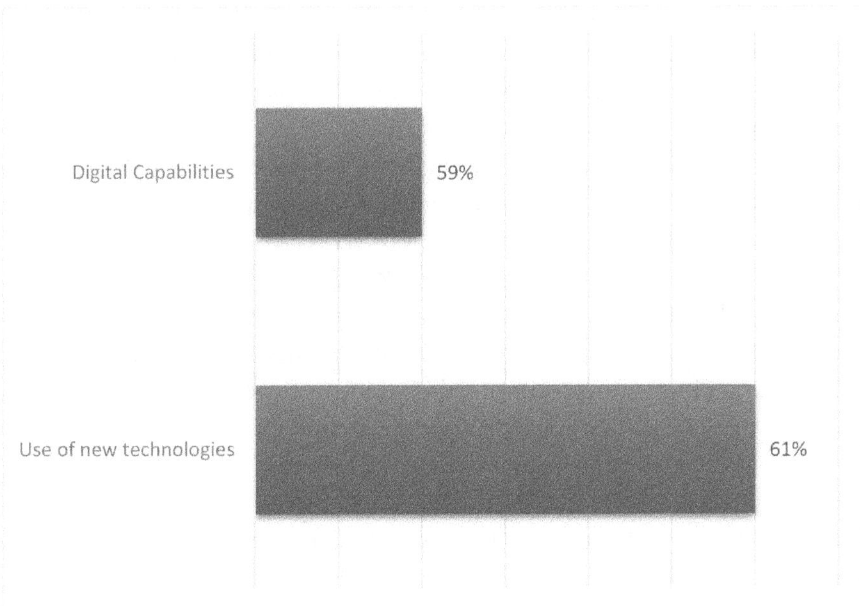

To prevail in the digital commercial centre, Malaysian privately-owned companies should coordinate their arrangements for digital change into the owner strategy. This planning should initially focus on the family's vision and mission for the business, generally held for the longer term. It is likewise significant for business leaders to have a clear mindset prior to coordinating such strategies. They need to expand the necessary arrangements for their workers who will require training to acquire the new vital skills to achieve their tasks. In the Family Business Survey 2021, PwC also suggested how NextGens can be the drivers of welcoming new technologies into the family business and implementing new strategies (PricewaterhouseCoopers, 2020).

Key actions that the NextGen leaders can consider in their leading role while spontaneously working with the owners:

Consider creating a digital budget policy: PwC believes that extracting 2 to 5% from the total business revenue for digital conversion will help the business accelerate and appear more competitive in the ever-evolving marketplace. However, the budgeting method may change when new demands and new and better technologies become more productive (PricewaterhouseCoopers, 2020).

Upskilling the employees: If given the scope, the company's employees will always show enthusiasm in learning new skills needed to improve the business and therefore keep their job in demand as well. Employees can develop micro-digital solutions that will welcome citizen-led modernization that will improve the business and its productivity drastically. Also, when employees are involved in making fundamental changes, their motivation level will rise (Hayward & Evennett, 2021).

Businesses need to be data-driven: Successful business leaders cannot stress enough how important it is for any business to be data-savvy. Information related to customer choices, trends in the market, and sales records are precious. The company understands this and appropriately manages its database will always be one step ahead of its competitors. In order to be data-savvy, companies ought to learn the process of data collection, storage and analysis (Hayward & Evennett, 2021).

In a recent story covered by thegadgetmarkets, Lim Chia Wei, head of Malacca Securities Sdn Bhd and a NextGen, had her first digitization project, which was the easy task of filtering existing customers' signature cards and carefully having them stored in the organization's database. This little yet very effective initiative helped her figure out how to instantly chop down the customer's ID confirmation check, which would have taken at least a few hours had she never changed her operation style. This action eventually made Lim's business quite successful, and her whole business process adopted a total digital transformation which then helped Lim take her business online. When asked, Lim shared that her family, especially her father, had been supportive when she suggested that the family business should start adapting to the digital world in order to remain competitive. She also added that her brother's love for new technologies made it easier for her to let her initiative run smoothly.

In another case, Ping Teo, MD of Centro Properties Gathering, is also a NextGen family business leader. One of the low-hanging organic products she zeroed in on was moving her organization's representative mileage claims measure online a couple of years prior. Before this, Teo clarifies, staff individuals needed to fill in a structure featuring their movement course utilizing Google Guides to present a case. The web-based framework that Teo is acquainted with can work out the mileage naturally and carefully present the case using a web-based human asset gateway. For NextGens, hoping to digitize their privately-run company's cycles, Teo stresses that set present moment "fast win" objectives that are not difficult to execute yet significantly affect the way staff individuals play out their positions. She adds that this will make it simpler to accumulate support from staff individuals and the board (Lim, 2020).

6.3.1.4. Focusing on Resilience and Sustainability

In the present fast-changing business climate with fluctuating business sector patterns, innovations and globalization constrain organizations to adjust their tasks routinely, knowing precisely what makes a privately-owned company competitive. One of the eminent benefits appreciated by some family-claimed organizations is their capacity to react rapidly to emergencies. The capacity to effectively move to full-time remote working has been critical to endurance during this time of vulnerability.

EY states that organization rule and design issues have regularly introduced difficulties for some family-owned companies because of relational intricacies. Those that put resources into sound administration systems will probably have the option to adjust rapidly during times of emergency. Recognizing a plan of action that empowers readiness and transformation is critical, close by essential arranging. Thus, privately-run companies frequently flourish because of their obligation to follow through on viable long-haul targets (Hayward & Evennett, 2021).

Further, the capacity of a business to draw in and hold ability is frequently a decent pointer of its strength. By and large, family-run companies are more effective at holding ability than most. A culture that assists drive with lowing staff turnover is valuable during a time of calamity when representative responsibility is vital. As the covid scene and public strategy keeps on developing, we see privately-run companies zeroed in on these aspects of versatility:

- Worker's wellbeing and prosperity
- Government and public plan
- Innovation and data security
- Store network and worldwide exchange
- Client and brand
- Ability and labor force
- Hazard
- Monetary and financial backer

- Protection and legitimate questions

Environmental, Social, and Governance (ESG)

Even though making a profit is a crucial motivation for any business to exist in the first place, it is different in the case of family-owned businesses. Most family-owned companies prioritize value creation instead of maximizing profits (PricewaterhouseCoopers, 2020). Malaysian family-run companies have established the family business as the primary asset and legacy. ESG can most certainly assist these family businesses in achieving those targets. For instance, leading towards running a sustainable business will help the organization save a significant portion of its cash flow and cash generation. Family businesses can additionally design their sustainability framework and present it to the marketplace, which later creates more potential business opportunities, expanding the business into new markets. However, the older generation often viewed ESG as regulation or some obligation to society and the environment but not as something to genuinely be motivated by. That is why they never considered sustainability one of the essential functions of their family business. Studies show that the 2nd generation, "NextGen", value the importance of sustainability for the betterment of the business and its communities. They understand that ESG not only helps the business save costs but also creates a better and stand-up image of the company, earning stakeholders' confidence and gaining customer loyalty as a result (PricewaterhouseCoopers, 2020). ESG is a must for any business that wants to survive. However, this commitment is set for the long term as the process takes time and cannot be done with an impatient mindset. So, the leaders yet to consider adapting to ESG should start acting now to create the right setting for their businesses and emphasize long-term values held by the family business.

PwC also suggests that Malaysian family-owned companies can begin adapting ESG by figuring out how to measure and convey their ESG plan to a more extensive shareholder board. Other than the conventional way of financing and reporting, organizations can also study how to value their ESG effects and compare them with their impacts on the procedures and venture decisions (PricewaterhouseCoopers, 2020).

Seeking Professional Help

Sometimes in running a business or any project, a third-party opinion seems logical. NextGen seems to understand this point, and they are willing to seek professional help whenever they find it necessary. Hundreds if not thousands of professional organizations in Malaysia currently work closely with many small and medium-sized family-owned businesses.

Sri Themudu, who ran a seasonal business called "Diyaa Confectionary" during Deepavali, shared his survival success story with Dave Grunebaum during the crisis (Grunebaum, 2020).

Diyaa Confectionary has, for a considerable length of time, taking into account Malaysian families and nearby organizations that purchase present crates of snacks like saltines, treats and coconut candy for Deepavali. The candies produced in his mother's kitchen sold for about $8 each. Mr. Themudu, at regular times, would visit his potential clients at his office and make a sales pitch right in front of them could not practice the same tradition this year due to the movement control order announced by the Malaysian Government. Besides, many of his long-term corporate clients cut their costs and ended up not buying his product like they usually would every year.

Feeling devastated and losing his sales confidence, Mr. Themudu went to a marketing/ videographer professional to renovate his business website and social media pages. His investment of around $1000 paid off with an enormous number of online orders. His success was so great that at one point, he could not help but stop taking further orders from clients, and the family failed to handle more requests. Diyaa's Confectionary revenue increased by 300% compared to last year's earnings. Mr. Themudu joyfully stated the "covid Year Sales Revenue" to be the best eight years in such business.

Since the beginning of the pandemic, numerous Malaysian organizations have rolled out critical improvements, for example, founding credit-only instalments and home delivery (Grunebaum, 2020).

Focusing on Social Impact

Like other organisations, family-owned companies are zeroing in further on their social and natural effects (Hayward & Evennett, 2021). From how they deal with their workers during an emergency to steps they take to offer back to and support their local networks, influential privately-run companies place a gigantic spotlight on culture, reason and worth in their tasks and strategy. Framing objectives around the close family and from the perspective of local networks can frequently assist with furnishing owners with a precise reason and concentration for how they need to utilise their budget, especially as new pioneers assume control over the reins. Developing the family-run business economically while assuming liability for others through charitable and social commitment ought to be a vital concentration for the leaders (Hayward & Evennett, 2021).

As family business leaders investigate the skyline, they expect an expanded spotlight on their organization's social effect and significance for their clients and workers. Studies have shown that 55% of family business employees would select to work for a socially mindful organization, regardless of whether the pay rates were lower. In comparison, 33% of customers search for socially dependable brands (Hayward & Evennett, 2021). The effect of covid-19 on these perspectives is yet to be ultimately perceived.

A recent survey shows Malaysian family-owned organizations' huge advancement in showing commitment towards the benefit of the local communities. While 12% of the world's privately-owned companies show interest in venture philanthropy, Malaysian privately-owned companies show an advancement of 6%. Be that as it may, Malaysia announced a 20% improvement in impact investments while the remainder of the world is simply behind by 2%. Concerning conventional charity, Malaysian family-claimed organizations show a vast increment of 55%, whereas it is just 42% throughout the planet. Lastly, 59% of Malaysian privately-owned companies communicated their premium in adding to the local communities, whereas in the remainder of the world, the sum is 62% (Hayward & Evennett, 2021).

Figure 6. Malaysian family businesses showing progress in contributing in social responsibilities

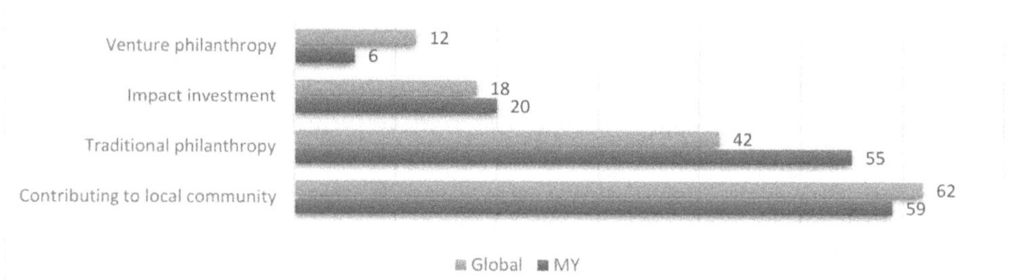

Diversifying Family Wealth

Family-owned companies can be jeopardized during leadership transition, primarily because of contention between the need to keep up with and follow old customs and adjust and advance the business in light of the evolving market. NextGens have an alternate vision for the future, for example, scouting innovation, broadening the organization's administrations or venturing into new business sectors (Hayward & Evennett, 2021). As organizations keep reacting to covid-19, there is a chance to investigate these conceivable outcomes and permit the new generation of leaders to acquire significant experience in management during a crisis. Hence, they are ready should a comparative circumstance emerge later on. Ey also stated that letting NextGen apply new thoughts and abilities to the business could have the effect between falling behind and prospering in the current situation. Welcoming even younger family members to help the business, making them participate in fundamental dynamics and correspondence so they can learn, grow, and experience the adaptation strategies in the changing business environment (Hayward & Evennett, 2021).

Financial Support From the Malaysian Government

To mitigate the country's economic situation, the government of Malaysia announced an "Economic Stimulus Package" in 2020. This new strategy bundle centres around three principal methodologies, which expect to speed up the financial exercises while using vital homegrown assets to create assurance. The 2020 Economic Stimulus Package includes an RM20 billion infusion into the Malaysian economy (The Government of Malaysia, 2020).

Table 6. Economic Stimulus Package 2020 total funding

Fund	RM (Billion)
Small projects	2.00
Other initiatives	1.50
3.50	
Loan	3.50
Additional Sources	13.00
Total	**20.00**

1st Strategy: It solely focuses on tackling the impact of the current pandemic. Strategy one consists of a total of 18 measures 14 of those measures directly helped various types of family businesses running in Malaysia. Each of those measures was designed to help the SMEs so they can at least hold on to their business and pay their employees during the lockdown (The Government of Malaysia, 2020).

2nd Strategy: This consists of 5 measures that focus on accelerating household spending and also supporting SMEs from specific sectors so they can keep their employees.

3rd Strategy: To support the energy of financial development, private utilization should be supplemented by speculation development. Towards this, the Government will have its influence in utilizing open ventures and give the motivation to empower private investments (The Government of Malaysia, 2020).

Table 7. Strategy 1, extenuating impact of covid-19

1st Strategy	
Measures	**Description**
1	Rebuilding and Loan Rescheduling To facilitate the monetary strain of borrowers that own any small or medium size businesses that were affected directly because of covid-19 were given economic alleviation by the local financial organization through rebuilding or rescheduling their credits. Additionally, 100% stamp duty exemption was given on the term that the original loan agreement had been duly stamped. Such exemption was implemented from 1 March 2020 to 31 December 2020 (The Government of Malaysia, 2020).
2	Implementing SRF, Special Relief Facility Bank Negara Malaysia (BNM) declared a RM2billion SRF that was offered to the affected businesses though a credit system which had an annual interest rate of 3.75%. The duration of such loan was 5.5 years with RM1million for each SME (The Government of Malaysia, 2020).
3	MRF, Micro Credit Facility by Bank Simpanan Nasional (BSN) Conveying the similar agenda, which was to help the local SMEs, BSN created a micro loan scheme of RM400million at a 4% interest rate instalment starting 6 months after the payout (The Government of Malaysia, 2020).
4	Revising the Income Tax and its deferment Organizations in the travel industry were allowed a delay of their month-to-month tax payment for 6 months from 1 April 2020 to 30 September 2020. Different organizations impacted by current financial turns of events, were permitted to revise their month-to-month tax payment in advance (The Government of Malaysia, 2020).
5	Tax Exemption for Hotels Businesses that provide accommodation services were given a service tax exemption for about 6 months from 1 March 2020 to 31 August 2020 (The Government of Malaysia, 2020).
6	Tax deduction in the purchase of personal protective equipment for workers Companies that required to spend on certain protective equipment for their workers were eligible for a deduction of tax. However, costs for non-dispensable PPE items can be guaranteed as capital recompense (The Government of Malaysia, 2020).
7	Further lowering tax on hotels that show expense related to training their employees The government encouraged the hotel owners to create a budget for training their workers service-related topic that are eligible under the Ministry of Tourism, Art and Culture. Companies that followed such process were allowed to claim double tax relief (The Government of Malaysia, 2020).
8	Human Resources Development Fund giving Exemption To assist with decreasing expenses for organizations impacted by covid-19, an exclusion from HRDF demands for a time of 6 months from 1 April 2020 to 30 September 2020 was be given. The 8 classifications of organizations covered by this exception are air travel, homegrown ground transport, conference halls, shopping centers, travel visit administrators, lodgings, establishments, and hypermarkets (The Government of Malaysia, 2020).
9	15% discount on Power bills To further tackle the economic impact of covid-19 to businesses, for a time of a half year from 1 April 2020 to 30 September 2020, a of 15% deduction on month-to-month power bills will be given to six classifications of organizations, in particular inn operators, travel services, shopping centers, conference halls also, amusement parks (The Government of Malaysia, 2020).
10	Changes on the regulation of the purchase of duty-free items The covid-19 has especially hit the retail businesses that operate in airports. This is because of the lower number of travelers. Along these lines, the qualification time frame for the acquisition of so-called duty-free products was diminished from 72 hours to 48 hours and the limit for merchandise is expanded from RM500 to RM1,000 from 1 April 2020 (The Government of Malaysia, 2020).
11	Domestic travel income tax rebate To encourage domestic tourism, an income tax duty alleviation of up to RM1,000 was be given to people to spend on domestic tourism from 1 March 2020 to 31 August 2020 yet restricted to: I) Accommodation costs at locations enlisted with Ministry of Tourism, Arts and Culture (MOTAC); and ii) Entrance charges (The Government of Malaysia, 2020).

continues on following page

Table 7. Continued

1st Strategy	
Measures	**Description**
12	Discount Vouchers for promoting domestic tourism To arouse interest for the traveling, the government pledged designate RM500 million for the accompanying measures: Travel rebate vouchers The Malaysian government teamed up with administrators of air travel, lodging and resort convenience booking destinations to offer rebate vouchers up to RM100 per individual. The organizations partaking were urged to offer extra awards for their clients. This scheme was presented in March 2020 (The Government of Malaysia, 2020). ii) *Galakan Melancong Malaysia* (GAMELAN) award GAMELAN was executed in 2019 with the goal to expand vacationer appearances, through open private coordinated effort on the travel industry advancement. To advance on the endorsed assignment RM60 million, Tourism Malaysia promised more noteworthy adaptability as far as using the corresponding award for Visit Malaysia Year 2020 promotion (The Government of Malaysia, 2020). iii) Promote Tourism With the normal decrease of sightseers particularly from China, Tourism Malaysia changed its focus to on regions including ASEAN, Middle East, Europe and South Asia. An extra distribution of RM30 million was given to Tourism Malaysia, well beyond the current Visit Malaysia Year 2020 the travel industry advancement allotment of RM90 million (The Government of Malaysia, 2020).
13	Employment Insurance System for saving jobs In case of employment misfortunes, EIS reserve was created to help the employees that needed it. This fund amounted to RM1.1 billion. EIS also promised to loosen up the qualification models for laborers from the most impacted areas, for example, postponing the base necessity of working commitment (The Government of Malaysia, 2020).
14	Skill Training Fund The government of Malaysia sees the current bump brought by covid-19 as a scope to elevate the skills of the labor forces in Malaysia especially from the most affected businesses. Therefore, the government added RM100 million to the Human Resource Development Fund which benefited over 40000 Malaysian workers. Later the government pledged and additional RM50 million specially to finance digital upskilling. Moreover, another financing of RM20 Million was promised in order to upskill Malaysian workers from the manufacturing sectors (The Government of Malaysia, 2020).

Succession Plan

Succession planning refers to a strategic plan that allows the successful replacement of leadership in any organization. Such a plan is required to successfully run the business even after the prominent face of the company retires and hands the responsibility to a new generation. Will also states that succession planning assesses every pioneer's ability, recognizing potential substitutions both inside and outside the organization and, on account of inward substitutions, preparing those members so that they are ready to dominate. This is anything but a single occasion; these plans ought to be reconsidered and conceivably refreshed every year. Family businesses need to fabricate structures for the success of the new generation. Long-term strategic planning is essential for accomplishing a drawn-out legacy. Hurried progress of control of business frequently may prompt underperformance. These cases can be better tended to through a very drafted and organized progression plan, which can empower preparing future pioneers as a business consistency plan (Krishnan, 2020).

Table 8. Strategy 2, extenuating impact of covid-19

2nd Strategy	
Measure	**Description**
1	Reduction in Employee Contribution to EPF From 1 April 2020 to 31 December 2020, the base worker commitment to the Employees Provident Fund (EPF) was decreased by 4%. This action will possibly expand cash in the possession of families by around RM10 billion (The Government of Malaysia, 2020).
2	Enhancement of *Bantuan Sara Hidup (BSH)* In the hope shared success, the Government improved BSH as follows: I) present BSH installment of RM200 booked by May 2020 to be paid in March 2020. ii) extra cash installment of RM100 made to all BSH beneficiaries in May 2020; and iii) a further RM50 directed via e-tunai (The Government of Malaysia, 2020).
3	Agrofood *Bank Negara Malaysia* (BNM) extended asset usage explicitly for SMEs associated with food manufacturing industries at the size of RM1 billion that can be utilized for working capital as well as for capital consumption. Asset will be presented at greatest 8 years residency, financing rate at 3.75% and RM5 million for every SMEs. Later the government announced an additional financing of RM40 million for the struggling SMEs (The Government of Malaysia, 2020).
4	Nationwide small projects helping SMEs Government proceeds to continue small scale project in metropolitan, sub-metropolitan and rustic regions and guarantee admittance to common conveniences and essential. Government financed near RM2 billion worth of ventures which would be done at different levels including Federal, State and Local Governments. These projects consequently helped multiple SMEs to stay in business (The Government of Malaysia, 2020).
5	Helping the Procurement Process Government changed the restriction of obtainment to accelerate the cycle and increment business exercises through improving the current interaction by expanding the edge for: I) Ballots increased by 100%; and ii) Quotation expanded by 300,0000 to RM800,000. Government likewise improved the assignment under the Malaysian Road Records System by permitting state legislatures stretch out use of the awards to cover extension (The Government of Malaysia, 2020).

Table 9. Strategy 3, extenuating impact of covid-19

3rd Strategy	
Measures	**Description**
1	SME Digital Upskilling and Automation BNM handed up to RM300 million for SMEs to overhaul, modernize and revive their useful resources. Financing could be utilized for buying gear, apparatus, ICTs and other immaterial resource for upgrading which will increase proficiency. This is going to be for 10 years and RM3 million for each SME at a 3.75% yearly interest rate (The Government of Malaysia, 2020).
2	Co-investment fund from the Securities Commission To advance private area investments especially in innovation and new development openings, up to RM500 million was given to private financial backers and Malaysian organizations (The Government of Malaysia, 2020).
3	Listing fees waiver for businesses that wish to be listed on ACE or LEAP To keep on empowering effective development of organizations to raise support with the help of stocks, both the Securities Commission and Bursa Malaysia forwent the listing fees for a year, their posting charges for organizations looking for listing on LEAP or ACE Market, just as companies with market capitalization of under RM500 million looking for posting on the Main Market (The Government of Malaysia, 2020).
4	Tax deduction on business renovation To elevate organizations to attempt remodel and repair in availability of the resulting upswing. Such expenses for business premises up to RM300,000 was be given tax discount from 1 March 2020 to 31 December 2020 (The Government of Malaysia, 2020).
5	Capital allowance for machinery and equipment To boost business investments interests, qualifying capital consumptions on gadgets and hardware gear were given Accelerated Capital Allowance that lasted from 1 March 2020 to 31 December 2020 (The Government of Malaysia, 2020).

Today, the developing impression of Malaysian family-run organizations can be seen across all business areas. The current pandemic has taught these family businesses how rapidly situations can turn for the worse. Therefore, it is crucial for any business to strategically plan for its future so the company can sustain itself. PwC suggests an Ownership Strategy that will enable both the old and new generations of the family to see and understand the responsibilities and roles of the owner and then draw out a practical framework for the future. A typical quality of best family-owned companies is that they see family starting things out and that attachment among relatives is critical to guarantee business coherence and achievement (PricewaterhouseCoopers, 2020). The current and NextGen hope to lead their privately-run company to long-term achievement. They need to comprehend the one-of-a-kind qualities of their family possession and administration structure to discover the responses to the difficulties they are confronting. This must be adjusted against the different interests and assumptions of members working for the business and those not. Fung shared that it is significant that the vision of the business is imparted to and perceived by all individuals from the family to adjust their activities towards accomplishing the common goal (Lin, 2020). This arrangement makes them start the organized course of formulating an owner strategy that joins the family methodology and business procedure and gives a structure to assist with tending to current and future emerging matters. She also suggested some questions that could be asked while creating such a strategy:

1. Who has the potential to be a stakeholder?
2. Does he/she understand succession principles?
3. What is the shared goal of the family business?
4. Which exact framework can the family apply in their business model?
5. How can they deal with conflicts?

NextGen's Role

It is pivotal to remember NextGens for the interaction, so they know about the obligations joined to their legacy. Their perspectives are additionally essential to bring a more prominent arrangement of family business techniques. According to PwC, NextGens can impart well and fabricate outstanding bonds with the administration and the proprietors. They can rehearse humilities, show development and act mindfully. They show love and enthusiasm for the business and, in this manner, support it with their best effort. Younger ages will, in general, be more receptive. Thus, they are less obstinate and continually able to learn from the errors that they make. They can also look for the point of view of outside experts when required (PricewaterhouseCoopers, 2020).

Figure 7. Family business owner strategy
(PricewaterhouseCoopers, 2020)

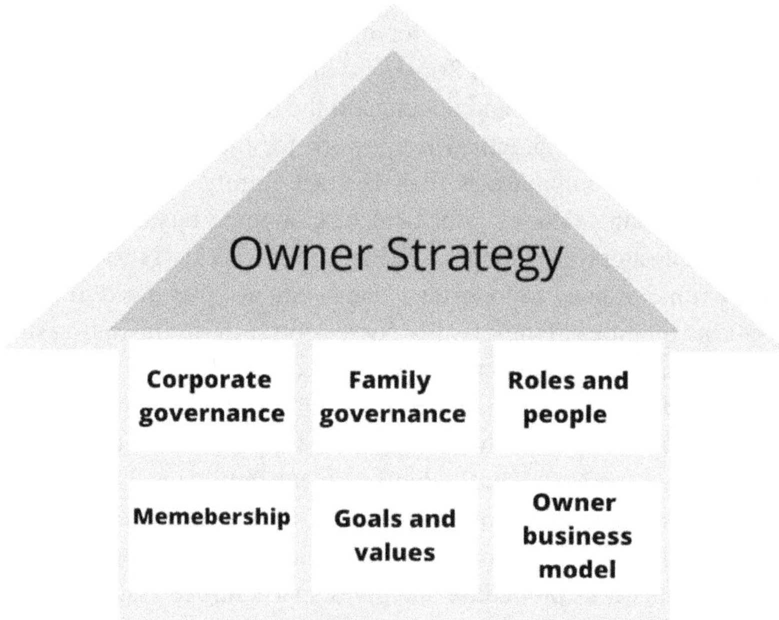

Outside Professionals

Alvin Yap suggests that it has become essential for Malaysian families-run companies to introduce professionalism in the business to have a better functioning governance structure (Yap). Applying a more organized measure closer to the administration of the business and the administration of the family seems more convenient today in Malaysia. The family office can assist with sorting out the family's resources globally to guarantee they are appropriately contributed, to secure the capital and let it grow. It will likewise empower families to part their business resources from individual resources and deal with their risks more globally and successfully. A few families may likewise decide to concentrate different capacities inside the family office, for example, an attendant service and the arrangement of assessment and other expert counsel to relatives. Trusted experts can offer a free voice between family conversations related to the business while adding to various abilities and ideas. These experts can likewise be helpful in specific circumstances to decrease clashing passionate components that might be available when deciding, especially on the family front (PricewaterhouseCoopers, 2020).

CONCLUSION

Malaysian family-run organizations structure a critical foundation of the country's financial map, offering dependability, a guarantee to the long haul, and an obligation to their networks and workers. Most of the businesses in this country are family-owned; therefore, the economic performance of the family businesses in Malaysia draws a more significant effect on its whole economy. The first and second Movement Control Orders, MCO 1.0 and MCO 2.0, in 2020 led to a vast economic downfall among many, if not all, family businesses in Malaysia. During MCO 1.0, the country's economy dipped by -17.2%, and when MCO 2.0 became effective, Malaysia lost RM600 daily. Alongside the financial difficulties brought by covid-19, Malaysian family-owned companies were battling with digital upskilling as the interest in e-commerce skyrocketed since the time people were locked inside their homes. Thus, that was something the older generations of the company struggled to manage since their conventional method of directing business had no dash of digital technologies. In any case, the young generation of those families understood the significance of innovation and digitalization. They will generally be sharper towards learning and quickly adjusting to the new era, which will, as an outcome, help their companies sustain even in times of crisis. Accordingly, numerous experts recommend that Malaysian privately-run companies have an essential succession plan so that when these youth come into power, they now have a better understanding of the general business and foster their thoughts and ideas to develop the quality of the business further. The economic circumstances began to recuperate rapidly as the NextGen business pioneers began to shape their companies to adjust to the digital world while sticking to the family's long-term vision for the business. They are now more hopeful that their financial condition will improve if they learn to adapt to the current business environment.

REFERENCES

Amran, N. A., & Ahmad, A. C. (2011). Board Mechanisms and Malaysian Family Companies' Performance. *Asian Journal of Accounting and Governance*, 15-26.

Arfa, A. (2021, July 8). *How Has MCO Affected The Malaysian Economy?* Taylors. https://university.taylors.edu.my/en/campus-life/news-and-events/news/how-has-mco-affected-the-malaysian-economy.html

Bowen, G. A. (2009). Document analysis as a qualitative research method. *Qualitative Research Journal*, *9*(2), 27–40. doi:10.3316/QRJ0902027

Cheng & Co. (2019, October 1). *Sustaining Family Businesses through Generations*. Cheng and Co. https://chengco.com.my/wp/2019/10/01/sustaining-family-businesses-through-generations/

Ernst & Young. (2020). *Economic impact of COVID-19: A Malaysian context.* Earnest and Young. eiscentre.perkeso.gov.my: https://eiscentre.perkeso.gov.my/wp-content/uploads/2020/04/COVID-19-Economic-Impact_Malaysia_080420.pdf

Grunebaum, D. (2020). *In Malaysia, Businesses Adapt to Survive COVID*. VOA News. https://www.voanews.com/a/east-asia-pacific_malaysia-businesses-adapt-survive-covid/6198371.html

Hayward, A., & Evennett, T. (2021). *Six things family business owners should be thinking about now*. EY. https://www.ey.com/en_uk/unlocking-ambitions-of-private-businesses-and-their-owners/six-things-family-business-owners-should-be-thinking-about-now

Hayward, A., & Evennett, T. (2021). *Six things family business owners should be thinking about now.* EY. www.ey.com: https://www.ey.com/en_uk/unlocking-ambitions-of-private-businesses-and-their-owners/six-things-family-business-owners-should-be-thinking-about-now

Kenton, W. (2020). Succession Planning. *Investopedia.* https://www.investopedia.com/terms/s/succession-planning.asp

Krishnan, R. (2020). Importance Of Succession Planning For Business Families. *Business World.* https://www.businessworld.in/article/Importance-Of-Succession-Planning-For-Business-Families-/03-10-2020-326948/

Lim, J. (2020). Family Business: A second look at the next generation of family business owners. *The Edge Markets.* https://www.theedgemarkets.com/article/family-business-second-look-next-generation-family-business-owners

Lin, F. M. (2020). *Developing the Owner Strategy for Family Businesses*. PWC. https://www.pwc.com/my/en/perspective/epb/200721-developing-the-owner-strategy-for-family-businesses.html

Ngui, C. (2002). *Asian family businesses: From riches to rags*. Malaysian Business.

PricewaterhouseCoopers. (2020). *Agents of change: Earning your licence to operate: PwC's NextGen Survey 2019 - Malaysia Report*. PWC. www.pwc.com/my: https://www.pwc.com/my/en/publications/2020/nextgen-survey.html

PricewaterhouseCoopers. (2021). *Family Business Survey 2021: The Malaysia Chapter.* PWC. www.pwc.com/my: https://www.pwc.com/my/en/assets/publications/2021/pwc-family-business-survey-2021-malaysia.pdf

The Government of Malaysia. (2020). *Economic Stimulus Package 2020 "Bolstering Confidence, Stimulating Growth, Protecting Jobs."* MOF. https://www.mof.gov.my/pdf/pre2020/Booklet_2020_Economic_Stimulus_Package.pdf

Yap, A. (n.d.). *Family and Business: Planning for the Future.* RHB Group. www.crowehorwath.com.my: https://www.rhbgroup.com/files/business/business-solution/sme-knowledge-center/Crowe%20Horwath%20Newsletter%20Succession%20Planning.pdf

Yusof, A. (2021). Timeline: How the COVID-19 pandemic has unfolded in Malaysia since January 2020. *Channel News Asia.* https://www.channelnewsasia.com/asia/timeline-how-covid-19-pandemic-has-unfolded-malaysia-january-2020-2082081

Chapter 5
The Impact of the COVID-19 Pandemic on the Small and Medium Family Businesses in Vietnam

Do Thi Thanh Nhan
Faculty of Finance and Banking, Ton Duc Thang University, Vietnam

Suu Duy Nguyen
Faculty of Finance and Banking, Ton Duc Thang University, Vietnam

Dao Le Kieu Oanh
Ho Chi Minh University of Banking, Vietnam

Le Ngoc Thuy Trang
Faculty of Management and Economic, Tomas Bata University in Zlín, Czech Republic

ABSTRACT

The Covid-19 pandemic has influenced the economy over the world. In Vietnam, Covid-19 emerged on January 23, 2020, and has encountered several outbreaks across the country, which has caused negative impacts on the economy. The Covid-19 has influenced all aspects of socio-economic life, creating difficulties for all businesses, especially small and medium family businesses (SMEs family businesses). SMEs account for most of Vietnam's firms and have important roles in the economy. Based on the current situation, the chapter explores the potential impacts of the Covid-19 pandemic outbreak on SME family businesses. Moreover, we discussed the strategies of SME family businesses and the government's policies during this period.

DOI: 10.4018/978-1-6684-7394-8.ch005

1. INTRODUCTION

Since reforming the economy in 1986, Vietnam has dramatically changed from a lowest-income country to a lower-middle-income country and has become one of the most dynamic economies. Moreover, Vietnam officially became the 150th member of the World Trade Organization in 2006. Then, Vietnam has become the destination of foreign direct investment and multinational corporations with deep integration.

When the covid-19 arose, the pandemic heavily affected Vietnam's economy. Nevertheless, Asia's economy is still top-performing, with a GDP growth of 2.9% in 2020 (World Bank, 2021). Notably, the covid-19 pandemic has had a negative impact on businesses' activities and significant effects on trade, services, and banking activities worldwide. However, only a few studies deeply and comprehensively research the effects of the covid-19 on the local economy. Meanwhile, different places affected differently by the covid-19 depend on their economic conditions. Therefore, studying the impact of the covid-19 on the locality's economic development is necessary. According to the Vietnam Academy of Social Sciences (VASS):

Most small and medium firms in Vietnam belong to families considered an essential part of the private sector and account for a large proportion of the Vietnamese business community (Hai, 2019).

Currently, Vietnam has about 541,753 SMEs family businesses with a total registered capital of about 130 billion USD, accounting for more than 30% of the capital of all enterprises (Vinh, 2021). Every year, they contribute about 40% of the GDP, 30% to the government's budget, 30% to exports, and attract nearly 60% of employees (Hai, 2019). Although the number is large, the number of medium-sized enterprises is only 1.6%, while the small and micro-enterprises represent a large proportion of SMEs family businesses.

Juergensen et al. (2020) indicated that SMEs are playing an important role in the economy. When covid 19 happened, SMEs are impacted in short term immediately. For long term, SMEs in different industries have various impacts, then the government should have suitable policies to help them. Moreover, Lu et al. (2020) conluded that covid 19 had a strong impact on the economy and SMEs. They have to face with a lot of difficulties during and after covid period. Thus, they need the support from the government. Furthermore, the covid-19 pandemic has put them in a problematic situation which causes many businesses to go bankrupt. The sector's revenue decreased, and firms in the service sector had the most revenue reduction, followed by industry and construction. Enterprises in the agriculture, forestry, and fishing sectors have the slightest revenue decrease. Furthermore, they also face a shortage of input materials. Currently, the domestic consumption market was also narrowed, with over two-thirds of enterprises saying that the domestic consumption market decreased sharply.

Additionally, the increased transportation and storage costs are also a concern. Therefore, the covid-19 has also caused disruptions and challenges to family businesses and the economy. Thus, the chapter's objective will focus on the family businesses during the covid-19 situation.

The first stage of the chapter summarises the covid-19 situation in Vietnam to analyse the process of preventing a health crisis. The following section presents the economic consequences due to the covid-19. The third section discusses the family businesses during the covid-19 period. The fourth section emphasises how family businesses in Vietnam can survive in the current situation. The final section discusses the strategies used by SMEs family businesses.

2. THE COVID-19 SITUATION IN VIETNAM

In Vietnam, the covid-19 pandemic caused by the SARS-CoV-2 virus was first confirmed on January 23, 2020. So far, through 4 outbreaks:

The first outbreak lasted from January 23, 2020, to April 16, 2020. There were 415 cases (106 locally acquired and 309 imported cases) (Ministry of health portal, 2021). With the first case appearing in Ho Chi Minh City, an imported case from Wuhan City (China), the disease spread to 13 provinces in all three North–Central–South regions. The government issued the Prime Minister's Directive No. 05/CT-TTg, toward combating the covid-19, with the principle of "protecting people's health first." Viet Nam has successfully and rapidly implemented necessary covid-19 prevention, detection, and control activities under the government's strong leadership and effective multi-sectoral coordination and collaboration.

The second wave of epidemics lasted from July 25, 2020, to January 27, 2021, but only peaked in 36 days (from July 25, 2020, to August 29, 2020) in Da Nang and only recorded 4 cases in the next 100 days in Ho Chi Minh City. With one patient at Hospital in Da Nang, the covid-19 spread out the second wave to 15 localities in all three North–Central–South regions. Although the outbreak was short-lived, the second outbreak recorded up to 1,136 infections, including 554 locally acquired cases and 582 imported cases (Ministry of health portal, 2021), more than 2.74 times higher than the first outbreak. On 21/01/2021, the second Vietnamese-made covid-19 vaccine (COVIVAC) by the Institute of Vaccines and Medical Biologicals (IVAC) had a human-clinical trial two months earlier than scheduled. Moreover, communications to the public focused on providing updates on outbreak situations and government actions, including stories on the ground, promoting protective measures, and countering rumours and misinformation. Messaging on protective measures had been repackaged as "5K": (1) Facemask; (2) Hygiene; (3) Safe distance; (4) Gathering; (5) Health declaration.

The third outbreak was about 57 days (from January 28, 2021, to March 25, 2021). The first patient from Hai Duong was positive when entering Japan. This time recorded, up to 910 patients with the covid-19 in the community, nearly double compared to the previous outbreak, mainly in the Hai Duong outbreak. The 3rd wave of the epidemic spread to 13 provinces and cities in all three regions.

On April 27, 2021, the fourth outbreak began when the patient was a hotel employee where Indian experts were isolated in Yen Bai province. Followed by case 2,899 covid-19 returned from Japan after completing 14-day isolation. The number of new infections recorded in the country during the outbreak from April 27 to July 31, 2021, was 142,834, including 141,877 locally acquired cases and 957 imported cases, of which 35,960 patients have been declared cured. The number of tests from April 27, 2021, to July 31, 2021, was 6,070,003 samples for 17,356,646 people (Ministry of health portal 2021). However, the 4th epidemic with a new strain is very complicated, infections and deaths increase daily, and there is no sign of stopping. Ho Chi Minh City is one of the hot spot areas in this epidemic. The rapid spread of SARS-CoV-2 with the Delta variant makes preventing and controlling the outbreak challenging, in which the treatment system in this city is overloaded.

For the first time, on March 31, 2020, Vietnam implemented social distancing to limit community spread when the number of cases in Vietnam increased rapidly day by day, while the number of patients in the world was 720,000 people and nearly 3.5 thousand deaths in 200 countries. After controlling the disease, there were outbreaks in some localities such as Da Nang, Ho Chi Minh City, Hai Duong, Binh Duong, etc. The high spread will implement partial or total social distancing depending on the number of cases and the level of disease control. This makes Vietnam one of the few countries that have well-controlled the epidemic situation when the number of cases is kept low and community transmission is limited.

Accumulating from January 2020 to the afternoon of July 31, 2021, Vietnam has 145,686 cases, including 2,239 imported cases and 143,447 locally acquired lab-confirmed cases. The total number of cured cases as of July 31, 2021are 38,734 cases. There were 441 critically ill patients treated in the ICU and 21 critical cases with ECMO (Ministry of health portal, 2021).

3. VIETNAM'S ECONOMY DURING THE COVID-19 PERIOD

According to the Business Registration Management Agency:

In the first nine months of 2020, 98,955 newly-established enterprises were down 3.2% compared to the same period in 2019. Meanwhile, the first nine months of 2015-2019 did not record a decrease in the number of newly-established enterprises, with an average growth rate of 14.3% per year (Hau, 2020).

The average registered capital per enterprise in the first nine months of 2020 reached 14.4 billion dongs, up 14.4% compared to the same period in 2019. Total registered capital for the first nine months of 2020 is 3,601,947 billion dongs (an increase of 19.2% over the same period in 2019), consisting of 1,428,482 billion dongs from newly established enterprises (up 10.7% over the same period in 2019) and 2,173,465 billion dongs from 29,540 operating enterprises for the additionally registered capital (up 25.6% over the same period in 2019) (Hau, 2020). The total number of newly-established enterprises registered employees in the first nine months of 2020 was 777,902, which decreased by 16.3% compared to the same period in 2019. In the early months of 2020, the additionally registered capital of operating enterprises decreased over the same period last year, indicating that the psychology of investors and entrepreneurs was significantly affected by the covid-19 pandemic. In the 3rd quarter of 2020, many indicators improved remarkably. The enterprises became more confident in seizing the opportunities to invest in production and business (the registered capital in 7/2020 increased by 72.0% compared to 6/2020, and the registered capital in 8/2020 increased by 20.7% compared to 7/2020).

Controlling the covid-19 very well is a critical factor that helps Vietnam become one of the bright spots for economic development in the world in 2020 when it maintains a positive economic growth momentum and controls inflation well. Although the GDP growth rate in 2020 only reached 2.91%, down from 7.02% in 2019, Vietnam was still one of the few countries to maintain positive growth momentum amid the complicated developments of the covid-19 outbreak. The CPI growth rate decreased from 3.6% in 2019 to 2.8% in 2020, showing that Vietnam has controlled inflation well (General Statistics Office, 2021). According to the loose monetary policy, the interest rate is maintained at a low level to contribute to the State Bank's growth and create conditions for commercial banks to develop their operations.

However, the covid-19 epidemic has caused many difficulties for foreign trade activities, leading to decreased output demand. The realised social investment capital had the lowest increase in the 2016-2020 period due to the negative impact of the covid-19 epidemic. Moreover, retail sales went down by 4.3% compared to the previous year, and the retail sales of goods were 80.6%, a slight increase (0.4%)

due to the recent popularity of online shopping by consumers. According to a report by the General Statistics Office (2021):

For the first seven months of 2021, nearly 79.7 thousand enterprises temporarily suspended their businesses, up to 25.5% over the same period in 2020.

Tourism is the most affected industry because the covid-19 epidemic occurred during the peak tourist season after Vietnam's Lunar New Year holiday. After that, other outbreaks of covid-19 caused many disadvantages for businesses in the tourism industry. Then, major tourism businesses stopped operating temporarily, and some hotels and restaurants must close. According to the year-end report of the General Statistics Office:

Because of covid-19, international visitors to Vietnam reduced by 79.5% compared to 2019; domestic tourists decreased by 34.1%; total tourism revenue went down 58.7% to 19 billion USD (Bao, 2021).

Besides that, the agriculture, forestry, and fishing industry are in a difficult situation because exporting, importing, circulating, and transporting goods are severely affected. Production costs increase, and agricultural business activities are interrupted, which puts pressure on storage costs for preservation. Agricultural products are getting stuck and delayed because of the customs clearance and trade of goods at border gates due to strict compliance with epidemic preventive measures and regulations.

Regarding the retail industry, because of the covid-19, many places are locked down, reducing consumers' purchasing power, and causing many challenges for the domestic retail industry. In that context, to maintain and develop, retail businesses need to quickly restructure and transform business forms such as multi-channel sales, online to in-person. Due to the impact of the covid-19 epidemic, the industry faced many difficulties but still achieved positive growth in the industrial field. The index of Industrial Production (IIP) increased by 5.25% over the previous year, the slowest growth rate in the last five years. The mining industry and manufacturing industry grew by 3.35% and 5.29%, respectively; production and distribution of electricity, gas, hot water, steam, and air-conditioning by 6.07%; water supply, waste, and wastewater management, and treatment activities went up by 3.26% over the previous year.

The added value of the whole industry for the entire year increased by 3.36% compared to last year, higher than the economy's overall growth rate. For real estate, the outbreak of the covid-19 has put the market into a "hibernation" state, which exacerbates finance and psychology. As a result, real estate is witnessing a sharp drop in demand and a downward trend in the supply of housing projects, especially in the social housing segment. The Socio-Economic Report of the General Statistics Office said:

In 2020, the construction industry in the whole country grew by 6.76%, which is the lowest growth rate in the 2016-2020 period. This is still higher than in 2011-2013.

Confronting unfavourable economic and market conditions, the number of new business establishments in real estate was 6,694 enterprises, which was reduced by 15.5% compared to 2019, with nearly 1000 firms completing dissolution procedures. The epidemic's negative impact is mainly due to economic disruption and a decline in investment demand. Economic disruption directly affects the short-term growth of the industry; conversely, a drop in investment demand will have a longer-term effect.

All businesses are greatly affected by the epidemic. The number of newly-established enterprises slowed down, and the amount of additional capital or commitment to put into business decreased compared to 2019. The covid-19 epidemic also has a significant impact on people's social life. Due to the epidemic, the working-age unemployment rate in 2020 was 2.48%, up 0.31% compared to 2019. Many groups of labour industries are seriously affected by the outbreak, such as transportation and warehousing services (79.7%), accommodation and food services (81.7%), and arts and entertainment (88.6%). At the same time, there is a significant shift in labour from the formal to the informal sector (General Statistics Office, 2021). According to the General Statistics Office (2021) report, per capita income decreased to only 5.5 million VND, down 0.128 million VND compared to the previous year.

3.1. Enterprises Dissolved or Temporarily Suspended Business

Statistics show that the number of enterprises withdrawing from the market and temporarily suspending business rose sharply in 2020. According to Business Registration Management Agency, in the first nine months of 2020, 78,306 enterprises were withdrawing from the market, including 38,629 enterprises registering business suspension for a definite time (an increase of 81.8% over the same period in 2019, 3.7 times higher than the average increase of 21.9% in the period 2015-2019), 27,855 enterprises waiting for dissolution procedures (down 2.4% over the same period in 2019, lower than the average increase of 2.9% in the period 2015-2019), 12,089 enterprises completing the procedures for dissolution (up 0.1% over the same period in 2019, the average increase in the period 2015-2019 was 12.1%) (Hau, 2020). On average, 8,701 enterprises withdrew from the market every month, up 27.2% compared to the average of the first nine months of 2019. According to historical data, the average increase rate of enterprises registering to suspend business temporarily in the first nine months of 2015-2019 was 21.9%. The sharp increase in the number of enterprises temporarily suspending business and the number of enterprises returning to operation shows a vital cleansing in the business community.

Figure 1. The number of enterprises suspending business by field of activity (Ministry of Planning and Investment, 2021)

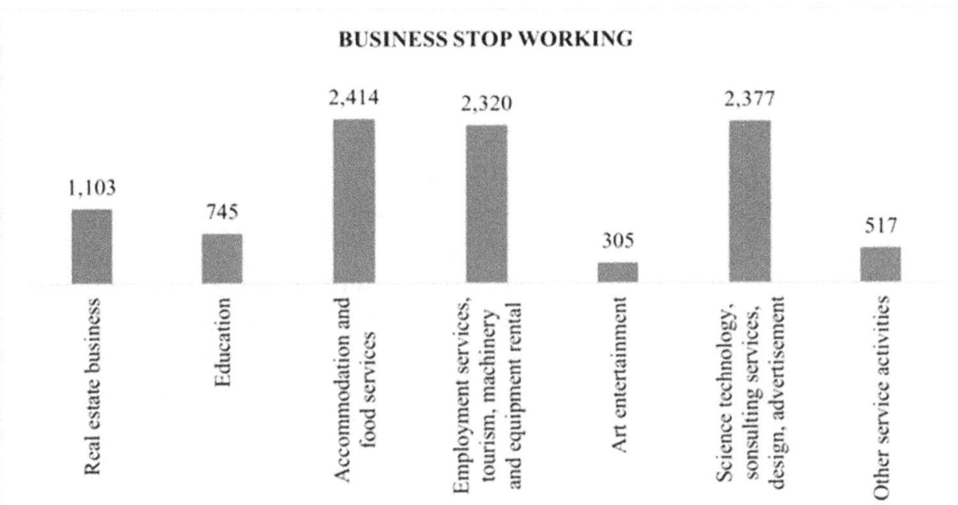

Enterprises registered to suspend business for a definite time in the first nine months of 2020 had total capital of 280,293 billion dongs and 277,180 employees (equivalent to 19.6% of total capital and 35.6% of total employees of newly-established enterprises in the first nine months of 2020). Remarkably, it was recorded 17/17 fields with a dramatic increase in the number of enterprises registered to temporarily stop their business compared to the same period in 2019. The industries and professions with the most substantial increase were real estate business (1,103 enterprises, up 161.4%), education and training (745 enterprises, up 129.9%), accommodation and food services (2,414 enterprises, up 120.3%), employment services, tourism, rental of machinery and equipment, utensils and other support services (2,320 enterprises, up 109.4%), arts, entertainment and recreation (305 enterprises, up 102.0%), other service activities (517 enterprises, up 97.3%), scientific and technical activities, consulting and design services, advertising and other professional activities (2,377 enterprises, up 81.5%). These are the most heavily affected sectors by the covid-19 pandemic.

3.2. The Impact of Covid-19 on Family Businesses in Vietnam

SMEs family businesses which are a critical portion of the private segment, have accounted for a significant proportion of Vietnam's economy. According to the General Statistics Office of Vietnam, there are about 541,753 SMEs family businesses with a total capital of around 130 billion USD. This shows that they play a crucial role in Vietnam's economy. Since 1986, with economic development and worldwide integration, SMEs family businesses have contributed significantly to Vietnam's economy. Furthermore, famous Vietnamese family brands such as Tan Hiep Phat Group, Thanh Thanh Cong Group, DOJI Jewelry Group, Hoang Cau Group, Minh Long, etc., also spread their businesses worldwide.

Additionally, SMEs family businesses make the economy dynamic because they are small, so they can easily change to suit the economy's needs. Additionally, SMEs family businesses often specialise in manufacturing a few parts to assemble a finished product. Besides, they are the primary key to the local economy. Suppose large enterprises are often based in the big cities of the country. In that case, SMEs family businesses are presented in all localities, essential contributors to the local budget, production, and job creation, contributing significantly to the country's GDP.

SMEs family businesses have advantages in organisation, strategy, or decision-making over other private or state-owned enterprises. However, most family businesses struggle to pass on to the second and subsequent generations because corporate governance issues arise. The vast majority of family businesses have difficulty dealing with this governance problem. Moreover, SMEs family businesses are confronting many challenges due to their small sizes, such as the capacity to access the funds to invest in modern technologies, lack of experience in corporate governance, and ability to compete. Besides, family businesses in Vietnam are young, with nearly two-thirds of the first generation as a major shareholders, compared with 43 per cent in Asia-Pacific and 32 per cent in the rest of the world. Moreover, the general trend of family businesses is to specialise, diversify, and develop multi-industry. At the same time, there is a management structure and personnel administration by personnel hired from outside rather than nepotism.

According to the PwC report:

33% of Vietnamese family businesses in the survey had a positive outlook for 2022, higher than the rate recorded at the regional level of 28% and globally 21%. Vietnamese family businesses focus on improving technology, and 55% of family business leaders confirm developing and bringing new products and services to the market. These strategies are also suitable for SMEs family businesses to main and grow, especially during covid-19.

Figure 2. The family business structure in 2020
(Source: According to a survey by PricewaterhouseCoopers Consulting (PwC). an auditing firm)

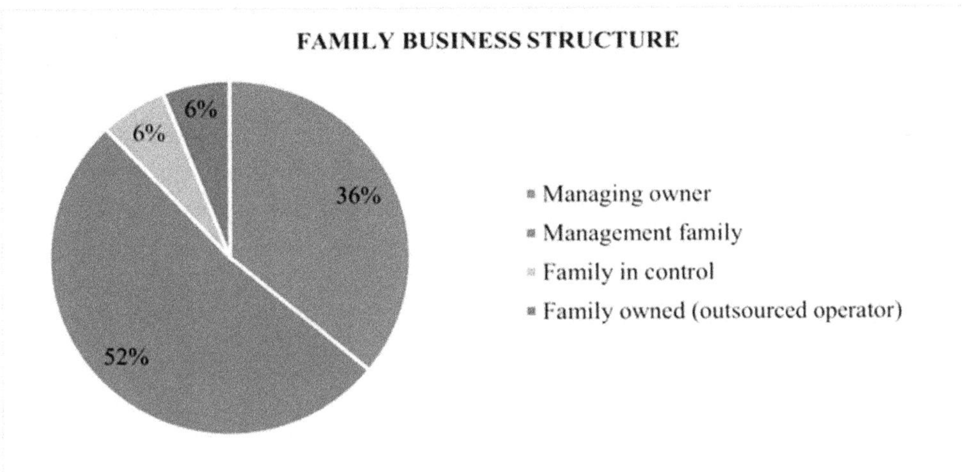

SMEs' family businesses are flexible because they can easily change the structure and make quick decision-making, but covid-19 has also influenced them. The number of SMEs family businesses shutting down increased in 2020. During the covid-19 period, many businesses have closed because they have fewer or no customers to maintain their businesses. Some are also concerned about losing their businesses temporarily. The rate of SMEs family businesses shutting down did not differ significantly among regions, areas of operation, or urban-rural locations.

According to the National Business registration portal in Vietnam, more than 90% of small family businesses temporarily closed or shut down in the first four months of 2021. In particular, the number of firms suspending business in the first four months of 2021 increased in all 17 fields: production and distribution, electricity, water, gas (269 enterprises, up 128%); health care and social assistance activities (89 businesses, increase 56.1%); education and training (606 enterprises, up 49.6%); mining (181 enterprises, up 40.3%); real estate business (842 enterprises, up 35.2%); science and technology; consulting and design services; advertising and other expertise (1,878 businesses, up 34.5%); employment service; travel; leasing of machinery, equipment, utensils and other supporting services (1,752 enterprises, up 32.6%) and information and communication (627 enterprises, up 30.1%) (Duong and Truong, 2021).

Notably, enterprises registered to suspend business are mainly small family businesses with a VND 0-10 billion capital scale with 25,919 enterprises (accounting for 91.4%, up 24.1% over the same period in 2020). At the scale of 10-20 billion VND, there are 1,366 enterprises (accounting for 4.8%, up 39.2% over the same period in 2020). From 20 to 50 billion dongs, there are 664 enterprises (accounting for 2.3%, up 29.2% over the same period in 2020). From 50 to 100 billion VND, there are 230 enterprises (accounting for 0.8%, up 13.9% over the same period in 2020). The scale of over 100 billion VND has 170 enterprises (accounting for 0.6%, up 49. 1% over the same period in 2020) (Duong and Truong, 2021).

The consumption market shrinks rapidly, with 57.7% of affected enterprises thinking that the consumption market dropped sharply. Notably, up to 47.2% of enterprises with export activities confirmed that manufactured goods could not be exported during all this time.

Figure 3. The rate of enterprises affected by the consumption market
(General Statistics Office, 2021)

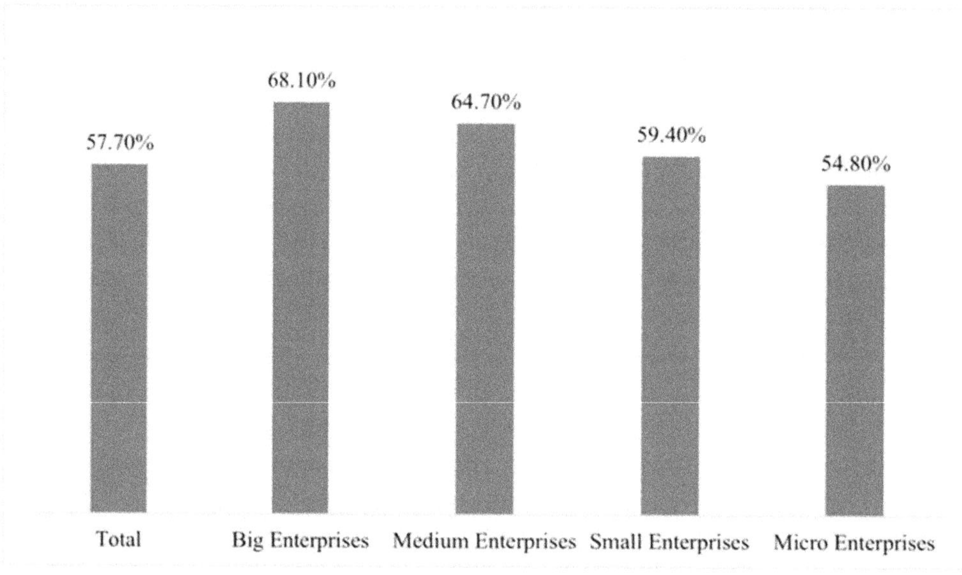

The larger the group of enterprises, the higher the raw and input materials shortage. This rate gradually decreases with the size of the enterprise. This does not mean that smaller enterprises face fewer difficulties in assessing input materials in the context of the pandemic. For SMEs family businesses, the shortage of raw and input materials is more worrying. At present, microenterprises have access to raw and input materials only to satisfy nearly 1/5 of the demand; this rate increases gradually with the size of the enterprise and is over 1/3 of the need for large enterprises. The domestic consumption market is narrowed when more than two-thirds of enterprises say that the domestic consumption market has decreased sharply. The rate of enterprises facing difficulties due to the narrowing export market is relatively high. Export enterprises with larger sizes have a higher rate of facing challenges due to the narrow export market. With the downward trend in export quantity and the difficulties in merchandise circulation in most enterprises, transportation and storage costs have also risen as a concern. Moreover, the longer the covid-19 epidemic lasted, the more the input material reserve of enterprises would be depleted. At the time of the survey, 22.1% of enterprises were in shortage of inputs.

Figure 4. The rate of enterprises affected by input factors

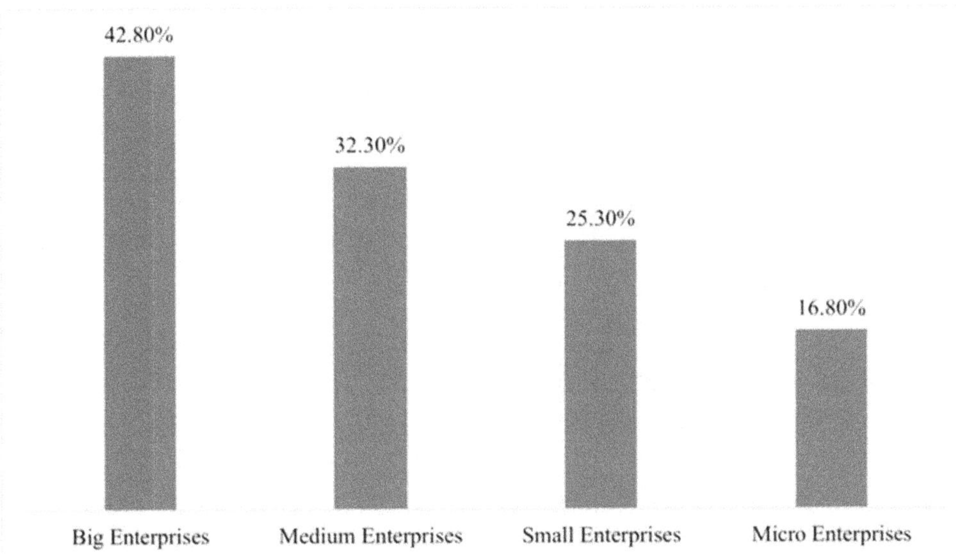

Shortage of capital for business operation: 45.4% of surveyed enterprises were in shortage of financing for their business operations, which is one of the most significant difficulties of current enterprises and the general situation of all other business sectors. In the context of the severe impact of the Covid-19 epidemic, businesses face many difficulties in cash flow. Currently, enterprises face five challenges: paying wages to employees, paying interest on bank loans, paying regular activities, rent expenses, and other activities. Some enterprises have to accept trade-offs to maintain production and business activities. However, many enterprises could not survive during this period. Most enterprises that suffered heavy losses have done the procedures to apply for tax reduction, tax payment extension, loan repayment extension, and call for support from the government. However, due to the influence of the covid -19 outbreak on the entire economy, it is difficult for the government to provide timely support to all enterprises.

Moreover, supply chain disruption also plays an important role in the economy. The long-lasting Covid-19 pandemic in 2020 and 2021 has caused the supply chain of goods. In addition, global supply chain disruption; increased cost and time of shipping increased; prolonged loading and unloading time; lack of customs and warehousing services; lack of means and two-way carriers from industrial zones and seaports; lack of private and public services aggravates the situation. These reasons cause more difficulties for SMEs firms to do their business.

Furthermore, access to technology and digital transformation is still limited. Most SMEs have small capital, and weak financial capacity, while professional and effective technological equipment and digital transformation solutions have huge costs. Besides, the lack of well-trained human resources and consulting also make it difficult for businesses to have enough resources to invest in digital transformation. In addition, most SMEs have to focus on the business for survival, they have very little time to focus on digital transformation for businesses.

Finally, Covid 19 changes customer tastes, behavior, and the way of consumption. Therefore, these changes will definitely affect enterprises' production and business activities.

4. HOW CAN THE FAMILY BUSINESS SURVIVE IN THE COVID-19?

The covid-19 pandemic severely affects small and medium enterprises' operations. Therefore, not many enterprises can survive the pandemic. Statistics show that more than 80% of businesses deal with many challenges to survive during the period. The number of enterprises dissolving and suspending operations increased sharply. To survive and overcome the pandemic, many enterprises have taken different methods to do their business. The business community, especially most SME family businesses, had to stop operating or reduce production because the production costs increased due to the implementation of epidemic prevention and the increase of input material. Then, they need support from all levels of government to operate and maintain their businesses during this time.

SMEs family businesses also need to change their ways of doing business, which helps them adapt to current conditions. With the current state of "health" of SMEs' family business sector and the consequences of the covid-19 pandemic on businesses and the economy. It is urgent to research and implement appropriate policies and solutions in the medium and long term. SMEs family businesses have recently implemented solutions such as changing sales approach, business diversification and converting essential products, investing in a niche market, and transforming the crisis into an opportunity.

Bai et al. (2021) sugguest that SMEs have to develop digital in doing businesses to boost their profit, especially after the covid 19 period. The firms can change from direct sales to online sales through online shopping applications such as Lazada, Sendo, Tiki, Shopee, VinID, GoFood, etc. This is considered a bright spot for firms when applying online sales methods successfully, taking advantage of scientific and technological developments and e-commerce in business activities. However, it also depends on the enterprises' items to determine the possibility of success in this approach. According to statistics, during the covid-19 outbreak, online sales have increased sharply for essential items such as food, medicine, hygiene tools, cosmetics, and baby supplies.

However, the covid-19 pandemic has strongly affected SME's family businesses in the retail industry under the effect of banning mass gatherings. Nevertheless, some enterprises need more conditions to switch to selling online, and their revenue decreases. The covid-19 pandemic has profoundly changed customers' needs and buying habits in the direction of shifting from face-to-face, traditional interactions to more online interactions. In that context, each firm needs to raise its awareness of rising, promoting its advantages, and improving its competitiveness.

SMEs family businesses have some preferences in commerce, including diversified market segments and wide customers with domestic, regional, and international commercial activities. To improve product quality and labour productivity, they need to increase investment, innovate technology, apply innovation in product design, production process, and process management and attach importance to investment in science and technology. This is the key to helping businesses overcome difficulties in the context of the covid-19 pandemic and take advantage of opportunities to recover and develop production and trade. SMEs family businesses can easily capture the needs and psychology of customers for each group and region by each enterprise's type and business line. Thus, SMEs family businesses can create solutions that help them focus on and promote in the current period. Additionally, enterprises should develop strategies with specific plans, clear visions, and operational missions.

Only a few enterprises can succeed, mainly manufacturing essential products such as pharmaceuticals and basic foods. Besides trading traditional goods, these enterprises provide more critical products to meet the needs during the pandemic.

The covid-19 epidemic has significantly changed Vietnamese people's behaviour and habits. Consumers prioritise local brands to support local businesses, communities, brands, and retailers. Thus, SME family businesses should develop supporting industries such as manufacturing components and accessories, spare parts, production for the textile and garment industry, and leather and footwear, and serving the high-tech industry. These are the areas that help Vietnamese family enterprises actively strengthen domestic supply chains. The better link between SMEs' family businesses and domestic supply chains; contributes to limiting the impact of disruptions to international supply chains and input supply activities due to the impact of the covid-19 pandemic while ensuring that they can take advantage of market opportunities, recover and develop, contributing to promoting Vietnam's economic growth.

SMEs' family businesses have transformed and are considered successful during the covid-19 period. Thaco has carried out digital transformation, starting from automating factory production lines, then gradually changing processes, technology, and management and achieved remarkable success. Thaco is still in digital transformation in all five investment areas, including automobile, agriculture, construction, logistics, trade, and service. Duy Khanh Engineering Company has implemented digital transformation and has become the pioneer in Ho Chi Minh City in this field. The results of digital transformation help the company save costs in the production process and increase business efficiency through automation.

Garment 10 Joint Stock Company has coped with the negative impacts of the covid-19 pandemic by transforming production processes and products and promoting the rapid transformation of traditional product structures into fast adaptive items. For example, when ordering with veston high-class, high-end shirts, etc. They then switch to workwear, knitwear, and traditional shirts; or increase the proportion of jackets, winter coats, and casual clothes at home; and produce cotton face masks, and protective clothing for the domestic market and export. The member units of Vietnam National Textile and Garment Group not only produce ordinary garments but also participate in the production of antibacterial fabric materials for making masks, their own antibacterial fabric mask product lines and sell them throughout the nationwide retail system, including Hanosimex, Chien Thang Garment, Nha Be Garment, Viet Tien, Nam Dinh Silk Textile Joint Stock Company, etc.

4.1 Reducing the Cost of Production

In the context of the covid-19 pandemic, SME family businesses must comply with health regulations such as using masks and hand sanitiser and keeping social distancing. Compliance with these regulations will increase the production and business costs of enterprises. To cut costs and create favourable conditions for reducing selling prices to maintain the market and stabilise revenue, they need to implement the following cost-cutting methods. Firstly, the firms should restructure production lines and areas, renew production technology, improve production processes towards increasing labour productivity and eliminate redundant operations. Secondly, designing a supply chain management system to ensure a smooth transition from receiving orders, determining raw material standards, selecting suppliers, and receiving and storing raw materials. Next, choosing the optimal amount of materials and goods in stock to minimise storage costs, safe storage costs, and purchasing costs, using diverse supply sources and logistics services. At the same time, they can perform well in forecasting demand for materials and raw materials to be proactive in production plans to minimise shortages and excesses of raw materials and finished products.

4.2 Support Policies from the Vietnamese Government

In 2020, flexible tax policy solutions were given by the government. In particular, the tax reduction and extension of nearly 124,000 billion VND have been approved to support all businesses, which will help them overcome the widespread challenges caused by the covid-19. Specifically, in September 2020, the government issued Decree 114/2020/ND-CP detailing the implementation of Resolution No. 116/2020/QH14 of the National Assembly on reducing 30% of corporate income tax (CIT) 2020 for all kinds of businesses. Besides corporate income tax, the tax extension deadline for payment of enterprises' first-half year of 2021 corporate income tax is three months from the end of the time limit for paying corporate income tax following the law on tax administration. Value-added and personal income tax of businesses and households is extended until December 31, 2021. However, according to some experts:

With the complicated developments of the covid-19 epidemic over time, businesses in many industries and fields have faced difficulties, production stagnation, and a decline in sales. Small-scale enterprises have had to reduce production or temporarily suspend operations if only tax extension or postponement would be the same as interest-free loans. SME family businesses that access capital from banks have encountered administrative procedures with many regulations. Instead, corporations and banks need to be equal because they operate under the Enterprise Law and share risks for development.

Most firms' management proposed to the government to support the extension of bank loans for businesses in the next six months for short-term and long-term loans. They asked to reduce 2%-3% of lending interest rates for businesses affected by covid-19 and delay paying taxes and social insurance in the next six months to help businesses have more cash flow for production and business activities. It is necessary to extend the duration of support packages for enterprises to restore production and business. At the same time, it is necessary to loosen up some conditions to ameliorate the procedures and processes for accessing support packages, especially the financial proofing procedure. Notably, the Prime Minister asked the Ministry of Finance to set up a fund for SME family businesses with VND 100,000 billion to support businesses without collateral. However, the firms must demonstrate healthy financial statements and contracts/orders within the next six months to receive the guarantee.

For instance, one of the big four groups, Agribank, spent VND 30,000 billion for SME family businesses to borrow at a very low-interest rate of 4.5% per year. Vietnam International Commercial Bank (VIB) also reduced interest rates for more than 8,500 SME family businesses, with an average interest rate reduction of 1.5 percentage points from July 2020. Intending to promote economic development, enhance banking capacity, and access to financial services for rural SME family businesses, Bac A Commercial Joint Stock Bank implements preferential program loans from the project "Rural Finance II". Accordingly, the maximum loan amount is 75% of the total cost, and the maximum loan limit is also up to 2.3 billion VND for each sub-project (Giang, 2021). These programs are necessary to help businesses to survive and develop during the covid-19 period.

In addition, the local banking industry also pays special attention to small and medium enterprises. For example, the State Bank of Vietnam Dong Nai branch informed that by the end of July 2021, outstanding loans to small and medium-sized enterprises of credit institutions in the province were estimated at more than 59,900 billion VND.

According to VCCI, by the end of July 2021, national and provincial levels have issued nearly 100 documents on supporting policies for businesses during the covid-19 pandemic. Overall, the support policies for SMEs are grouped into three packages. Firstly, fiscal policy (exemption, reduction of taxes, fees, charges, extension of deadline for VAT payment, corporate income tax). The government reduces an extensive personal income tax for family enterprises and land rent. Likewise, they also have credit support policies such as interest rate support for enterprises to borrow to develop production (a credit support package of VND 250,000 billion) (Minh, 2021).

Secondly, the government has given the "3 on the spot" policy to maintain their businesses during covid-19. Furthermore, Vietnam's government allowed the firms to implement "3 on the spot" or "1 road, 2 destinations". The firms added overtime pay to encourage employees to participate and provided an additional bonus. The enterprise also offers four meals daily, coffee, and milk, creating conditions for workers to entertain themselves after work, on weekends, etc. However, this method has also brought many problems, especially for family businesses, because of their lack of capacity. Remarkably, the most severe difficulty for businesses when implementing "3 on the spot" is that their infrastructure is not qualified to meet epidemic prevention, and the implementation cost is high. Moreover, the regulations and guidelines of this policy are not specific and inconsistent, which makes enterprises confused in the implementation process. Consequently, most firms have the plan to stop their businesses because of the above reasons.

Thirdly, the Vietnamese government has many support policies for corporations' labour. For example, the staff working in all corporations receive support packages, including food and money from the government. Especially the government has more significant care for the staffs of SMEs family businesses who have a strong influence because of the pandemic. All activities encourage the business community, showing a positive message about accompanying the government with SMEs' family businesses. However, the government must regularly exchange with the business community to find a familiar voice in promoting effective policy implementation. Then, the government can improve policies to support businesses during the covid -19 epidemic.

5. CONCLUSION

The covid-19 pandemic has significantly impacted the development of Vietnam's economy, including SMEs and family businesses. The epidemic has affected substantially some specified sectors of SMEs' family businesses, including accommodation and food service, tourism industry, education, real estate, agricultural products, and retail, because they get more challenges in accessing customers. Moreover, the supply chain of many enterprises has been interrupted, significantly affecting the production schedule, which causes reduced orders and output, delaying investment progress. Besides, this group is more disadvantaged because of the difficulties with resources. The negative impact of the epidemic is mainly through two factors, namely economic disruption and a decline in investment demand. In which, economic disruption directly affects the short-term growth of the industry; conversely, a decline in investment demand will have a longer-term effect. Then, the government should have more support policies to help them maintain production and business activities during the covid-19 pandemic.

Several solutions are applied to help SMEs' family businesses. One of the essential solutions from the government is reducing corporate income tax and value-added tax for some industries heavily affected by the epidemic. Additionally, the government should add more tax reductions for major affected industries such as tourism, restaurants, hotels, and transportation. Currently, 30% is the current tax discounted rate for all firms, and this support tax level needs to be expanded to 50% to help SME family businesses to recover after the covid-19 epidemic. A recommended additional solution is to support businesses with covid-19 epidemic prevention costs of maintaining production, which directly supports SME family businesses to face the difficulties. This policy is also fair when businesses try to implement the government's policy on maintaining their operations to boost economic recovery. Besides, the government should find solutions to reduce the cost of essential commodities such as electricity and petrol to reduce the input cost for all firms. The covid-19 pandemic is still complicated development, and then SME family businesses should change the management, production, and distribution enterprises to maintain and develop their businesses during this period. In addition, they should apply digital technology, adapt quickly, and transform working and management forms which can turn difficulties into opportunities.

The covid-19 is tightening the tolerance threshold of people and businesses in terms of goods and cash flow. To overcome the crisis and the government's support solutions, rebuilding internal resources by applying technology, cutting costs, and changing strategies for business recovery is necessary.

REFERENCES

Anh, M. (2021). *Commercial and service activities continue to be affected by the COVID-19 epidemic.* ChinhPhu. https://thanglong.chinhphu.vn/hoat-dong-thuong-mai-dich-vu-tiep-tuc-chiu-anh-huong-tu-dich-covid-19

Bai, C., Quayson, M., & Sarkis, J. (2021). COVID-19 pandemic digitization lessons for sustainable development of micro-and small-enterprises. *Sustainable production and consumption, 27*, 1989-2001.

Dat, H. (2021). Looking back at the impact of the Covid-19 epidemic on Vietnam's tourism and development trends in 2021. *Figures & Event review of the GSO.* https://consosukien.vn/nhin-lai-tac-dong-cua-dich-covid-19-doi-voi-du-lich-viet-nam-va-xu-huong-phat-trien-nam-2021.htm

Duong, T., & Truong, X. (2021). *Tax policy to support SMEs during the pandemic in Vietnam compared to some countries.* Phaply. https://phaply.net.vn/chinh-sach-thue-ho-tro-doanh-nghiep-vua-va-nho-trong-dai-dich-cua-viet-nam-so-voi-mot-so-nuoc-a250797.html

General statistics office. (2021). *Tourism in 2020 suffering because of COVID-19.* Hanoi General statistics office. https://www.gso.gov.vn/du-lieu-va-so-lieu-thong-ke/2021/01/du-lich-nam-2020-lao-dao-vi-covid-19/

General statistics office. (2021). *Vietnam economy 2020: A year of charges of growth.* Hanoi General statistics office.

Giang, H. (2021). *Vietnam national Union of Bank workers.* VNUBW. http://vnubw.org.vn/tin-tuc/t6927/ngan-hang-tang-cuong-ho-tro-doanh-nghiep-nho-va-vua-vuot-kho.html

Ha, L. (2020). Some solutions to promote industrial and commercial development; remove difficulties in production and business. *Department of industry and trade - Lang Son province, 1*. https://soct.langson.gov.vn/vi/mot-so-giai-phap-day-manh-phat-trien-cong-nghiep-thuong-mai-thao-go-kho-khan-trong-san-xuat-kinh

Hai, C. T. (2019). Vietnam Social Sciences. *Vietnam Journals Online*. https://vjol.info.vn/index.php/khxhvn/issue/view/4236

Hau, M. (2020). *Ministry of Planning and Investment.* MPI. https://www.mpi.gov.vn/Pages/tinbai.aspx?idTin=47732&idcm=188

Huong, D. (2021). The Government of the socialist republic of Vietnam. *Baochinhphu*. https://baochinhphu.vn/Kinh-te/Gia-tri-xuat-khau-nong-lam-thuy-san-tang-manh-bat-chap-dich-COVID19/436310.vgp

Juergensen, J., Guimón, J., & Narula, R. (2020). European SMEs amidst the COVID-19 crisis: Assessing impact and policy responses. *Economia e Politica Industriale*, *47*(3), 499–510. doi:10.100740812-020-00169-4

Linh, K. (2021). *How does Covid-19 affect Vietnamese businesses?* Baokiem to annhanuoc. http://baokiemtoannhanuoc.vn/kiem-toan-trong-nuoc/covid-19-tac-dong-den-cac-doanh-nghiep-viet-nam-nhu-the-nao-147152

Lu, Y., Wu, J., Peng, J., & Lu, L. (2020). The perceived impact of the Covid-19 epidemic: Evidence from a sample of 4807 SMEs in Sichuan Province, China. *Environmental Hazards*, *19*(4), 323–340. doi:10.1080/17477891.2020.1763902

Minh, A. (2021). *Vietnam government portal.* Bao Chin Phu. https://baochinhphu.vn/Kinh-te/Doanh-nghiep-danh-gia-cao-muc-do-huu-ich-cua-cac-chinh-sach-ho-tro/440223.vgp

Minh, V. (2021). *Website of the Vietnamese Party Committee.* HCMCPV. https://hcmcpv.org.vn/tin-tuc/nganh-du-lich-tang-cuong-cac-bien-phap-phong-chong-dich-covid-19-1491878889

Ministry of health portal. 2021. *COVID-19 epidemic bulletin of the Ministry of Health on the evening of July 31: An additional 4,564 cases of COVID-19, bringing the total number of cases of the day to 8,624.* Hanoi Ministry of health portal. https://moh.gov.vn/tin-lien-quan/-/asset_publisher/vjYyM7O9aWnX/content/ban-tin-dich-covid-19-cua-bo-y-te-toi-31-7-them-4-564-ca-mac-covid-19-nang-tong-so-mac-trong-ngay-len-8-624-ca

Ministry of Planning and Investment. (2019). *Vietnam Enterprise White Paper 2019.* Hanoi Ministry of Planning and Investment.

Ministry of Planning and Investment. (2021). *Socio-economic targets in 2020.* Ministry of Planning and Investment.

PricewaterhouseCoopers. (2021). Family Business Survey 2021. Vietnam: PricewaterhouseCoopers. .

Bao, Q. (2021). *International visitors decrease by 1 billion, 2020 becomes the 'catastrophe' year of the tourism industry.* Vietnam National Administration of Tourism.

Quynh, N. (2021). *Drive retail growth with digital transformation.* Bao Ninh Binh. https://baoninhbinh.org.vn/thuc-day-tang-truong-nganh-ban-le-bang-viec-chuyen-doi-so/d20210708082546 37.htm

Trang, L. (2021). *Nhan Dan (The People).* 3 1. Accessed 6 9, 2021. https://nhandan.vn/dien-dan-dulich/du-lich-viet-nam-2020-phat-huy-noi-luc-trong-bao-covid-19-630469/

Trang, T. 2021. *News.* 12 3. Accessed 5 25, 2021. https://baotintuc.vn/kinh-te/gan-90-doanh-nghiep-tai-viet-nam-bi-anh-huong-boi-dich-benh-covid19-20210312100553768.htm

Truong Thu Huong, Do Van Chuc. (2021). Solutions for small and medium-sized businesses to survive the Covid-19 pandemic. *Financial magazine,* 72.

Vietnam Association of Seafood Exporters and Producers Seafood. (2021). *Export of agricultural, forestry and fishery products: Quality of growth is a measure.* Vietnam Association of Seafood Exporters and Producers Seafood.

Vinh, B. T. (2021). Factors affecting the access of small and medium-sized enterprises to loan provided by Vietinbank - Tay Tien Giang branch. *Industry and trade magazine.* https://tapchicongthuong.vn/bai-viet/cac-yeu-to-anh-huong-den-doanh-nghiep-vua-va-nho-vay-von-tai-ngan-hang-vietinbank-tay-tien-giang-79930.htm

World Bank. (2021). *The world Bank in Vietnam.* World Bank. https://www.worldbank.org/en/country/vietnam/overview

World health Organization. (2021). *WHO Viet Nam situation reports by date.* World health Organization.

Chapter 6
COVID-19 Pandemic:
How Do the Family Businesses in India Cope With the Crisis?

Garima Madaan Dua
Denmark Technical University, Denmark

Gaurav Gupta
Amity University, Noida, India

Divya Jain
Sharda University, India

Kanhiya Garg
CHRIST University (Deemed), India

ABSTRACT

The Covid-19 pandemic brought about a major economic breakdown throughout the world due to the shutting down of businesses and organizations. Covid –19 took a toll on India also, the second-most populous country. In India, family-run businesses are the deep-rooted, oldest, and most widespread form of business ownership. Most family businesses, while keeping the welfare of their customers, employees, and communities in mind, have resorted to remote work and halting non-essential work. The government of India took measures mainly consisting of an increased moratorium period, corporate tax cuts, lower interest on delayed tax payments, extension in return filing deadline, and other policy decisions. This study discusses the impact of Covid-19 on family businesses and how family businesses cope with the shock to the system. In addition, it covers innovative and strategic solutions adopted by the family businesses as a shield to their business against the impact of the crisis and to grow progressively overcoming the pandemic situation.

DOI: 10.4018/978-1-6684-7394-8.ch006

1. INTRODUCTION

The ongoing outbreak of Covid-19, a respiratory infection initially diagnosed in December 2019, is the most recent threat to world health. A novel coronavirus was discovered to be responsible, with structural similarities to the virus that causes severe acute respiratory syndrome (SARS) (Fauci, Lane, and Redfield, 2020). The virus initially arose in the People's Republic of China's Hubei Province, and it has since spread to a number of other countries. Based on rising case notification rates in China and around the world, the WHO Emergency Committee declared a global health emergency in January 2020 (Velavan, Thirumalaisamy, & Christian 2020). The world has paid a high price in terms of human lives lost, economic ramifications, and increased poverty since the initial pandemic.

This pandemic was so severe that it exposed vulnerabilities in worldwide healthcare systems, which were unprepared to handle a large number of patients who required respiratory assistance in a short period of time. Health officials were compelled to cease all non-urgent medical treatments and convert units into ICUs or sub-ICUs as a result of the situation. Because of the epidemic, scientists have had to band together to tackle this unusual infection (Ciotti et al., 2020).

According to the International Monetary Fund, the world economy would drop by more than 3% in 2020, the greatest decline since the 1930s Great Depression. The pandemic has pushed the global economy into a state of recession, which means that economies are shrinking rather than increasing. During the coronavirus pandemic, some governments throughout the world adopted lockdowns to "level the curve" of the infection. As a result of the lockdowns, millions of individuals were confined to their homes, businesses were closed, and virtually all economic activity was suspended (Indian Express 2020).

The pandemic wreaked havoc on the economy and society, causing tens of millions of people at risk of falling into abject poverty (Chriscaden, 2020). However, governments had no choice but to impose restrictions on the movement of people to enable social distancing, which resulted in national economies and businesses counting the consequences such as millions of jobs lost, hospitalizations, and hospitalizations, among other things (Chriscaden, 2020: Jones, Palumbo, & Brown, 2021). Governments all throughout the world are working hard to ensure that people are vaccinated. With all of the work that has gone into developing new vaccines. There is still no guarantee that the pandemic situation will improve. The Covid-19 pandemic has claimed many lives around the world, and it poses an unprecedented threat to public health, food systems, workplaces, enterprises, and the global economy.

2. THE COVID - 19 SITUATION IN INDIA

On January 30, 2020, India reported the first instance of the disease. The number of instances has consistently and considerably climbed since then. The Indian government enforced a two-month state-wide lockdown on March 25, 2020, to prevent the virus from spreading (Dev and Sengupta, 2020). India was placed on national lockdown for an extended length of time during the first wave, with a substantially lower number of peak cases. The first wave was almost entirely urban in nature. There were more cases in cities than in rural areas throughout the first five months of the pandemic (Kumar 2021). After recovering successfully from the first wave, India was hit far worse in terms of fatalities by the second wave. Coronavirus cases began to rise again in India in the first week of March 2021, nearly six months after the first wave peaked in September 2020, signaling the start of the country's second wave of pandemics (TOI 2021). Rural areas began reporting more cases than urban areas in the second wave as early as the second month. The absence of medical facilities in rural regions exacerbated the problem, as did the rush of patients from villages and small towns to urban areas. On May 31, 2021, the Indian government announced that the economy had shrunk by 7.3 percent in the fiscal year 2020-21. Since India's independence in 1947, it has experienced the most significant contraction (Kumar 2021). The second wave has resulted in more state-mandated lockdowns, which have harmed the economy and imposed severe limitations on critical industries. This was followed by a slowdown in labour-intensive businesses such as manufacturing, real estate, construction, and infrastructure, due to a lack of manpower during this time (Nexdigm 2021).

Figure 1 depicts the worsening condition of India, despite the fact that India is prepared for a probable third wave of Covid-19, the country saw a 4% drop in coronavirus infections for the week ending August 8, 2021. According to figures from the Union Health Ministry, the explanation of this is a substantial decrease in Covid-19 cases in a number of north-eastern states. According to data issued by the Union Health Ministry on Monday, India had 35,499 new coronavirus infections on August 9, 2021, increasing the overall number of infections to 31,969,954 and the death toll to 428,309, with 447 new fatalities (9th August 2021).

In August, the country's vaccine vaccination drive accelerated, which is a positive trend. According to data from the Ministry of Health, the daily average increased to 51.45 lakh doses for the week of July 31 to August 6, up from 48.26 lakh doses the week before. India's cumulative vaccination coverage passed the 50-crore mark on August 7, making it the world's second-highest behind China. Another encouraging discovery is that an ICMR (Indian Council of Medical Research) research found that combining the Covishield and Covaxin vaccinations improves immune protection (E online 2021).

Figure 1. State-wise total number of cases in India
Image Source: Author's Compilation
Data Source: https://www.covid19india.org/

Figure 2. Top 10 recipients of FDI inflows in 2020
Image Source: Author's Compilation
Data Source: RBI Bulletinhttps://timesofindia.indiatimes.com/business/india-business/indian-economy-in-explained-10-charts/articleshow/84465093.cms.

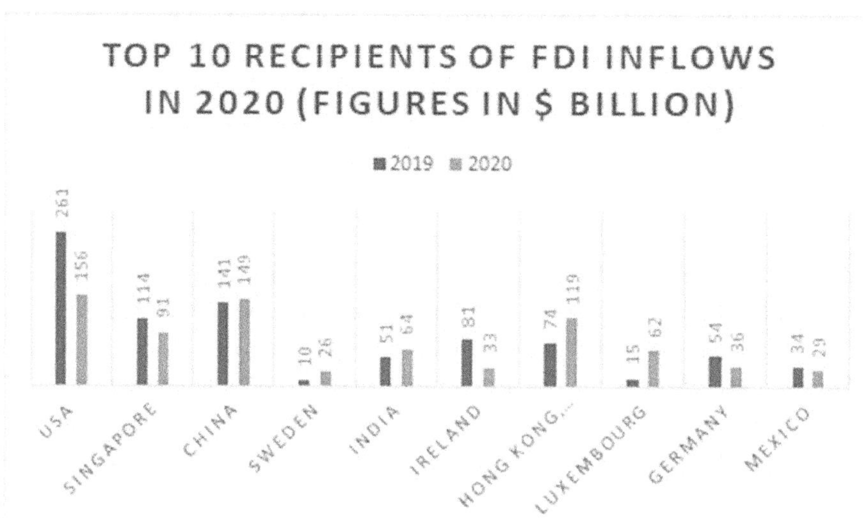

According to the World Investment Report 2021 (WIR) published by the United Nations Conference on Trade and Development (UNCTAD), India was the world's fifth-largest receiver of Foreign Direct Investment (FDI) inflows in 2020. In the first five months of 2021 (January to May), gross FDI inflows totalled $32 billion, accounting for about 37% of total inflows in 2020 (*In Charts: State Of Covid-Hit Indian Economy,* 2021).

In 2021, global FDI is anticipated to regain some lost ground, with Asia expected to be the primary beneficiary. The production linked incentive (PLI) programme, according to the RBI, has been recognised as a game changer in attracting export-oriented investments, resulting in a recovery in FDI into the manufacturing sector (*In Charts: State Of Covid-Hit Indian Economy*, 2021).

3. IMPACT OF COVID 19 ON THE WORLD ECONOMY AND INDIAN ECONOMY

Initially, the Covid-19 pandemic was assumed to be limited to China. As a result of human movement, it later spread over the world. The economic suffering became severe as individuals were asked to stay at home, and it was felt across the economy, with travel prohibitions hitting the airline business, athletic event cancellations affecting the sports industry, and mass gathering ban affecting the events and entertainment industries. As a result, several governments made rash policy decisions with far-reaching good and bad economic implications, with some countries facing recession. Many countries implemented social distancing measures and lockdown limitations, and there have been claims that such policies can cause a recession.

Ozili and Arun (2020) revealed in their study that a 30-day social separation policy or lockdown limitation harms the economy by lowering the level of general economic activity and negatively impacting stock prices. Covid-19 has had a significant and widespread economic impact. The unprecedented lockdowns to restrict the spread of Covid-19 caused GDP to drop substantially in 2020 Q2 (-24.4 percent year on year). In 2020 Q3, the decline eased to -7.4% year on year, and growth returned to positive territory in 2020 Q4 and 2021 Q1, at 0.5 and 1.6 percent, respectively. In the most recent preliminary estimate, the national statistics agency revised GDP growth for FY 2020/21 to -7.3 percent (Policy Responses to Covid-19, IMF 2021).

The Covid-19 pandemic has resulted in a significant increase in uncertainty. Almost every aspect of the virus's infectiousness, prevalence, and lethality is shrouded in mystery: the virus's infectiousness, prevalence, and lethality; the availability and deployment of antigen and antibody tests; healthcare systems' ability to meet an unprecedented challenge; and how long it will take to develop and deploy safe vaccines (Baker et al., 2020). The effects of the Covid-19 crisis may be seen in a variety of industries, including global financial markets, travel and tourism, aviation sector, industrial production, sales and investments, hotel industry, and so on. Governments all across the world are adopting various measures to deal with the aftermath of the corona issue.

Various rescue packages for enterprises most impacted by the Covid-19 spread, lower reserve requirements for banks, cash transfers to residents and SMEs, and delayed tax payments to travel and tourist discounts are just a few of the alternatives (Boshkoska and Nikolche, 2020). According to official estimates released by the ministry of statistics and program implementation, the Indian GDP contracted by 7.3 percent in the April-June quarter of the fiscal year 2021. Since the government began collecting GDP numbers quarterly in 1996, this is the greatest reduction. Following the imposition of the lockdown in 2020, an estimated 10 million migrant workers returned to their homes (Mangla 2021).

The major industries impacted by Covid-19 in India are:

- Hospitality sector

Restaurants, bed & breakfasts, taverns, bars, nightclubs, and other enterprises are all part of the hospitality industries. States have put restrictions and curfews on the sector, which contributes a significant percentage of India's yearly GDP.

- Tourism sector

After the first wave, the sector that employs millions of Indians began to recover, but the second wave of Covid-19 was ready to wreak havoc! The tourist industry accounts for about 7% of India's yearly GDP. The second wave's limitations have devastated the tourist industry, which was already trying to recover from the firms' first losses in 2020.

- Automobile sector

Due to Covid-19 scenario in India, the car sector is anticipated to continue under pressure in the foreseeable future.

- Real estate and construction sector

During the second wave, real estate and construction operations began to be disrupted as a huge number of migrant workers fled metropolitan regions. As of 2020, the situation for this industry has not been dire (Mangla 2021).

- Aviation and transport

Due to losses and difficult circumstances, the Covid-19 pandemic had a significant impact on the Indian aviation industry in 2020, with major airlines laying off employees, sending them on leave without pay, or slashing their compensation. The government had to extend the deadline for submitting bids for Air India five times in 2021. The impact of this disruption could be estimated using the loss numbers of India's two largest airlines. In the first and second quarters of this fiscal year, IndiGo lost Rs 2,884 crore and Rs 1,194 crore, respectively. In the first and second quarters, SpiceJet lost Rs 600 crore and Rs 112 crore, respectively (Kumar 2021).

One of the key industries that has been badly impacted by the Covid-19 epidemic is transportation. The Centre for Public Policy Research (CPPR) conducted a poll among specialists in the transportation sector from June to July 2020 to learn about their perceptions on the pandemic's effects on the sector in India. A total of 15 specialists were interviewed, including academics, practitioners, policymakers, and researchers from various regions of the country who worked directly with the transportation industry. Many worries about the future of India's passenger transportation business arise as the country continues to deal with the epidemic and an unpredictable conclusion to the issue (CPPR 2020).

4. HOW THE COVID -19 IMPACTED BUSINESSES

The Covid-19 has had an influence on enterprises, which has had an impact on the economy. All businesses, large and small, have been affected; the severity of the effects varies. There is little demand in the market, resulting in no revenue and a reduction in staff compensation. Some businesses, such as daily vendors, clothing stores, restaurants, and luxury goods stores, have totally shut down. While some firms, such as technical sectors, are mildly impacted because they are totally digital and employees can easily work from home, a smaller segment of enterprises that deal with groceries and everyday vital commodities has seen either a profit increase or a profit decrease (Vatsa 2020).

The overall impact on Indian businesses can be observed from the following parameters:

1. Industrial production
2. Business confidence
3. Capacity utilization

Figure 3. Industrial Production
Image Source: Author's Compilation
Data Source: Ministry of Statistics and Programme Implementation (MOSPI) https://www.economy.com/india/industrial-production

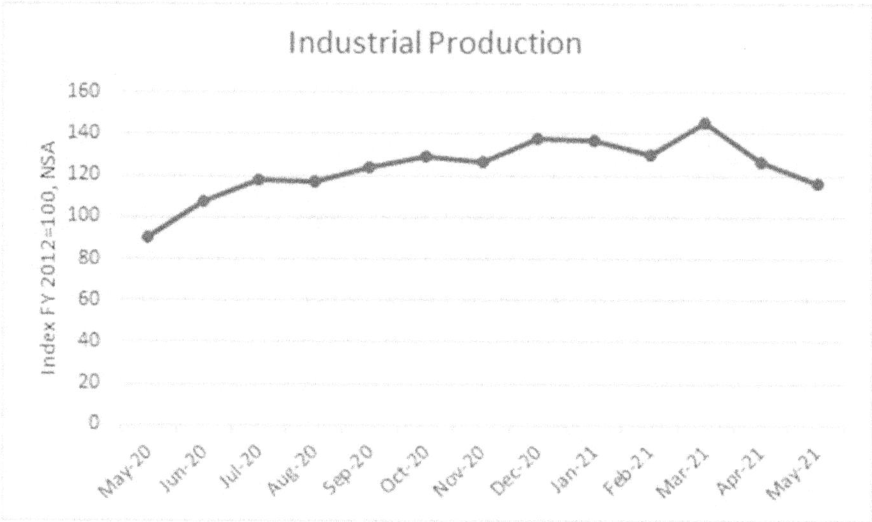

In Figure 3 the magnitude of the Index of Industrial Production (IIP) indicates the status of production of products individually and collectively as an industrial group for a particular period of time. The inputs and technologies utilised in the manufacture of the goods in question may or may not be the same. In a strict sense, the IIP is a short-term measure of organized-sector industrial development until the findings of the Annual Survey of Industries (ASI) become available. This indicator is critical for the government's planning objectives, and it is also widely utilised by a variety of organisations, including industry, research, and academic institutions. The indicator of industrial output is a numerical index that measures the production of products in physical terms. The index is calculated by comparing the amounts of goods produced during the current month to the base year's average monthly output. The current series of IIP (base 2011-12) is based on UNSD's ISIC-Rev. 4 and follows the National Industrial Classification 2008 (NIC-2008) (Moody's Analytics 2021).

Coming to the overview of analysis by the Indian Central Bank, The Reserve Bank of India's industrial outlook survey is a quarterly study that collects data on manufacturing industry mood. The stronger the indicator of confidence, the larger the 'net reaction.' The numbers presented are 'net responses,' which are calculated as the difference in percentage share between firms reporting 'optimistic' (positive) and 'pessimistic' (negative) answers. There are no reactions to change that are rejected. The fiscal year in India runs from April 1 to March 31, YYYY+1. Fiscal year 2020-2021, for example, goes from April 1, 2020 to March 31, 2021 (Moody's Analytics 2021).

Figure 4. Business Confidence
Image Source: Author's Compilation
Data Source: Reserve Bank of India Available https://www.economy.com/india/industrial-production

Figure 5. Capacity Utilization
Image Source: Author's Compilation
Data Source: Reserve Bank of India https://www.economy.com/india/industrial-production

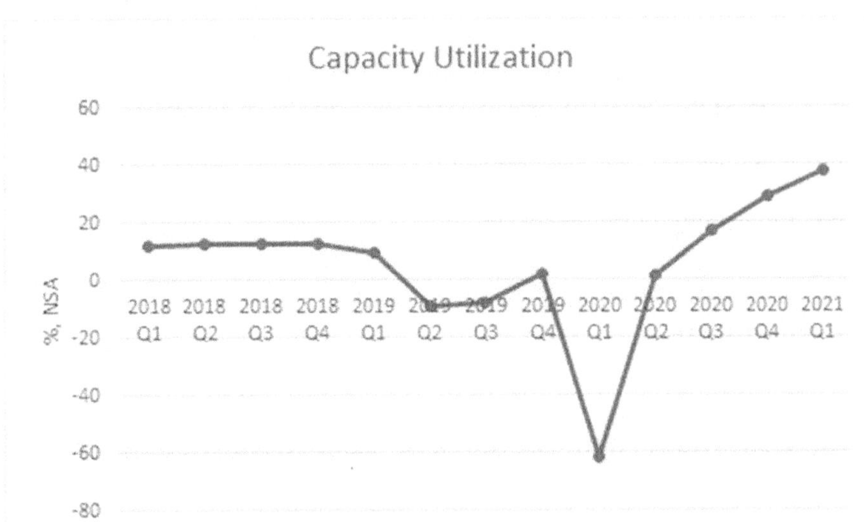

The Reserve Bank of India's industrial outlook survey is a quarterly study that collects data on manufacturing industry mood. The stronger the indicator of confidence, the larger the 'net reaction.' The numbers presented are 'net responses,' which are calculated as the difference in percentage share between firms reporting 'optimistic' (positive) and 'pessimistic' (negative) answers. There are no reactions to change that are rejected (Moody's Analytics 2021).

Amidst all of this, family businesses in India have taken a huge hit. They were doing pretty well before the advent of the Covid-19 global pandemic outbreak and were filled to the brim with a positive outlook towards their future prospects and growth. But, the virus came like a nightmare and has had adverse effects on family businesses especially the MSMEs owned and managed by joint families.

5. FAMILY BUSINESS

A family business is referred to an organisation that is involved in commercial activities on a regular basis for the purpose of earning profits by providing products or services in their respective industry markets and is run or controlled by multiple generations of the same family - related by blood, marriage, or adoption.

Family businesses in India have had a pretty glorious history with diversity and culture blooming throughout the nation. During the early days of the eighteenth century, the agrarian economy was the major operating factor for the Indian economy and our social system was deeply caste-based which often shaped the choices for occupation in India. Agriculture was the primary source of occupation, income, and livelihood followed by manufacturing industries that were few in number, and most of them were based on textiles or handicrafts. The setting of the 18th Century saw the huge shift from mercantile capitalism to industrial capitalism in India. Birlas, Tatas, Walchands, Lalbhai, and Kasturbhai emerged as the leading businessmen during this time of the industrial revolution in the Indian economy.

This form of business is one of the most ancient forms of business in India and started out as a part of the bazaar system. In the bazaar system, the family businesses mostly dealt in trading and money-lending.

5.1. The Advent of Industries and How They Evolved From Bazaars

The family businesses, as we see today, were not always so big or operated in the form of industries. Family businesses are the oldest and most popular business model in the world, ranging from small local firms to global conglomerates such as Wal-Mart and Heineken and so is the case in India. Maintaining family ownership of a firm is a deeply ingrained habit in India. India has a richness of family business ranging from small businesses to big conglomerates. Many family businesses have proven their ability to expand quickly from small beginnings and contribute significantly to the economy (Saigal, Mehrotra, and Mukadam 2018).

The rapid shift from bazaar form to industrial form in a family business in India came very recently around the beginning of 1992. Most of the transformation dates back to the **British Rule in India** and **the First World War**. One of the major catalysts and examples of the transformation was **Cawasji Davar** who set up his very first Cotton Mill in **Bombay** (*now known as Mumbai*) in **1854.** It was also the first manufacturing enterprise owned by a family in India. Following suit, many other trading communities started their own textile mills in Mumbai and Ahmedabad in the last half of the 19th Century.

Since India's independence from the United Kingdom in 1947, family business conglomerates have dominated the Indian economy's private sector (Manikutty, 2000). In India, family members are allowed to work together in the family businesses (92 percent), spouses/partners own shares in the family businesses together (3/4th), and many also work together in the family businesses (2/3rd). In India, 73 percent of family firms include the next generation in business, compared to an average of 65 percent globally, and the majority (60 percent) pass on the ownership to the next generation (Ganesh Raju and N V Sivakumar 2019). The right to private property possession and inheritance has played a significant role in promoting the family company in India's manufacturing sector. The evolution of entrepreneurial enterprises correlates with the emergence of family business firms (Kurma, 2020).

After the economic liberalization, India was now facing stiff competition from foreign multinational companies, it opened up the way for private players to enter the segments which were previously only exclusively accessible by the public sector. According to a study conducted by Bang, Ray and Ramachandran (2017), around 1,222 Family-Business Group Firms (FBGF) and 1,464 Stand-alone Family Firms (SFF) were incorporated in 1900-1990.

When the family businesses first started out in India, they were mainly opened and operated by two communities - **the Jains** and **the Marwaris.** The geographical location of the businesses was mostly confined to **Northern India** (Sinha, 2014). As time passed, the family businesses started forming the majority of the Indian economy and its contribution to the national income of India kept on growing. Seeing this, almost all communities started joining the group of the family businesses and some of them turned out to be big players in the segment. The concentration of family businesses divided amidst the various communities of India was as follows:

In the North:

- the Aggarwals

- the Guptas

In the South:

- the Chettiars

In the West:

- the Parsees
- the Gujarati Jains
- the Banias
- the Muslim Khojas
- the Memons

Centrally, all over India:

- Marwaris, *later on, the Aggarwals came to be commonly referred to as Marwaris*

According to a report by PwC India (2019), 90% of family-owned businesses in India are associated with philanthropic work which is concerned with donating financial resources. Philanthropy in India is often associated with donating money to a charity/NGO where it's put to some good use for society. However, what's more remarkable is that 89% of the businesses are also involved with philanthropic activities that go beyond just donating money and are often serving society with their services. The family-based ownership model is considered to be a major driving factor behind this philanthropic ideology of most businesses and many families have solely or jointly set up their own organisations to help society. To compare, with the global average of family-owned businesses being involved in philanthropic activities, the number was significantly lower at 68%.

5.2. Family Businesses in Today's World

In India, there's still a large portion of the business population that is operating as a family. The family businesses have contributed a significant amount of wealth and prosperity to the wealth of India. According to a report prepared by India Corporate Solutions Group, the family businesses in India contributed 79% to the GDP of India. In the same report, India Corporate Solutions Group mentioned that India was the third-largest country based on the number of publicly-listed operating family businesses in the world amounting to a staggering 108.

In Indian economy, the family businesses contribute significantly to wealth creation, wealth preservation, and wealth distribution, and their unique strategy of looking at their businesses through generations and as an investment for the future is commendable, ensuring that decisions are made with a long-term perspective and providing economic stability (ICSG, Alvarez and Marsal, 2018). According to a study that looked at companies with a market valuation of $250 million or more, India ranked third on the list of countries with the most family-owned enterprises in 2018, with 111 family-owned businesses. China and the United States came in first and second, respectively, with 159 and 121 businesses, respectively (Almeida 2021).

A few examples of big family businesses operating in India are Ambani, Godrej, Hinduja, and Adani. The Ambani family is India's wealthiest family, with a worth of Rs 3,80,700 crore (Rs 3.80 lakh crore). The Ambani family, in fact, is Asia's wealthiest, with a billion-dollar home in Maharashtra. The family owns Reliance Industries Limited (RIL), an oil-to-telecom conglomerate with operations in textiles, plastics, gas, petroleum, and other industries. RIL also has plans to join the retail sector. Mukesh Ambani is India's richest man and the most well-known member of the Ambani family.

The Godrej Group was founded in 1897, and its roots may be traced back to India's independence and the Swadeshi movement. Ardeshir Godrej, the company's founder and a lawyer-turned-serial entrepreneur, tried a few other enterprises before finding success with a lock company. The Godrej family has amassed a net worth of Rs 1,57,000 crore, making them one of India's wealthiest families (Rs 1.57 lakh crore). With a revenue of over USD 4.1 billion, Godrej is one of India's largest and oldest consumer goods companies.

Parmanand Deepchand Hinduja, a self-made young entrepreneur from Shikarpur, formed the Hinduja Group. In 1919, Hinduja established a branch in Iran and joined the global market. Merchant banking and trade were the two foundations of the company. The Group's headquarters were in Iran until 1979. Then it travelled to Europe. Hinduja The family has an estimated net worth of Rs 1.86,500 crore (1.86 lakh crore).

With a worth of Rs 1,20,900 crore, the Adani family is also on the list (Rs 1.20 lakh crore). With a total turnover of $13 billion, the Adani Group is an integrated multinational conglomerate. It consists of six publicly traded companies. Adani was created in 1988 and is a global integrated infrastructure player with operations in natural resources, logistics, energy, and agriculture (ET Now Digital 2020).

According to research conducted by PwC India in 2019 (PwC 2019), the family businesses operating in the country showed a tremendous annual growth of 76% which was significantly higher than the global average annual growth rate of family businesses which stood at 69%. What's even more remarkable is that around 58%

of the family businesses showed a double-digit growth which is 24% higher than the global growth rate of 34%.

5.3. Challenges Faced by Family Businesses in India

Although the family businesses in India have shown tremendous growth and contributed significantly to the national GDP, they still face a lot of challenges in today's dynamic business environment which is changing more frequently than ever in the history of global business. The first challenge that most family-owned businesses are facing is the advent of digital technologies and the shortcomings because of not having stepped on the bandwagon in its earlier stages. Most of the modern-day businesses in India and all over the world have started going digital with their websites, applications, and social media where they allow the consumers to go through the details of the company, their products, and services and make purchase decisions smartly and with minimal use of time at the convenience of their homes. But, family-owned businesses in India have been historically resilient in adapting to new technological advancements. Lack of awareness amongst family business leaders in India regarding technology has caused them to face a major slowdown in growth. They are not aware of how to take advantage of the technological paradigm shift in India because of which they are left behind in today's rapidly changing business environment.

Another problem being faced by Family Businesses in India is the passing on of management to the next generation of their family or hiring managers outside family relations for more professional management of the business. They are now facing strict governance guidelines which hold them accountable for the performance of the businesses and their contribution to the economy which has put them in a difficult position between deciding amongst their next generation and outside managers.

5.3.1. Comparison with Rest of the World

India, Indonesia, Germany, the USA, and the UK are the top five global economies of the world and for the sake of clear and fair comparison, we are going to take a closer look at family businesses in all of these economies and contrast them with the structure, working, and performance of family businesses in India (Alderson, Keanon & Shane, Scott 2018).

The economies of the US, the UK and Germany are similar in terms of their family business contribution to the GDP whereas India and Indonesia are close counterparts in terms of their family business contribution. The US and the UK just have 5% of their top companies as family-owned businesses whereas the number is 40% in the case of India and Indonesia respectively.

Table 1.

Country	% of businesses owned by Families
India	95%
France	83%
Australia	67%
UK	65%
Canada	45%
Romania	20%
(Sorted according to %)	

India and Indonesia are quite similar in terms of the structure of their family-owned businesses. Most of the businesses are owned and actively managed by families i.e. the owners and the managers are the families themself. Family-owned businesses in the US, the UK, and Germany are mostly managed by managers hired by the owners and they mostly just play the part of stakeholders in the organisations.

Diving deep into this structure formation and analysing the reason behind the adverse differences between such diversity in the management structure of family businesses in the economies, we discovered that India is still majorly dependent on families for its functioning. Marriages are still arranged by parents. It is normal for children to stay with their parents in their houses even after marriage. The families of India are often brought up amidst the values of ancient writings like Mahabharata and Ramayana that predominantly focused on family values.

Meanwhile, in the US, UK, and Germany, the concept of individualism is very common and parents often prefer their children to find their own passion and work towards it rather than join their family businesses. Most of the children move out once they reach their teenage years and start learning the concept of individualism. Hence, most of the owners of family businesses in these economies prefer to be passive investors in the businesses (Sinha 2014).

India and Indonesia have a large chunk of their GDP being contributed to by their family businesses so credit acquisition is fairly easier for them as compared to other economies which make the performance mindset of these businesses risk-oriented. Hence, these businesses grow much faster as compared to the US, UK, and Germany. When compared to individually-owned businesses, family businesses have shown constantly better performance in India. Owing to the risk-taking mindset, these businesses are also consistent in delivering better returns to their stakeholders.

Family-owned businesses in the US, UK, and Germany are generally not that risk-taking and they are viewed as a way of families trying to conserve and safely grow their wealth. Very few family-owned businesses like Nike and Hyatt have taken the risk in these economies and turned out successful but even they did not actively pass on the management to their heir and later on became passive investors in the organisation.

The family businesses in India are very optimistic regarding their future growth and aimed to grow by 44-45% in the succeeding 2 years. Their growth capital requirement would be funded by borrowing from banks, credit lines and also internal sources. Many business leaders also mentioned private equity/venture capital funding or getting listed on a stock exchange. According to a report by PwC India (2019), 89% of the family-owned businesses in India use bank loans and credits as a major source of their funding. However, an interesting outcome in the report also showed that 58% of the family business leaders preferred getting listed on a stock exchange as a source of their funding (PwC India).

The Indian GDP was on a steep rise before the advent of the Covid-19 global pandemic. Although not a rapid spike was being seen in the growth but a gradual growth was most definitely visible. However, due to the outbreak of the virus, the entire country had to go through two phases of full lockdowns that lasted months on months and caused businesses to stay shut and halt their operations. This caused a huge economic downfall in the entire country and resulted in farmers committing suicides, MSMEs shutting down, and banks going empty for even giving small loans.

5.4. The Covid-19 Impact on Family Businesses in India

Families and companies around the world have faced enormous hurdles as a result of the abrupt breakout of the Covid-19 epidemic, forcing them to adapt to the new reality. For most firms, this has been a trying moment. Supply chain disruptions, a drop in client demand, inconsistent labour supply, and a slew of other challenges have put them under a lot of stress on the operational side (Sankhe, 2020). The first reaction was to reduce spending and labour costs. Some family businesses turned to government programmes for financial aid. Others thought about how they could adjust their businesses to the reality of a changing global market. In order to retain their governance procedures and commitments to all of its stakeholders, families reiterated their mission and beliefs (KPMG 2017).

Family companies account for 60-70 percent of GDP in most developed and growing countries. India is no exception. Because Indian family businesses form the "backbone" of the Indian economy, it is critical to extending their lives so that the economy can benefit from their contributions in the future (CII 2021).

The Covid-19 pandemic is imparting many lessons about readiness, agility, and adaptation to the family businesses. It also emphasises the importance of critical self-evaluation—taking a hard look at what works, what doesn't, and what isn't even being talked about but should be. Building resilience is what today's effective governance is all about (*The Resilient Family Enterprise*, 2021). According to the research, the family businesses took few steps to deal with Covid-19's immediate impact, adapt to the problems and opportunities it brought, and expedite family members' involvement in future planning.

They made steps to address the pandemic's impact not only on their family and business, but also on the overall well-being of society and the requirements of all their stakeholders, including employees, customers, suppliers, and local communities. During the pandemic, the family businesses were found to be 42% more likely than non-family enterprises to employ business transformation initiatives. When compared to single-generation family enterprises, multigenerational family businesses were 45% more likely to implement a business transformation strategy.

The paper also highlights two important factors that influenced family strategy decisions. First, whether the company is managed by a family or non-family CEO; and second, whether the company's ownership is distributed among a small or large number of family members (Badwe 2021). According to a new report by the Successful Transgenerational Entrepreneurship Practices (STEP) Project Global Consortium and KPMG Private Enterprise, family firms' unique structure has allowed them to adjust to the effects of Covid-19 and has aided the global economy's recovery. The study discovered that the family's engagement and long-term outlook helped them to show resilience in the face of the epidemic, putting them in a critical position to lead the economic recovery.

The study report, titled 'Mastering a comeback: How family companies are triumphing over Covid-19,' includes data from almost 2,500 family firms and over 500 non-family enterprises from 75 nations (Phaniharan 2021). "Lower percent of firms in India (29%) took steps to reduce/eliminate labour expenses when compared to the worldwide average of 36%. In India, there was a greater emphasis on cost reduction by decreasing operational costs, reducing investments, restructuring, postponing payments and expenses, and lowering the senior management team's remuneration than in other countries." stated Dr. Nupur Pavan Bang, Associate Director, Thomas Schmidheiny Centre for Family Enterprise (India Education Diary 2021).

5.5. Impact on MSME and SMEs

Micro, small, and medium enterprises (MSME) make up a significant portion of India's manufacturing sector and play a vital role in creating large-scale employment. According to recent yearly studies on MSMEs, the sector generates roughly 30% of India's GDP, employs around 50% of industrial workers, and accounts for half of all exports, according to conservative estimates. Among the MSME, 94% are microbusinesses (Dev and Sengupta, 2020).

Although the epidemic has impacted all firms, the MSME sector would be particularly hard to hurt by the state-wide lockdown's reduced cash flow. Their supply chain has been interrupted, and they have been harmed by migrant labour exodus, limits on raw material availability, disruptions in exports and imports, as well as broad travel prohibitions, closures of malls, hotels, theatres, and educational institutions, among other things. As a result, the MSMEs have been severely impacted (Dev and Sengupta, 2020).

The MSMEs owned by the family businesses in India are really concerned regarding their future prospects since 2017 and the global pandemic that started post-2019 has put them in an even deeper problem. As much as 35% of MSMEs are expected to shut-down due to cash-crunch and late technological adoption by 2025 in India (Dev and Sengupta, 2020).

Small and Medium Enterprises (SMEs) are having a terrible time, with many closing their doors due to rising costs and depleted financial reserves. The SMEs are already experiencing layoffs and business closures as a result of the Covid-19 epidemic, as well as staff turnover, slow small business growth, and a variety of other issues. In every country, the SMEs have a bad reputation (Kumar and Ayedee 2021).To handle the havoc the pandemic has wreaked on supply chains and to tackle numerous logistics and supply chain concerns in the future, it is vital to adapt to digitization (*Dun & Bradstreet: Over 82% of Smes Had Negative Impact During Covid-19,* 2021). As a result of financial constraints and limited working capital, small firms and merchants suffered the brunt of the second wave's early impact. Businesses are likely to receive 70% of pre-covid revenue as the second wave stabilises. The healthcare infrastructure was the hardest hit, as systemic flaws made it impossible to keep up with the exponential increase in cases during the second half of the year (Nexdigm 2021).

India's falling exports, ranging from pearls and jewellery to clothing/attire and ocean depths, are primarily supplied to these countries, affecting a large number of employment. The MSMEs, who make up the backbone of India's international travel industry, accounting for about half of the country's fares, require special attention in order to get back on track. Furthermore, the blockade in these countries has caused disruptions in supply chains and production systems across segments, all of which have had an impact on India's manufacturing, trade, work, and development (Baragde and Jadhav, 2021).

The manufacturing industry was impacted in numerous ways as a result of the pandemic, including reduced production volumes and low-scale operations. This has a negative impact on turnover and income over time (Nexdigm 2021). The IHS Markit India Manufacturing Purchasing Managers' Index (PMI) fell to 55.4 in March 2021 from 57.5 in February 2021, a seven-month low. After falling to a seven-month low of 55.4 in March, data for April shows a little rebound to 55.5. The reality that "the headwinds facing manufacturers cannot be disregarded" is not obscured by this minor gain. When enterprises' financials are already vulnerable to the hurdle of growing worldwide prices, the increase of Covid-19 cases could depress demand even more (Sharma 2021).

The pandemic is predicted to have long-term effects on employment markets. An expansion in the pool of unemployed workers will have a direct influence on their negotiating power and, as a result, salaries (Kapoor and Chirag 2021). In India, a state-wide lockdown to prevent the spread of Covid-19 has left labour migrants in a state of despair, leaving them jobless, homeless, hungry, and forcing them to return to their villages in large numbers. Thousands of migrant workers walking with their children on major highways across India exposed our society's flaws (Ranjan 2021).

The issue of labour migration has left deep bruises on the sentiments of labour societies in India and a lot of them had to wipe their hands off their lives because of carelessness in supplies and facilities for Indian Labours. This has made acquiring labour a lot harder than before, especially during the time of Covid-19 where there's no certainty about daily wages and labour-intensive projects (Ranjan 2021).

Prior to the Covid-19 epidemic, Indian businesses worked on interconnected and lean supply chains to close gaps by increasing supply chain efficiency. However, due to unknown supply chain weaknesses, the pandemic has exposed most Indian enterprises to severe supply chain disruptions (SCDs). The Covid-19 pandemic-related limitations have had a significant impact on cargo traffic volume at India's 12 major ports. Shipping transportation disruptions have merged with road and aviation freight transit disruptions, resulting in severe SCDs (Sudan and Taggar 2021).

India saw significant delays in its cargo-flight shipments and most of the businesses that depended on order supplies for their income had to shut down temporarily and some even permanently. The cost of supplies went drastically high making it really difficult for MSMEs to deliver shipments on time hence leading to excessive cancellation in orders and creating another hole in the loss statement of these businesses. Around 70% of total orders were cancelled on average combining all the MSMEs in India (Sudan and Taggar 2021).

The fiscal support measures taken by India's federal government may be classified into two categories:

1. Above-the-line measures such as government spending (approximately 3.5% of GDP, of which about 2.2% was estimated to have been used in the previous fiscal year), foregone or deferred revenues (approximately 0.3% of GDP due in the previous fiscal year), and expedited spending (approximately 0.3% of GDP due in the previous fiscal year);
2. Below-the-line policies aimed at assisting companies and bolstering loan availability to a variety of sectors (about 5.3% of GDP). Above-the-line spending initiatives in the early phases of the pandemic response were largely focused on social protection and healthcare. In-kind (food, cooking gas) and cash transfers to low-income households (1.2% of GDP); wage support, and other measures are among them (Policy 2021). The central government invested Rs. 14,500 crore (US$ 1.99 billion) in non-interest-bearing bonds in the Central Bank of India, Indian Overseas Bank, Bank of India, and UCO Bank in March 2021 (*Brand India*, 2021).

Finance Minister Smt. Nirmala Sitharaman announces a relief package of Rs 6,28,993 crore to support the Indian economy in the fight against the Covid-19 pandemic. Circular on ISS and PRI for short-term agricultural loans during the years 2018-19 and 2019-20 was issued on June 4, 2020, extending the moratorium period until August 31, 2020. On April 17, 2020, it was decided that the 90-day NPA norm would exclude the moratorium period for all accounts for which lending institutions decide to grant a moratorium or deferment, and which were standard as of March 1, 2020, i.e., all such accounts would have an asset classification standstill from March 1, 2020 to May 31, 2020. Simultaneously, banks will be required to maintain a higher provision of 10% on all such accounts during the standstill, which will be spread over two quarters, i.e. March 2020 and June 2020, in order to ensure that they have sufficient buffers and are adequately provisioned to meet future challenges. These provisions can be modified subsequently based on the provisioning required for real account slippages.

Laws concerning taxation and other matters (Relaxations of Certain Provisions) Ordinance 2020 made it easier to comply with and enforce a variety of economic regulations. All pending income-tax refunds up to $5 lakh, as well as all pending GST and customs refunds, will be released immediately, totalling $18,000 crore in reimbursements. The "Distressed Assets Fund - Subordinate Debt for Stressed MSMEs" was established by the Indian government. A credit guarantee scheme for subordinate debt (CGSSD) was created, under which guarantee coverage will be offered to SCBs that are CGTMSE member lending institutions (MLIs) to help the MSMEs stress. The credit guarantee scheme's goal is to make it easier for promoters of challenged MSMEs to get loans from banks to use as equity or quasi-equity in their businesses (RBI 2021).

A collateral-free lending programme with a 100% credit guarantee, subordinate debt with a partial credit guarantee for stressed MSMEs, a partial credit guarantee scheme for public sector banks on borrowings from non-bank financial companies, housing finance companies (HFCs), and micro finance institutions, a Fund of Funds for equity infusion in the MSMEs, and a partial credit guarantee scheme for public sector banks on borrowings from non-bank financial companies, housing finance companies (HFCs), and micro finance institutions are among the relief measures Concessional financing for farmers and a credit facility for street vendors (PM SVANidhi) are two examples (PIB 2020).

Finance Minister Nirmala Sitharaman announced new economic relief measures on Monday, 21st June 2021, the first since the second Covid-19 wave. The new economic measure emphasis on giving loan guarantees and concessional loans to pandemic-affected industries, as well as investments to increase hospital capacity. The overall financial consequences of the package, which included the reiteration of certain previously announced measures such as the distribution of food grains to the needy until November and greater fertiliser subsidies, were estimated to be Rs 6,28,993 crore by the government. Ms. Sitharaman announced a 1.5 lakh crore increase in the existing Emergency Credit Line Guarantee Scheme (ECLGS). She also launched a new $7.500 crore plan to guarantee loans up to Rs. 1.25 lakh to small borrowers via microfinance institutions (The Hindu 2021).

Emergency working capital assistance for companies, particularly the MSMEs, worth INR 3,000 billion (US$40.14 billion). Additional working capital funding of 20% of existing credit (as of February 29, 2020) in the form of a term loan at a concessionary rate of interest will be offered to enterprises to provide relief. Units having an outstanding credit of up to INR 250 million (US$3.34 million) and a turnover of up to INR 1 billion (US$13.38 million) will be eligible. The Indian government would fully guarantee this money, giving more than 4.5 million MSMEs with total liquidity of INR 3,000 billion (US$40.14 billion) (Bhardwaj 2021).

6. CONCLUSION

The pandemic's forced stop has, in some ways, helped families reorganise and reassess their priorities. During this crisis, one of the most significant issues faced by many families has been business continuity planning. It is suggested that each family form an investment committee that will operate in a fiduciary role and report to the family council on the family's portfolio. The investment committee will be in charge of all assets owned by or held in trust for the portfolio's investment. A systematic management information system should be in place for the family's finances, investment portfolio, including the family's share in the group enterprises, and any other difficulties that may occur (Sankhe 2020).

As a family business owner, one may find that the epidemic forces him to alter his personal wealth protection approach. He should consider the implications for his estate and tax planning, as well as his private assets in different asset classes. In addition, many countries are enacting emergency tax rules, and it's critical to understand how they can be affected.

Today's family businesses necessitate a strong sense of family solidarity. The owners of a family firm must band together, demonstrate their devotion to the enterprise, and speak with one voice. They must provide a clear statement that they support the company to their employees, business partners, and the broader public. If they do things correctly and do not compromise their convictions, they will build trust and confidence, which will help them when the economy rebounds (Englisch and Ambrosini, 2021).

REFERENCES

Alderson, K., & Shane, S. (2018). *Understanding the Family Business Exploring the Differences Between Family and Nonfamily Businesses* (2nd ed.). Entrepreneurship and Small Business Management Collection.

AlmeidaAron. (2021). Top Founder/Promoter Family Managed Companies in India! *Trade Brains*. https://tradebrains.in/promoter-family-managed-companies-india/

Alvarez & Marsal. (2021). *Family Business in India*. ICSG. https://www.alvarezandmarsal.com/sites/default/files/77597_tag_india_familybusinessreport_05_singles.pdf

Moody's Analytics. (2021). *India - Industrial Production*. Moody's Analytics. https://www.economy.com/india/industrial-production

Badwe, A. (2021). Family Businesses SHOWED Resilience During COVID-19 Pandemic. *The Bridge Chronicle*. https://www.thebridgechronicle.com/business/family-businesses-showed-resilience-during-Covid-19-pandemic

Baker, S. R., Bloom, N., Davis, S. J., & Terry, S. J. (2020). Covid-induced economic uncertainty (No. w26983). National Bureau of Economic Research.

Bang, N. P., Ray, S., & Ramachandran, K. (2017). *Family businesses: The emerging landscape 1990-2015*. Thomas Schmidheiny Centre for Family Enterprise, Indian School of Business.

Baragde, D. B., & Jadhav, A. U. (2021). Impact of COVID-19 on Indian SMEs and Survival Strategies. In *Handbook of Research on Strategies and Interventions to Mitigate COVID-19 Impact on SMEs* (pp. 280–298). IGI Global. doi:10.4018/978-1-7998-7436-2.ch014

Boshkoska, M., & Jankulovski, N. (2020). Coronavirus impact on global economy. Annals of the 'Constantin Brâncuşi" University of Târgu Jiu. *Economy Series*, *4*, 18–23.

IBEF. (2021). *Brand India.* IBEF. https://www.ibef.org/industry/services.aspx

CII. (2021). *Family Business CII.* https://www.cii.in/sectors.aspx?enc-prvePUj2bd MGTmvPwvisYH+tEnGjyGXO9hLECvTuNt8Yt8MGwm3xVypjS9tGblw.

Chriscaden, K. (2020). Impact of COVID-19 on people's livelihoods, their health, and our food systems. World Health Organization.

Ciotti, M., Ciccozzi, M., Terrinoni, A., Jiang, W. C., Wang, C. B., & Bernardini, S. (2020). The COVID-19 pandemic. *Critical Reviews in Clinical Laboratory Sciences*, *57*(6), 365–388. doi:10.1080/10408363.2020.1783198 PMID:32645276

Correspondent, S. (2021). Govt. Unveils ₹6.28 Lakh Cr STIMULUS Post Second Covid Wave. *The Hindu.* https://www.thehindu.com/business/Economy/nirmala-sitharaman-unveils-new-covid-recovery-package-expands-credit-relief/article35020572.ece

Dev, S. M., & Sengupta, R. (2020). Covid-19: Impact on the Indian economy. *Indira Gandhi Institute of Development Research, Mumbai April.*

Dun & Bradstreet: Over 82% of Smes Had Negative Impact During Covid-19. (2021, April 22). The Economic Times. https://economictimes.indiatimes.com/small-biz/sme-sector/dun-bradstreet-over-82-of-smes-had-negative-impact-during-Covid-19/articleshow/82197779.cms?from=mdr

Englisch, P., & Ambrosini, F. (2020). Family Businesses and COVID-19: Our support and recommendations.

Indian Express. (2020). Explained: How Covid-19 Has Affected the Global Economy. *The Indian Express.* https://indianexpress.com/article/explained/explained-how-has-Covid-19-affected-the-global-economy-6410494/

Your Article Library. (2014). *Family Business in India: A Historical Perspective (with Example).* Your Article Library. https://www.yourarticlelibrary.com/essay/family-business-in-india-a-historical-perspective-with-example/41128

Fauci, A. S., Lane, H. C., & Redfield, R. R. (2020). Covid-19—Navigating the uncharted. *The New England Journal of Medicine, 382*(13), 1268–1269. doi:10.1056/NEJMe2002387 PMID:32109011

Ministry of Finance. (2020). *Fiscal and Monetary Policies to Deal with Slowdown Due to Covid-19.* Press Information Bureau. https://pib.gov.in/PressReleasePage.aspx?PRID=1656925

Press Information Bureau. (2021). *Fiscal and Monetary Policies to Deal with Slowdown Due to Covid-19.* Press Information Bureau. https://pib.gov.in/PressReleasePage.aspx?PRID=1656925

Times Now News. (2021). From Ambanis To Wadias: Here Are 10 Richest Families of India. *Business News.* https://www.timesnownews.com/business-economy/companies/article/from-ambani-to-wadia-here-are-10-richest-families-of-india/592759

World Health Organization. (2021). Impact of Covid-19 on People's Livelihoods, Their Health and Our Food Systems. World Health Organization. https://www.who.int/news/item/13-10-2020-impact-of-Covid-19-on-people's-livelihoods-their-health-and-our-food-systems

In Charts: State Of Covid-Hit Indian Economy. (2021, July 16.) Times of India. https://timesofindia.indiatimes.com/business/india-business/indian-economy-in-explained-10-charts/articleshow/84465093.cms

IBN. (2021). *India's COVID Stimulus MEASURES: Indirect Relief, Short-Term Goals.* India Briefing News. https://www.india-briefing.com/news/india-covid-stimulus-indirect-relief-credit-guarantee-loans-compliance-relaxations-22588.html/

Jones, L., Palumbo, D., & Brown, D. (2021, January 24). *Coronavirus: How the Pandemic Has Changed the World Economy.* BBC News. https://www.bbc.com/news/business-51706225

Kumar, M., & Ayedee, D. (2021). Technology Adoption: A Solution for SMEs to overcome problems during COVID-19. *Forthcoming. Academy of Marketing Studies Journal, 25*(1).

Kurma S. (2020, June 11). A case study on entrepreneurship and small family business in indian tourism industry. *London Journal of Research in Management and Business.*

Nexdigm Private Limited. (2021). Impact of Covid-19 on the Manufacturing Sector In India - Coronavirus (COVID-19) - India. *Welcome to Mondaq*. Nexdigm Private Limited. https://www.mondaq.com/india/operational-impacts-and-strategy/1086172/impact-of-Covid-19-on-the-manufacturing-sector-in-india

Manikutty, S. (2000). Family Business Groups in India: A Resource-Based View of the Emerging Trends. *Family Business Review*, *13*(4), 279–292. doi:10.1111/j.1741-6248.2000.00299.x

C. P. P. R. (2020). Effects of Covid-19 On Transportation: What the Experts Say." Centre for Public Policy Research (CPPR), September 24, 2020. https://www.cppr.in/centre-for-urban-studies/effects-of-Covid-19-on-transportation-what-the-experts-say

Online, F. E. "Impact on Indian Economy after the Covid-19 Second Wave." The Financial Express. The Financial Express, June 21, 2021. https://www.financialexpress.com/economy/impact-on-indian-economy-after-the-Covid-19-second-wave/2275353/

Online, F. E. "Coronavirus Latest Highlights: Kerala May See up to 5 Lakh Cases till August 20, Central Team Raises Alarm over Onam Festivities." The Financial Express, August 10, 2021. https://www.financialexpress.com/lifestyle/health/coronavirus-in-india-latest-update-live-ahead-of-Covid-19-third-wave-indias-weekly-cases-decline-several-states-reopen-schools-for-offline-classes/2306949

Ozili, P. K., & Arun, T. 2020. Spillover of COVID-19: Impact on the Global Economy. SSRN *Electronic Journal*. doi:10.2139/ssrn.3562570

Phaniharan, V. R. C. (2021, April 4). "Resilient Mindset of Family Business Helped Sail through Pandemic." The Hans India. The Hans India. Retrieved from https://www.thehansindia.com/news/cities/hyderabad/resilient-mindset-of-family-business-helped-sail-through-pandemic-680086

IMF. (2021). *Policy Responses to covid19*. IMF. https://www.imf.org/en/Topics/imf-and-covid19/Policy-Responses-to-COVID-19

Raju, G. & Sivakumar, N. V. (2019). *PwC India Family Business Survey 2019*. PWC.

Reserve bank of India. (2021). *Annual report*. Reserve Bank of India. https://rbi.org.in/scripts/AnnualReportPublications.aspx?Id=1327

Saigal, M., Mehrotra, S., & Mukadam, S. (2018). *Family Businesses In India*. Alvarez and Marsal. https://www.alvarezandmarsal.com/sites/default/files/77597_tag_india_familybusinessreport_05_singles.pdf

Sankhe, R. (2020). Managing Family Businesses during Covid-19. Fortune India: Business News, Strategy, Finance and Corporate Insight. *Fortune India*. https://www.fortuneindia.com/opinion/managing-family-businesses-during-Covid-19/104733

Sudan, T., & Taggar, R. (2021). Recovering supply chain disruptions in post-COVID-19 pandemic through transport intelligence and logistics systems: India's experiences and policy options. *Frontiers in Future Transportation*, *2*, 660116. doi:10.3389/ffutr.2021.660116

Hindustan Times. (2019). The Global Variations in Family Business Structures. *Hindustan Times*. https://www.hindustantimes.com/analysis/the-global-variations-in-family-business-structures/story-NrikbnqLCGQUVlw0VEwTcO.html

(KPMG. (2021). *The Impact of Covid-19 on Family Businesses*. KPMG. https://home.kpmg/xx/en/home/insights/2021/03/the-impact-of-Covid-19-on-family-businesses.html.

The Impact of Covid-19 on India's Manufacturing Sector. (2021). The Wire. https://thewire.in/economy/the-impact-of-Covid-19-on-indias-manufacturing-sector

The Resilient Family Enterprise. (2021, June 2). Deloitte. https://www2.deloitte.com/global/en/pages/about-deloitte/articles/Covid-19/the-resilient-family-enterprise.htm

Times of India. (2021). First vs Second Wave of COVID-19 in India: Things You Need to Know. *The Times of India*. https://timesofindia.indiatimes.com/india/first-vs-second-wave-of-Covid-19-in-india-things-you-need-to-know/articleshow/82143427.cms

Vatsa, S. (2020.) A Study On The Impact Of Covid-19 On Businesses In Indian Economy.

Velavan, T. P., & Meyer, C. G. (2020). The COVID-19 epidemic. *Tropical Medicine & International Health*, *25*(3), 278–280. doi:10.1111/tmi.13383 PMID:32052514

Chapter 7
Christian Ethics and Xinyong Practices Leading to Longevity Post COVID-19 Pandemic Among Chinese Family Businesses in Indonesia and Malaysia

Lee Kean Yew
University of Malaya, Malaysia

Jacob Donald Tan
Universitas Pelita Harapan, Indonesia

ABSTRACT

The emergence of the novel Coronavirus disease (Covid-19) has changed our norms and lifestyles. In facing this crisis, businesses in general are often struggling to sustain their livelihood and legacy. For Chinese family dynasties that are in their third generations, i.e. YTL Corporation Berhad in Malaysia and Lippo Group in Indonesia, they are able to apply Christian ethics and xinyong "信用" virtues that enable longevity and fostering workplace innovation during the Covid-19 crisis. Christianity business ethics and xinyong practices can be connected through routine applications of Christ-centered decision-makings that are evident in business environments and social impacts. Nevertheless, integrating cultural norms and Chinese confucion virtues such as xinyong in family businesses can be challenging in ensuring the CFBs sustainability. Hence, this chapter sheds light on the journey of the two families' Chinese dynasties, as they apply Christian faith and xinyong along with impactful actions to develop new solutions leading to longevity.

DOI: 10.4018/978-1-6684-7394-8.ch007

INTRODUCTION

Living out the Christian ethics is a natural transformation of a new person in Christ. The old is gone, the new has come. Nevertheless, this transformation is a process that requires time and often a conundrum when encountered with cultural norms in Chinese confucion virtues such as *xinyong*, as well as the local country's business practices such as in Indonesia and Malaysia. The Covid-19 pandemic has led us to an emergency that has revolutionised our lives, our way of working and living daily life. Chinese family dynasties such as YTL and Lippo are in their third generations, and they are able to apply Christian ethics and *xinyong* virtues that enable longevity and fostering workplace innovation during the Covid-19 crisis. Christianity business ethics and *xinyong* practices can be connected through routine applications of Christ-centered decision makings that are evident in business environments and social impacts. This chapter sheds light on the journey of the two family Chinese dynasties, as they apply Christian faith and *xinyong* along with impactful actions such as time, skills and experience to develop new solutuions leading to longevity.

Romans 12:2 NIV

"Do not conform to the pattern of this world, but be transformed by the renewing of your mind. Then you will be able to test and approve what God's will is —his good, pleasing, and perfect will."

Secrets to Longevity: Family Businesses and Xinyang

In most countries, family businesses are an important part of economic growth as they provide job opportunities to over 85 percent of the employed population and contribute greatly towards over 75 percent of the Gross Domestic Product (GDP) worldwide (Anderson & Reeb, 2003; Astrachan & Shanker, 2003). In the USA (Heck & Trent, 1999; Astrachan & Shanker, 2003) and European Union (Botero, Cruz, Massis, & Nordqvist, 2015), they constitute about half of the GDP. Moreover, in several countries, their economy is dominated by family firms. For instance, among the companies listed on the stock exchange in France and Germany, family enterprises constitute 57 percent and 51 percent, respectively (Wallau & Kayser 2001).

A similar situation is seen in Southeast Asia (Lee & Gomez, 2014; Nishida & Redding, 1992). Specifically, in Malaysia and Indonesia, people of Chinese origin are known for their great involvement in industry and trade (Lee & Xavier, 2022; Tan, Supratikno, Pramono, Purba, & Bernarto, 2019). In Malaysia, ethnic Chinese have a dominant presence in business, whether they act as family businesses or SMEs[1] like trading companies and groceries (Jesudason, 1989), or corporation sectors such as construction and steel making (Gomez, 2007). According to the Malaysian Department of Statistics (2021), SMEs contributed 38.3 percent to the GDP in 2018, and in the following year, the amount increased to 38.9 percent. A similar scenario is observed in Indonesia. Although Chinese Indonesians only comprise of 7 percent of Indonesia's population, they are significant in terms of controlling the majority of the country's commerce and wealth (Backman, 2001; Chua, 2004; Globe Asia, 2016).

In Chinese society, traditional Confucianism regards family as the epicenter of all relations (Wah, 2001). Other aspects of life such as group conformity, education, social ethics, centralized authoritarian values, employment, and business matters (Lin & Huang, 2014; Wang, Li, & Sun, 2018) are also influenced by traditional Confucianism. Hence, it is common for Chinese Family Business (CFB)—a single or dynasty-governed business that works towards achieving the vision set within a family (Lee, 2021; Tong, 1996)—to practise Confucianism. In this philosophical belief, to become *junzi* "君子", who is an ethical and righteous person (Ahn, 2008), one must exhibit these virtues: *lijie* (empathy), *ren* (humanity), and *xinyong* (trust). Also known as "moralistic trust" is a moral commadment to treat people as if they were trustworthy (Uslaner, 2002), Luhmann (1979) described *xinyong* as a person with business credibility which is an impression that is formed based on their reputation in keeping their words. For instance, if business partners are cooperative and can be trusted to keep their promises, this business relationship will be sustainable (Rathbun, 2012). Not surprisingly, CFB modes of practicing *xinyong* dominate in most Southeast Asian economies from SMEs to conglomerate diversified groups (Chen & Eweje, 2019; Leung, Lai, Chan, & Wong, 2005).

Moral issues of finance and business are not new topics in the business literature, as these have been discussed since the sixteenth century (Alves & Moreira, 2013; Chafuen, 1986; Hoffmann-Holland, 2009). However, CFB practices often contradict with western values. While the CFB focuses on social relations, hierarchy, and *guanxi* networking, western values rely on reason as anticipated by ancient Greece (Hooker, 2003) and emphasize on "scientific rationality" and "universalizing rationality" (Wong & Tam, 2000). Moreover, the West's secularism is based on a religious foundation provided by Judaism through Christianity (Hooker, 2003). In the contemporary studies, the religious practices of the ethnic Chinese business leaders make an interesting debate for exploring how leadership, ethics and perspective are argued because of the sharp distinction made between 'before' and 'after'.

Business ethics applied to economics and business has a long tradition (Shawn, 2009). While business ethics remain important in the business, closer attention to religion ethics — including human values from the religion ethics such as Buddhism and Christian ethics (two important religion practices among ethnic Chinese business leaders in Southeast Asia) in leading business longevity, all occurring in rapidly transforming multicultural contexts— can provide deeper insights into unexpected aspects of religious humanism and social change in Southeast Asia (Dean, 2020). While Buddhism focuses on experientially-based ethical consciousness to develop the business with self-responsibility, Christian faith brings about principles, criteria, and guidelines for actions that are relevant in the marketplace (Cao, 2019). Furthermore, these Christian actions are based on unconditional devotion to God, which naturally derived from the Christian faith and thus non-transactional.

Although an extensive research has been conducted to understand the contributing factors of family business longevity (e.g., Simarasl, Jiang, Kellermanns, & Debicki, 2020), limited sources are available regarding the practice of *xinyong* values and Christian ethics to maintain longevity in the context of Malaysian and Indonesian CFBs. A great majority of overseas Chinese, especially older generations, have grown up in the backgrounds of Chinese religion as well as Buddhism and Taoist beliefs in Asian societies (Wong, 1988; Tan, 1995). Most of them convert to Christianity in their later age and are aware of their new identity and the requirements of their new faith. Yang (1999) study on Asian Christians and entrepreneurs in the United States, these overseas Christians and entrepreneurs particularly from Chinese community participated actively in Chinese festivals and identified with Chinese traditional virtues, identified as 'Confucian ethics', which obviously include filial piety, diligence, tolerance, harmonious relationships such as finding trustworty business partners in foreign land. In The *Protestant Ethic*, believers were concerned to prove to themselves and to God, in The *Protestant Sect*, they proved to their fellows that they were hardworking, discipline, and trustworthy (Weber 1947b: 321).

Only a 'true' Christian will want to hold accountability to God and to his fellow believers; and thus qualify him to be a potential trustworthy partner. The heart of the matter is *xinyong* (trustworthiness) and dependability. This is especially important in a situation like CFBs in Malaysia and Indonesia whereby 'the secret to business survival under political changes (both NEP and the New Order)' is important to form business ties in forming business alliances between CFBs and Malay/Indonesian communities. Under the political changes in Malaysia and Indonesia, seeing that ethnic Chinese companies had to come under state control or be privately Malay or *Pribumi*-controlled, some of the CFBs felt insecure and hence chose to heighten the importance of *xinyong* in knowing people or business partners that can be trusted, and of course greatly strengthens the centripetal pull of a religious community such as Chinese Christian entrepreneurs community (Lee & Tan, 2022). It was common for Christian ethics to think that a 'true' believer would recognize God's compassion and kindness and pay it forward, thus reducing the tendency of opportunism and corruption. In the event of a Christian entrepreneur betraying the *xinyong* of his or her co-believers, he or she would be seen as betraying not only his brothers and sisters, but also God and his faith, which would result difficulties in building genuine, honest, and candid relationships with her stakeholders towards longevity business opportunities.

In the Book of Acts 2:44, the event exemplified the xingyong / trustworthiness among the Christians to contribute their assets and resources to meet the essentials of others. This incident transpired, as the Christians understood the purpose of their life to serve God utilizing their resources. This spirit of Godly purpose driven compassion and kindness, based on unconditional love, is imprinted in the first generation of YTL and Lippo to the next. This imprinting is "a process whereby, during a brief period of susceptibility, a focal entity develops characteristics that reflect prominent features of the environment, and these characteristics continue to persist despite significant environmental changes in subsequent periods." (Marquis & Tilcsik, 2013, p. 201) Once imprinted, the new phase of cultures –Godly traditions- become the fundamental elements for the success and longevity of the two Chinese businesses (e.g., Anteby & Molnar, 2012; Suddaby & Jaskiewicz, 2020).

To shed more light on this issue, in the current work, the two Christian-based CFBs, YTL Corporation Berhad and Lippo Group, are studied in a comparative perspective. To discuss this topic, this study aims to answer two main questions. First, what differentiates these CFBs (both YTL and Lippo) that have shown the capacity to keep longevity by practising Christian ethics and *xinyong* practices? Second, why is it that these CFBs have emerged as major conglomerate diversified business even in the post Covid-19 pandemic?

Linking Christian Ethics Fostering Workplace Innovation Post Covid-19

Many researchers have studied a systems perspective in defining family business with a number of models (Gersick, Lansberg, Desjardins, & Dunn, 1999; Lee & Gomez, 2014; Tognazzo & Neubaum, 2020). Generally, an actual family business is regarded as a "total system" involving the founding entrepreneur and family-member (Le Breton-Miller & Miller, 2018; Simarasl, Jiang, Kellermanns, & Debicki, 2020). In the model of CFB which adopts kinship-based ownership structures, the familism model and its aspects, namely family ownership, paternalism, and nepotism, are influenced by the values of Chinese culture (Wong, 1993). Clearly, each sub-system in CFB possesses its own criteria, as it progresses through its own life-cycle. Nevertheless, it is challenging to improve performance of a conglomerate multinational group when involving family members during the process of succession mostly in second generation. Not only can it be detrimental for the organisation, when the decision-making process falls in the hands of incompetent managers through nepotism, this can also lead to sibling rivalry (Lee & Gomez, 2014; Wong, 1993). In short, the integration of cultural values in CFB (Wong, 1993) and the power dominance through kinship-based ownership (Zhu & Warner, 2004) are the main characteristics that differentiate Chinese managerial systems from others. Although knowledge innovation is crucial to survive intense market competition in CFB (Lee, 2021), applying workplace innovation or religion and spirituality in the organisation is another important topic to be discussed in the post Covid-19 pandemic era (Tan, Musa, & Su, 2022; Yin & Mahrous, 2022).

Due to the role of religion in shaping a person's principles and ethics, it is assumed that it can influence a person's moral norms in business and society (Tan, Musa, & Su, 2022). According to the Malaysian Department of Statistics (2021), a majority of the Malaysian population (61.3%) practises Islam with all Malays being legally Muslims, followed by Buddhism (19.8%), Christianity (9.2%), and Hinduism (6.3%). Most of the Indians (86.2%) and the Chinese (83.6%) are Hindus and Buddhists, respectively, while the indigenous people or *Orang Asli*, the *Orang Asli* are the indigenous minority in Peninsular Malaysia within the Negrito (Semang), Senoi and Aboriginal-Malay groups are mainly Muslims (40.4%) and Christians (46.5%) (Malaysian Department of Statistics, 2021). Half of the Indonesia population is comprised of Javanese (40%) and Sundanese (15.5%), meanwhile religion-wise, about 87% of the population are Muslims, followed by Protestants or Catholics (9.90%), Hindus (1.69%), Buddhists (0.72%), and Confucianists (0.05%) (Hefner, 2021).

In countries in Southeast Asia with other religions and beliefs, generally, Western business ethics is recognized as having Judeo-Christian roots (Lynn, Naughton, & VanderVeen, 2009). By assessing western business ethics, this will provide the fundamental basis for the evaluation of ethical aspect and their impacts on behavior. Recently, companies and CEOs in United States who described themselves as "Christians" are gaining attention (Ibrahim, Rue, McDougall, & Greene, 1991). It is believed that by integrating Biblical principles and economic activities, this will maintain the business longevity. In one study, Christian values seem to have an influence on the success of economic activities (Ibrahim & Angelidis, 2005). A similar trend is observed in Malaysia and Indonesia, where several Christian CEOs of CFBs are professing as Christians. This can be seen based on their public documents and speeches, even in a non-religious context. Recently, both Francis Yeoh of YTL Corporation- one of the richest businessmen in Southeast Asia's (Doebele, 2005) and Mochtar Riady of Lippo Group- one of the Indonesia's richest businessmen for 2018 (Karmali, 2018)- are devout Christian businessmen.

The emergence of Coronavirus disease (COVID-19) brought about tremendous negative impact on the global financial, social, and economic developments. According to World Bank (2022), growth in emerging and developing economies will be around 4% below their pre-pandemic expectations. This disrupted growth of economic activity can be seen as a result of strict regulations to curb the spread of Covid-19 (Clark, Davila, Regis, & Kraus, 2020; Breier, Kallmuenzer, Clauss, Gast,

Kraus, & Tiberius, 2021), and this situation posed challenges for business, large and small, as they struggled to sustain. For surviving businesses, they faced long-lasting impacts such as placing organisational resilience in their corporate agenda, shifting the way people operate their business, and adopting a digital workplace. In fostering workplace innovation, working remotely in a digital workplace has become a new norm (Clauss, Breier, Kraus, Durst, & Mahto, 2022; Yin & Mahrous, 2022). On top of the innovation that the CFBs have to adopt in the pandemic, it is essential to assess the role of Chinese values and religion in sustaining a long-lasting business corporation.

Methodology: Case Studies

Weber was prepared to acknowledge that the Chinese "would be quite capable ... of assimilating capitalism which has technically and economically been fully developed in the modern cultural area" (Weber 1964:248, 242). Therefore, it is important to explore the success of overseas Chinese entrepreneurs in Southeast Asia who were establishing capitalistic businesses from the end of the nineteenth century until now.

Barbalet (2016) has recently pointed out the new ways to conceptualize the impact of elements of Chinese civilizational techniques (including mentalities as well as ritual technologies) on the rise of capitalism in Southeast Asia. Kuhn (2008) points to the importance of kinship, Chinese association, religion practices and place of worship in the establishment of economic niches within chain migration within the Chinese diaspora in Southeast Asia. In the current work, two Christian based CFBs namely YTL Corporation Berhad and Lippo Group in Southeast Asia are studied in a comparative perspective in terms of their history, Christian ethics, and *xinyong* practices. On top of their good reputation in marketing products with international or national acclaim, these CFBs are commonly linked with a certain brand service or product such as YTL developer (cement) and Lippo bank.

In the contemporary context, strong connections with internal and external stakeholders characterize Chinese principles of business practice. These extensive business practices provide useful intelligence and support in the global business context. Obviously, its role in Chinese business has engendered significant debate (Kao & Sek-Hong, 1995; Chatterjee, 2001). For example, Morris and Schindebutte (2005) argued that different cultural backgrounds impact on business practices. For Asians, they note a Chinese traditional values heritage involving Confucian dynamism, fidelity, altruism and unspecified obligations of reciprocity norms in securing their business even during the turbulent time and crisis. These CFBs are among the multinational conglomerate companies in Malaysia and Indonesia that lasted more than three generations. In fact, these businesses were founded in the colonial period and managed to sustain their legacy until now by practising

Chinese human values. Throughout the years, they have faced several crises, which in some cases, threatened them with business collapse during financial crises and the Covid-19 pandemic.

YTL Corporation Berhad - Most Influential Developers

At first, the YTL group mainly involved in power supply, and water supply and treatment. However, in the past three decades, this group has expanded into other activities, including manufacturing, cement production, information technology, hotel and resort management. Among its famous acquisitions are the Ritz-Carlton hotel in Kuala Lumpur; PowerSeraya Ltd., a major electricity supplier in Singapore; and Wessex Water Ltd. in the United Kingdom. Known as one of Malaysia's biggest conglomerate, since its establishment in 1985, the YTL has developed from a single entity to seven of them, both domestic and abroad. The success behind this corporation is the managing director, Tan Sri Francis Yeoh.

Originally from Fujian province in China, Francis Yeoh's grandfather came to Malaysia in 1920[2] and started a timber business. In 1955, Yeoh Tiong Lay, Francis Yeoh's father, founded Yeoh Tiong Lay Building Co., which later known simply as YTL. In the beginning, this company was involved in the construction of low-cost housing, hospitals, and military garrisons. Being the eldest son, Francis Yeoh acted as the *head boy*[3] to assist his father at work and he offered to quit his schooling when he was 16 years old. However, his decision was denied by his father. His father was never compromise on education and supported him until he attended Kingston Polytechnic at London. The family business was badly hit during the 1970s oil crisis, and when he returned to Malaysia in 1978, he was chosen by his father to be the new managing director of YTL at the age of 24. Under his management, the construction business was transformed into a multi-disciplinary conglomerate. He was named as "one of Asia's most powerful and influential business personalities" by Fortune and Business Week. In his interviews, he shares his Christian values about life, family, and business. As a religious man, he attributed everything that he has achieved as a blessing and inspiration from God, which guided him in managing his company (Rovnick, 2009).

Jacob Yeoh is one of the sons for Francis Yeoh. His son told the press from the Edge by saying that Rome wasn't build in a day to be one of Asia's most influential business personalities even the group belongs to family business. Jacob Yeoh has been taught by his father to believe that nothing was given, and that everything had to be earned. He grew up in the Christian family and Francis Yeoh has reminded him to hate evil, corruption and other activities that do not benefit people's live as mentioned in the Christian ethics. Christian ethics and *xinyong* practice have helped YTL in fostering the concept of stewardship to secure many mega projects. Francis

Yeoh vehemently denied the group's political connection with top politician will always secure the tender projects from government. Francis Yeoh has long been seen as a business crony of former Prime Minister Tun Mahathir, but the group atrributed Christian values to their group's administration by introducing innovative ideas and strictly meet the guidelines in fulfilling condictions for contract renewal.

Recently in January 2023, YTL Power's wholly owned subsidiary in Singapore is collaborating with Tenaga Nasional Berhad (TNB) unit for contract renewal to supply 100 megawatts (MW) of electricity from Malaysia to Singapore via the newly upgraded interconnector. The agreement marks the first time electricity from Malaysia will be supplied to Singapore on a commercial basis, adhering to the Energy Commission's Guide for Cross-Border Electricity Sales. Francis Yeoh believed that if the family values of Christian ethics and xinyong practice continue to thrive and the group is able to win more mega projects, there may be reasons to believe that YTL may survive the fifth genetic line or even more generations to come.

The YTL board is dominated by Yeoh's family members where they hold 8 of the 13 seats. This clan is ranked Malaysia's sixth-richest clan, as the extended family's net worth is approximated at RM 30.1 billion (US$7.1 billion). With a total asset of RM74.7 billion (USD18.2 billion) has been appointed, Francis Yeoh's sibling, Tan Sri Dato Michael Yeoh Sock Siong has been appointed as new managing director for Lagrage cement. Combining the values of its listed entities in the country (YTL Power International Berhad, YTL Land & Development Berhad, and YTL Hospitality REIT), YTL Corp has a market capitalization of about RM21.2 billion (USD5.2 billion) in 2019. Additionally, YTL Corp has a stake Starhill Global Real Estate Investment Trust (REIT), which is a Singapore-based real estate investment trust investing primarily in real estate used for retail and office purposes and possesses retail assets in multiple countries, namely Singapore, Malaysia, Australia, China and Japan. While the parent company is traded in Tokyo, shares of YTL and six other entities in the YTL group are listed in Malaysia. Having a philosophy to produce "world-class products at competitive prices", this has allowed the corporation to attract a massive customer base over the last three decades.

Lippo Group - Most Diversified Conglomerate

Born in Malang, East Java, Indonesia in 1929, the founder of Lippo Group, Dr. Mochtar Riady spent his early years in Xin Dian Village in Fujian, China with his grandmother who gave him wise advice and encouraged him to bring blessings back to his home village. Until this day, he firmly believes in the Chinese idiom "饮水思源" which means one should always remember the source of blessings. In 1935, he returned to Malang and received his education in Nanqiang, Malang which is a school for the Hokkien descendants. Dr. Mochtar learned about money management and Sun Tzu's art of war from his beloved father, Li A Pi, who also taught him about family values, Chinese traditions, and culture. Dr. Mochtar experienced the Japanese occupation in 1942 and married his wife, Li Li Mei, in 1951. Then, under his management, he turned his mother-in-law's convenience store in Jember into the largest one in the area. In 1954, he moved to Jakarta and started selling bicycles and accessories. Although this business was not profitable, his shipping business was successful, thanks to his social networking.

In 1959, Dr. Mochtar began his banking business and career as President Director of Kemakmuran Bank (partnership with Andi Gappa). In his banking career, Dr. Mochtar was involved in Buana Bank, Panin Bank, and Bank Central Asia (BCA). He was well-known as the "banking doctor" in the industry, as he was able to resolve bank mismanagement issues and reversing the fortunes of financial institutions. His target for BCA then was to make it an official clearing house besides the Indonesian Central Bank. Lippo Bank was established in 1989 and became the first bank to go public in Indonesia). In the following year, Lippo Karawaci Tbk. was public-listed. Dr. Mochtar understood the importance of information accessibility and networking; thus, PT Multipolar was established in 1975 to handle the information flow of companies such as Lippo Life Insurance Co.

Overall, Dr. Mochtar Riady and his family have successfully diversified their business and investment portfolio, starting from banking, to other areas including real estate (e.g., Lippo Karawaci, Lippo Cikarang, etc.), education (e.g., Universitas Pelita Harapan, Sekolah Pelita Harapan, Sekolah Dian Haparan, Sekolah Lantera Harapan, UPH College), hospitals (e.g, Siloam Hospital), supermarkets (e.g., Hypermart), malls (e.g., Lippo Mall Puri, Lippo Mall Cikarang, Lippo Mall Kemang, Lippo Mall Kuta), and telecommunications (e.g., Firstmedia). He also established Mochtar Riady Institute for Nanotechnology (MRIN) in 2006 and Mochtar Riady Comprehensive Cancer Centre (MCCC) in 2007.

During the pandemic, Lippo Group's Siloam Hospital served the Indonesia patients by dedicating four of its 40 hospitals to Covid-19 patients, and there was even an increase in the number of patients who needed cancer treatments or others, as the government imposed travel restrictions (Suhartono & Baigorri, 2022). In 2021, Siloam's net income increased by 480% from the previous year. This denotes the *xinyong* effect of what Lippo stands for in the communities and societies through their diversified portfolio investments such as Siloam Hospital, as well as of their Christian worldview, that is to impact the lives of people altruistically in the regions they invested in.

Another example is Pelita Harapan Foundation -co-founded by Dr. James Riady and a subsidiary of Lippo Group- that epitomizes the practice of *xinyong* and Christian worldview in building the nation through education. One of the highlights is the educational outreach by the foundation to Papua since 2012, with the heart to improve quality of education there. Due to the shortage of teachers in the province of Papua, some teachers there have had been sent to study in Universitas Pelita Harapan (UPH); upon graduation, they would return to contribute to the schools in the province. As the geographical location inhibits Papuans from accessing education, Pelita Harapan Foundation built four schools in the province to support the development of Papuan children's education (Kusuma, 2017). This outreach to the eastern side of Indonesia is an exemplar of the potential need and growth in the education industry, in which Lippo has established its footprint.

CHRISTIAN VALUES, XINYONG IN BUSINESS, AND WORKPLACE INNOVATION

Christian Ethics and Assurance in God

In both YTL Corporation Berhad and Lippo Group, the government's efforts to promote industrialization are aligned with the country's economic policies. In Malaysia, Second Industrial Master Plan 1996–2005 (IMP2) and Third Industrial Master Plan 2006–2020 (IMP3) are introduced during the economic crisis of 1997–1998 which also aligned with Malaysia's *vision for 2020* (Mohamed, Abd Kadir, & Raof, 2021). However, in Indonesia, the recent state of the industrial policy in Indonesia begins with its National Industrial Policy as announced in the Presidential Regulation No. 28 in 2008, which are the 2008 National Industrial Policy and the Indonesian Master Plan for Acceleration and Expansion of Indonesia Economic Development (MP3EI) which was introduced in 2011 in facing the global financial crisis (Aswicahyono, Hill, & Narjoko, 2010). These public endeavors contributed to an increase in the annual sales growth for CFBs for both YTL and Lippo that are involved in industrialization, property development and manufacturing.

However, SMEs in both countries were negatively impacted by the Asian financial crisis (1998-2000) and the global financial crisis[4] (2007-2009). To handle these crises, well-capitalized YTL Corporation acquired cheap assets in tough markets. Besides devising strategies to cope with bad situations, he believes that his Christian faith was influential in ensuring YTL's success. When Francis Yeoh began managing YTL, he was inspired by former Malaysian Prime Minister Mahathir Mohamed's privatisation drive. In 1993, this corporation achieved the government's first independent power producer contract, and since then, YTL was built conservatively. Due to the practice of *xinyong* and gaining trusts from business networks, each of YTL's subsidiaries managed to secure long-term contracts and generate recurring revenues. Thus, this corporation gains a continuous flow of income regardless of the economic climate. Just to name a few examples, YTL Corp. has 53 years left to operate the express train service from Kuala Lumpur Airport to Central station; Wessex Water has a rolling 25-year license to provide water supply and treatment services in England; the majority of YTL Power's power plant have over 15 years of contracts; and the retailers in Starhill Gallery have agreed to long-term leases.

In his interview, when Asiamoney.com inquired about his strategy in managing the company's financial effectively, Francis Yeoh responded with references to his Christian faith. Humbly declaring himself as the steward of God's wealth, he agreed that such sentiment might be unsettling for unbelievers. In managing a business, rather than aiming for short-term profits, he suggested others to consider the "needs of future shareholders" by following the Christian way (Rovnick, 2009).

According to Indonesia's Ministry of Home Affairs in 2021, the people are known to be one of the most religous, where they believe that worshipping God is essential (Iswara, 2020; Kusnandar, 2021). However, worshipping God and having assurance in God are two contrasting attitudes. Assurance in God means surrendering and accepting whatever incidents that happen in life -especially during the pandemic- by accepting that God is still in control of the circumstances (Hermanto, 2020; Lincoln, 2020; Wong-McDonald & Gorsuch, 2000).

In Christianity, life that is driven by a purpose is emphasized and encouraged to revolve around the daily activities. As mentioned by Aglozo, Akotia, Osei-Tutu, and Annor (2021), an individual's spirituality and cognizance of the meaning of life can influence how the individual appraises his or her life, and affect the experiences of positive and negative emotions. Thus assurance in God in Christian faith induces honorable actions of kindness and goodness regardless of the situations.

Dr. Mochtar Riady became a Christian in his 60s. He was listening to an Indonesian evangelist, Dr. Stephen Tong, preaching about the sinful nature of human beings, and he realized that every person needs Christ. Dr. James and Dr. Stephen also became believers in the early 1990s and they believe that the purpose of life is to worship God and lead their daily lives based on the lessons in the Bible (Chua, 2009).

Dr. Stephen Riady:

"I think as Christians, we should know what the purpose of life is. The Bible tells us that the purpose of life is to know Christ and to grow in Him. So, our purpose here is not just to make money. We want to glorify Him. And the way to do this is through our daily life, our experiences in family, business, and so on." (Chua, 2009)

Being devout believers, Dr. Mochtar Riady and his family strives to build up better communities throughout Indonesia and bringing blessings for others through education and health care.

Dr. James Riady:

"My father [Mochtar Riady] is a senior banker. He's probably the most senior banker right now in Indonesia and he has always believed that in life we must contribute to nation building and to society by generating economic growth, investments, jobs [and so on], while at the same time, support social causes — and we do that through education and health care. That has been a tradition. Through hard work and sensible management of our companies, we have come this far." (Knowledge at Wharton Staff, 2009)

This is in line with Dr. James's belief that education is the foundation of a country's development. In 1993, Dr. James established Yayasan Pendidikan Pelita Harapan (Pelita Harapan Education Foundation) with the motto: True Knowledge, Faith in Christ, and Godly Character. This motto value is transcended throughout all the educational institutions to remind the stakeholders of Christian values, love, and respect for the societies. Dr. James also established Teachers College to train teachers and even offering scholarships. Recently, Dr. James and his wife, Aileen Riady established Yayasan Pendidikan Harapan Papua (YPHPapua) which is an educational foundation focusing to provide access to education to children in this remote area (Djono, 2020). According to Knowledge at Wharton Staff (2009), Dr. James Riady is very proud of his contributions towards transforming healthcare and education in Indonesia.

Just like her husband who is a dedicated Christian, Aileen Riady shows her care and compassion by helping children of Indonesia even to the remote areas of Papua (e.g., Tumdungbon in the District of Pegunungan Bintang). Dr. Mochtar himself had funded the establishment of Putian University in Fujian and Ma Chung University in Malang, Indonesia. There is a total of 45 K-12 schools and 3 university campuses around the country. When giving a statement about the family enterprise (Richter, 2014), the Senior Advisor & Board Member of the Pelita Harapan Education Foundation, Dr. Niel Nielson applauded the Riady's family efforts in enhancing the society and country through the gospel.

As mentioned by John Riady (CEO of Lippo Karawaci, Tbk. & President Commissioner of Siloam Hospitals) in The Business Times (2019), Lippo's real estate business jumped by 86% in home sales, and its health care unit also performed well (Permatasari & Amin, 2022). Siloam's net income increased by 480% in 2021 from the previous year (Suhartono & Baigorri, 2022). John Riady took the leadership position in 2019. His future vision is to expand Lippo into new projects such as in the new capital city planning in East Kalimantan province, by building health care centers and educational institutions.

Xinyong and Trustworthiness in Chinese Family Business

In both YTL and Lippo, it is well stated that CFB could benefit from focusing on *xinyong* or trustworthiness values to sustain the business (Rathbun, 2012). Decisions relating to apply *xinyong* are often strategic in that it ensures business success and survival (Uslaner, 2002). When the suppliers are convinced with the trustworthiness of the family enterprises, this will encourage the growth of the customer base. These links of acquaintances and *xinyong* are clearly significant for any research and development projects in the family business. Without the presence of trust and respect, it is difficult to form a meaningful and long lasting relationship with promising suppliers, customers, and acquaintances, since *xinyong* a is one of the fundamental virtues to see whether business partners are reliable or not to form trustworthiness business relationship in the long run (Chen & Eweje, 2019).

In Christian faith, xinyong or trustworthiness is emphasized so that the Great Commission for evangelism and discipleship can be achieved through the work of many stakeholders in one body, all having the same purpose to serve God unconditionally. The teaching of working together is based on xinyong or trust; if not everyone would think they are the heads and no one wants to be the feet. In the same way with business, the robust integration of value chains yields the benefits of economic growth and employment opportunities for any country. However, without xinyong or trustworthiness, these chains of value will not exist to benefit the economic and social impacts for consumers as well as the sustainability of businesses.

From business relationship to business longevity, YTL and Lippo always strive to offer assistance when their business partners need it. While engaging in quid pro quo is common in business affairs, it is righteous to genuinely help others out of good intention in sustaining the business longevity. Both YTL and Lippo have agreed many corrupt employers who faced business collapse would have experienced a different outcome if they had practised *xinyong* ethics and trustworthiness. For example, during the Asia financial crisis, the ringgit value plummeted and they were unable to repay the costly debt after receiving loans in US dollars. Francis Yeoh, on the other hand, expected the risks of making an abroad loan. In the early 1990s, he declared that when necessary, YTL should only receive loans locally and do all transactions in Malaysian ringgit. This borrowing strategy was proven to be more reliable, as YTL's profits increased in 1997 and 1998.

In common, although the company might have missed out on some money-making opportunities[5], both YTL and Lippo have never regretted their decisions. In some cases, clever investment will be paid off in the long run. In 2002, YTL Power bought Wessex Water Limited for £1.2 billion, which is £1.4 billion cheaper than what Enron originally paid for it. Currently, Wessex Water generates recurring revenues through a 25-year license to provide water supply and treatment services in England. When interviewed by the KL Lifestyle, Francis Yeoh mentioned that having a long lasting business relationship is essential, profit is not everything if we lose out the business relationship. On the contrary, he felt the urge to do the right thing which comes from "intrinsic human feelings".

"We asked our business partners what were they afraid of when we became the owners, and they said they were afraid that we would be like any other owner who would strip the company of its assets and take short cuts to make profits. We assured them that wasn't what YTL was about, but they had to do us a favor and grow the company with us." (KL Lifestyle Magazine, 2012)

"If you are a rich man, and you have faith, the wealth doesn't really matter to you. It is just something that makes people ask questions, as people always like to hear from the rich, to give their testimony. People always ask me what my secret of success is and I give back the truth humbly and truthfully; my secret is the Lord Jesus Christ." (KL Lifestyle Magazine, 2012)

For Lippo group, Dr. Mochtar holds strongly to the trustworthiness or *xinyong*. He heeds his father's advice to not be greedy and to never inflict losses on others. Described as "a disciplined, full of principle, full of dedication, and futuristic person" by his grandson, John Riady, Dr. Mochtar possesses a multinational mentality that believes in the importance of global networking to access capital markets such as in the United States and Hong Kong. He applied the Chinese idiom "骑马找马" that insists on connecting with genuine overseas partnerships. Networking is one of Lippo's extensive capital both in business and non-profit environments. The wide-ranging scale connections of the CFB prove that applying trust in their business is relevant worldwide.

In his book (Riady, 2016), Dr. Mochtar Riady wrote, "When I graduated from school, I was already thinking about being a banker. My opinion was, the bank's commodity is not money, it is trust. As long as I can have people's trust, I can be a banker." Believing that the foundation of the banking industry is infinite trust, Dr. Mochtar made this value the key philosophy of his management. In banking, the Lippo group had been accountable in managing depositors' money in Lippo Bank by keeping the loan-to-deposit ratio at a maximum of 75 percent that helped the family bank to survive the 1998 Asian economic crisis.

Besides *xinyong*, Dr. Mochtar also applied *xinren* (entrustment). He entrusted his grandson, John Riady, with a number of digital ventures before John took up the CEO position at Lippo Karawaci. Assigning successors with tasks and allow them to make mistakes is also part of Dr. Mochtar's philosophy of management. John Riady had been assigned to manage two projects MatahariMall.com and OVO; while one was unsuccessful, the other was. As an experienced businessman, Dr. Mochtar understood that failures are part of the journey to success in the process of *xinren*. While John's performance in the handling of the online mall did not impress Dr. Mochtar, John made up for it with e-money (Suzuki, 2018, para. 8). John was the managing partner in Venturra Capital, leading the development of OVO, a digital payment platform (e-wallet) that successfully attained unicorn (US$1 Billion valuation) status in 2019 and processing transactions worth US$4 billion in the first half of the year (Muskita, 2019). With Lippo Group that invests in at least 40 startups such as Grab, Fave, Ruangguru.com, and Sociolla, John has transformed the whole group (Siagian, 2022). When interviewed by The Business Times (2019), John Riady commented, "It's a big role, so I don't take it lightly. You have a responsibility not only to the family but to the minority shareholders at large. That's real."

He also emphasized the managerial concept of "presence in absence" by setting strong firm governance to motivate and monitor members in organisations, even when the top leader is not around. *Xinyong* and *xinren* is founded on the Lippo group's management and work ethics. Dr. Mochtar advised his two sons to apply the Word of God in their personal lives, families, and businesses. In 1989, at the age of 60, Dr. Mochtar had begun to trust Dr. James Riady and Dr. Stephen Riady in the autonomy of managing the family enterprise. Dr. Mochtar underlined love, tolerance, harmony, and hard work in the Lippo family group by quoting a Chinese idiom: "家和万事兴", which means when family members are harmonious, tens of thousands of undertakings will prosper.

Dr. Stephen Riady (Son of Dr. Mochtar) remarks after the global financial crisis in 2008:

"There is too much greed and over-confidence. That's why so many people make wrong decisions and create so many kinds of crises. We must learn to be responsible. [...]. That is why when we face a problem or crisis, testing and temptation come at the same time. We have to keep learning and improving ourselves because our environment is constantly changing." (Christian Today, 2009)

Workplace Innovation Post Covid-19 Pandemic

In order to with the speed of industry changes, both YTL and Lippo emphasize on workplace innovation and upskilling. To assist employees in upgrading their language and soft skills, a free online platform was created by YTL. Via YTL Learning Academy, employees are able to undergo training through a "Train the Trainer" program and attend recreational classes both onsite and offsite. At YTL, they emphasize in mastering the three languages in the workplace which are the languages of God (integrity), Man (confidence), and Machine (technology). Besides innovation, YTL is committed towards sustainability in all aspects namely workplace, environment, marketplace, and community.

Both YTL and Lippo stresses that a big corporation must benefit of people, for instance, through CSR corporate social responsibility (CSR)[6]. By being involved in CSR during the post-pandemic times, this involvement may be useful for future oriented market (Clauss et al., 2022). In line with this, workplace innovations in both YTL and Lippo after the Covid-19 pandemic have shown that firms' innovative attitudes are needed for handling a crisis.

The third generation CEO of YTL Land & Development, Pei Teeng Yeoh expressed her admiration for how well her team dealt with the implementation of Malaysia's Movement Control Order (MCO) in property development.

"I don't foresee the future of YTL Land & Development to be completely office-free, construction on several YTL projects were still at a halt, with the sales and marketing team showing units to customers via teleconferencing." (Jayatilaka, 2020)

"Digital platforms are adequate for property browsing. However, the buying experience is very different. Both man and machine have kept the organisation intact during these trying times. Learning from this, we're redefining our workplace to build a more resilient work culture." (Jayatilaka, 2020)

In Lippo Group, the legacy of Dr. Mochtar is in the third generation of the family dynasty. He is aware of "富不过三代" (family wealth not lasting for more than 3 generations), and fostering family members must be based on their integrity and competency in order to participate in the businesses. Lippo is one of the experts in applying co-innovation during the pandemic, Co-innovation involves the collaboration and co-creation among firms, partner organisations, external institutions, and customers (Saragih & Tan, 2018). This allows Lippo to produce new products, a value chain, business model, and customer base.

Lippo has at least 16,000 employees in Indonesia, not including Singapore and other Asian countries' operations, let alone the educational institutions. On average, each employee has had 38.8 hours of training and development annually during the pandemic. Lippo believes that employees must share the same vision and mission as the company, embrace challenges, execute strategies in an effective manner. There are active communications on the wellness program "Lippo Fun Club" through email blasts, a WhatsApp group, and social media. More engagements are initiated to facilitate feedback and people-to-people interactions through town hall meetings, informal lunch meetings, and focus group discussions (FGDs). Keeping the "family" togetherness is key for Lippo, especially during the pandemic. Online trainings for the internal audit teams were also held by The Institute of Internal Auditors Indonesia. Management Development Programs (MDPs) have been ongoingly effective in updating and nurturing employees in managerial levels. Professors at Pelita Harapan University established by Lippo were invited to share their knowledge and skills. In health care, a systematic e-Learning system was also developed for hospital personnel to enhance their skills to serve the high demand of patients during the pandemic.

John Riady (CEO of Lippo Karawaci, Tbk. & President Commissioner of Siloam Hospitals):

"I see the Covid-19 pandemic giving us the opportunity to be able to share and become a blessing for Indonesia through Siloam." (in the webinar The Untold Story of Next Generation Leaders, Saturday (13/3). (Bahfein, 2021)

CONCLUSION

The current work reveals that CFB such as YTL and Lippo that can last a several generations needs to make full use of the distinctive Christian ethics and *xinyong* with trustworthiness. By forming this interpersonal relationship pattern found in the overseas Chinese community, whereby religious freedom is important in advancing the human values and fully mobilizes family members, stakeholders, and other acquaintances to strengthen communication and trust. This practice allows a conglomerate to diversify businesses more easily.

Lippo and YTL are building their families to last for generations are developing their organisational pathway cemented on the foundation of Christ. In the book of Proverbs 22:1 (NIV), King Solomon, the richest man in the world in his time, gave one of his best advices: *"A good name is more desirable than great riches; to be esteemed is better than silver or gold"*. In Christianity, the sovereignty of God is the main theme of the Bible with forgiveness of sins through the unconditional sacrifice of Jesus Christ. This unconditional love in sacrifice is exemplary for CFBs to follow in applying sacrificial trust within the family that emanates throughout the family's stewardship. This is in contrast with the invisible hand concept by Adam Smith that when all parties act on their self-interests, unintended benefits are generated (Smith, 2010). On the other hand, the notion of *xinyong* means yielding or sacrificing one's self-interest to align oneself towards the betterment of the whole family. Overall, to break the curse of "富不过三代", CFBs requires the heart of stewardship (Tan, 2021) and early preparations for the next generations.

There are also a few caveats about workplace innovation management by emphasizing on the Christian faith and Chinese virtues such as *xinyong* with trustworthiness where a central transformation of the organisation's business philosophy and culture may be necessary. It entails an organisation to rethink its business to motivation and basing the decision-making process on ideals like intuition, creativity, and trusworthiness. Without *xinyong*, there will be no *xinren* and no family harmony and togetherness in the family enterprise.

In facing the challenges during the pandemic or generational change, the most prominent difficulty is the diversity of working experiences and religious traditions of the individual employee (Breier et al., 2021). In instilling the company's Christian values, both YTL and Lippo may face resistance in changing their religious views. Thus, the organisation must explain the importance of engaging in Christian ethics towards the company goals to the employees, as suggested by Hooker (2003). Lastly, it is vital for corporations to show the practical value of business longevity through dynamic empirical studies built on a solid theoretical framework. Seeing the significance of managing workplace innovation after the Covid-19 pandemic, it is important for researchers in this field to devise initiatives that are practical for organisations.

ACKNOWLEDGMENT

The authors are thankful to the University of Malaya (Department of Chinese Studies and Malaysian Chinese Research Centre) and Universitas Pelita Harapan (Faculty of Economics and Business) for supporting this research. Appreciation is also extended to all the stakeholders who are willing to openly share their ideas on how Christian based Chinese family enterprises function in Malaysia and Indonesia. We thank the anonymous reviewers for their insightful comments and suggestions for improving our manuscript.

REFERENCES

Aglozo, E. Y., Akotia, C. S., Osei-Tutu, A., & Annor, F. (2021). Spirituality and subjective well-being among Ghanaian older adults: Optimism and meaning in life as mediators. *Aging & Mental Health*, *25*(2), 306–315. doi:10.1080/13607863.2019.1697203 PMID:31814428

Ahn, H. (2008). Junzi as a tragic person: A self psychological interpretation of the Analects. *Pastoral Psychology*, *57*(1), 101–113. doi:10.100711089-008-0133-2

Alves, A. A., & Moreira, J. M. (2013). *Business ethics in the school of Salamanca. Handbook of the philosophical foundations of business ethics*. Springer.

Anderson, R. C., & Reeb, D. M. (2003). Founding-family ownership and firm performance: Evidence from the S&P 500. *The Journal of Finance*, *58*(3), 1301–1328. doi:10.1111/1540-6261.00567

Anteby, M., & Molnar, V. (2012). Collective memory meets organizational identity: Remembering to forget in a firm's rhetorical history. *Academy of Management Journal*, *55*(3), 515–540. doi:10.5465/amj.2010.0245

Asia, G. (2016, August). 100 top groups. *Globe Asia*, *10*(Special Issue), 42–79.

Astrachan, J. H., & Shanker, M. C. (2003). Family businesses' contribution to the US economy: A closer look. *Family Business Review*, *16*(3), 211–219. doi:10.1177/08944865030160030601

Aswicahyono, H., Hill, H., & Narjoko, D. (2010). Industrialisation after a deep economic crisis: Indonesia. *The Journal of Development Studies*, *46*(6), 1084–1108. doi:10.1080/00220380903318087

Backman, M. (2001). *Asian eclipse: Exposing the dark side of business in Asia*. John Wiley.

Bahfein, S. (2021). *John Riady anggap pandemi COVID-19 berkah bagi Lippo*. Kompas.com. https://properti.kompas.com/read/2021/03/14/070000221/john-riady-anggap-pandemi-covid-19-berkah-bagi-lippo

Barbalet, J. (2016). *Confucianism and the Chinese State: Reexamining Max Weber's China*. Palgrave Macmillan.

Botero, I. C., Cruz, C., Massis, A. D., & Nordqvist, M. (2015). Family business research in the European context. *European Journal of International Management*, *9*(2), 139–159. doi:10.1504/EJIM.2015.067858

Breier, M., Kallmuenzer, A., Clauss, T., Gast, J., Kraus, S., & Tiberius, V. (2021). The role of business model innovation in the hospitality industry during the COVID-19 crisis. *International Journal of Hospitality Management*, *92*, 102723. doi:10.1016/j.ijhm.2020.102723 PMID:36919038

Cao, N. (2019). A Sinicized world religion?: Chinese christianity at the contemporary moment of globalization. *Religions*, *10*(8), 459. doi:10.3390/rel10080459

Chafuen, A. A. (1986). *Christians for freedom: Late-scholastic economics*. Ignatius Press.

Chatterjee, S. R. (2001). Relevance of traditional value frameworks in contemporary chinese work organizations: Implications for managerial transition. *Journal of Human Values*, *7*(1), 21–32. doi:10.1177/097168580100700103

Chen, M. S., & Eweje, G. (2019). Establishing ethical Guanxi (interpersonal relationships) through confucian virtues of Xinyong (trust), Lijie (empathy) and Ren (humanity). *Corporate Governance: The International Journal of Business in Society*, *20*(1), 1–15. doi:10.1108/CG-01-2019-0015

Christian Today. (2009). The Christian billionaire's approach to the financial crisis. *Christian Today*. https://www.christiantoday.com/article/the.christian.billionaires.approach.to.the.financial.crisis/22926.htm

Chua, C. (2004). Defining Indonesian Chineseness under the new order. *Journal of Contemporary Asia*, *34*(4), 465–479. doi:10.1080/00472330480000221

Chua, E. (2009, March 26). *Billionaire: Remember purpose of life amid recession*. The Christian Post. https://www.christianpost.com/news/billionaire-remember-purpose-of-life-amid-recession.html

Clark, C., Davila, A., Regis, M., & Kraus, S. (2020). Predictors of COVID-19 voluntary compliance behaviors: An international investigation. *Global Transitions*, *2*, 76–82. doi:10.1016/j.glt.2020.06.003 PMID:32835202

Clauss, T., Breier, M., Kraus, S., Durst, S., & Mahto, R. V. (2022). Temporary business model innovation–SMEs' innovation response to the Covid-19 crisis. *R & D Management*, *52*(2), 294–312. doi:10.1111/radm.12498

Dean, K. (2020). Religion and the Chinese diaspora in Southeast Asia. *Review of Religion and Chinese Society*, *7*(2), 220–249. doi:10.1163/22143955-00702005

Djono, A. L. (2020). *Mendidik anak papua dengan hati*. Berita Satu. https://www.beritasatu.com/archive/652931/mendidik-anak-papua-dengan-hati

Doebele, J. (2005). Southeast Asia's 40 richest. *Forbes*. https://www.forbes.com/2005/09/078/southeast-asia -richest-cz_05seal

Gersick, K. E., Lansberg, I., Desjardins, M., & Dunn, B. (1999). Stages and transitions: Managing change in the family business. *Family Business Review*, *12*(4), 287–297. doi:10.1111/j.1741-6248.1999.00287.x

Gomez, E. T. (2007). Family firms, generational change and identity formation: The Chinese in Britain and Malaysia. *East Asia: An International Quarterly*, *24*(2), 153–172. doi:10.100712140-007-9012-1

Heck, R. K. Z., & Trent, E. (1999). The prevalence of family business from a household sample. *Family Business Review, 12*(3), 209–224. doi:10.1111/j.1741-6248.1999.00209.x

Hefner, R. W. (2021). Islam and institutional religious freedom in Indonesia. *Religions, 12*(6), 415. doi:10.3390/rel12060415

Hermanto, Y. P. (2020). True response to COVID-19 plague reviewed from the perspective of Christian faith. *IOSR Journal of Humanities and Social Science, 25*, 33–36.

Hoffmann-Holland, K. (2009). *Ethics and human rights in a globalized world: An interdisciplinary and international approach*. Mohr Siebeck.

Hooker, J. (2003). *Working Across Cultures*. Stanford University Press. https://dailysocial.id/post/lippo-groups-john-riady-takes-on-the-conglomerate-investment-in-the-technology-landscape

Ibrahim, N. A., & Angelidis, J. P. (2005). The long-term performance of small businesses: Are there differences between "Christian-based" companies and their secular counterparts? *Journal of Business Ethics, 58*(1), 187–193. doi:10.100710551-005-1413-8

Ibrahim, N. A., Rue, L. W., McDougall, P. P., & Greene, G. R. (1991). Characteristics and practices of "Christian-based" companies. *Journal of Business Ethics, 10*(2), 123–132. doi:10.1007/BF00383615

Iswara, M. A. (2020, July 31, 2020). Indonesia ranks among most religious countries in Pew study. *The Jakarta Post*. https://www.thejakartapost.com/news/2020/07/30/indonesia-ranks-among-most-religious-countries-in-pew-study.html

Jayatilaka, T. (2020). *Tatler in Culture & Travel: "Post-Covid-19 era: Is working in the office still relevant?"* Tatler. https://www.tatlerasia.com/culture/travel/sg-how-relevant-is-the-office-in-the-post-covid-era-ytl-land-development-zalora-malaysia?tool=addthis#.Yx2SSasAnBY.link

Jesudason, J. V. (1989). *Ethnicity and the economy: The state, Chinese business, and multinationals in Malaysia*. Oxford University Press.

Kao, H. S. R., & Sek-Hong, N. (1995). Chinese values in work organization: An alternative approach to change and development. *Journal of Human Values, 1*(2), 173–189. doi:10.1177/097168589500100203

Karmali, N. (2018). Indonesia's Richest 2018: Mochtar Riady's Lippo Group Faces Fresh Challenge. *Forbes*. https://www.forbes.com/sites/naazneenkarmali/2018/12/12/indonesias-richest-2018-driven-to-diversify/?sh=67890b571962

Knowledge at Wharton Staff. (2009). *Lippo Group CEO James Riady: 'Money and power are a blessing and a curse'*. Wharton. https://knowledge.wharton.upenn.edu/article/lippo-group-ceo-james-riady-money-and-power-are-a-blessing-and-a-curse/

Kuhn, P. (2008). *Chinese among Others: Emigration in Modern Times*. National University of Singapore Press.

Kusnandar, V. B. (2021). Sebanyak 86,88% Penduduk Indonesia Beragama Islam. *Katadata Media Networks*. https://databoks.katadata.co.id/datapublish/2021/09/30/sebanyak-8688-penduduk-indonesia-beragama-islam

Kusuma, B. (2017, July 22). Papua Education, The Key to Overcome Separatism. *Republika.co.id*. https://www.republika.co.id /berita/oth7t2413/papua-education-the-key-to-overcome-separatism

Le Breton-Miller, I., & Miller, D. (2018). Beyond the firm: Business families as entrepreneurs. *Entrepreneurship Theory and Practice*, *42*(4), 527–536. doi:10.1177/1042258717739004

Lee, J. K. Y. (2021). Still a Chinese Family Business? *Journal of Chinese Overseas*, *17*(2), 399–418. doi:10.1163/17932548-12341450

Lee, J. K. Y., & Gomez, E. T. (2014). Advancing tacit knowledge: Malaysian family SMEs in Manufacturing. *Asian Economic Papers*, *13*(2), 1–24. doi:10.1162/ASEP_a_00275

Lee, J. K. Y., & Tan, J. D. (2022). Adapting to local markets and political changes: Chinese businesses in Malaysia and Indonesia. *South East Asia Research*, *30*(4), 452–471. doi:10.1080/0967828X.2022.2145989

Lee, J. K. Y., & Xavier, J. A. (2022). Strategizing family business with a Chandlerian perspective on 3Ms: A case study of London Biscuits Berhad in Malaysia. *Journal of Asia Business Studies*, *16*(1), 181–199. doi:10.1108/JABS-10-2019-0302

Leung, T. K. P., Lai, K. H., Chan, R. Y., & Wong, Y. H. (2005). The roles of xinyong and guanxi in Chinese relationship marketing. *European Journal of Marketing*, *39*(5/6), 528–559. doi:10.1108/03090560510590700

Lifestyle Magazine, K. L. (2012). Tan Sri Francis Yeoh – Steering YTL with vision. *KL Lifestyle Magazine*. https://www.ytlcommunity.com/shownews.asp?newsID=1197

Lin, K. W., & Huang, K. P. (2014). Moral judgment and ethical leadership in Chinese management: The role of Confucianism and collectivism. *Quality & Quantity*, *48*(1), 37–47. doi:10.100711135-012-9747-7

Lincoln, A. T. (2020). Reading Hebrews in a Time of Pandemic: Heroism and Hope in the Face of Fear. *The Expository Times*, *131*(11), 471–479. doi:10.1177/0014524620946689

Loo, D. (2008, June 23). *Lippo to invest $10 billion in Asia in 5 yrs*. Reuters. https://www.reuters.com/article/us-property-summit-lippo-idUKSP7151220080623

Luhmann, N. (1979). *Trust and Power*. Wiley.

Lynn, M., Naughton, M., & VanderVeen, S. (2009). Faith at work scale (FWS): Justification, development, and validation of a measure of Judeo-Christian religion in the workplace. *Journal of Business Ethics*, *85*(2), 227–243. doi:10.100710551-008-9767-3

Malaysian Department of Statistics. (2021). *Demographic Statistics First Quarter 2021, Malaysia*. Malaysian Department of Statistics. https://www.dosm.gov.my/v1/index.php?r=column/pdfPrev&id=aVlJRDAvbjhWWEhQa1YvSWhsSjF3QT09

Marquis, C., & Tilcsik, A. (2013). Imprinting: Toward a Multilevel Theory. *The Academy of Management Annals*, *7*(1), 195–245. doi:10.5465/19416520.2013.766076

Mohamed, Z., Abd Kadir, Z., & Raof, N. A. A. (2018). Malaysia Industrial Master Plans (IMPs) and the focus on the nation technology and innovation development. *Journal of Science. Technology and Innovation Policy*, *4*(2), 11–19.

Morris, M., & Schindebutte, M. (2005). Entrepreneurial values and the ethnic entrepreneur: An examination of six sub-cultures. *Journal of Small Business Management*, *43*(4), 453–479. doi:10.1111/j.1540-627X.2005.00147.x

Muskita, P. (2019). Ovo confirms unicorn status. *Tech in Asia*. https://www.techinasia.com/ovo-confirms-unicorn-status

Nishida, J. M., & Redding, S. G. (1992). Firm development and diversification strategies as products of economic cultures: the Japanese and Hong Kong cotton textile. *European Business Systems: Firms and Markets in Their National Contexts*, 241.

Permatasari, S., & Amin, H. (2022, May 29). *Lippo tycoon eyes hospitals, schools for Jokowi's new capital*. BNN Bloomberg. https://www.bnnbloomberg.ca/lippo-tycoon-eyes-hospitals-schools-for-jokowi-s-new-capital-1.1772150

Rathbun, B. C. (2012). From vicious to virtuous circle: Moralistic trust, diffuse reciprocity, and the American security commitment to Europe. *European Journal of International Relations*, *18*(2), 323–344. doi:10.1177/1354066110391308

Riady, M. (2016). *Manusia Ide*. PT Kompas Media Nusantara.

Richter, P. (2014). Invitation to Indonesia. *The Geospel Coalition.* https://www.thegospelcoalition.org/article/indonesia-invitation/

Rovnick, N. (2009, January 23). *Interview: Francis Yeoh explains YTL's divine performance*. Global Capital Asia. https://www.globalcapital.com/asia/article/28mvfg22uqekr0unx7x1c/emerging-markets/interview-francis-yeoh-explains-ytls-divine-performance

Saragih, H. S., & Tan, J. D. (2018). Co-innovation: A review and conceptual framework. *International Journal of Business Innovation and Research*, *17*(3), 361–377. doi:10.1504/IJBIR.2018.095542

Shaw, W. (2009). Marxism, business ethics, and corporate social responsibility. *Journal of Business Ethics*, *84*(4), 565–575. doi:10.100710551-008-9725-0

Siagian, K. (2022). *Lippo Group's John Riady takes on the conglomerate investment in the technology landscape*. Daily Social.

Simarasl, N., Jiang, D. S., Kellermanns, F. W., & Debicki, B. J. (2020). Unmasking the social ghost in the machine: How the need to belong and family business potency affect family firm performance. *Family Business Review*, *33*(4), 351–371. doi:10.1177/0894486520948992

Smith, A. (2010). *The wealth of nations: An inquiry into the nature and causes of the wealth of nations*. Harriman House Limited.

Suddaby, R., & Jaskiewicz, P. (2020). Managing traditions: A critical capability for family business success. *Family Business Review*, *33*(3), 234–243. doi:10.1177/0894486520942611

Suhartono, H., & Baigorri, M. (2022, August 25). *Lippo Karawaci Mulls Buying CVC's Siloam Hospitals Stake*. Bloomberg. https://www.bloomberg.com/news/articles/2022-08-25/lippo-karawaci-said-to-mull-buying-cvc-s-siloam-hospitals-stake

Suzuki, J. (2018). *Lippo tycoon looks to young-gun grandson to build digital empire*. Asia Nikkei. https://asia.nikkei.com/Spotlight/Asian-Family-Conglomerates/Lippo-tycoon-looks-to-young-gun-grandson-to-build-digital-empire

Tan, C.-B. (1995). The study of Chinese religions in Southeast Asia. In L. Suryadinata (Ed.), *Southeast Asian Chinese: The Socio-Cultural Dimension*. Times Academic Press.

Tan, J. D. (2021). *The panorama of succession: nurturing transgenerational entrepreneurship in family business (parent-child dyad)*. Penerbit Andi.

Tan, J. D., Supratikno, H., Pramono, R., Purba, J. T., & Bernarto, I. (2019). Nurturing transgenerational entrepreneurship in ethnic Chinese family SMEs: Exploring Indonesia. *Journal of Asia Business Studies, 13*(2), 294–325. doi:10.1108/JABS-04-2018-0132

Tan, M. M., Musa, A. F., & Su, T. T. (2022). The role of religion in mitigating the COVID-19 pandemic: the Malaysian multi-faith perspectives. *Health Promotion International, 37*(1), daab041.

The Business Times. (2019, September 13). Riady scion takes action to revive Lippo flagship. *The Business Times*. https://www.businesstimes.com.sg/real-estate/riady-scion-takes-action-to-revive-lippo-flagship

Tognazzo, A., & Neubaum, D. O. (2020). Family business leaders' metaphors and firm performance: Exploring the "roots" and "shoots" of symbolic meanings. *Family Business Review, 33*(2), 130–151. doi:10.1177/0894486520910874

Tong, C. K. (1996). Centripetal authority, differentiated networks: The social organisation of Chinese firms in Singapore. In Gary Hamilton (Ed.), Asian Business Networks (pp. 133–56). de Gruyter.

Uslaner, E. M. (2002). *The Moral Foundations of Trust*. Cambridge University Press.

Wah, S. S. (2001). Chinese cultural values and their implication to Chinese management. *Singapore Management Review, 23*(2), 75–83.

Wallau, F., & Kayser, G. (2001). In the federation of German industries (Ed.), Das industrielle Familienunternehmen—Kontinuität im Wandel. Berlin: Bundesverband der Deutschen Industrie (BDI e.V) and Ernst & Young.

Wang, X., Li, F., & Sun, Q. (2018). Confucian ethics, moral foundations, and shareholder value perspectives: An exploratory study. *Business Ethics (Oxford, England), 27*(3), 260–271. doi:10.1111/beer.12186

Weber, M. (1947b). The protestant sects and the spirit of capitalism. In *From Max Weber* (H. H. Gerth & C. W. Mills, Trans.). Oxford University Press.

Weber, M. (1964). The religion of China: Confucianism and Taoism, (trans. Hans H. Gerth). New York: Free Press.

Wong, S. (1988). *Emigrant entrepreneurs: Shanghai industrialists in Hong Kong*. Hong Kong: Oxford University Press: Wong, Y. H., & Tam, J. L. (2000). Mapping relationships in China: Guanxi dynamic approach. *Journal of Business and Industrial Marketing*, *15*(1), 57–70. doi:10.1108/08858620010311557

Wong, S. L. (1993). The Chinese family firm: A model. *Family Business Review*, *6*(3), 327–340. doi:10.1111/j.1741-6248.1993.00327.x

Wong-McDonald, A., & Gorsuch, R. L. (2000). Surrender to God: An additional coping style? *Journal of Psychology and Theology*, *28*(2), 149–161. doi:10.1177/009164710002800207

World Bank. (2022). *Global Growth to Slow through 2023, Adding to Risk of 'Hard Landing' in Developing Economies*. World Bank. https://www.worldbank.org/en/news/press-release/2022/01/11/global-recovery-economics-debt-commodity-inequality

Yang, F. (1999). *Chinese Christians in America: Conversion, assimilation, and adhesive identities*. The Pennsylvania State University Press.

Yin, E., & Mahrous, A. (2022). Covid-19 global pandemic, workplace spirituality and the rise of spirituality-driven organisations in the post-digital era. *Journal of Humanities and Applied Social Sciences*.

Zhu, Y., & Warner, M. (2004). Changing patterns of human resource management in contemporary China: WTO accession and enterprise responses. *Industrial Relations Journal*, *35*(4), 311–328. doi:10.1111/j.1468-2338.2004.00316.x

ENDNOTES

1 SMEs refer to "firms with sales turnover not exceeding RM20 million OR number of full-time employees not exceeding 75". In contrast, firms in Indonesia can be categorized as SMEs with sales revenue not more than Rp 50 million.

2 During the British rule period, hundreds of thousands of Chinese people from China migrated to Malaya and Indonesia. Coming from different dialect groups, these migrants have unique practices which reflect their geographical origins and ancestors' beliefs. Some of these Chinese cultural values remain practised in Southeast Asia.

3 Confucian theories dictate that family responsibilities fall on the shoulders of male family members, particularly the eldest son.

4 Following the 2009-2010, for example, YTL Corporation chose not to make costly acquisitions during the global financial crisis. Francis Yeoh aggressively bought cheap assets during 2008-2009. For Lippo Group, their operations are mostly in Indonesia (70%) such as Lippo Karawaci and Lippo Cikarang. According to Reuters (Loo, 2008), in April 2008, Lippo planned to invest $10 billion in Asia by selling off its ownership in Robinson –a Singapore retailer- to United Arab Emirates group Al Futtaim in a deal worth $409 million. Despite a poor market for new REITs, Lippo group would still plan to list three property trusts in Asia, and was getting ready to incorporate a set of projects into the trusts.

5 In 2006, although People criticized YTL "for a low return on equity in YTL Power", YTL still being conservative and keep trustworthiness. Francis Yeoh is focuses on *xinyong* to avoid short term profits and he concentrated on long-term business relationship even YTL suffered from a poor rating of their stocks. For Lippo Group, Mokhtar Riady always keeps his promise or *xinyong* to convince which business owners from top-class businesses to support his plan to establish a reliable bank for Chinese. After forming a partnership with powerful businessmen, Mokhtar Riady bought Bank Buana which kickstarted his banking business.

6 Through BUILDS, the CSR team of YTL Cement has donated 7,000 COVID-19 Care Kits and distributed essential cleaning equipment to educators and pupils from 24 schools across Peninsula Malaysia. YTL has built on the rural renewable energy program during the pandemic around YTL Jawa Timur (YTLJT) in Java, Indonesia, to reduce the negative health impacts of dangerous indoor fumes on June 2020. For Lippo Group, Lippo Cikarang's CSR team distributed food supply and mask to the Bekasi Regency Indonesian Chamber of Commerce (KADIN) on April 22, 2020. To combat the virus spread, Lippo Cikarang showed an initiative to spray disinfectants in Lippo Cikarang as well as maximizing online communication media.

Chapter 8
Longterm Cycles of Innovation in Europe's Textile Business

Bernd Hallier
European Retail Academy, Germany

Violena Hubenova Nencheva
European Retail Academy, Mexico

ABSTRACT

The textile business is an excellent example for permanent transformations of the lifestyle of consumers. The first cycle in the Darwinism of the European textile sector was dominated by traders' knowledge about the sources of the product-materials and opportunities for processing. In a second phase covering the start of industrial mass-production and professional mass-distribution, outlets for textiles were established with benchmarks at high frequency spots in down-towns of acclomerations like Berlin, Cologne, London, or Paris. Department stores became the anchor of cities and for life-style driven citizens. In the third phasis the outlet-dominance is attacked by IT-driven businesses by the development of tools like the European article numbering-system, chips and QR-codes, clouds for big data and data mining, artificial intelligence, and virtual reality. For the textile traders it is an improvement of the efficiency by the ability to control the total supply chain electronically. Of course, this is resulting in big changes for the supply patterns.

DOI: 10.4018/978-1-6684-7394-8.ch008

INTRODUCTION

Textile Business as an Innovator

This Chapter deals with the long-term role of innovation within the textile sector as well as by the sector in society because consumer habits are heavily influenced. A special focus does have family-businesses as the textile sector has big clusters of small and medium-sized companies with families as owners. In the beginning of the 20ies of this century the sector is challenged not only by a unique speed of sector internal factors but also by unprecedented external factors. The question for the sector is if there will be resilience in the near future or if the market will be reduced in volume and number of players for the ongoing time.

Internal Factors of Innovation of Businesses

The innovation of businesses is a permanent process initiated by thousands of individual decisions either to cut costs or to increase sales volume by product adaption. Academic pioneers to analyse emperial data about those processes are Kondratieff (1926) for macro-economics and Schumpeter (1961) for micro-economics. Innovation cycles in retail/wholesale as a sector-analysis has been systematically documented firstly by Hallier (1999a, 1999b, 2022a) based on reports about sub-groups of this spectrum (Hahn 1984; Hauptmann 1943; Birchall 1997; Bauer and Hallier, 1999, pp. 162-192; Zola 2004; Hallier et al. 2002, p. 155; Hallier et al. 2002, p. 210-212) or own observations.

The impact of innovations for the entrepreneurs and the changes of consumerism within the centuries as well as a prognosis of the future within the next decades can be summarized for example by the sub-group Textile Trade. Starting in the 20ies of this century shopping in an affluent society is mixing with entertainment: in future also inclusive gaming in a virtual world with avatares being sponsored by the branded goods industry of textiles or by outlet-chains. The final outfit of customers might be co-determind by long-distance partners in those games or it might be a decision tool for the planning of a meeting of a group of shoppers in a specific outlet at a certain date. The real world and the virtual world mix in a Metaversum.

Figure 1. Long-term Innovation Cycles
Source: Hallier, B.

Steam Engine	Railways	Electrical Engeneering	Petrochemial Industrie	Information Technology	Lithium Industry
Cotton	Steel Production	Chemestry	Automobiles	Global Trade	Smart Economics
1800	1850	1900	1950	2000	2050
imperial import / export domestic commerce	local consumes cooperatives start of department houses	first national buying groups start of mail-order companies	supermarkets big boxes shopping centers information technology	chip technology RFID internet B2B/B2C omni-Channel mobile shopping	data-clouds block-chain technology Internet of Things Artificial Inteligence Retail Knowledge Consortia

Source : Prof.Dr.Bernd Hallier : Dec.2020

Origions of Textile Trade as Family-Business

Tracing family businesses in the textile sector in Europe one impressive example from the Middle Ages is the Fugger Clan from the city of Augsburg/Germany (Hallier et al. 2002, p. 12 ff). The family was named by the Latin word „fucare "standing for the technical process to create from neutral cotton the basis for coulered clothes. The Fugger brothers Hans and Ulin started in 1367 and 1377 their businesses in Augsburg: importing cotton from Egypt via Venice/today Italy, transporting the cotton over the Alpes-mountain-range and coulering the stuff in cooperation with small local manufacturers. The next Fugger generation expanded the internationalization to cover also the East of Europe and the Baltic Sea. Additionally, they started to diversify into the metal business (mining gold/silver) in Austria and Hungary – finally also banking mainly for the Pope but also for Cesar Maximilian and Cesar Karl V.

In 1517 like Cesar Maximilian also Jakob II Fugger ordered a portrait painted by Albrecht Dürer (Hallier et al. 2002, p. 15) – while Ulrich II Fugger asked Hans Holbein the Older to draw him. The paintings and the outfit of the aristocrates and the traders are documents for the desire of emancipation between the upper classes – also seen in detailled regulations for dress-codes by the Augsburg Administration in 1537, 1551 and 1581.

Figure 2. Jakob II Fugger

Figure 3. Niclas de Respaigne
Source: Hallier, B.

Dressing for Image "could be called also a portrait of the trader Niclas de Respaigne from Amsterdam who had moved his business from Venice to the textile center of the Middle East of that time Aleppo (Turkey/Syria). Peter Paul Rubens painted him in 1619 when de Respaigne was getting to marry (Hallier et al. 2002, p. 259). He was painted dressed in the Oriental (Ottoman-/Turkish) Style standing on an Anatolian carpet. Cloth styles and accessoires grew in importance.

Start of Mass-Production and - Distribution

A new epoche started with the discovery of America and the import of cotton from there. In response to increased demand on the one hand side and new sources for import on the other side: the painting of Rembrandt van Reijn in 1662 is titled „Quality Control "and showes the Guilde of the Amsterdam Textile Traders checking the quality of their imports (Hallier et al. 2002, p. 255).

Figure 4. Amsterdam Guilde of Textile Importers
Source: Hallier, B.

This trend of mass-distribution of textiles is also taken as a topic by the French impressionist Edgar Degas who visited parts of his family who lived in New Orleans/ USA earning their livings in the textile business (Bauer and Hallier, 1999, p. 129).

His painting „Office of a cotton-trader in New Orleans "in 1873 has to be connected with his letters reporting about his stay in the USA comparing it with Paris in France: „All day we speak about cotton and credits; the ships from Europe to fetch the cotton-exports are coming in a frequency like the buses at the Paris-station "! The global supply chain and the importance of capital for increased markets became of big importance for the textile business.

Figure 5. New Orleans Cotton Exporters
Source: Hallier, B.

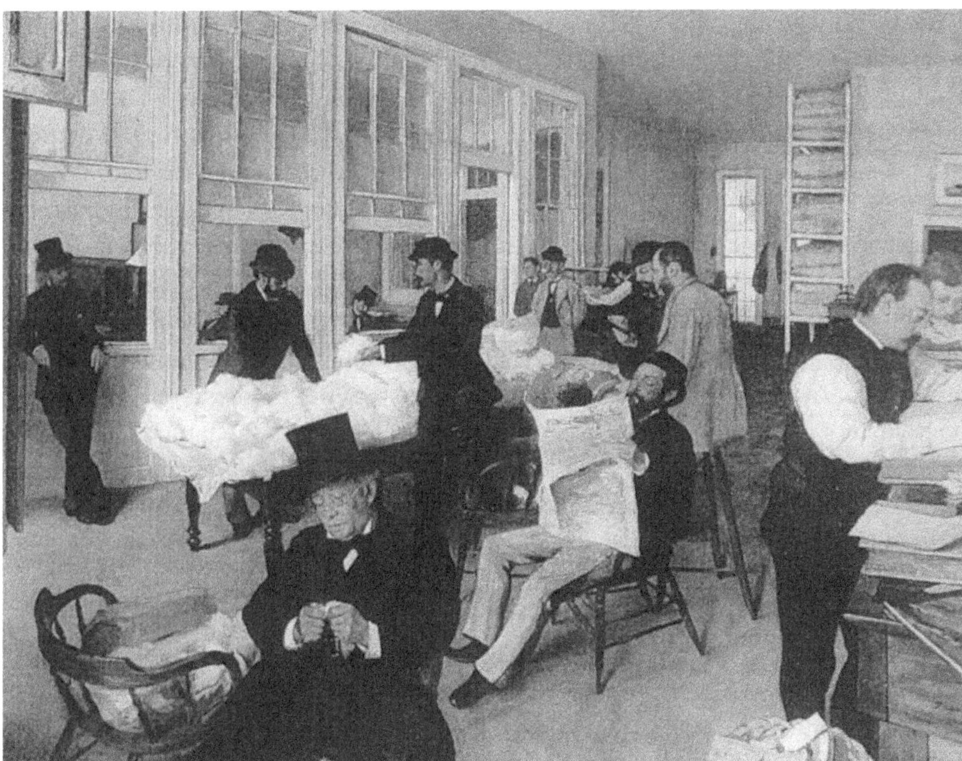

Urban LifeStyle and Segmentation

That century had another impact on the textile industry also in macro-economics in general: the range of consumers was broadened beside the upper classes due to industrialization also consimers with lower budgets could be reached. Additionally, it was the start of exhibitions about the beginning of an international competition about the results of the industrialization. In 1811 for example the city of Düsseldorf/

Germany prepared an exhibition for the French Cesar Napoleon I. to demonstrate the potential of the occupied Rhineland-area. It was several times repeated and was one of the origions to organize later EXPOs for the „jet-set" society of that time which travelled by the new cross-border railway-systems to explore the life-style of other countries (Hallier 2022b). In Paris Gustave Eiffel designed for the Paris Expo the famous tower which was planned to stay only for the period of the exhibition – but actually became the landmark of the city of Paris till today. Other places like Milano in Italy are also still „bundler"of all local/national producers of the textile sector to exhibit the latest fashion of Italy. In Germany after World War II Düsseldorf took over this function from the divided capital Berlin – but lost its unique sales position in West Germany after the reunification of Germany after 1990 when Berlin started to be again the number 1 trend-setter of life-style. Fashion Today reported in its News of KW 27/2022 that the Berlin exhibitions Premium, Seek and The Ground had invited also 25 international buying directors to arrange proactively meetings with the exhibitors (Fashion Today 2022). Furtheron, they announced that in 2023 the events of the Premium Group would be organized parallel to the Berlin Fashion Week. The business-competence of textile traders was for more than a century linked to those hot-spots where designers, producers, models, high-level distributors and the high society were meeting like in circus-events watched by the public.

Important to mention that it was also Gustave Eifel who designed the fashion-show-room Au Bon Marche: a department-store with a sales-area of 25.000 squaremeters – desribed by the French writer Emile Zola in his famous „Paradise for Ladies" (Zola 2004) – which was showing the social impact also for the small businesses which started to be eliminated by the big players. Paris was competing in the ranking of consumers of the upper classes with London, Cologne, Berlin and Moscow. In 1902 Tietz in Cologne (today Kaufhof) was quoted to state that his sales-people were able to serve customers in 8 languages (Hallier et al. 2002, p. 155). Interestingly in Germany all the big department-stores started with textiles and only later diversified by an enlargement of the assortment.

Others like C&A, P&C (with their tradition to trade textiles in the triangle Belgium, Netherlands and Germany) or many local players remained in the textile sector for partly for more than two centuries: others like H&M or Zara joined in an international expansion drive but being focused on special target groups. Lately in Germany for cheap offers special textile discounters like Takko or Kik followed in down-town locations which became as outlets too small for food-stores like modern supermarkets or which are placed especially in low-income areas. Last but not least food-discounters like ALDI or Lidl as well as coffee-shops like Tchibo use textiles for weekly offers to get a higher frequency to their shops or to cash-in with additional assortments from those customers which can be reached by on-the-spot offers. As a result of those promotions the food-discounter ALDI is within the Top 10 textile retailers in Germany and the coffee-shop Tchibo has pushed the special offers to over 50 percent of its total turnover.

For labels the alternatives are high-level flagship-stores to promote the brand within an umbrella-strategy and to offer in factory outlet centers (FOC) a limited assortment which is on average 15 percent lower in its sales-prices and is additionally run by slogans like „over run“, „factory seconds“, „damaged“, „past season“, „samples“ or „discontinued items“. Very often those factory outlets are in agglomerations of at least five label-producers with a minimum of 4500 squaremeters sales area (Hallier 1999c).

This evolution of the mix of target-groups enlarged also the potential tools of marketing: the store-format, its target- group's financial situation, its range of assortment, the presentation-style became equally important like the product itself. One example of the latest trend to catch the eye and the heart of upper- level consumers is the new store of the French top-designer Christian Dior in Paris who in 2022 upgraded his store by adding to the sales-floor also three gardens, one restaurant, one cafe and one patisserie. Another example is in Berlin P&C opening its first Mega Eco Store responding by this with a Corporate Social Responsibility strategy to the trend of many people in Germany to go shopping in stores which are constructed according to environmental aspects, presenting products which fit ecological standards and which are produced under fair conditions and transported with a low footprint (*Mode ohne schlechtes Gewissen* [*Fashion without a guilty conscience*], 2022). The business became more complex – more and other abilities were needed beside the product-knowledge.

This increasing spectrum for retailers has also an impact on exhibitions: in this context it has to be remembered that it had been fairs like the EXPO in Paris which became the mirrows of the latest life-styles. After World War II there had been two competing trends: the revitalization of traditional department stores with beautiful decorated windows – and on the other hand the American Way of Life by modern sales technologies (Hallier 2022b). Both trends for better sales was the idea to launch the exhibition EuroShop and still is the basis of the success of the world-leading triannual shopfitting exhibition in Düsseldorf which was started in 1966 by the same fair-management which was responsible for the fashion shows of IGEDO, which was the show-room of West Germany for fashion. The flagship of shopfitting EuroShop again reacted in 1997 to follow the latest consumer trends by segmenting its IT-shows under the name of EuroCIS and to exhibit annually for this target-group of IT-managers in retail/wholesale also to follow the speed of technical/digital innovation in this segment.

From Big Boxes to Big Data

Especially since the middle of the 70ies the growth of the big players was supported by innovations in the IT-Sector (Hallier 1987; Heidel 1990; EHI 1994; Hallier 1995, Hallier 1999d). Only by the electronic control of the articles in the shelf of the outlets or the delivery systems the efficiency of big groups of outlets could/can be checked. Due to the multiplication of outlets per chain the single outlets could be no longer visited permanently by the owner of the businesses or by Board-members but had to be delegated and to be controlled by new technology.

As an example, for the innovation of the key-elements of the retail technology is the EAN-barcode which was introduced in 1975. It contains the country of origion, the manufacturer and the product. By this the inventory within the depots and the stores could be quickly followed up. Actually, the POINT of MANAGEMENT DECISION (PMD) could be turned from the head of a manager in the headquarter of a company towards the POINT of DATA COLLECTION (PDC). Benetton for example changed the production of its cloths no longer in connection to spring/summer/autumn/winter trade fairs/collections but permanently due to the incoming data from the cash-zones of its outlets.

At about the year 2000 the printed barcode was replaced step by step by the chip technology which was able to integrate more data than the printed version and enabled interconnectivity with other systems without manual intervention. Machines started to take over from human beings: AI (Automated Intelligence) became the key-word. The UK retailer Morrisons is quoted at EuroCIS 2022 to cover already more than 90 percent of its product movements by AI of their IT provider Blue Yonder. The French department store Bonprix claimed at the same event to have survived well the decreased sales caused by the Covid Crisis due to AI software which had speeded up the data mining.

Other advantages of the chip-technology and its connectivity with data clouds is the Internet of Things (IoT): the capacity allows to demonstrate details for the application of the bought products and to attach marketing communication. Last but not least the QR-code (Quick Response) allows the consumer to read advertising in different media and to order by a photo of the code the product immediately (Hallier 2011, p.148 ff).

The role of a wholesaler for the physical flow of products could change to be B2B – or even B2C-platform providers in the virtual world and deliveries will come increasingly by a delivery-partner with sub-partners. The definition „institutional wholesaler/retailer"will show less members than the „functional wholesaler/retailer". There will be a great boom in segmentation, diversification and partnering. One example of such recent cooperations is C & A Germany which started in July 2022 to place selective items at the German Site Amazon.de: the launch at the Dutch, the French, the Italian and the Spanish Sites are planned to follow.

The importance of data could be seen already after World War I when department houses were destroyed and the lack of capital did not allow new brick-and-stone outlets. In Nürnberg/Germany the Schickedanz family started a mail-order system based on the send-out of catalogues and data of customers (Hallier et al. 2002, p. 210); his company Quelle (the German word for „Source") became a benchmark for success and was copied by others like OTTO after World War II. (Hallier et al. 2002, p. 112 f).

Modern IT/digitalization became the competitor for the printed catalogues and the brick-and-stone outlets. Parallel to EuroShop 2008 in Germany the fashion online supplier Zalando was founded. In 2022 it has 35 million customers within 17 countries in Europe. Per minute 7500 online-orders are registered. This success of course is stimulating not only newcomers but also traditional business to react with omni-channel strategies – selling instore as well as online trying to push each channel by the visibility or the comfort of the other.

But even industry is involved in the search for direct contacts with the consumer. In summer 2022 for example Beiersdorf is promoting its range of sun-creams and beauty-articles by in-store activities with trade partners in Germany. Consumers are offered a free-of-charge bathing towel if they send in a cash-slip of having bought Beiersdorf products in the value of 20.- Euro (plus) to the address of the company. Of course, also the address of the shopper has to be sent for the mailing of the towel-parcel. The fabrics in this case of course are no sales-items but calculated as part of the promotion costs.

VIRTUAL REALITY, AVATARES, AND METAVERSUM

The latest trend comes via Virtual Reality (VR) and will be encluded in a Metaversum. Within interactive games avatars will have the image of the player/players. The play-background can be the image of outlets combined with images of products. Within the game the player and co-players can dress alternatively the avatar and those being in the players 'team can decide together the final outfit or meet based on those discussions in a real store of that fashion supplier. Those games could be developed and promoted by producers or retailers or in cooperation between those two groups. It might be also seen as a potential new income for those who keep the owner-rights of those income. In the end of this thought, it might happen that the products 'profit might be Zero – and the economic gain is the profit by advertising within the games as a kind of „listing price for the product" or selling the data of the trends as a service of market research – similarly like in the Beiersdorf case-study.

But also, C2C platforms as a kind of semi-professional business can be put into this new trend. Via eBay or other platforms consumers sell own used stuff or buy second hand for discounts of 30 to 60 percent for second hand. There are even offers of top brands of the textile or from the accessoire-market for reuse by consumers who could not afford to pay for those products the price of the first user. Influencers with recommendations do have their own communities as followers who want to copy their stars. Influencers earn by clicks or from advertising partners.

External Impact Factors

Also, in the past very often more than one sector of national economies has been affected by external factors like Wars, Disruptions of traditional supply chains, Exploration of New Trade Routes or Markets, Innovations like Industrialization or new Infrastructure like rail-ways.

In the context of this Chapter the major external global challenges of the 20ies of this century are listed as key-words. They are influencing the potential return on investment of the whole textile sector in general but also especially the family businesses.

Climate Change

The warming of the global climate caused in many densly populated areas of the world either draughts or extrem floods. Millions of people have lost by this own food supply and often even their homes. As a result, their budget for new textiles is at the moment very low – which is backed in theory by the Consumption Pyramid of Richard Musgrave.

The World Climate Conference in Paris had agreed to limit its global CO2-emissions to reduce the increase of the worldwide warming-up to 1.5 degrees Celsius within the next decade. The follow-up Conference in Egypt in November 2022 showed no consence about the split of country-individual goals to reach the average of the 1.5 target – and also not about the tactical steps to reach such a goal. Some countries want to stop all fossile sources for industry or households, others want even to increase coal as an exception for their countries – or at least an exception for some decades – others want compensation for the problems caused by too much CO2 output from other countries. The disagreement is also not only about the volume of financial compensation but also about who has to pay the bill.

Meanwhile floods increase in Asia for example in Bangladesh, India and Pakistan – in Australia and Florida/USA – and whole island countries in the Pacific like the Maledives or Tonga are threatened to be eliminated partly or totally by the increase of the water-level. And even in Europe scenarios show that big cities along the coast of the Atlantic will be lost in a foreseeable period because the shelters to protect those cities and farming areas is so cost-intensive that most probably not enough financial resources will be available.

On the other hand, there a draughts which turn former prosperous farm-land into deserts like in the Southern Africa, California/USA or the south of Spain. Connected with those draughts are often extrem fires like in the last years in Australia, USA or around the Mediteranean countries Portugal, Spain, France, Italy, Greece and Turkey.

All three factors: floods, draughts and fires spoil cultivated land or endanger cities directly – but additionally they contribute also additionally to push the spiral of the warming up of the globe.

Migration

Due to the climate change and due to wars in quite a number of areas of the world millions of people have become migrants. Their individual budgets but also that of national and international NGOs are extremely stressed. New textiles are ranking low in comparison with food, drinks or shelters to survive.

While in Asia till the end of World War II the colonial occupation covered the area of IndoChina the emancipation of the colonial military forces in the Commonwealth as well as the expansion of communism from China to Cambodia, Laos, Vietnam and Korea caused major shifts within the very diverse tribes of population. India broke down in two steps: first Pakistan was separated, then Bangladesh did split away. But even within the state of India about 48 different ethnic groups are under one roof – very often also in local/regional conflicts with each other.

Similar diversities of ethnical tribes are in Cambodia, Laos, Vietnam and partly in Korea and Thailand.Those countries in this group have been/are still partly involved in the conflict of communism versus the Western style of government. Taken China as one of the major drivers in this geopolitical controversy migration of millions of people towards Taiwan and Hongkong had been within the awareness of the countries in Western Europe a rather normal development and was mainly solved within Asia.

For Western Europe countries like Spain and France have been threats of increasing migrants coming from their former colonial activities in Northern Africa. Their "gates" have been Ceuta/Gibralta or crossing the Mediterana by boat to Greece or Italy. Those spotlights of migration have increased within the last years dramatically by refugees from a lot of African countries which suffer by local/regional wars or by draughts due to the warming up of climate.

Other pressure for migration towards Western Europe comes since about 2015 from the Middle East conflicts in Syria and Iraque – and lately additional from Afganistan after Western troops left the country. It has to be mentioned that the origin of the Brexit for the UK was a conflict about the EU-migration-policy which was too liberal in the British eyes.

The latest push of migration started in spring 2022 by the invasion of the Ukraine by Russian troops. About 10 million people are either within the Ukraine migrating or towards EU countries. Due to destroyed water and energy supplies and urgent need for food and medicine within the Ukraine and Moldovia financial resources in the West are extremely stressed – and demand for new textiles/fashion is rather low.

Covid-19

The break-out of Covid in the end of 2019 was and is still connected for example in China with a close-down of whole cities, regions or even in West European countries. The result are lower incomes for employees and brick-and-stone outlets for example also textile stores. Additionally, consumers working in home-office reduce the number of suites and dresses – and working already with computers at home tend to go shopping by internet. Those companies not being present by own HomeSites are losing market-shares and profits.

With the exception of stores for food countries like Italy, Spain, Austria or Germany ordered stores to lock-down their business for weeks or limited the access for even longer periods for the number of shoppers within the outlets. Customers had to wait in front of the store or had to arrange a specific date with the sales-people. Spontaneous shopping down-town or in shopping centers had not been possible. Being in an affluent society in Western Europewhere shopping is mainly fun but not a necessity for the daily survival and therefore such situation of no frequency of shoppers results in dramatic decreases of sales.

For textile/fashion the situation of not selling the stocks from the shelves is different then for shops of other non-food items as fashion depends on the four seasons spring, summer, autumn and winter. Independant of the sales-situation for example in spring already the stocks have to be ordered and paid for summer. The cash-flow has a sudden gap in such a system. The banks see such gaps and are not always happy to increase in such a situation the volumre for credits or charge higher interest-rates for their higher risk. In the other hand the retailer has to discount his stocks to get the shelves empty for the products of the next season – by this he is reducing his margins which is again seen by the banks as an additional risk.

But the Covid impact did hit the outlets also already by the disruption due to lock-downs in countries of production of textiles for example in Bangladesh, Vietnam or China - and also by problems within the global total supply chain because of lock-downs of harbours like Shanghai or others. For the outlets in Germany or other countries in Western Europe it now happened that the local lock-down had ended – shoppers returned to the textile stores, but the expected new season products did not have arrived: the customer left the shop disappointed, the retailer had no sales and the bank saw an increase of risk again.

In 2022 the situation increased additionally by high energy costs due to the oil and gaz disruptions by the Russian invasion of the Ukraine. Costs for energy increased already often by 100 percent and might increase even more during the winter 2023. This means economically for the textile retailers the loss of sales volume and the decrease of margin additionally is worsened by increasing costs for the daily operations. Last but not least the employees suffering from increasing prices for their daily life ask for higher compensation by higher salaries.

On the other hand, consumers who have learnt by home-office to use daily the internet and who saved time of travelling from their home towards company offices started to order textiles by electronic platforms. The advantage for them is saving time for going down-town, having the convenience to get the textiles delivered free to their homes and to resend them free of costs if they do not fit; and lower prices for the textiles than in the down-town shops as the depots of the textile deliveries are out of town with lower rent and lower saleries for the employed people as in Germany they do not belong to the Union of textile-employees but to the Union of transport which have lower salaries because the qualification of jobs is estimated to be lower than having skills/knowledge for consumer-consulting about the textile products.

Department-stores like KarstadtKaufhofGaleria in Germany or H&M UK announce therefore in November 2022 to consider to close down about 30 percent of their outlets in Germany respectively the UK.

Russian Invasion of Ukraine

The Russian invasion of the Ukraine in February 2022 is causing additional problems not only for the two countries involved directly but on production, distribution and consumption patterns globally.

Due to reduced imports and exports the volume of all participants in the markets is decreasing which are losses in the end for consumption on all levels and categories. Food prices are in the end of 2022 up by 70 percent because the Ukraine and Russia had been the main grain exporters to Western Europe and Africa. Now in summer and autumn 2022 the war resulted of the destruction of the infra-structure in the Ukraine to export its grain – and on the other end the Western Alliance did cut the imports from Russia to cut Russia's buying power for weapons.

The shortage of grain but also oil from sun-flowers is decreasing the global supply for those products which in Western Europe leads to higher consumer prices for food and in poor countries in Asia and Africa to food shortage. Hunger again in Africa leads to more migration to those countries in Western Europe which still have food on their shelves.

Beside the shortage of food due to less corn from Russia and the Ukraine there are tremendous price increases for energy as Russia was a main supplier of gaz and oil for Western Europe. Again, this has impacts for consumers' budgets but also the cost-structure for production and distribution. In Germany in December the department store-chain KarstadtKaufhofGaleria is considering to close at least 30 percent of its 139 outlets – as does also announced by H&M UK for its operations there. Alone at those two big companies several thousand employees will be out of job – having reduced incomes. But also, for textile producers such close downs means that there are thousands of shelves not to be stocked in 2023/2024.

The competition of producers for the remaining retailers in the market will grow as will be the competition of retailers with omni-channel tactics to attract consumers which eagerly due to decreasing income will search for best value for their money.

Each dollar spent by governments for weapons in that war or for restoring destroyed infra-structure is no longer available as input for human consumption. This has short-term effects for today's consumerism but also for the next generations.

Accumulation of Problems

All listed external problems each by each are already heavy burdens on business in the near future. What it makes different to earlier days is its accumulation and complexity of a world which became globally so interconnected in the last 25 years like never before. There are no strategies developed which had forecasted this situation.

Taken Western Europe after World War II it was already a great political deal between the former enemies of the war to create the roots of todays EU in the first step by 6 countries and then in further steps to enlarge it – after the fall of the Berlin Wall and the fall of the former Sowjet Union even by countries of the former COMECON.

The start of Economic Zones in China by the former Chairman Deng and later the Vision of a Revival of the Traditional Silk Road to interconnect Europe and Asia kicked of the dream of a Global House of Harmony based on an optimization of the triangle between Economics, Ecology and Ethics.

This dream of a joined civil society with respect to each other has been broken abruptly by geopolitical power-plays about the Aims to Limit the rise of the World Climate, the growing number of immigrants due to climate change and wars and last but not least the Covid pandemy which is widening the gap between rich and poor people within the single countries but also between rich and poor countries globally.

Lack of Theory

The theoretical models used within the last century were based on the optimization of work-processes (Adam Smith) or the national/international exchange of products

(David Ricardo / Michael Porter). There had been no considerations about the possibilities that a global optimization could be disrupted for geopolitical interests. But now the global freedom of trade with international work-division has crashed. Models for Resilience have yet to be developed.

In the 70ies of the last century there was started a discussion about "The Limits of Growth" – now in the end 2022 we have to revitalize that topic. We realize that already within 6 months per year we are using 100 percent of the really available resources of our globe for each year.

Consumption has to be reduced – food waste has to be reduced – packaging and transportation has to be reduced. Sending textiles free of charge and with no charge for returns – and destroying returned textiles because it is cheaper than to clean them and to store them again is no longer acceptable if a theory and application of such a theory is charging the real price for the production/distribution and also the redistribution/and used resources for both ways.

CONCLUSION ABOUT THE PRESENT SITUATION AND THE FUTURE

Especially for family-businesses the present situation caused by the speed of sector-internal innovations as well as by external macro-effects is a unique challenge.

Speed and Complexity

Compared with the development of innovation cycles in the last 200 years the speed of the evolutionary permanent wheel of retail has turned in the last 25 years into a revolutionary retail-tornado. (Izraeli, 1973; Hallier, 2011).

Overall Lack of Theory

Having an overall lack of theory means also to have a lack of measures for resilience for individual sectors and of course for small and medium-sized businesses – many of them family owned.

Pioneer of Niche-Markets

The traditional family textile trader as a specialist making decisions alone by creating ideas just in his head will no longer be able to innovate and execute all alternative processing in mass-distribution. But if he is speedy enough to adapt quickly in a permanent changing market he will remain a potential pioneer in niche-markets.

Big business needs a broad knowledge of different abilities in management - no longer to be in the hands of single persons (or only in exceptional cases) or run by people with experience in one sector only. Also, family-businesses will have to integrate know-how from external Human Resources which in the end is changing the character of a "family-business".

One of the profiles beside the long-term human commitment of family-members perhaps over generations is also to back the processes of operations by own capital/ risk. Smaller markets or disruptions of markets do not allow to accumulate big sizes of own capital. Disruptions unfortunately decrease capital for the running operations as well as for innovation.

Joint Capital or Share of Outlets

The internal and the external disruptions cause a big need for fresh financial capital. Family business have therefore to check cooperations like by franchise of whole stores or shop-in-the shop depots – sometimes perhaps even for a broader visibility the chance to display products in pop-up shops in a cross-sector environment. Such cross-selling could be either from textile stores to interested groups like in Stuttgart/ Germany Breuninger Textiles with exhibitions of Porsche sportscars as both come from the same area or Soccer Fan Clubs with offers of T-shirts or other textile items for the fans of those specific clubs.

Cooperations could be also on the technical level like a joint IT-platform for more visibility for fashion of a region or a country. Possible are in such a category mono-sector platforms like "Wear of India" or "New Fashion of Pan-Africa" which both had been cases in discussions with staff of the European Retail Academy.

But also, platforms like "Irland" or "Buy Scottish" could bring visibility for cross-sector target groups which perhaps have a faible for everything from Irland or Scotland: Irish butter, Irish whiskey, Irish cakes ...

Retail Knowledge Consortia

Looking beyond the sector of textile-business one can see that companies like AMAZON or ALIBABA but also data-collectors like Google / Microsoft or DHL delivery start to act as partners within Retail Knowledge Consortia (Hallier 2022c). The future success will depend on the way leaders of companies will be able to bridge different company cultures for united ambitions – or they have to limit their activities to the function of Holdings for Shares.

In the retail-theory in Germany there had been in the 60ies/70ies of the last century the main stream to focus retail by dividing between institutional approaches like neighbourhood-store, discounter, supermarket, hypermarket and other outlet-definitions according to the store-size or the number of articles being offered or by the functional approach of being a retailer only selling to the level of individual consumers or being a wholesaler only to deliver to other retailers or to HORECA sector of hotels, reaurants, pubs. That time in Germany was reflecting in research and teaching by the analysis of segmentation and diversification as means of profiling companies by stores as a physical point of differentiation. Store branding was a key-element of retail marketing at that time. It has to be reminded that the exhibition "EuroShop" started in 1966 in Düsseldorf.

Now with the start of the 20ies of the present century the new stress of analysis is put to the functional processes and elements of marketing: a supermarket concept is no longer limited to 800 squaremeters sales area and an assortment of 10.000 items – but if it is the assortment-mix and the appearance by POS-tools like a supermarket it can have also for example 2500 squaremeters and 25.000 items plus service counters.

Insofar the range of "retailers" as well as the physical outlets have changed in size, assortment and targeting; traditional definitions are becoming just history- they are no longer relevant for modern applied sciences.

Knowledge and Skills are the future elements in functional retail; sharing cross-sector knowledge is decreasing costs for alternative own development of innovative tools or data-panels and within the Darwinism of retail it is quicker to conquer new markets.

Shift and Split of Profits

And finally, it has to be realized that the traditional split of profit along the Total Supply Chain will switch from production and trade towards companies with data-competences /digital marketing experiences – even like game-developers. This could mean that for example no longer a range of textiles is produced targeting own consumer-groups but delivering textiles ordered by other companies some of the own sector or others from cross-sectors.

The main point is to check permanently the total supply chain for cheaper processes than own operations or to share the discovery of new markets for better profits with partners to speed up relevant market shares which could be not caught by own force.

Urban Future

On local, regional, and national level within City Marketing Concepts department- or textile stores are anchors for urban lifestyle. The closure of such players can cause problems for a whole cluster of other stores or restaurants/pubs being linked/ dependant on the high frequency at the anchor business. A collapse of the key-player can endanger the wealth of such areas. The domino effect are less customers for the suppliers, less jobs for employees – but also less income for the house-owners or shopping center-owners.

City Marketing for down-town activities started by URBANICOM as a cooperation between urban institutions and commerce as a counter measure against shopping centers outside of the cities when mobility of consumers started by the explosion of the number of private cars in the 60ies in West Europe.

Interestingly in November 2022 at BBC tv world-program two advertisements could be watched: one about the city of Istanbul as a target for shopping in a mix of traditional Souks and shops down-town; at another advertisement spot from Dubai showed one of the world's biggest modern shopping-centers.

The learning from those examples from Western Europe and the Middle East is that the understanding about what can be expected about concepts of future cities does differ extremely from country to country. Textile fashion is not automatically like 100 years ago Urban LifeStyle promoted in London or Paris – but the main future stream of fashion might be created and influenced by fashion designers from Africa or India who are potentially able to communicate their concepts via new media in times of reliance from the present problems.

Rich and Poor Countries

In macro-economic terms it will create big problems for developing countries if they do not have the skills or digital connections to participate with a fair share in the value-chain but if they remain just in the competition of offering the cheapest labour internationally (Hallier 2022d; Hallier 2022e).

The task for international political and other leaders of the Global Community would be to keep the markets in the rich countries open for exports from the poorer countries and to support the developing countries with the technical infra-structure for digital communication and sales – and last but not least by guarantees for capital for necessary innovations.

REFERENCES

Bauer, H. J., & Hallier, B. (1999). *Kultur und Geschichte des Handels* [*Culture and history of trade.*]. EHI-EuroHandelsinst.

Birchall, J. (1997). *The international co-operative movement.* Manchester University Press.

EHI. (1994). Scannersysteme – Neue Impulse für Organisation und Marketing. [Scanner systems – New impulses for organization and marketing.] Köln.

EHI. (1999). Factory Outlet Center.

Fashion TodayKW 27/2022

Hahn, H. W. (1984). *Geschichte des Deutschen Zollvereins: Kleine Vandenhoeck-Reihe*.

Hallier, B. (1987). Sich ins Regal hineinrechnen. [Count yourself on the shelf.]. *Absatzwirtschaft*, *10*, 87.

Hallier, B. (1995). Der Handel auf dem Weg zur Marketingführerschaft. [Retail on the way to marketing leadership.] *Absatzwirtschaft, A*.

Hallier, B. (1999b). EHI – Factory Outlet Center.

Hallier, B. (1999d). Wird ECR zum Club der Grossen? [Will ECR become a club of the big ones?] In: von der Heydt (ed.) *A: Handbuch Efficient Consume Response–Konzepte, Erfahrungen, Herasuforderungen, S*, 55-61.

Hallier, B. (2002). *Sammler, Stifter und Mäzene des Handels* [*Collector, benefactor and patron of the trade*.]. EHI.

Hallier, B. (2011a). *Von der Krise zur Kompetenz. [From crisis to competence*.]

Hallier, B. (2011b). Smart Phones and QR-Codes. In: Pantano, E. & Timmermans, H. (eds.), Advanced Technology Management for Retailing: Frame works and Cases. IGI Global.

Hallier, B. (2011c). The Evolution Tornado Retail. In Advanced Technologies Management for Retailing: Frameworks and Cases (pp. 26-40). IGI Global. doi:10.4018/978-1-60960-738-8.ch002

Hallier, B. (2022a). 50 Years Perspective.

Hallier, B. (2022b). Promoting Life-Style.

Hallier, B. (2022c). Empowered Logistics.

Hallier, B. (2022d). Darwinism in the Textile Sector.

Hallier, B. (2022e). Accelleration by Disruption.

Hauptmann, G. (1943). *Die Weber* [[*The weavers]*]. Vol. 2). Suhrkamp.

Heidel, B. (2013). *Scannerdaten im Einzelhandelsmarketing* (Vol. 68). Springer-Verlag. [*Scanner data in retail marketing* (Vol. 68).]

Izraeli, D. (1973). The three wheels of retailing: A theoretical note. *European Journal of Marketing*, *7*(1), 70–74. doi:10.1108/EUM0000000005101

Kondratieff, N. D. (1926). Die langen wellen der konjunktur. [The long waves of the economy.]. *Archiv für Sozialwissenschaft und Sozialpolitik*, *56*(3), 573–609.

Mode ohne schlechtes Gewissen [Fashion without a guilty conscience]. (2022, August 12). Kölner Stadt-Anzeiger.

Pantano, E., & Timmermans, H. J. (2011). *Advanced technologies management for retailing: frameworks and cases*. Business Science Reference. doi:10.4018/978-1-60960-738-8

Schumpeter, J. A. (1961). Konjunkturzyklen. *Eine theoretische, historische und statistische Analyse des kapitalistischen.* Prozesses Bd. I.

Zola, E. (2004). *Paradies der Damen* [*[Ladies' paradise*]].

Chapter 9
Cognitive Biases Affecting Business Transmission Planning in Family Firms:
A Theoretical Framework Exploring the Impact of Biases During Family Firm Succession

Filippo Ferrari
Department of Management, Bologna University, Italy

ABSTRACT

The business succession is the most critical event in the life of a family business, and represents a challenging scenario for the decisions that must be made. It therefore becomes a strategic objective to avoid factors that can negatively influence the assessment of the situation by the actors involved. This chapter explores the cognitive mechanisms (biases) that influence the decision-making process at the basis of the business transmission. Although already known and empirically supported in many fields of business and management, these cognitive factors have systematically been overlooked by previous family business literature. By exploring how these biases play a role in affecting business succession planning, and by putting emphasis on the human nature of the decision process of the incumbent, this study adds new insights to recent succession literature that highlights the central role of the cognitive processes during family firm succession.

DOI: 10.4018/978-1-6684-7394-8.ch009

INTRODUCTION

The field of organizational studies offers extensive research on family firms, defined by Chua, Chrisman, Sharma (1999, 35) as "organizations for economic purposes owned and / or managed [...] by a coalition of members of the same family or a few families, in such a way as to be potentially sustainable across generations." According to this definition, a noteworthy feature is that such firms have also non-economic goals (Astrachan, Jaskiewicz, 2008; Berrone et al., 2012; Chua, Chrisman, & Sharma, 1999; Zellweger & Astrachan, 2008), and by definition (Chua et al., 1999), one of the most important non-economic goals is corporate sustainability across generations. Business succession is a process, not an event (Chittoor & Das, 2007; Gimenez & Novo, 2020; Porfirio et al., 2020). It goes through several distinct phases including initiation, integration, joint reign, then withdrawal (Cadieux, 2007; Le Breton-Miller, Miller, & Steier, 2004). This long-term scenario requires the family business to adapt to the surrounding complex environment, and the outcome is often negative. In fact, family businesses show a long-term survival problem: about 40% make a positive transition to the second generation and only 12% to the third (Bridge et al., 2003).

In management and complex adaptive systems literature, *exploration* refers to the search for new, useful adaptations, and *exploitation* refers to the use and propagation of known adaptations (March 1991; Mitchell 1996). Hence, exploration seems to ensure more adaptive capabilities for organizations, from a long-term perspective. However, 'lazy organizations' often utilized exploitation due to immediate and certain return (Denrell and March, 2001), but could experience future failures and economic losses. Furthermore, sometimes exploitation could also become an 'invisible trap' for these organizations: in fact, it's possible that the current situation could be appraised as profitable and overall as excellent by organizations, in terms of effectiveness and efficiency, but at the same time neglecting reliability in the long term. As cited by Fang et al. (2010, 626), Holland (1992, p. 69) generalized such a dilemma as follows: "Deciding to what degree the present should be mortgaged for the future is a classic problem for all systems that adapt and learn."

Indeed, business transmission process should be future oriented, and pursuing organizational reliability in the long term. The strategic choices made at a given moment have an impact on subsequent periods. In a turbulent and unpredictable era, full of unexpected socio-economic phenomena, the ability to plan business transmission properly becomes a fundamental asset for business continuity. Both *exploitation* and *exploration* are primarily cognitive processes, and as such they must be investigated. In the business transmission it is necessary to enhance what is already available (exploitation) and to find new organizational structures (exploration). But the available literature highlights that both of these processes are prone to biases (Picone et al., 2021).

While literature suggests the intention itself to hand over the firm to the next generation has potential positive effects (De Massis et al., 2016), it exposes the company to the risk of an eluded, demanded or even traumatic succession and related negative consequences for business continuity (Ferrari 2021; 2021a; Piantoni, 1990; Wilson, 2015). Much has been written about the factors influencing both the intention (De Massis et al., 2016) and the implementation of the succession process (De Massis et al., 2008; Sharma, Chrisman, & Chua, 2003; Sharma et al., 2001; Venter et al., 2005). However, to date little attention has been given to investigating the reasons *why* intra-family succession might not take place when there is an intention to do so and a potential successor is available (De Massis, 2008). A promising stream of research is arising from a socio-cognitive approach investigating biases and shortcuts affecting decision-making processes within family firms (De Massis, Foss, 2018; Picone et al., 2021). Although already known and empirically supported in many fields of business and management, these cognitive factors have systematically been overlooked by previous family business literature. Therefore, the purpose of this chapter is to explore if and how biases play a role in affecting business succession planning. In doing so, and by putting emphasis on the human nature of the decision process of the incumbent, this study adds new insights to recent succession literature that highlights the central role of the cognitive processes during family firm succession (Cadieux, 2007; Ahrens, 2019; Ahrens *et al.*, 2018b; Picone et al., 2021).

THEORETICAL FRAMEWORK

Interest in family businesses has steadily grown over the past two decades, as evidenced by the growing number of articles published in the most impactful journals (Kotlar et al., 2018; Neckebrouck et al., 2018). The business succession is probably the most investigated issue in the family business field of research. But, although broad and articulated, this body of knowledge still shows limitations. For example, the situation in which the succession is accepted by the incumbent, the successor is already present and active in the firm and available to run the business but the succession is not formally planned, is still under investigated. Empirical evidence often shows a lack of consistency between the intention to pass the company on to the next generation, despite the desirability of the succession, the social norms supporting the succession, the perceived feasibility of the succession itself (Ferrari, 2021; Sharma, Chrisman and Chua, 2003; Wilson, 2015). In these situations, family firms seem to face difficulties in the process of transforming intention/attitude into action, thus undermining its reliability. The attention for intergenerational transmission of family businesses has been highlighted by different approaches:

Socio Emotional Wealth (SEW) (e.g. Astrachan, Jaskiewicz, 2008; Berrone et al., 2012; Chua, Chrisman, & Sharma, 1999; Zellweger & Astrachan, 2008 and others); *Theory of Planned behaviour* - TPB (Carr & Sequeira, 2007; Ferrari, 2021; Sharma et al., 2003; Wilson 2015); *Transgenerational intent* – TI (Chua et al., 1999; Wright & Kellermanns, 2011; Williams et al., 2013), incumbents' attitude toward *intrafamily succession* (IFS) (De Massis et al., 2016). Until now, none of these approaches have yet been able to definitively explain why small family businesses are so resistant to really planning the business transmission, even in a very favourable, clear and shared situation. Paradoxically, the ability to plan for the future becomes even more important in an unpredictable situation. High Reliability Organizations approach (HROs: Weick, Sutcliffe, 2005; Weick et al., 1999) has shown empirically that owning a strategy is a success factor in itself, because it provides guidance in conditions of uncertainty, reducing consumption of organizational and cognitive resources to cope with uncertainty (Weick, Sutcliffe, 2005). Given this theoretical scenario and its limitations, this chapter aims to present and discuss cognitive factors affecting the business succession attitude, thus explaining why often the business succession is not properly planned but postponed or even eluded.

COGNITIVE FACTORS AFFECTING BUSINESS TRANSMISSION PLANNING

Scholars' knowledge about individual-level determinants of the incumbent's intention for intrafamily succession (De Massis et al., 2016), and more generally, the succession process and its performance outcomes (Le Breton-Miller et al.,, 2004) are still limited by researchers' difficulty to theoretically and empirically locate the proximate causes of such aspects at the micro-level of analysis. Recently, a promising approach is constituted by microfoundations (e.g. De Massis, Foss 2018), which aims to explain the mechanisms underlying decisions in an organizational context. this approach aims to identify at the micro level the factors that contribute to explaining a phenomenon. For instance, how psychological attributes and biases affect strategic choices and firm performance, an aspect that has been rather neglected in prior family business research (Nicholson, 2008). As advocated by recent literature, there are still several questions about the microfoundations of succession to be investigated. The area literature has identified two types of biases. According to available literature (Benson 2016), cognitive biases affecting attitude toward business succession planning could be active in two domains, a) attitude to risk and probability and b) taking action.

The first set of biases can affect if and how the incumbent makes the decision of act business succession in the presence of uncertainty and risk or with probabilistic outcomes. Undoubtedly, business succession is a process full of risks, of highly uncertain outcome, and positive in a limited number of cases. It is therefore highly probable that in this situation cognitive biases relating to the estimation of risk and consequences are activated, as actor-observer bias, illusion of control, optimism bias, confirmation bias, and availability bias especially. Given this theoretical foundation, it's possible to set up the first theoretical proposition:

P1: in a family firm facing business transmission, the assessment of the situation, the risk orientation and the perceived probability of success are influenced by cognitive biases.

Regarding the second set of biases, once information is available and has been evaluated sufficiently to allow action to be taken, other cognitive biases may have an effect on the actions incumbent takes, perhaps delaying or prolonging the action of planning. The above cited approaches (SEW, TPB, TI) highlight a weakness in the transition from intention to action. It is therefore likely that other biases are active at this stage affecting the actual implementation of business succession planning (confirmation bias, choice-supportive bias, endowment effect, and escalation of commitment bias especially). Basically, incumbents do not revise their beliefs sufficiently when presented with new evidence because of conservatism bias (Azzopardi, 2010).

Given this theoretical foundation, it's possible to set up the second theoretical proposition:

P2: in a family firm facing business transmission, taking action and decision-making are influenced by cognitive biases.

a) Biases affecting social judgment, **a**ttitude to risk and probability emerging from literature review

Naive realism, in social psychology, is the human tendency to believe that we see the world around us objectively and that people who disagree with us must be uninformed, irrational, or prejudiced (Ross, & Ward, 1996). Naive realism provides a theoretical basis for many other cognitive biases, which are systematic errors when it comes to thinking and making decisions.

Actor-Observer Bias In essence, individuals make different attributions when they view themselves as actors or observers of a situation. Also, people tend to separate themselves from things that have negative outcomes. Consequently, individuals are better judges when they observe, interpret and evaluate a situation involving other people; on the contrary, they demonstrate subjectivity of judgment and indulgence when they have to explain the same situation involving themselves. In the case of business succession, this bias leads to more easily identifying the criticalities in the situations of others (inadequate CV, next generation unfitting the entrepreneurial role etc.), and to underestimate the criticalities in one's own.

Fundamental Attribution Error The fundamental attribution error refers to the tendency of a person observing another person's behaviour to attribute it to internal factors or personality and to underestimate the effect of situational causes (i.e., external influences) (Jones & Nisbett, 1971; van der Pligt & Eiser 1983). In other words, individuals believe that others do what they do because of their internal disposition. Sherman (2014): the bankruptcy of other companies is due to internal causes (CV of the next generation, wrong strategic choices), it does not happen to them because they are different 'This bias can lead to postpone business transmission as it leads to the belief that other family businesses fail due to their inability to plan succession, while at the same time living their situation with fatalism. In the perception of entrepreneurs "the other entrepreneurs fail in underestimating the problem, and postponing the business succession, but with us the situation is not yet ready for the succession '.

Availability Bias. It is a mental shortcut that relies on immediate examples that come to a particular person's mind when evaluating a specific topic, concept, method or decision. The availability heuristic assumes that if something can be easily recalled it must be important, or at least more important than alternative solutions that are not so readily recallable (Esgate & Groome, 2005). This refers to the overestimation of risks that are easily available in memory. How easily things come to mind is a heuristic that makes people overestimate the importance of certain kinds of information. If something is difficult to remember, one will assume that it is less likely to occur. For instance, when asked to give examples of next generation successes and failures, respondents report recent, mostly positive, episodes, neglecting past negative episodes occurred to other family businesses.

False Consensus Effect People have a tendency to overestimate the extent to which other people share their attitudes, behaviours, beliefs, preferences and opinions. Individuals tend to think that others think the same way they do (Ross et al., 1977). For example, entrepreneurs argue that "most other entrepreneurs do like us, they DON'T plan (or: plan)", or "if you ask any entrepreneur, it makes no sense to hire a non-family member for a managerial position, it would be a waste if the next generation is willing to join'. In other words, some people assume that everyone else thinks like them. This alleged agreement is statistically unfounded and leads to the perception of a consensus that does not exist. This logical fallacy causes a group or individual to believe that their opinions, beliefs and preferences are generally more prevalent in a population than they really are. The consequences are a bias that influences decision making, leading the decision maker to comply with a false majority.

Blind Spot Bias. A consequence of naive realism is termed "blind spot bias," which is the ability to recognize cognitive and motivational biases in others while failing to recognize the impact of biases on the self (Pronin et al., 2002). People tend to have a bias blind spot, meaning that they are more likely to rate themselves as being less susceptible to biases (this includes cognitive biases) than others. We are also more able to detect biases in others than in ourselves. (Reo, 2015). As already explained above, there is a perception that other companies have underestimated the risks of the business transmission by postponing planning, while for the entrepreneur in his/her specific situation it is not yet time for succession; or again, "the others brought their children into [the company] on the basis of belonging, they did not have an adequate CV; while our children (especially the daughters) are committed and they like what they do, so they will have no problem growing as entrepreneurs.

Optimism Bias This refers to the tendency to be overly optimistic about favourable outcomes. Neuroscience and social sciences agree that the human being is more optimistic than realistic, despite the fact that people like to think that they are rational creatures capable of making correct predictions based on objective assessments. This tendency to perceive the bright future, even comparing it to the past and the present, is known as optimism bias (Sharot, 2011; Sharot et al., 2007). In other words, the human mind gets by imagining a difficult future for the community but not for themselves. People do not believe that bad things will happen to them (Evatt, 2010). When the catastrophic statistics on the failure rate in business succession are shared during the interview, the entrepreneur's answer is "why should this happen to us?"

Golden age bias. By this term we mean the belief that things once "were better". This cognitive phenomenon is also known as 'rosy retrospection' (Mitchell, Thompson, 1994). This is a kind of mythology that accompanies the history of almost every people, and the belief that things used to be better has been investigated by the cognitive sciences (Pinker, 2011). Rosy retrospection is also related to the concept of declinism, such as people saying "things were better in the old days" or "back in my day...". Declinism is particularly the predisposition, caused by cognitive biases such as rosy retrospection, to view the past more favourably and the future more negatively. According with this bias, a common perception among entrepreneurs could be that 'once it was easier to do business, fewer rules, fewer taxes, the market was protected, less competition'. The perception of a past golden age could lead the incumbent entrepreneur to postpone business transmission, in order to protect the new generation.

b) Biases affecting taking action emerging from literature review

Choice-Supportive Bias

It's the tendency to remember one's choices as better than they actually were. In this respect, people tend to over attribute positive features to options they chose and negative features to options not chosen (Mather, Johnson, 2000) . Choice-supportive bias is therefore the tendency for people making a decision to remember their choice as being better than it actually was simply because they made it (Lind et al., 2017). Basically, we overrate options we selected and underrate options that were rejected (Henkel, Mather, 2007). This bias could lead the entrepreneurial family to overestimate the goodness of the decisions made, even though they turned out to be clearly wrong.

Confirmation Bias

Once people form an opinion they "embrace information that confirms that view while ignoring, or rejecting, information that casts doubt on it … Thus, we may become prisoners of our assumptions" (Heshmat, 2015). People tend to favour a prior view even when presented with new information or evidence, i.e., there is a tendency to stick to old information and a reluctance to accept something new. People do not revise their beliefs sufficiently when presented with new evidence because of conservatism bias. Conservatism bias is related to status quo bias (Azzopardi (2010). This type of bas could lead an entrepreneur to persevere in a decision made, systematically ignoring any additional information that might emerge. According to this bias, once the entrepreneur has developed a negative evaluation of the qualities of the successor, he does not change his mind, despite any successes shown by the next generation.

Endowment Effect

It consists in the tendency of people to assign greater value to what they already have, compared to what they do not have. This is a very common cognitive error, amply demonstrated by scholars through experiments conducted with groups of people (Morewedge & Giblin, 2015). According to cognitive psychologists (Kahneman, Knetsch, & Thaler, 1991) this error stems from our innate aversion to loss: having to part with something we own (no matter if bought with our money or given as a gift) is painful in its own way, and therefore we demand a reward greater than the value of the asset. which would be attributed in other circumstances. In business transmission, this bias could lead to refusal of offers from third parties interested in taking over the company, even when the next generation is not willing to continue the business, or does not have the skills. This bias could generate perseverance in the wrong choices related to business transmission or, more generally, to strategic choices related to business continuity.

Escalation of Commitment Bias

Also known as sunk cost fallacy, it's the tendency for an individual or a group to stick with a failing decision or action rather than accepting that a mistake was made and alter course (Staw, 1007). This cognitive bias leads a person to evaluate in a non-rational but emotional way their choices, actions, situations, based on the investments and costs previously incurred, and now no longer recoverable, for something. The sunk cost represents an investment that can no longer be recovered, be it money, time, mental, physical or emotional commitment.

There is a reluctance to admit that the original decision was wrong even when there is clear evidence that this is the case. This bias could lead the owner family to continue investing in the human capital of the next generation, even when this is refractory to any development in performance (Woods, Dalziel, & Barton, 2012).

Ikea Effect

There is a tendency for people to overvalue and overrate objects they made or assembled by themselves such as IKEA furniture, regardless of the actual quality of the finished product (Landers, 2012). However, this effect seems to only exist when the labour resulted in the successful completion of the project. If subjects did not complete the task, the IKEA effect disappeared (Norton, Mochon, & Ariely, 2012).

According to this bias, in a first generation family business, the founder built the business, and this can generate an extreme reluctance to hand it over to the next generation.

Illusion of Control

It is a bias first defined by Langer (1975) and is characterized by an increased confidence in one's chances of success (overconfidence). People tend to overestimate how much control they have over external factors such as prices, costs, demand, and the stock market. In some cases, people actually believe that they can control the outcome of something that is totally random such as the toss of dice (Presson & Benassi, 1996). This bias can induce in the incumbent the false perception of having everything under control, even in the future.

Starting from this theoretical propositions, it's possible to highlight several common themes related to attitude and take in action biases, as discussed in the following section.

DISCUSSION

Family business literature shows an inconsistency between attitude and implemented behaviour (Sharma et al., 2003). Furthermore, contrary to what was claimed by other approaches (SEW, TPB, TI), empirical research highlights that the business succession does not actually take place, despite the genuine desire of incumbents to maintain the business control within the family. Sharma et al. (2003) had noticed that planning takes place (if and when it happens) due to the availability of a willing and trusted successor rather than due to the willingness of the seniors to leave, but they had not been able to explain why. Often, business transfer does not happen even when the second generation is willing. Therefore, other factors (cognitive rather than motivational) intervene to moderate the relationship between intention and behaviour.

By adopting a cognitive framework in exploring family business dynamics, this study suggests that cognitive factors can play a role in business succession planning attitudes (Picone et al., 2021). These factors affect the decision-making process related to business succession planning, shifting the evaluation to an optimistic stance. Although literature (Bentgsson, Ekeblon, 2014) documents that entrepreneurial optimism may not be a behavioural bias that gives rise to irrational decision-making, this does not seem to be the case with business succession. In family firms, a bias in the assessment of the situation can to be confirmed: the decision-makers are aware of the criticalities in business succession in general, but are optimistic about their specific case. This framework hence suggests that in business succession, many biases could play an important role.

In summary, this theoretical framework support both Propositions (*P1: in a family firm facing business transmission, the assessment of the situation, the risk orientation and the perceived probability of success are influenced by cognitive biases; P2: in a family firm facing business transmission, taking action and decision-making are influenced by cognitive biases*) and suggests that business succession planning can be a process affected by cognitive factors and prone to biases. These biases often lead decision-makers to a fatalistic assessment of their situation (Kanheman et al., 1991; Pohl, 2017; Rotter, 1990).. As a result, business transmission attitude often results in a postponed succession planning, thus exposing family firms to the risk of an eluded or even traumatic succession. For example, gender stereotypes shared among all the involved people result in the unavailability of the daughters for the succession of the business, even by self-exclusion (Overbecke et al., 2013).

IMPLICATION FOR PRACTICE: HOW TO MANAGE COGNITIVE BIASES

Unlike traditional approaches that have investigated at the macro level the factors that influence strategic decisions in family firms, this chapter offers the tools to intervene at the micro level. The detailed description of the possible practical uses of the tools to manage or even cancel the distortions of judgment due to biases would go beyond the scope of this paper. Here, however, we want to provide some examples related to how to tackle cognitive biases during the business succession process.

It is possible to design and deliver specific training to help understand how to manage the specific biases affecting that specific company. An approach based on microfoundations necessarily has an extreme level of customization. The consequence is that it is not possible for a family business engaged in a successful business to acquire generic knowledge. The known biases can be at the base of the construction of appropriate check-lists for the consultant's use (the so called 'de-biasing list'). Furthermore, there has been evidence for many years of the effectiveness of quasi-experimental situations focused on specific biases to increase the effectiveness of training sessions (Bazerman, Moore, 2012). The management literature also suggests numerous strategies for countering cognitive biases (e.g. Klynn, 2021; Soll et al., 2015).

While cognitive biases can be unconscious, there are a number of things people can do to reduce their likelihood. During a business succession process, the decision makers are usually the incumbents, so they are the main target of training and advice. 1. *Be aware*. The first tip to overcome cognitive biases related to business succession is to acknowledge that they exist. When incumbents and their heirs know there are factors that can alter the way they see business succession, they're more likely to be careful as they form judgments or make decisions. 2. *Consider current factors that may be influencing your decision*. Is there anything in the firm's specific current situation that could lead a business family to feel overconfident in their convictions? Or cause them to ignore certain information? For instance, incumbents make sure not to fall victim to the 'bandwagon effect', or adopt attitudes simply because others incumbents are. 3. *Reflect on the past*. Look for patterns in how they've perceived prior situations and where they might have made mistakes. If, for example, incumbents see that they tend to ignore facts or overemphasize intuition. Then lean into opportunities to further explore data presented to you. 4. *Be curious*. Being curious can help incumbents avoid cognitive biases. Curiosity can help them pause long enough to ask questions to a consultant. It stops them from assuming they're right. 5. *Strive for a growth mindset*. People with growth mindsets believe that cognitive ability can be developed and tend to learn from criticism. Rather than covering up mistakes, they see them as an opportunity to learn. They don't believe that factors are "fixed" or unchangeable. Cognitive bias modification is possible with some work and effort. A growth mindset is one of many heuristics that can help move incumbents in the right direction. 6. *Identify what makes you uncomfortable.* Are there people or situations that rub incumbent the wrong way? Trainers and consultants should help incumbents ask themselves what makes them respond this way and whether they could have a bias that's impacting their perspective. 7. *Embrace the opposite.* Trying to understand an issue from both sides can make the incumbent a stronger critical thinker and help them see the world with more empathy. Trainers and consultants should help incumbents push themselves to believe the opposite of their initial reaction and pay attention to what happens. 8. *Seek multiple perspectives.* Trainers and consultants should provide feedback and perspectives to incumbents. Asking others for their input can help incumbents find potential blind spots and stop them from being overconfident. 9. *Look for disconfirming evidence.* Incumbents should be stimulated to go out of their way to seek out information that runs counter to their existing belief. 10. *Practice intellectual humility.* Intellectual humility is about remaining open to the idea that you might be wrong. Rather than blindly standing by their convictions, incumbents should ask to themselves, "what am I missing here?"

MAIN CONTRIBUTIONS

The theoretical development of this chapter offers new points of view to extend and integrate what is suggested by family business literature. For instance, De Massis & Foss (2018) see the need for future research on the psychological foundations of management in family businesses. According to these authors, this chapter explore how the characteristics of real judgment and decision-making processes within such companies (De Bondt & Thaler, 1995) challenge current predictions on the behaviour of family businesses, based on relevant psychological research (Pastorino & Doyle- Portillo, 2013).

The propositions here developed suggest investigating at a deeper level the relationship between non-economic objectives and decision-making processes. The biases and heuristics that afflict the decision maker (the incumbent especially) provide an important lens for interpreting and explaining the mistakes made in planning and carrying out the business transmission.

As suggested by Picone et al., (2021), psychological research can allow scholars of family businesses to broaden and enrich the current predictions on the behaviour of family businesses (Gagné et al., 2014) and therefore on their heterogeneity compared to others. businesses and between family businesses.

CONCLUSION

Business continuity is, without doubt, one of the most challenging non-economic goals for a family business (Berrone et al., 2010; 2012; Chua et al., 2009; Ferrari, 2020; 2021; Gomez-Mejia et al., 2007). In addition to objective motivations related to the available actors and socio-economic conditions (De Massis et al., 2008; De Massis et al. 2016), up to now the literature has investigated the cognitive factors preventing business transmission. There is therefore a clear need to empirically investigate whether and under what conditions the biases described in this study are activated, and to what extent they play a role in preventing business succession.

The current socio-economic scenario, unpredictable and complex, does not allow entrepreneurs to make decisions by relying only on common sense and experience, but requires the use of a scientifically based approach. The socio-cognitive literature has amply demonstrated that decision-makers are prone to biases, especially when they decide on particularly salient issues from a psychological and emotional point of view. This is the case with the business transmission in family businesses.

REFERENCES

Ahrens, J.-P., Calabrò, A., Huybrechts, J., & Woywode, M. (2019). The Enigma of the Family Successor–Firm Performance Relationship: A Methodological Reflection and Reconciliation Attempt. *Entrepreneurship Theory and Practice*, *43*(3), 437–474. doi:10.1177/1042258718816290

Ahrens, J. P., Uhlaner, L., Woywode, M., & Zybura, J. (2018). „Shadow Emperor" or "loyal Paladin"? The Janus Face of Previous Owner Involvement in Family Firm Successions. *Journal Of Family Business Strategy*, *9*(1), 73–90. doi:10.1016/j.jfbs.2017.11.003

Astrachan, J. H., & Jaskiewicz, P. (2008). Emotional returns and emotional costs in privately held family businesses: Advancing traditional business valuation. *Family Business Review*, *21*(2), 139–149. doi:10.1111/j.1741-6248.2008.00115.x

Bazerman, M. H., & Moore, D. A. (2012). *Judgment in Managerial Decision Making*. John Wiley & Sons.

Berrone, P., Cruz, C. L., & Gómez-Mejía, R. (2012). Socioemotional wealth in family firms theoretical dimensions, assessment approaches, and agenda for future research. *Family Business Review*, *25*(3), 258–279. doi:10.1177/0894486511435355

Bridge, S., O'Neill, K., & Cromie, S. (2003). *Understanding Enterprise, Entrepreneurship and Small Business* (2nd ed.). Palgrave Macmillan, Basingstoke.

Cadieux, L. (2007). Succession in Small and Medium-Sized Family Businesses: Toward a Typology of Predecessor Roles During and After Instatement of the Successor. *Family Business Review*, *20*(2), 95–109. doi:10.1111/j.1741-6248.2007.00089.x

Carr, J. C., & Sequeira, J. M. (2007). Prior Family Business Exposure as Intergenerational Influence and Entrepreneurial Intent: A Theory of Planned Behavior Approach. *Journal of Business Research*, *60*(10), 1090–1098. doi:10.1016/j.jbusres.2006.12.016

Chittoor, R., & Das, R. (2007). Professionalization of Management and Succession Performance—A Vital Linkage. *Family Business Review*, *20*(1), 65–79. doi:10.1111/j.1741-6248.2007.00084.x

Chua, J. H., Chrisman, J. J., & Bergiel, E. B. (2009). An agency theoretic analysis of the professionalized family firm. *Entrepreneurship Theory and Practice*, *33*(2), 355–372. doi:10.1111/j.1540-6520.2009.00294.x

Chua, J. H., Chrisman, J. J., & Sharma, P. (1999). Defining the family business by behavior. *Entrepreneurship Theory and Practice*, *23*(4), 19–39. doi:10.1177/104225879902300402

De Massis, A., Chua, J., & Chrisman, J. J. (2008). Factors Preventing Intra-Family Succession. *Family Business Review*, *21*(2), 183–199. doi:10.1111/j.1741-6248.2008.00118.x

De Massis, A., Sieger, P., Chua, J. H., & Vismara, S. (2016). 'Incumbents' Attitudes towards Intrafamily Succession: An Investigation of its Antecedents,'. *Family Business Review*, *29*(3), 278–300. doi:10.1177/0894486516656276

Denrell, J., & March, J. G. (2001). Adaptation as information restriction: The hot stove effect. *Organization Science*, *12*(5), 523–538. doi:10.1287/orsc.12.5.523.10092

Esgate, A., & Groome, D. (2005). *An Introduction to Applied Cognitive Psychology*. Psychology Press.

Evatt, C. (2010). *Brain biases*. Brain Shortcuts. http://brainshortcuts.blogspot.com/2010/11/optimism-bias.html

Fang, C., Lee, J., & Schilling, M. A. (2009). Balancing Exploration and Exploitation Through Structural Design: The Isolation of Subgroups and Organizational Learning. *Organization Science*, *21*(3), 625–642. doi:10.1287/orsc.1090.0468

Ferrari, F. (2017). 'The tragedy of having a daughter. Construction and reproduction of gender stereotypes in Italian family SMEs', *Reti. Italian Juournal of Cognitive Sciences*, *01*, 133–151.

Ferrari, F. (2019). In the mother's shadow: Exploring power dynamics in family business succession. *Gender in Management*, *34*(22), 121–139. doi:10.1108/GM-07-2017-0091

Ferrari, F. (2019a), The Daughters' Career in Family Firms: A Reflection on the Cultural/Contextual Aspects, Pereira E.T. and Paoloni P.(Eds), Global Perspectives on Women in Management and the Labor Markets, IGI Global Publishing.

Ferrari, F. (2019b), Investigating Inner Dynamics in Family Firms. A Multilevel Model of Analysis, Camisón C. and González T. (eds), Competitiveness, Organizational Management, and Governance in Family Firms, IGI Global Publishing.

Ferrari, F. (2020). Exploring the side effects of Socio-Emotional Wealth. A multilevel analysis approach to the dysfunctional dynamics in family business succession. International Journal of Entrepreneurship and Small Business, 40(1), 128-146. doi:10.1504/IJESB.2020.106943

Ferrari F. (2021). The postponed succession: an investigation of the obstacles hindering business transmission planning in family firms. *Journal of Family Business Management*. doi:10.1108/JFBM-09-2020-0088

Ferrari, F. (2021a). The Eluded Succession: Readiness to Change and Resistance to Retirement among Elderly Family Business Founders and Owners. *Change Management: An International Journal*, *21*(2), 1–19. doi:10.18848/2327-798X/CGP/v21i02/1-19

Giménez, E., & Novo, J. A. (2020). A Theory of Succession in Family Firms. *Journal of Family and Economic Issues*, *41*(1), 96–120. doi:10.100710834-019-09646-y

Gomez-Mejia, L. R., Haynes, K. T., Nunez-Nickel, M., Jacobson, K. J. L., & Moyano-Fuentes, J. (2007). Socioemotional wealth and business risks in family-controlled firms: Evidence from Spanish olive oil mills. *Administrative Science Quarterly*, *52*(1), 106–137. doi:10.2189/asqu.52.1.106

Henkel, L. A., & Mather, M. (2007). Memory attributions for choices: How beliefs shape our memories. *Journal of Memory and Language*, *57*(2), 163–176. doi:10.1016/j.jml.2006.08.012

Holland, J. (1992). Genetic algorithms. *Scientific American*, *267*(1), 66–72. doi:1 0.1038cientificamerican0792-66

Johnson, J., & Powell, P. (1994). Decision making, risk and gender: Are managers different? *British Journal of Management*, *5*(2), 123–138. doi:10.1111/j.1467-8551.1994.tb00073.x

Jones, E., & Nisbett, R. (1971). *The actor and the observer: Divergent perceptions of the causes of behavior*. General Learning Press.

Kahneman, D., Knetsch, J., & Thaler, R. (1991). Anomalies: The Endowment Effect, Aversion, and Status Quo Bias. *The Journal of Economic Perspectives*, *5*(1), 193–206. doi:10.1257/jep.5.1.193

Klynn, B. (2021). Cognitive bias: What it is and how to overcome it. *BetterUp*. https://www.betterup.com/blog/cognitive-bias.

Kotlar, J., Signori, A., De Massis, A., & Vismara, S. (2018). Financial wealth, socioemotional wealth, and IPO underpricing in family firms: A two-stage gamble model. *Academy of Management Journal*, *61*(3), 1073–1099. doi:10.5465/amj.2016.0256

Landers, R. (2012). Unfolding the IKEA Effect: Why We Love the Things We Build. *Journal of Consumer Psychology*, *22*(3), 453–460. doi:10.1016/j.jcps.2011.08.002

Langer, E. J. (1975). The Illusion of Control. *Journal of Personality and Social Psychology*, *32*(2), 311–328. doi:10.1037/0022-3514.32.2.311

Le Breton-Miller, I., Miller, D., & Steier, L. P. (2004). Towards an Integrative Model of Effective FOB Succession. *Entrepreneurship Theory and Practice*, *28*(4), 305–328. doi:10.1111/j.1540-6520.2004.00047.x

Lind, M., Visentini, M., Mäntylä, T., & Del Missier, F. (2017). Choice-Supportive Misremembering: A New Taxonomy and Review. *Frontiers in Psychology*, *8*, 2062. doi:10.3389/fpsyg.2017.02062 PMID:29255436

March, J. G. (1991). Exploration and exploitation in organizational learning. *Organization Science*, *2*(1), 71–87. doi:10.1287/orsc.2.1.71Martínez-Romero, M., & Rojo Ramírez, A. (2016, January-June). SEW: Looking for a definition and controversial issues. *European Journal of Family Business*, *6*(1), 1–9. doi:10.1016/j.ejfb.2015.09.001

Mather, M., & Johnson, M. K. (2000). Choice-supportive source monitoring: Do our decisions seem better to us as we age? *Psychology and Aging*, *15*(4), 596–606. doi:10.1037/0882-7974.15.4.596 PMID:11144319

Mitchell, M. (1996). *An Introduction to Genetic Algorithms*. MIT Press.

Mitchell, T., & Thompson, L. (1994). A theory of temporal adjustments of the evaluation of events: Rosy Prospection & Rosy Retrospection. In C. Stubbart, J. Porac, & J. Meindl (Eds.), *Advances in managerial cognition and organizational information-processing* (Vol. 5, pp. 85–114). JAI press.

Morewedge, C. K., & Giblin, C. E. (2015). Explanations of the endowment effect: An integrative review. *Trends in Cognitive Sciences, 19*(6), 339–348. doi:10.1016/j.tics.2015.04.004 PMID:25939336

Neckebrouck, J., Schulze, W., & Zellweger, T. (2018). Are family firms good employers? *Academy of Management Journal, 61*(2), 553–585. doi:10.5465/amj.2016.0765

Norton, M. I., Mochon, D., & Ariely, D. (2012). The IKEA effect: When labor leads to love. *Journal of Consumer Psychology, 22*(3), 453–460. doi:10.1016/j.jcps.2011.08.002

Overbecke, K. K., Bilimoria, D., & Perelli, S. (2013). The dearth of daughter successors in family businesses: Gendered norms, blindness to possibility, and invisibility. *Journal of Family Business Strategy, 4*(3), 201–212. doi:10.1016/j.jfbs.2013.07.002

Piantoni, G. (1990). *La successione familiare in azienda. Continuità dell'impresa e ricambio generazionale*. EtasLibri.

Picone, P. M., De Massis, A., Tang, Y., & Piccolo, R. F. (2021). The Psychological Foundations of Management in Family Firms: Values, Biases, and Heuristics. *Family Business Review, 34*(1), 12–32. Advance online publication. doi:10.1177/0894486520985630

Pinker, S. (2011). *The Better Angels of our Nature*. Viking.

Pohl, R. F. (2017). *Cognitive illusions: Intriguing phenomena in thinking, judgment, and memory*. Routledge.

Porfírio, J. A., Felício, J. A., & Carrilho, T. (2020). Family business succession: Analysis of the drivers of success based on entrepreneurship theory. *Journal of Business Research, 115*, 250–257. doi:10.1016/j.jbusres.2019.11.054

Powell, M., & Ansic, D. (1997). Gender differences in risk behavior in financial decisionmaking: An experimental analysis. *Journal of Economic Psychology, 18*(6), 605–628. doi:10.1016/S0167-4870(97)00026-3

Presson, P. K., & Benassi, V. A. (1996). Illusion of control: A meta-analytic review. *Journal of Social Behavior and Personality, 11*(3), 493–510.

Pronin, E., Lin, D. Y., & Ross, L. (2002). The Bias Blind Spot: Perceptions of Bias in Self Versus Others. In Personality and Social Psychology Bulletin, 28, 369–381, DOI: doi:10.1177/0146167202286008

Ross, L., Greene, D., & House, P. (1977). The false consensus effect: An egocentric bias in social perception and attribution processes. *Journal of Experimental Social Psychology*, *13*(3), 279–301. doi:10.1016/0022-1031(77)90049-X

Ross, L., & Ward, A. (1996). Naive realism in everyday life: Implications for social conflict and misunderstanding. In T. Brown, E. S. Reed, & E. Turiel (Eds.), *Values and Knowledge* (pp. 103–135). Erlbaum.

Rotter, J. B. (1990). Internal versus external control of reinforcement: A case history of a variable. *The American Psychologist*, *45*(4), 489–493. doi:10.1037/0003-066X.45.4.489

Sharma, P., Chrisman, J. J., & Chua, J. H. (1997). Strategic Management of the Family Business: Past Research and Future Challenges. *Family Business Review*, *10*(1), 1–35. doi:10.1111/j.1741-6248.1997.00001.x

Sharma, P., Chrisman, J. J., & Chua, J. H. (2003). Predictors of Satisfaction with the Succession Process in Family Firms. *Journal of Business Venturing*, *18*(5), 667–687. doi:10.1016/S0883-9026(03)00015-6

Sharma, P., Chrisman, J. J., Pablo, A. L., & Chua, J. H. (2001). Determinants of Initial Satisfaction with the Succession Process in Family Firms: A Conceptual Model. *Entrepreneurship Theory and Practice*, *25*(3), 1–19. doi:10.1177/104225870102500302

Sharma, P., Chua, J. H., & Chrisman, J. J. (2000). Perceptions about the extent of succession planning in Canadian family firms. *Canadian Journal of Administrative Sciences*, *17*(3), 233–244. doi:10.1111/j.1936-4490.2000.tb00223.x

Sharot, T. (2011). *The Optimism Bias: A Tour of The Irrationally Positive Brain*. Pantheon. doi:10.1016/j.cub.2011.10.030

Sharot, T., Riccardi, A. M., Raio, M. C., & Phelp, E. A. (2007). *Neural Mechanism Mediating Optimism Bias*. Nature Publisching Group. doi:10.1038/nature06280

Shepperd, B. H., Hartwick, J., & Warshaw, P. R. (1988). The theory of reasoned action: A meta-analysis of past research with recommendations for modifications and future research. *The Journal of Consumer Research*, *15*(3), 325–343. doi:10.1086/209170

Soll, J. B., Milkman, K. L., & Payne, J. W. (2015). Outsmart Your Own Biases. *Harvard Business Review*, pp.64–71. https://hbr.org/2015/05/outsmart-your-own-biases

Staw, B. M. (1997). The escalation of commitment: An update and appraisal. In Shapira, Zur (ed.). Organizational Decision Making. Cambridge University Press.

van der Pligt, J., & Eiser, J. R. (1983). Actors and observers attributions, self-serving bias and positivity bias. *European Journal of Social Psychology*, *13*(1), 95–104. doi:10.1002/ejsp.2420130107

Venter, E., Boshoff, C., & Maas, G. (2005). The influence of successor-related factors on the succession process in small and medium-sized family businesses. *Family Business Review*, *18*(4), 283–303. doi:10.1111/j.1741-6248.2005.00049.x

Weick, K. E., & Sutcliffe, K. M. (2005). *Managing the unexpected. Resilient performance in an age of uncertainty*. Wiley.

Weick, K. E., Sutcliffe, K. M., & Obstfeld, D. (1999). Organizing for high reliability: processes for collective mindfulness. In B. Staw & R. Sutton (Eds.), *Research in Organizational Behavior* (pp. 81–124). JAI Press.

Williams, D., Zorn, M. L., Crook, T. R., & Combs, J. G. (2013). Passing the Torch: Factors Influencing Transgenerational Intent in Family Firms. *Family Relations*, *62*(3), 415–428. doi:10.1111/fare.12016

Wilson, S. L. (2015). *Antecedents to business succession planning in small relationship- dependent service businesses.* [Unpublished PhD Thesis, Graduate College of the Oklahoma State University] https://hdl.handle.net/11244/45386

Woods, J. A., Dalziel, T., & Barton, S. L. (2012). Escalation of commitment in private family businesses: The influence of outside board members. *Journal of Family Business Strategy*, *3*(1), 18–27. doi:10.1016/j.jfbs.2012.01.002

Wright, M., & Kellermanns, F. W. (2011). What can family firm research learn from management and entrepreneurship? *Journal of Family Business Strategy*, *2*(4), 187–198. doi:10.1016/j.jfbs.2011.10.002

Zellweger, T. M., & Astrachan, J. H. (2008). On the emotional value of owning a firm. *Family Business Review*, *21*(4), 347–363. doi:10.1177/08944865080210040106

Chapter 10
The Digitalization of Micro, Small, and Medium Enterprises in Indonesia as a Part of Policy Implementation in Overcoming the COVID-19 Pandemic

Yuhilza Hanum
Universitas Gunadarma, Indonesia

ABSTRACT

The COVID-19 pandemic affects all aspects of life for everyone in this world. In Indonesia, micro, small, and medium enterprises (MSMEs), which are mostly family businesses, are among the worst hit, since they do not have the stable capital backup as is the case in big enterprises. Since MSMEs contribute significantly to Indonesia's GDP, this problem needs government assistance for its recovery. Policies at several levels are put to practice and to be implemented. Digitalization of businesses has started even before the pandemic, and is more widely utilized in this condition. Therefore, the policies emphasize regulating the digitalization of MSMEs from the provision of the internet to accommodating their transactions.

DOI: 10.4018/978-1-6684-7394-8.ch010

INTRODUCTION

The COVID-19 pandemic that started in Wuhan, China, in 2019, has its effect on every aspect of life. Some people who were used to working in offices must now do their work from home. Students of kindergarten right through universities must take their classes from home. Their teachers either teach from home or from school that is now empty from academic activities. Some companies, such as transportation and accommodation companies, even have to close down, or at least cut down on their employees and branch offices.

In this pandemic condition, changes in every aspect of life must be managed in order, so that Indonesia as a nation will be able to survive. The government draws up policies, rules, and regulations, and develops programs that will overcome the present condition. Institutions such as Indonesia's Central Bank (Bank Indonesia (BI)), and ministries develop policies and programs that are related to their authorization. These are policies at the macro level since they are made at the national level. One of them is the Law of the Republic of Indonesia No. 11 of 2020 on Job Creation that replaced the Law of the Republic of Indonesia number 20 of 2008 on Micro, Small, and Medium Enterprises. On December 30th 2022, Law No. 11 of 2020 on Job Creation is replaced by Government Regulation in Lieu of Law (PERPU: Peraturan Pemerintah Pengganti Undang-undang) No. 2 of 2022. According to Indonesian law No. 12 of 2011, PERPU is at equal level with the law. The content of the PERPU is the same with Law No. 11 of 2020 except for clauses on specific time work agreement. The Central Bank develops some programs in accordance with these laws and other policies. Many aspects are addressed in these policies and programs; however, this analysis is on the digitalization component of the whole system.

BACKGROUND

The COVID-19 pandemic that spread throughout the world has its impact on every scale of businesses, from global companies to micro, small, and medium enterprises (MSMEs). Big businesses have to cut down their production, employees, and even close down some branches. The same goes with medium-sized ones and MSMEs as well. The Statistic Indonesia (BPS, 2020a, p. 15) note that from an economic perspective, COVID-19 pandemic has resulted in a recession in almost all countries, including Indonesia. This can be seen from the slowdown in economic growth in the first quarter of 2020 and negative economic growth in the second and third quarters of 2020. Sectors that are experiencing a decline during the pandemic are:

1. The accommodation, food, and beverage sectors experienced a decline in revenue due to decreasing number of foreign tourists and the cancellation of various activities such as meetings at hotels by government agencies and businesses.
2. The processing industry sector, especially the food and beverage industry, experienced a slowdown due to declining foreign demand, which was reflected in the decrease in exports of food and beverage commodities.
3. Rail and air transportation declined due to decreasing number of passengers from the cancellation of train and plane trips to reduce the spread of COVID-19.

The three sectors are operated by the government and private companies. Some of the private companies are family businesses. Family business comes in every size of entrepreneurship. The so-called, top performers in many countries, or the world at large, are family businesses that have gone through many generations of successors. PwC (a merger of two firms, Price Waterhouse and Coopers & Lybrand) conducted a survey on Indonesia's family business in 2014. It revealed that more than 95 percent of Indonesia's business is owned by families (PwC, 2014). The family businesses are ubiquitous (Poza and Daugherty, 2014). Every nation in the world has its own family businesses. In Indonesia there are big family businesses such as Sampoerna, Indofood, Djarum, Bakrie Group, and many more. However, MSMEs are easier to be started as family businesses. Data for the year 2019 from the Statistics Indonesia shows that the number of micro and small enterprises (MSEs) reached more than 26 million businesses or 98.68 percent of the total non-agricultural businesses in Indonesia. The MSEs are also able to absorb more than 59 million Indonesian workers or around 75.33 percent of the total non-agricultural workforce.

Those figures show that the pandemic affects many people on this scale of entrepreneurship. A survey conducted by Statistics Indonesia in 2020 listed the obstacles faced by SMEs impacted by the pandemic as shown in Table 1. The percentages add up to more than 100, which means that some SMEs face more than one obstacle.

Table 1. SMEs percentage according to obstacles during the COVID-19 pandemic

No.	Obstacle	Percentage(%)
1	Financial problem	62.21
2	Employee cut down	33.23
3	Decreasing income	84.20
4	Decreasing demand	78.35

Source: (BPS, 2020a) (data processed)

This analysis is put on family owned MSMEs for their uniqueness, either in terms of a family business or as MSMEs. MSMEs that are able to survive in this pandemic usually seize the opportunity in specific products and markets. This is one of the traits of family businesses, the agility to adapt. Furthermore, Arshed and Danson (2016) put down those statistics across countries suggest that 60 percent to 70 percent of all small firms (less than 50 employees) are family-owned.

Issues of 2021 and 2022 discussed by Statistics Indonesia (BPS, 2021a, 2022) do not specifically cover or give emphasize on small and medium enterprises anymore, since the COVID-19 is on the stage of recovery. SMEs issue that is mentioned at a glance in 2021 report is that women workers who are under-skilled usually work in informal SMEs. This condition made them survive the employee cut down mentioned in Table 1 both at enterprise level and individual level. MSMEs implement digitalization for their transaction, at the very least, hence the focus of this chapter.

FAMILY BUSINESS

There are a great variety of different types of family firms, as they can range from small lifestyle businesses to large multinational corporations. However, researchers cannot come to a single definition of a family business. Poza and Daugherty (2014) considered family businesses to constitute a complete range of enterprises in which one or more family members strategically influence the firm. The small and medium-sized business sector in most countries is dominated by family businesses.

Poza and Daugherty (2014) further explained the costs of family businesses. Comparison of total costs between family businesses and other businesses shows that while financing costs for other businesses can range from 25-30 percent for venture capital to bank financing, the family business owner controls 100 percent of the stock and reinvestment can be done without paying out dividends or loan interest. Therefore, family businesses acquire a lower cost of capital than other businesses. The same goes for the administrative cost that is lower for family.

In a family firm, owner and manager responsibilities sometimes overlap. This can lead to advantages, such as reduced administrative costs and speedier decision-making, that result in streamlined and less-costly decision making. Family firms may routinely be able to make decisions more quickly. The family-management-ownership interaction can also produce significant adaptive capacity and competitive advantage. On the situation of shrinking product life cycles experienced in this pandemic, the owners may quickly decide to be more innovative or adapt and renew their strategies. Kelly and Marchese (2015) discussed that many of the best and brightest of the millennial generation are showing themselves to value autonomy and independence, gravitating toward smaller businesses and more flexible employment arrangements.

As in any other business, the family businesses also go through the stages of procuring and deploying new products and new product/service combinations in supply-chain channels. Ever since the beginning of the Internet, the family businesses have been using it to make a "dot com" presentation of the firm right through practically anything in the present e-commerce era. Through the use of new digital technologies, family companies can deepen their traditionally strong relationships with customers, restructure channel dynamics, take on strategic partners in the value chain, and get closer to the end customer (Poza and Daugherty, 2014).

Data on the exact number of family businesses in Indonesia is not available. However, informal observation can be conducted. Big family businesses like the ones mentioned in the introduction section are public companies with shares available at the stock exchange. The families usually possess a majority of the shares, such as described as one of the characteristics of family business. MSMEs as family businesses are much more in numbers for the reason explained in the previous paragraph. Observation of one's surrounding can reveal the fact that many MSMEs in the neighborhood are family-owned, from the laundry franchise to Padang restaurants, and many other examples. The author once visited one Padang restaurant in South Jakarta and met the owner, who said that he owns Padang restaurants by the same name in that area. Aside from this chapter, it seems that a survey is needed to just record the number of MSMEs of every kind from Sabang (the western-most regency in Indonesia) to Merauke (the eastern-most).

MICRO, SMALL, AND MEDIUM ENTERPRISES (MSMEs)

MSMEs in Indonesia used to be regulated by the Law of the Republic of Indonesia number 20 of 2008 on Micro, Small, and Medium Enterprises (MSMEs). According to this law, micro, small, and medium enterprises are based on the principles of kinship, economic democracy, togetherness, justice efficiency, sustainability, environment friendly, independence, progress balanced, and national economic unity.

In more detailed points, the criteria stated in this law are (1) Micro Enterprises must possess the net asset of a maximum of fifty million rupiah (Note: the exchange rate in 2008 is 1US$=Rp10,950), excluding the sites and buildings of the enterprise; and annual sale income of maximum three hundred million rupiah; (2) Small Enterprise must own the net capital of more than fifty million rupiah, excluding the sites and the buildings of the enterprise; or owning the annual sale income of more than three hundred million rupiah up to the maximum of two billion five hundred million rupiah; (3) Medium Enterprises must own the net asset of more than five hundred million rupiah up to ten billion rupiah excluding the sites and the buildings of the enterprise, or own the annual sale income of more than two billion five hundred million rupiah up to the maximum of fifty billion rupiah.

To prove the government's concern, these criteria are redefined in the Government Regulation in Lieu of Law No. 2 of 2022 on Job Creation on the 12th of December 2022. It is stated in Chapter five, article 6, paragraph 1 and 2 that the criteria for Micro, Small and Medium Enterprises can include business capital, net worth indicators, annual sales results or investment value, incentives and disincentives, application of environmentally friendly technology, local content, or the number of workers in accordance with the criteria for each business sector; Further provisions regarding the criteria for Micro, Small and Medium Enterprises are regulated in a Government Regulation.

Micro, small, and medium enterprises (MSMEs) play a significant part in Indonesia's economy. The MSMEs role in Indonesia's gross domestic product (GDP) is illustrated by the Ministry of Cooperatives, Small and Medium Enterprises as shown in Figure 1. This figure shows the MSMEs contribution to GDP based on constant base price and current price. It can be seen that since 2019 the MSMEs contribution to GDP has been greater than 50 percent.

Figure 1. MSMEs contribution to Indonesia's GDP
Source: Katadata, 2021a, & BPS, 2021b
(data processed)

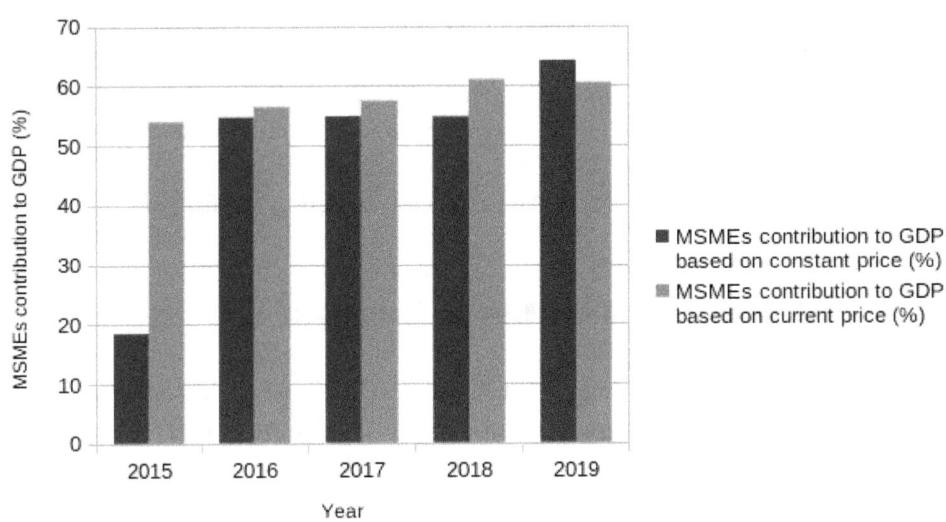

The result of Statistics Indonesia census on Economy in 2016 reveals that there are 15 sectors of Indonesia's SMEs, which are:

1. Mining and quarry.
2. Processing industry.
3. Procurement of gas electricity/steam hot water and cold air.
4. Water management, wastewater management, waste management and recycling, and remediation activities.
5. Construction.
6. Wholesale and retail trade, repair and maintenance of cars and motorcycles.
7. Freight and warehousing.
8. Provision of accommodation and provision of food and drink.
9. Information and communication.
10. Financial and insurance activities.
11. Real estate.
12. Company services.
13. Education.
14. Human health activities and social activities.
15. Other services.

Three sectors most affected by the pandemic are provision of accommodation and provision of food and drink, other services, and freight and warehousing (BPS, 2020b). Three sectors least affected are 1). the water management, wastewater management, waste management and recycling, and remediation activities; 2). procurement of gas electricity/steam hot water and cold air; and 3). real estate. Based on Figure 1, it can be concluded that every step must be taken to save these MSMEs. This is also supported by the MSMEs data on manpower absorption explained in the introduction section. The impact is further explained in the following section.

THE COVID-19 PANDEMIC IMPACT ON MSMEs

Approaching the end of the year 2020, Statistics Indonesia released data on the percentage of companies based on operational status under the COVID-19 condition (2021c). The survey is on 35,992 business subjects, which consisted of 28,923 micro and small enterprises, 4,289 medium and big enterprises. Other business subject is agriculture that is not categorized as micro, small, medium, or big enterprise. This business subject is comprised of 2,780 units. The result is shown in Table 2.

Table 2. Micro and small enterprises' operational status as a result of the COVID-19 pandemic

No.	Operational status	Percentage(%)
1	Continue operating by conducting working from home (remote or teleworking) for some of the employees.	7.00
2	Continue operating by conducting working from home (remote or teleworking) for all employees.	5.17
3	Continue operating by reducing capacity (working hours, machines, and labor).	28.45
4	Continue operating, with higher capacity.	3.17
5	Operating as usual.	38.99
6	Closed temporarily.	17.22

Source: (BPS, 2021c)

The survey also revealed that 67.77% percent of micro and small enterprises still suffered decreasing revenue in the third trimester of 2020 (BPS, 2021c). This resulted mostly from marketing/selling problems, debt payment, operational cost and employee salaries, bill payment, raw material, and rental payment. Business partners who are also affected by the pandemic are another cause for the decreasing revenue. Considering that an enterprise interacts with employees, customers, suppliers, and business partners, this situation calls for major recovery steps, not only at the micro-level, but more from the macro level. Strategies must not only be taken by the individual enterprise but must be managed from the highest level, that is, the government.

To emphasize this interconnection between an organization, be it an MSME or even a big enterprise, Figure 2 shows parties that are connected to it. The picture shows an information system of an organization, but on the other hand, it reflects the relationship between an enterprise and those connected to it. It can be seen that any disturbance experienced by suppliers, customers, stockholders, and even competitors, will make the enterprise shaky as well. Especially when those disturbances happen in the environment such as this COVID-19 pandemic. Regulatory agencies, on the other hand, play their part in assisting all parties involved to overcome the obstacles caused by the crisis.

Figure 2. An organization (e.g. enterprise) and its related parties
Source: Laudon & Laudon, 2014

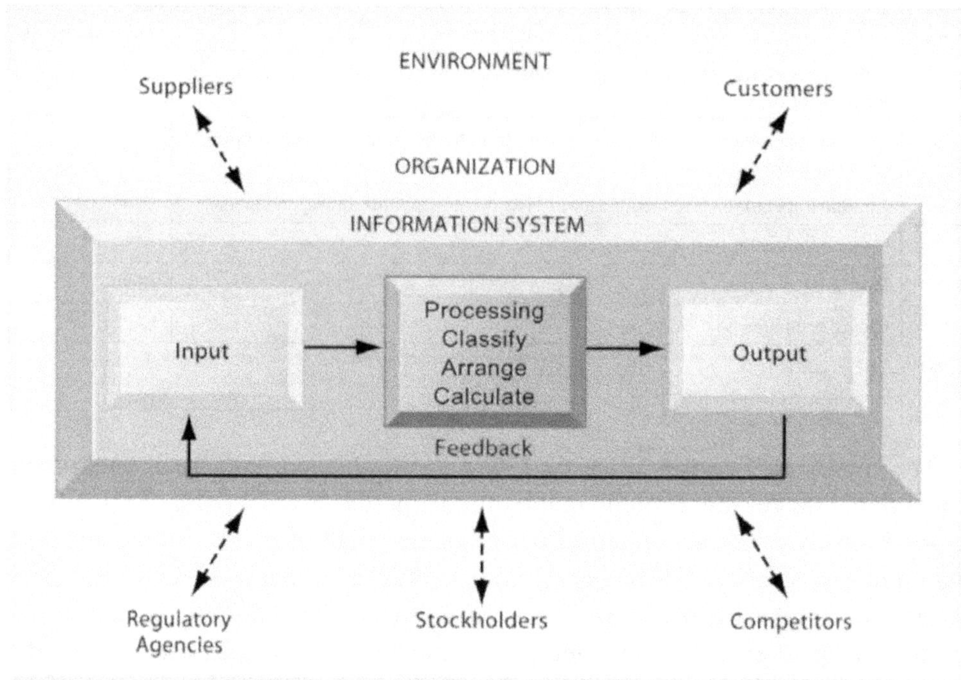

STRATEGY

Besanko, Dranove, Shanley, and Schaefer (2016) stated that strategies are—and should be—the adaptive, but principled, responses of firms to their surroundings. The infrastructure and market conditions of business do not uniquely determine the strategies that firms choose. In the present condition, the MSMEs main purpose is to survive by keeping their businesses sustain. Their "surroundings" are not (yet) the competitors and market condition. Infrastructure, on the other hand, plays an important role in this condition of surviving. In this present condition of almost equal quality of transportation throughout Indonesia, it is mainly the Internet connection that has an important influence on businesses.

Ferrell and Hartline (2014) explained that a developed marketing plan must be preceded by, among others, situation analysis. In doing this analysis, three environments (internal, customer, external) must be tracked simultaneously. Figure 3 shows the relationship of these environments' components.

Figure 3. The relationship among the internal, customer, and external environments
Source: Ferrell & Hartline, 2014

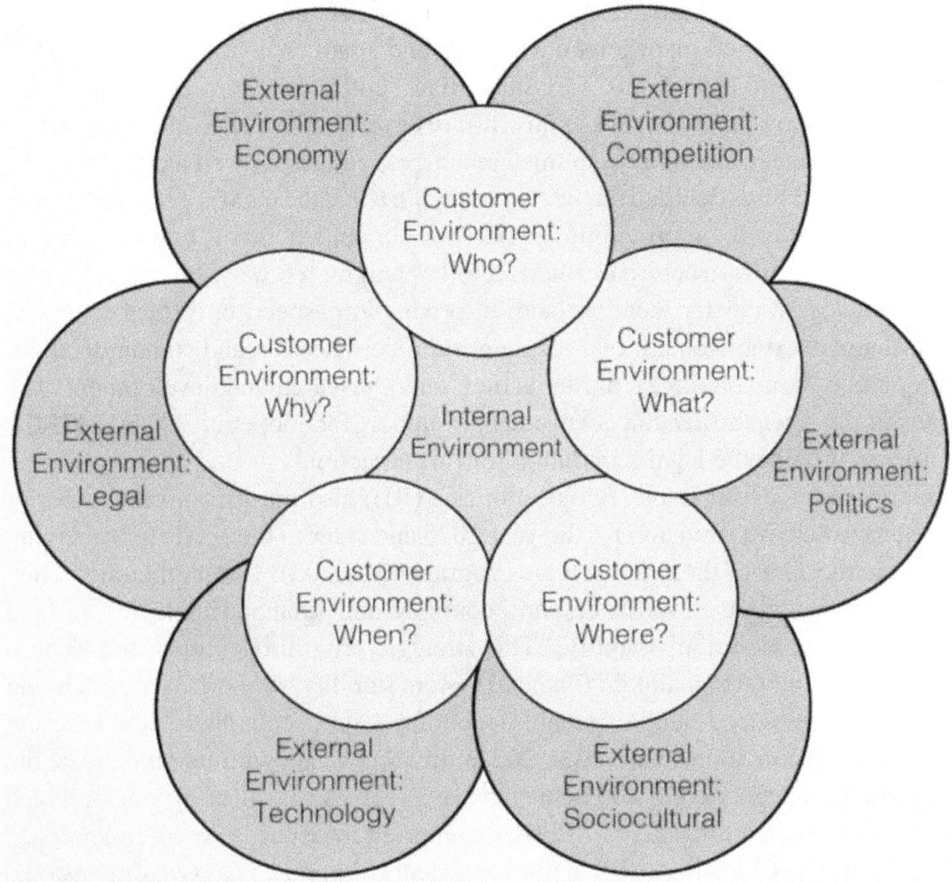

It can be concluded from Figure 3 that the major component of the present condition is sociocultural affected by the pandemic. At the same time, legal and political components can be put into practice in doing the simultaneous handling as mentioned previously. The technology aspect will support the steps taken in the form of digitalization.

LEGAL ENVIRONMENT

The Law of the Republic of Indonesia number 20 of 2008 on micro, small, and medium enterprises was then substituted by the Law of the Republic of Indonesia No. 11 of 2020 on Job Creation on the 2nd of November 2020, which was next replaced by Government Regulation in Lieu of Law No. 2 of 2022 on Job Creation on the 12th of December 2022. Chapter five of this law state the simplification, protection, dan empowerment of cooperatives, and MSMEs. In more detail, part five of this chapter explains the integrated management of micro and small enterprises. Furthermore, article 89, paragraph 5 of this part states that central government and regional governments carry out assistance as an effort to develop micro and small enterprises to provide management support, human resources, budget, as well as facilities and infrastructure. This is detailed further in paragraph 6 that the central government and regional governments in providing support for human resources, budgets, as well as facilities and infrastructure as referred to in paragraph 5 must provide facilities which include: a. cluster location land; b. production aspect; c. infrastructure; d. value chain; e. establishment of a legal entity; f. certification and standardization; g. promotion; h. marketing; i. digitalization; and j. research and development. The details in this law confirm the government's support for cooperatives and MSMEs in order to provide the legal foundation for further actions.

Indonesia's Central Bank (Bank Indonesia (BI)) also put forward a number of strategies to achieve its vision for the year 2025 and cater to the needs for surviving the pandemic. One of them is Strategic Program 03 (PS 03): "Strengthening policy and macroprudential surveillance and economic and financial inclusion to help maintain financial system stability." This strategic program is part of the Central Bank policy strategy to maintain financial system stability, support credit/financing growth for a balanced and sustainable economy, and accelerated economic and financial inclusion (Bank Indonesia, 2021). In accordance with its objectives, the successful achievement of PS 03 in the next five years is measured by, one of which is: (iv) development progress of MSMEs supported by access to bank financing.

According to Clement (2010), a macroprudential approach has two dimensions, pointing to distinct policy implications. One referred to the financial cycle of mutually amplifying processes between the financial system and the real economy. The other dimension was about risk distribution within the financial system or "cross-sectional dimension". The focus was on interconnections between institutions facing similar conditions. This explains the decision of the Central Bank to conduct this approach since every institution on every level has been facing the pandemic condition since the first quarter of 2020. Referring to the MSMEs' problem related to their customers, employees, suppliers, and business partners, this is the needed approach to be taken at the macro level. A significant number of research have been conducted on macroprudential policies. Juhro, Prabheesh, and Lubis (2021) concluded that those studies clearly suggest that the macro-prudential policies are crucial to maintaining financial stability when the economy is exposed to global financial conditions, like the one the whole world is facing at present.

In accordance with the Central Bank medium-term planning for the period of 2020-2025 and the conditions to be achieved by PS 03 in 2025, one of the steps to be carried out is: "c. Acceleration of access, and economic and financial inclusion, especially for MSMEs, including by encouraging the digitalization of MSMEs." PS 03 is not the only Central Bank strategy that is connected to MSMEs. Another one is Strategic Program 06 (PS 06): "Strengthening the synergy between the Central Bank policies with the government policies and the Financial Services Authority (Otoritas Jasa Keuangan – OJK) to develop digital economy and finance".

On the 4th of March 2021, the President of the Republic of Indonesia released the presidential decree on Task Force of Acceleration and Expansion of Regional Digitalization. The task force was formed with the aim of accelerating and expanding regional digitalization especially for, among others, supporting the development of public digital payment transactions, realizing financial inclusion, and enhance economic integration, and national digital finance.

From the ten facilities that the government has to provide that are described in the law of job creation, the one that will be discussed in this chapter is digitalization. The discussion will include the basic theory of digitalization, technologies adopted by the MSMEs, and the result of this conversion.

DIGITIZATION, DIGITALIZATION, AND DIGITAL TRANSFORMATION

Many sources on digitization, digitalization, and digital transformation have been available for quite some time. The explanation in this chapter refers to Gupta (2021) on the ARC Advisory Group website. Figure 4, also copied from this article, shows the relation between these three terms that form a digital transformation pyramid.

Digitization refers to creating a digital representation of physical objects or attributes. An example is scanning a paper document and saving it in either PDF, JPG, or other formats. The purpose of this process is so that the object can be used in a computerized system or program.

Digitalization refers to enabling or improving processes by leveraging digital technologies and digitized data. Examples might be an automated shutdown logic in case an error occurred, or a scheduled shutdown is met. Digitalization increases productivity and efficiency while reducing costs. Another explanation from I-scoop (2021) is that digitalization means the use of digital technologies and of data (digitized and natively digital) in order to create revenue, improve business, replace/transform business processes (not simply digitizing them) and create an environment for digital business.

Figure 4. Digital transformation pyramid
Source: Gupta, 2021

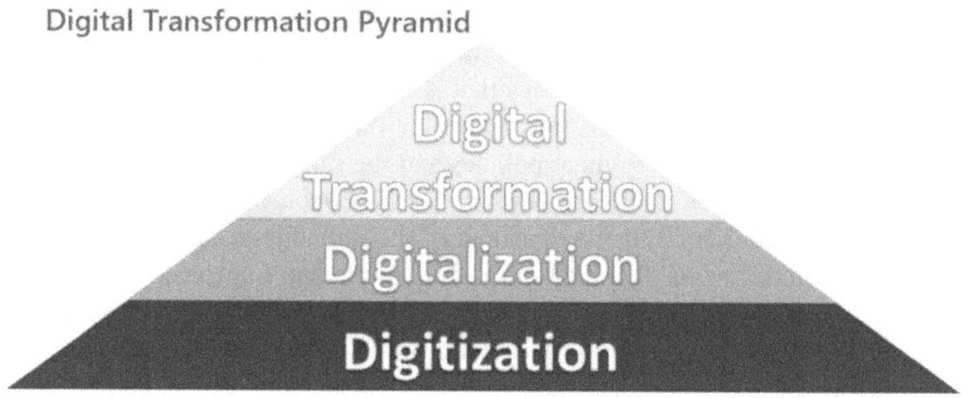

Digital transformation is the term most frequently discussed compared to digitization and digitalization. Digital transformation is business transformation enabled by digitalization. The essence of digital transformation is the changing of business processes enabled or forced by digitalization technologies. An example is the integration of customer sales volumes feeding through a company's raw material vendors, thus integrating sales and supply chain for greater efficiency. Referring to Figure 4, it can be concluded that digital transformation is digitalization in a more formal, purposeful, and directed form in a company/enterprise.

Parviainen, Kääriäinen, Tihinen, and Teppola (2017) explained the positioning of a company in digitalization. They developed a model that can be used in tackling digital transformation in a company. This model (shown in Figure 5) illustrates that the steps in positioning a company in digitalization, which are identifying digitalization impacts, digitalization drivers, digitalization scenarios, and digitalization goals might form a cycle or be done iteratively for improvement.

Parviainen et al. (2017) conclude that digitalization is not about turning existing processes into digital versions but rethinking current operations from new perspectives enabled by digital technology. Work is needed to reach goals, based on identifying the gap from the current state. A roadmap for success must be planned systematically and implemented into practice.

Figure 5. Model for tackling digital transformation
Source: Parviainen, Kääriäinen, Tihinen, & Teppola, 2017

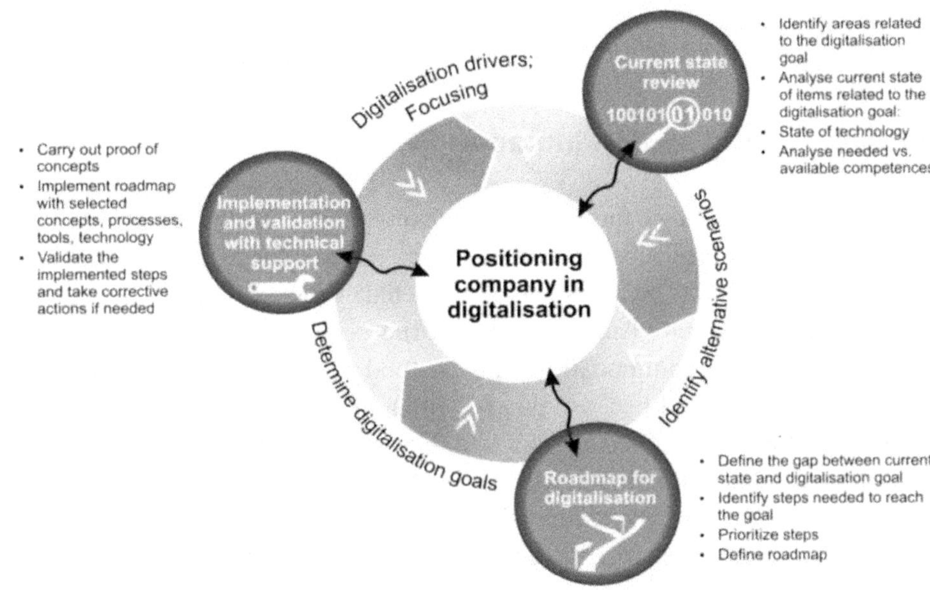

DIGITALIZATION IN INDONESIA

Indonesia like any other countries has entered the digitalization decades. Edamadaka and Seike (2019) from BayCurrent Consulting describes digitalization in Indonesia at large, not limited to MSMEs. They identified that the drivers of the digital economy in Indonesia are:

- Political: digital-friendly policy, strong digital content laws, and changing digital taxation policy.
- Economical: strong growth.
- Social: mass acceptance of Internet.
- Technological: strong digital buyer growth.

There are two challenges for digitalization in Indonesia, which are physical issues such as infrastructure maintenance and political issues such as conflicts with existing businesses. However, in 2017, some facts that can be stated are that online buyers are in the age group of 18 to 34 years, with the majority of the shopping through smartphones. Those item categories bought online are fashion, toys, hobby, and DIY (do-it-yourself). The fast penetration of smartphones will increase demand for digital services in areas of entertainment and services. This analysis is in accordance with the explanation of Figure 3, as well as the model in Figure 5.

Digitalization in Indonesia can be analyzed using the model proposed by Parviainen et al. (2017). There are 4 steps in the model depicted in Figure 5, and each step is explained by the potential and condition of Indonesia's MSMEs accordingly.

Identifying Digitalization Impacts

COVID-19 pandemic has the greatest impact on the sector of provision of accommodation and provision of food and drink (BPS, 2020c). Ninety-two points for seven percent (92,47%) of this sector is impacted by the pandemic. The provision of accommodation and provision of food and drink sector is actually can be divided into two, that is 1). accommodation, and 2). food & drink. The accommodation sector is greatly impacted because people withhold from traveling and staying in hotels or any other form of accommodation. However, since these sectors are used to be promoted online, digitalization is not new for them. The accommodation sector might just add new components by using the already available channels, such as using virtual or augmented reality so that the guests have a more realistic preview of their place.

The food and drink sector alone survives better in this condition. People restrain from eating in a restaurant, but they turn to order online. Analyzing from the perspective of costs, this will affect the mixed cost of the MSMEs. Mixed costs are the annual/monthly expenses that include both fixed and variable cost components, e.g. monthly costs such as insurance, advertising, transportation, and others (Tooch, 2015).

Advertising, promotion, and selling processes are now conducted over the Internet. This has been going on even before the pandemic, as already explained. Therefore, the digitalization of advertising, promotion, and selling affected the composition of costs. It seems that with outlets closed down, costs such as electricity and rent will be spared. MSMEs must be careful in managing this change since they might just be shifting the cost of outlets to electricity and rent in an informal place of business activities.

Digitalization Drivers

As mentioned by Edamadaka and Seike (2019), the drivers of Indonesia's digital economy are digital-friendly policy, strong digital content laws, changing digital taxation policy, strong economic growth, mass acceptance of the Internet, and strong digital buyer growth. Policy in the form of laws is already explained. The economic growth has been proven by Indonesia's 7.07 percent figure in the second quarter of 2021.

Mass acceptance of the Internet and technological drivers need a special explanation. As mentioned by Edamadaka and Seike (2019), the fast penetration of smartphones will increase the demand for digital services. People no longer need a high-end personal computer to access services over the Internet. All services on the Internet can now be accessed from a smartphone that can be carried everywhere. This access is made easier by mobile operators that provide several types of packages so that consumers can choose the appropriate one that caters to their needs.

From the communication infrastructure regulation, Regulation of the Minister of Communication and Informatics of the Republic of Indonesia number 14 the year 2021 concerning The Third Amendment to Regulation of the Minister of Communication and Informatics number 13 the year 2019 concerning the provision of telecommunication services was released on the 29th of December 2021. It states the obligations of telecommunication providers who offer services from delivering simple text messages to Internet access. The telecommunication consumers in this case are individuals, legal entities, and government agencies.

For the last few years, online shops have been available in Indonesia. The ones mentioned by Edamadaka and Seike are Tokopedia (established in 2009) and Bukalapak (established in 2012). These online shops are formally called "marketplace" or "digital platform", defined by Statistics Indonesia (BPS, 2020c) as "a place for buying and selling products where sellers and consumers meet on a platform". BPS further identify social media (Facebook, Instagram, and Twitter), and instant messages services (WhatsApp, Line, and Telegram) as other media for the online transaction.

These marketplaces / digital platforms are under a bigger grouping, named e-commerce. E-commerce based on the Organization for Economic Co-Operation and Development (OECD) 2009 is the sale or purchase of goods/services, which are carried out through computer networks with methods specifically designed for the purpose of receiving or placing orders. However, payment and the main delivery of goods/services do not have to be done online (BPS, 2020c). E-commerce in the meaning of online shops seems to prosper for increasing demand for their goods and services. Chronologically, some MSMEs have already used online marketing and online transaction in their business. Statistics Indonesia data shows that 47.75 percent of companies (all kinds of enterprises) have been using Internet and IT marketing ever since before the pandemic, 46.5 percent do not use it at all, and 5.76 percent have begun using it after the hit of the pandemic (BPS, 2020c). Just like any other application, e-commerce is usually developed by an IT consultant. Services provided by e-commerce can be varied as shown in Figure 6, which are the ones provided by Ayaa Technologies.

Figure 6. Typical e-commerce services offered by an IT consultant
Source: Ayaa Technologies, 2021

Another important service catered by e-commerce is the E-Wallet. It is used to pay for transactions on more than one marketplace. Ovo, Dana, GoPay, LinkAja, Kredivo, AkuLaku, and PayLater are E-Wallets commonly used in Indonesia, although in 2019 E-Wallets only ranked in fourth place after COD (cash on delivery), transfer by ATM, and credit card (BPS, 2020c). The use might increase in this pandemic condition since consumers only have to put an adequate amount of money for multiple transactions. It also serves as an alternative to mobile banking and credit card methods.

Assembling the services explained previously, it can be concluded that MSMEs do not have to develop the application of their own. They can simply sell their merchandise on one or more of the online shops. Transactions are conducted easily and user friendly by using these online shops' applications that can be installed from the PlayStore or any other application distributors. Merchandise that is sold in these online shops varies from electricity vouchers to ready-to-eat food. This greatly simplifies the business process of MSMEs or even big enterprises, since these shops provide advertising, promotion, and handle transaction and delivery processes as well.

Some merchandise, especially ready-to-eat food and drink requires fast transportation. Transportation services are provided by several operators, such as Go-Jek, and Grab. They do not only provide transportation for people but also goods. There is a component in their application that presents restaurants and their menu so that people can place their order, pay with electronic money, and just wait for the food to be delivered. For the owners of restaurants, just like with online shops, this simplifies their business process in advertising, promoting, selling, and delivery.

Research by the Institute of Economic and Community Research, Faculty of Economics and Business, University of Indonesia, shows that the number of MSMEs that put their merchandise in Tokopedia increased from March to August of 2020. March 2020 is the beginning of the pandemic in Indonesia. The closing of schools, offices, and other public places began at that time. Figure 7 shows this significant increase compared to the January-February period.

Figure 7. The increasing number of MSMEs in Tokopedia during COVID-19 pandemic
Source: Katadata, 2021b
(data processed)

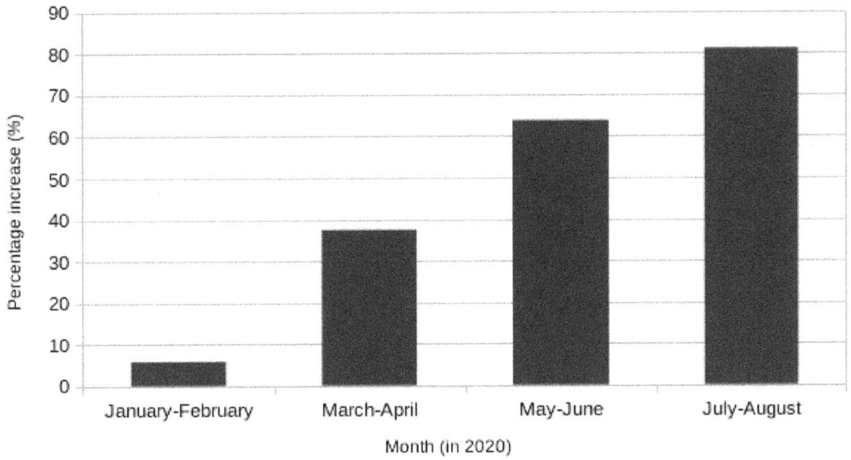

Figure 7 shows that MSMEs are aware of the services, facilities, or even infrastructure, available, and are making use of them extensively. For the ones who had been using it before the pandemic, this means that there will be more competitors. This is confronted by putting special promotions, such as a free delivery fee for a minimum transaction of a certain value.

Katadata Insight Center (KIC) in May 2021 listed services provided by marketplaces as assisting promotion, giving big promotion, secure transaction, ease of use, fast and good response from administrators, providing complete education, assisting export, and other services. Figure 8 shows these services against the percentage of MSMEs that use them in marketing their products.

Figure 8. Percentage of MSMEs that use marketplace services
Source: Katadata, 2021c
(data processed)

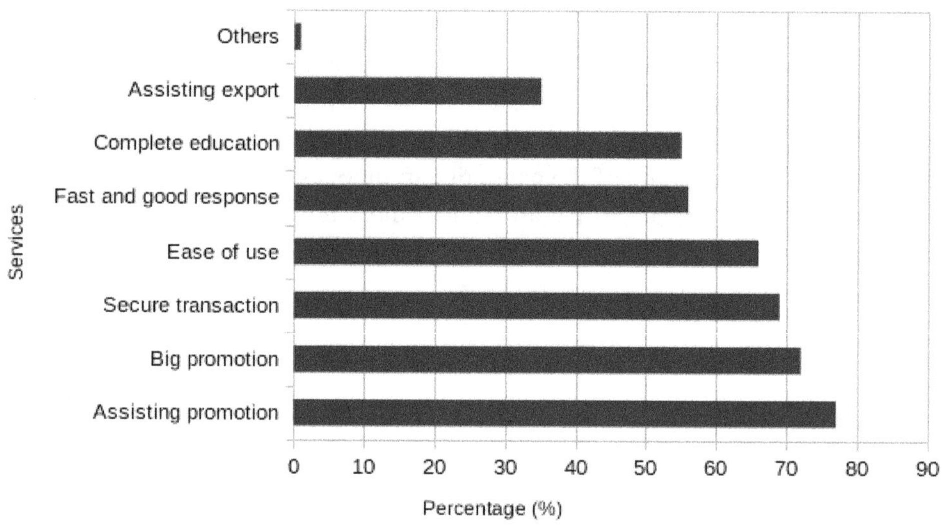

This step in the model proposed by Parviainen et al. takes the most extensive explanation since the digitalization drivers are used to support the MSMEs decision to "go digital" in some part of their business process.

Digitalization Scenarios

A digital scenario will conform to the pyramid in Figure 4. When the MSMEs have specified the part of their business that will be enabled by the digitalization technologies, realized and implemented the technology, then it is said that the digital transformation is established. For a family business of food and drink, the processing of raw material can certainly not be part of digitalization. The stages that can be put into digitalization are the promotion and transaction, that is the MSMEs can put it onto an online shop platform, or the delivery service. They will take customers' orders, respond, fill the orders, and make the payment by just using the platform. Expanding this digitalization is when inventory or stock is connected to the supplier by another digital platform so that they would not be a failure of filling orders for lack of raw material.

Various types of businesses will develop a different digitalization scenario from each other since their business processes are different. The accommodation sector might develop a digitalization scenario that consists of promotion, payment, the connection between its entities (e.g. front desk, housekeeping, kitchen, etc.), and also the connection to its suppliers.

Digitalization Goals

When digitalization is done correctly, it might achieve the objective of increasing productivity and efficiency while reducing costs, creating revenue, and therefore improving business. As in making scenarios, different MSMEs might have different goals although they are not doing business in different sectors. Some might prioritize sales, not necessarily profit, while some have the main objective of maximum profit. On the other hand, MSMEs might just try to achieve digital resilience. Casalino, Żuchowski, Labrinos, Nieto, and Martín-Jiménez (2019) described that digital resilience is about balance and collaboration. The balance between seizing the opportunities and managing the digital risks off the enterprise, and the balance between people (management and employee), processes, and technology as each needs to play their role. Collaboration is the key to success, that is, collaboration between the leadership team and their risk, security, and technology teams as well as collaboration with other key business stakeholders (communication, public relations, marketing, legal, procurement, etc.).

RECENT ISSUES

The Quick Response Indonesian Standard (QRIS) Adoption

There have been quite a number of methods in identifying a product. There are codes for goods that are stored and recorded in inventory. For many years, bar codes are used as the identification for goods so that, for example, cashiers in stores have only to scan these codes from people's purchases, and the price will appear in the cash register.

A Quick Response (QR) code is a type of two-dimensional matrix barcode. In practice, QR codes often contain data for a locator, identifier, or tracker that points to a website or application. A QR code uses four standardized encoding modes (numeric, alphanumeric, byte/binary, and kanji) to store data efficiently. Extensions may also be used, as explained in Wikipedia (2021).

The QRIS unites various kinds of QR from various Payment System Service Providers (PJSP) using a QR Code. The QRIS was developed by the payment system industry together with Central Bank of Indonesia so that the transaction process with the QR code can be easier, faster, and secure. All payment system service providers who will use QR code payments must implement QRIS (QRIS, 2021).

The Central Bank of Indonesia survey in January 2021 shows that the use of QRIS by MSMEs increased by 316 percent during the pandemic (Katadata, 2021d). Most of the merchants are the MSMEs from micro-enterprises (3.6 million) and small businesses (1.3 million). Figure 9 shows this development from 22nd of March 2020 to 30th of December 2020 for five categories of merchants.

Figure 9. Total adoption of QRIS by five categories of merchants
Source: Katadata, 2021d

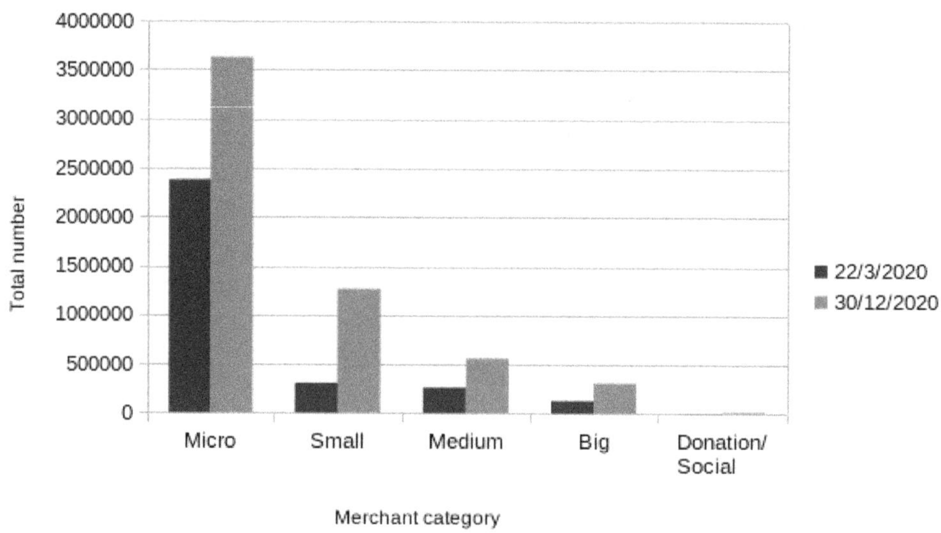

Needed Assistance

Despite the available support of regulations, infrastructure, services, and technology, the MSMEs still need more assistance at present compared to the time before the pandemic. The Institute of Economic and Community Research, Faculty of Economics and Business, University of Indonesia, revealed as a result of their survey that assistance mostly needed are affordable Internet connection, business funding, market creation, reduction of business costs, ease of doing business, ease of taxation, employment assistance, consulting service, and others, as shown in Figure 10.

Affordable Internet is the support mostly needed by the MSMEs. This is related to the Regulation of the Minister of Communication and Informatics of the Republic of Indonesia number 14 the year 2021 concerning The Third Amendment to Regulation of the Minister of Communication and Informatics number 13 the year 2019 concerning the provision of telecommunication services. The document states the obligations of telecommunication providers who offer services from delivering simple text messages to Internet access. Telecommunication providers offer any type of, so-called, data or Internet packages. Wireless connection packages can also be installed in houses, supporting the MSMEs that use a house or living place to operate their business.

Figure 10. Assistance needed by MSMEs to face the COVID-19 pandemic against the percentage of MSMEs who needed them
Source: Katadata, 2021e

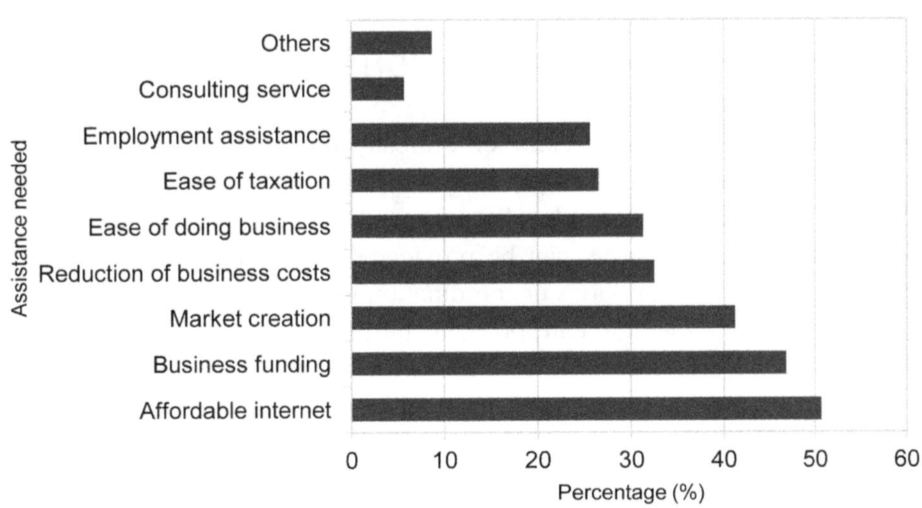

Business funding is managed at the macro level by the Central Bank. Recalling that the successful achievement of its PS 03 in the next five years is measured by, one of which is the development progress of MSMEs supported by access to bank financing. Market creation does not actually need support from the macro level. The MSMEs themselves are able to create their own market by putting their creativity and innovative ideas to good use. Prior to the pandemic, some of them has already used online shops and social media to promote and sell their products.

In reducing business costs, family owned MSMEs have already had the advantage as explained in the previous section, such as lower costs in capital and administrative costs. Problems with suppliers, business partners, and customers who also suffered the impact of the pandemic are those that the Bank Central works on with its macroprudential approaches.

Ease of doing business and ease of taxation is regulated by the Government Regulation in Lieu of Law No. 2 of 2022 on Job Creation. Support in employment is not actually needed by family-owned micro and small enterprises, since they usually employ their own relatives, and salary can be more easily negotiated. This will also help in employing those who were laid off by the companies they previously worked for. The support in employment is more needed by the medium scale enterprises, though they can propose for financial aid provided by the government.

Family-owned MSMEs can also look for consulting services by themselves. This is easier for big families that consist of, not only parents, spouses, and children, but include uncles, aunties, cousins, grandparents, and also in-laws. This kind of family management to overcome regular or special problems is explained in detail in Poza and Daugherty (2014) right down to the family meetings.

SOLUTIONS AND RECOMMENDATIONS

Policies at national level must be, and some already have been, detailed at the lower level, whether ministry-wise or regional-wise. These details can be implemented by related divisions at provincial level or regency level. Affordable Internet, which is the most needed assistance, can be provided by the ministry of Ministry of Communications and Informatics in coordination with private sectors.

Micro, small, and medium enterprises as family businesses require assistance along with close monitoring and guidance from related parties, either government or private. Koperasi, which is the Indonesian traditional grouping and management of MSMEs might have an important role in this assistance. The government's intention to keep this koperasi can be seen by the availability of Ministry of Cooperatives and SMEs, as well as SMEs Development and Consumer Protection Department in Bank Indonesia.

FUTURE RESEARCH DIRECTIONS

Future research along this line can be done by analyzing the policy implementation at micro level, especially since this discussion is mostly about family MSMEs. Several branches can be taken as well, such as analysis of the contributing factors of MSMEs' digitalization success, the impact of MSMEs digitalization on public welfare, its contribution to Original Local Government Revenue, and assessment of digital infrastructure.

CONCLUSION

Micro, small, and medium enterprises have been having a significant contribution to Indonesia's economy. Their contribution is more than half of the nation's PDB. Therefore, the problems they have in relation to customers, suppliers, employees, and business partners must be overcome with the help of macro policies from the government.

Family businesses in the scale of micro, small, and medium enterprises are not well recorded by related institutions, even though we can see them in our immediate environment, i.e. the neighborhood. A study focusing on the family owned MSMEs is needed so that complete data is available, and related research can be conducted.

Provision of accommodation and provision of food and drink is the sector most affected by the COVID-19 pandemic. However, the food and drink sector by itself is able to gain momentum due to the fact that food and drink are one of the people's basic needs. This sector has to make adjustments to cope with the pandemic, one of which is by using electronic commerce in promoting, selling, and delivering the products.

Legal aspects in the form of regulations are already provided by the Indonesian government from the presidential to ministry level in order to support MSMEs during this pandemic time. These regulations are periodically evaluated and changed if necessary. The Central Bank of Indonesia (Bank Indonesia-BI) also takes role in supporting the MSMEs with programs related to financial aid, since business funding is one of the assistances needed.

Digitalization is the step taken from a technological aspect to overcome the difficulties faced by the MSMEs, even though some of them have used it for several years. As one component in the process of digitalization, the marketplace or digital platform provides services that are needed and used by MSMEs. Several technological services that are increasingly used by MSMEs, among others, are QR codes and E-Wallets. Electronic commerce provides services that are useful for MSMEs in the digitalization of their business process.

Digitalization in Indonesia caters to MSMEs needs to face the obstacles during this pandemic, but it must be combined with and supported by other aspects, such as regulations and infrastructure to become a comprehensive strategy. However, family owned MSMEs seem able to cope with the crisis. This is proof that family business has the ability and agility in adapting to any conditions, whether they are negative, positive, or new ways to do business, such as new technology.

REFERENCES

Arshed, N., & Danson, M. (2016). Enterprise: Concepts and Issues. In J. Sanders (Ed.), *Family Business* (pp. 113–130). Goodfellow Publishers.

Ayaa Technologies. (2020). *E-commerce development*. Ayaa Technologies. https://ayaatechnologies.com/ecommerce-development/

Bank Indonesia. (2021). *Laporan Tahunan Bank Indonesia 2020*. Bank Indonesia.

Besanko, D., Dranove, D., Shanley, M., & Schaefer, S. (2016). *Economics of Strategy* (7th ed.). Wiley.

BPS. (2020a). *Analisis Isu Terkini 2020*. BPS RI.

BPS. (2020b). *Analisis Hasil Survei Dampak COVID-19 Terhadap Pelaku Usaha*. BPS RI.

BPS. (2020c). *Statistik E-Commerce 2020*. BPS RI.

BPS. (2021a). *Analisis Isu Terkini 2021*. BPS RI.

BPS. (2021b). *PDB seri*. BPS RI. https://www.bps.go.id/indicator/11/65/3/-seri-2010-pdb-seri-2010.html

BPS. (2021c). *Analisis Hasil Survei Dampak COVID-19 Terhadap Pelaku Usaha Jilid 2*. BPS RI.

BPS. (2022). *Analisis Isu Terkini 2022*. BPS RI.

Casalino, N., Żuchowski, I., Labrinos, N., Nieto, Á. L. M., & Martín-Jiménez, J. A. (2019). Digital strategies and organizational performances of SMEs in the age of Coronavirus: Balancing digital transformation with an effective business resilience. *Law and Economics Yearly Review*, *8*(2), 347–380. doi:10.2139srn.3563426

Clement, P. (2010). The term "macroprudential": Origins and evolution. *BIS Quarterly Review*, (March), 59–67.

Edamadaka, P., & Seike, I. (2019). *Digitalization in Indonesia*. Singapore: SBayCurrent Consulting.

Ferrell, O. C., & Hartline, M. D. (2014). *Marketing Strategy: Text and Cases* (6th ed.). Cengage Learning.

Gupta, M. S. (2021). *What is Digitization, Digitalization, and Digital Transformation?* Arc Web. https://www.arcweb.com

I-scoop. (2021). *Digitization, digitalization, digital and transformation disruption*. I-Scoop. https://www.i-scoop.eu/digital-transformation/digitization-digitalization-digital-transformation-disruption/

Juhro, S. M., Prabheesh, K. P., & Lubis, A. (2021). The Effectiveness of Trilemma Policy Choice in the Presence of Macroprudential Policies: Evidence from Emerging Economies. *The Singapore Economic Review*, *66*(3), 1–45. doi:10.1142/S0217590821410058

Katadata. (2021a). *Kontribusi UMKM Terhadap Ekonomi Terus Meningkat*. Katadata. https://databoks.katadata.co.id/datapublish/2021/08/13/kontribusi-umkm-terhadap-ekonomi-terus-meningkat

Katadata. (2021b). *Jumlah Pelaku UMKM di Tokopedia Meningkat Selama Pandemi COVID-19*. Katadata. https://databoks.katadata.co.id/datapublish/2021/03/25/jumlah-pelaku-umkm-di-tokopedia-meningkat-selama-pandemi-COVID-19

Katadata. (2021c). *Lewat Market Place 77 UMKM Terbantu Pasarkan Produk Saat Pandemi COVID-19*. Katadata. https://databoks.katadata.co.id/datapublish/2021/05/05/lewat-marketplace-77-umkm-terbantu-pasarkan-produk-saat-pandemi-COVID-19

Katadata. (2021d). *QRIS*. Katadata. https://databoks.katadata.co.id/search/cse/qris

Katadata. (2021e). *Internet Terjangkau Bantuan Paling Dibutuhkan UMKM Saat Pandemi*. Retrieved September 11, 2021, from https://databoks.katadata.co.id/datapublish/2021/03/24/internet-terjangkau-bantuan-paling-dibutuhkan-umkm-saat-pandemi

Kelly, E., & Marchese, K. (2015). Supply chains and value webs. In M. Canning & E. Kelly (Eds.), *Business ecosystems come of age* (pp. 55–62). Deloitte University Press.

Kementerian Komunikasi dan Informatika Republik Indonesia. (2021). *Peraturan Menteri Komunikasi dan Informatika tentang Perubahan Ketiga atas Peraturan Menteri Komunikasi dan Informatika Nomor 13 Tahun 2019 tentang Penyelenggaraan Jasa Telekomunikasi*. Informatika Republik Indonesia. https://peraturan.bpk.go.id/Home/Details/203125/permenkominfo-no-14-tahun-2021

Laudon, K. C., & Laudon, J. P. (2014). *Management Information Systems: Managing the Digital Firm* (13th ed.). Pearson.

Parviainen, P., Kääriäinen, J., Tihinen, M., & Teppola, S. (2017). Tackling the digitalization challenge: How to benefit from digitalization in practice. *International Journal of Information Systems and Project Management*, *5*(1), 63–77. doi:10.12821/ijispm050104

Pemerintah Republik Indonesia. (2022). *Peraturan Pemerintah Pengganti Undang-Undang (Perpu) tentang Cipta Kerja*. Peraturan. https://peraturan.bpk.go.id/Home/Details/234926/perpu-no-2-tahun-2022

Poza, E. J., & Daugherty, M. S. (2014). *Family Business* (4th ed.). Cengage Learning.

PwC. (2014). *Survey Bisnis Keluarga 2014: Indonesia*. PWC. https://www.pwc.com/id/en/publications/assets/indonesia-report-family-business-survey-2014.pdf

QRIS. (2021). *Satu QR Code untuk semua payment*. QRIS. https://qris.id/homepage/

Tooch, D. E. (2015). *Effective Accounting for Small Business: A Guide to Business and Personal Financial Success*. Cognella Academic Publishing.

Wikipedia. (2021). *QR code*. Wikipedia. https://en.wikipedia.org/wiki/QR_code

Chapter 11
Exploring How Family Businesses Turn COVID-19 Challenges Into Opportunities:
A Qualitative Enquiry on the Floriculture Sector in Sri Lanka

Kanchana Wijayawardena
University of Wollongong, Australia

Chandra Padmini
Sri Lanka Council for Agricultural Research Policy, Sri Lanka

Vilani Sachitra
University of Sri Jayewardenepura, Sri Lanka

ABSTRACT

The sudden spread of Covid-19 around the world is causing significant damages to the corporate sector. Family businesses are not an exception to the crisis. During a pandemic, one of the most distinctive traits of a family business may be to react effectively to keep the business afloat. Family firms have been exposed to be better equipped to survive periods of political uncertainty and natural disasters with the courses of a mix of long-term horizon, and social and political capital. Conceptually, little is still acknowledged about how they survive and sustain during the COVID-19 pandemic, and the implications of family control on the ability of firms to overcome a pandemic are unclear. The authors explore how family businesses in the floriculture sector in Sri Lanka react and cope with this unexpected crisis, COVID-19. This study reveals how institutional theory links with macro, micro, and meso levels of interactions, and the model offers a richer understanding of the survival, resilience, and renewal process of floriculture family businesses in Sri Lanka.

DOI: 10.4018/978-1-6684-7394-8.ch011

INTRODUCTION

Family business context inspires the creation of strong, enduring, and the most innovative organizations globally (De Massis et al., 2018). Family businesses are firms with significant involvement and influence of family members who are related by blood, adoption, or marriage and exert significant influence on all or major strategic decisions of the firm, which has implications for the firm's performance, productivity, survival, and growth (Afredo et al., 2014). Moreover, family businesses are often motivated by the desire to pass on a healthy business to descendants and thus exhibit longer time-possibilities in decision-making, higher reputational concerns, and a stronger attachment to the business. The aspiration to thrive in the long run is among the most distinctive traits of a family business.

We know that the sudden spread of Covid-19 around the world is causing significant damages to the corporate sector. Family businesses are not an exception to the crisis. The pandemic has already created major changes into the business environment, and that will overwhelmingly impact the businesses for years to come, and it does alter how people live, think, and manage and organize their societies (Wright, 2020). During a pandemic, one of the most distinctive traits of a family business may be to react effectively to keep the business afloat. Family firms have been exposed to be better equipped to survive periods of political uncertainty and natural disasters with the courses of a mix of long-term horizon, and social and political capital. Conceptually, little is still acknowledged about how they survive and sustain during the COVID-19 pandemic and the implications of family control on the ability of firms to overcome a pandemic are unclear. In this gloomy scenario, factors driving family businesses resilience will prove decisive to discern the ability of firms to overcome the current crisis.

The literature exclusively seems to cover five crisis phases; precrisis normality, crisis emergence, crisis occurrence, crisis aftermath, and post-crisis normality (Pramono et al., 2020). In such emerging pandemic scenarios, Crisis Management (CM) decisions play a vital role, and different sectors adhere to different CM strategies to either move forward or survive. Here, the agriculture sector receives great attention because COVID-19, as a health crisis, may lead to a food security crisis (Food and Agriculture Organization, 2020).

Sri Lanka and Covid-19

The first person infected with Covid-19 was reported on March 10 2020, in Sri Lanka. As an immediate precaution, the government declared the closure of nationwide schools. Following the medical experts' opinions, a nationwide curfew was imposed for 07 days effecting from March 20, 2020, and employees (public and private) were requested to continue essential services using the work-from-home approach. On March 19, the government declared a partial shutdown of all the ports and international airports until August 01, 2020. To neutralize the difficulties encountered in several economic activities such as utility services, rural agricultural production, essential product distribution, controlling price of essential foods and services, a presidential task force was formed on March 26th. Accordingly, proactive measures were initiated to mitigate the pandemic's impact, such as cash transfers to marginalized communities and postponed tax payments and leasing instalments. However, exports were functioned while ensuring national food security (rice was not allowed to export). With its unique pandemic management strategy, 'test, trace, treat', and continuous efforts and commitments of all the people, Sri Lanka ensured that the first and second wave were contained effectively. In the middle of March 2021, the government started the vaccination deployment programme. Unfortunately, a rapid increase in cases were reported during April and May 2021 due to the failure in following health precautions in celebrating cultural events. As a result, a nationwide curfew was again imposed for 30 days in May 2021.

Concerning Sri Lanka's economic performance in 2020, 3.6 percent contraction in the gross domestic product was reported, indicating the worst growth performance on record. Sectors like tourism, transportation, construction, textile, and education are severely damaged by the actions taken in containing and fighting this global crisis.

Sri Lanka and Agriculture

Though we are positioned in the 4th industrial revolution, Sri Lankan economy has traditionally been dominated by the agriculture sector. The sector is dominated by smallholding farm families and constitutes 7 percent of GDP and 23.3 percent of export earnings in 2020 (Central Bank Report, 2020) and provided employment to about 25.3 percent of the labour force (Sri Lanka Labour Force Survey Annual Report, 2019). Out of the total land area, 24 percent are recognized as agricultural land (Department of Census and Statistics, 2021). The COVID-19 pandemic affected the food security status of the country and puts the agriculture sector on test to sustain self-sufficiency.

The concept of home garden and rooftop gardening were introduced as a remedy to secure people to stay at home and maintain food and nutrient security among them. Cultivating of flowers and vegetables was made attractive since there was active engagement by all family members. However, its ability to rescue the country as planned is limited. Even though the government has allowed farming to continue unrestricted, uncertainties surrounding the temporary lifting of curfew hours and means of distributing essential goods to households have resulted in wastage and slowdowns in the supply. However, there were no restrictions on the export of agricultural commodities, except the export of rice to ensure national food security (IPS Report, 2020).

The trade volume in the global aspect is expected to tumble between 13% and 32% in 2020 (WTO, 2020 a, b). Trade in agricultural products has been relatively resistant to these disturbances, at least over the short run. Interestingly, in line with our observations, the official trade data insisted that the agricultural export sector in Sri Lanka seemed to experience smaller trade impacts, where floriculture exports have remained to reach clients in the global markets. However, due to high freight cost, foliage exports have been declined relatively to the others (Refer to Annexure 1). For instance, the floriculture sector comprised 12.62 US$ Mn of export earnings in 2019 and offered around 5000 direct employment and over 15,000 indirect employments (EDB trade Analysis System, 2021). The floriculture sector is dominated by family businesses since around 10000 families are actively engaged. One of the main intentions behind the sector is to empower women labor force while achieving socio-economic development in Sri Lanka. Consequently, there is a potential to focus on floriculture related value propositions coupled with floriculture which could lead to gain foreign exchange to the country (Table 1).

The ability to reach global markets during the pandemic period is a strong determinant of Sri Lanka's capability to trade. These shed a light that though there were strong public health and government policies imposed to respond to the pandemic, the Sri Lankan floriculture trade is in a good position to uphold its inclusive trade profile during the pandemic. Thus, this will lead to \an advantage of a quick global economic recovery.

On these notes, this study aims to: (1) Identify the key challenges experienced by floriculture family businesses in Sri Lanka in the COVID 19 pandemic; (2) Explore the survival, resilience and renewal strategies of floriculture family businesses in Sri Lanka in the COVID 19 pandemic and (3) Propose crisis survival, resilience and renewal model for floriculture family businesses.

The study classified family business as an entity led by a Manager/Director/CEO/ Chairman belonging to the controlling family. Thus, we believe that identifying the survival and resilience strategies of a family business during a long-lasting crisis will contribute to the existing literature in crisis management. We further intend to contribute to the stream of literature by revealing the fact that not only business owner adjustment strategies but also simultaneous government and inter-organizational intervention on family business can be helpful in thriving the business during the pandemic. This will lead to providing recommendations for family businesses on how to remain competitive and contribute to the national economy during a pandemic through resilience and renewal strategies.

Table 1. Earnings of floriculture exports

Code	Description	2016		2017		2018		2019		2020		2021 (May)	
		Quantity	Value	Quantity	Value	Quantity	Value	Quantity	Value	Quantity	Value	Quantity	Value
S.0602	Foliage	3,782,729	12.07	4,217,011	14.19	4,491,248	13.75	4,279,690	13.94	2,448,992	8.56	1,455,968	6.67
		15,428,963 No	1.2	16,178,145 No	1.24	16,710,519 No	1.38	17,570,925 No	1.54	16,080,929 No	2.08	13,055,873 No	1.46
S.0604	Floriculture Seeds	2,724	1.37	3,296	0.89	4,704	0.75	19,301	1.24	10,157	1.31	73,401	0.56
S.0603	Aquatic plants	28,996	0.24	28,748	0.28	31,725	0.28	98,498	0.69	73,919	0.57	3,976	0.44
S.0601	Cut Flowers	133,286	0.12	132,630	0.15	80,643	0.09	90,270	0.1	73,822	0.09	26,119	0.07
	Total:		**15**		**16.74**		**16.25**		**17.5**		**12.62**		**9.2**

*Quantity in Kg.; Value in US Dollars Millions

Source: Sri Lanka Customs

The book chapter is organized as follows. In the next section, the relevant literature is outlined. This is followed by a section that presents and describes the methodology chosen. Then the findings are presented. Based on that, an analytical framework is presented and discussed. Finally, conclusion section is explained the contribution of the study and further research opportunities.

Literature Review

The institutional theory offers a theoretic framework to explain certain organizational phenomena and facilitates the inspection of structural variations, mainly as a response to environmental forces (Selznick, 1996). It further considers the legitimacy, the embeddedness of organizational fields, and the centrality of classification, routines, scripts and schema (Greenwood & Hinings, 1996). How institutions emerge with distinct forms, processes, strategies and competencies when there are environmental pressures are explained in the institutional theory.

In the case of the family businesses, family and capitalism become the central logic (Friedland & Alford, 1991). Family businesses account for a great number of private companies, and are perceived as the backbone of the world's economy and as sustainable business models (Hategan et al., 2019). The unified systems model states that the family represents history, traditions and life cycle of the family; where the business subsystem represents the strategies and structures utilized to generate wealth. Accordingly the individual family member represents the interests, skills and life stage of the participating family owners/managers (Habbershon et al., 2006). A family business of today serves to provide more than the accumulation of wealth under a system of capitalism and provides an opportunity to extend positive family relationships. Accordingly, the family business converts all social relations into mutual and unrestricted obligations oriented to the propagation of family members.

Acknowledging the institutional theory, the literature describes three dimensions of family business: (Olson, 2000), cohesion (the emotional bonding that family members have towards one another), flexibility (the amount of change in its leadership, role relationships and relationship rules), and communication (facilitating dimension). Family can aid as a resource enhancer and stress shield when disruption is encountered. This is called resilience capacity (Danes *et al.*, 2002); the accumulation of trust and creativity in problem solving in a family can be more easily and quickly tapped and adapted to dynamic environment. Communication style in a family business is a unique feature to control disruptions. As Winter & Morris (1996) noted, family business uses indirect communication extensively. Using nonverbal language to convey meaning could affect disruptions, procedures, and accomplishments in the firms.

Simultaneously, Oliver (1997) notes that the achievement of legitimacy gained through social acceptance, together with economic optimization of structure and processes, contribute to institutional success and survival of the family business. As such, the theoretic framework of institutionalism predicts the adjustment of organizational attributes, such as relationships, structures and strategies, as responses to environmental pressures or disruptions. Disruptions in family business can be classified as normative and non-normative. Normative family disruptions are those related with aging and family formation, whereas non-normative disruptions are not predictable or highly infrequent like the Covid pandemic.

Family businesses have always been capable of outperforming non-family companies in a dynamic environment with respect of decision-making, of adapting to economic changes, and of creating their competitive advantage (Miller and Breton-Miller, 2006). At a crisis scenario, family businesses leverage their opportunities by taking advantage of their attributes, such as shareholder structure, family legacy, the involvement of family members in the business, family governance, long-term vision, and risk-averse orientation. Furthermore, family businesses are characterized as agile with a craving for trustworthiness and creative, which dwellings them to perform better than non-family businesses.

Leaptrott (2005) argued that understanding how family business performance under various rates of change in combinations of task and environment could lead us to better descriptive models of success and survival in family businesses. Moreover, responding strategies towards environmental changes would extend the knowledge of institutionalization of survival strategies. On these notes, it suggests that institutional theory is useful in identifying that portion of conglomeration present in family businesses with respect to the differences in their structure and emblematic nature.

Resiliency is the owning family's use of an ability to adjust processes to disruptions (Danes, 2006). There have been a number of reasons posited for the less survival of family businesses during crisis situations (Tienda and Raijman, 2004); the relative nonattendance of role model; the low position of business ownership, human capital restraints in the form of business knowledge, experience, and skills of management; critical for raising financial capital and limited social and business networks. It is further opined that a positive interdependence between family, business process, and public community is productive for responding to the environmental changes (Niehm et al., 2007); family business can be destroyed if the boundaries are too diffuse (Stafford *et al.*, 1999); during times of distractions, family member CEO/ managers must renovate processes to safeguard sustainability (Danes *et al.*, 2005); resource and interpersonal processes should jointly utilize to optimize achievement of the objectives during the time of disruption (Danes, 2006).

Particularly, Danes et al. (2008) insisted that business-owning families may classify the need for an additional family structure, namely, a family council to handle specific issues that created the major changes into the business environment. Personal grounding is another unique feature in family business where the business owner is self-promoting when other family members are contributing to the business. Once the family business owners engage with cooperative working culture, it is likely to get the beneficial effect from the family member (Danes et al. 2007). In here, collective cultures are highly allied with cooperative personal grounding. Aforementioned, key characteristics of family business are concurrent roles, shared identity, a lifelong common history, emotional involvement, private language, mutual awareness, privacy, and the symbolic meaning of the family company (Stafford et al., 1999). Subsequently, the dimensions of the family business that determine its success and sustainability are the task structure, the legitimizing structure, and family organizational behavior.

Recent evidence suggest that family business governance and firm's leadership approaches create long-term investment capability and a valuable perspective in a dynamic environment, which position them as sustainable business organizations in the world (Cioca et al., 2020). Crisis management research inclines to be performed in large and or multinational organizations; however, the focus on family business is still fragmented (Bundy et al., 2017). In general, there is a misconception that family businesses seem to be too small and unimportant, however they are having extensive experience on the market, more stabilize, business heritage from generation to generation, and real economic contributions (Cioca et al., 2020). Having a closer look at prevailing literature on responses of family businesses towards different types of crises primarily focus on either susceptibility or the flexibility of such businesses (Quansah & Hartz, 2021; Jaskiewicz et al., 2020; Pramono et al., 2020; Kraus et al., 2020) and an individual's actions to recover or survive from disruptions (Combs et al., 2020).

In line with the decision-making process, Dyer (2010) specified four types of family culture characteristics that affect the company's survival decisions: (1) paternalistic culture—a fusion of the past values and present trends; (2) laissez-faire culture—employees are empowered to make decisions by themselves; (3) participative culture—a mixture of paternalistic and laissez-faire; and (4) professional culture—involvement of professional managers in the family business, result-oriented strategy. Moreover, the family group interaction, social interaction and inter-organizational interaction have been found to be vital in understanding why some family businesses are able to survive and why others cannot or take longer to do so. Thereby, family business studies rather extended in a new direction considering a macro, micro and meso level perspective. The micro level of analysis focuses on family firm owner's behaviour as an entity (Jaskiewicz et al., 2015). The meso-related factors focus on the interpersonal relationships that influence decisions in family businesses. It is important to understand how social trends influence the way family businesses evolve. The macro level refers to pressure emerging from professional associations such as government and organizational networks.

There are substantial challenges in developing a macro, micro and meso level model integrated with institutional theory on family business survival (Shepherd, 2009). The number of strategic business actions in their decision-making process in the short term will create business opportunities for the long-term results. In this context, "keeping up with the crises", the family business learns to change its dynamism and to learn to have a more agile behavior. Indeed, it is important to understand why some family businesses are able to survive and why others cannot or take longer to do so. Against this background, the overall aim of the present study is to explore how family businesses in the floriculture sector in Sri Lanka react and cope with this unexpected crisis, COVID-19. Our study reveals how institutional theory links with macro, micro and meso levels of interactions and the model offers a richer understanding of the survival, resilience and renewal process of floriculture family businesses in Sri Lanka.

Methods

As the target population, floricultural family businesses in Western Province were selected. The highest number of growers and exporters are inhabited in Western province due to the facility availableness in terms of exporting and local market access. Our paramount attention was given to individual cases, stressing the story of sequential nature of the floriculture family businesses. The owners of Family Businesses were carefully selected based on their economic contribution, years of experience, and number of employees. In order to select the policymakers, we considered their legitimate position, expertise, and involvement with the floriculture sector. On these notes, we used qualitative human judgement methodology to examine subjective human experience. The qualitative approach was suitable since it allows describing experiences of the participants through formal or informal interviews (Creswell, 2013) and it facilitates the researchers to link to the phenomena under investigation. This approach needs vigilant exploration because it depends on the knowledge and experience of the participants. It is further required to consider individual differences regarding the study design and participants, despite the desire to be able to replicate and other homogeneous factors. In this vein, the study considered individual differences of the participants with regard to the participant's attributes like years of experience and education.

The number of interviews conducted was decided with the emergence of saturation of themes (Saunders et al., 2017). The sampling was purposive; six to eight is recommended as an appropriate number of participants (Smith and Eatough, 2006) and opportunism and convenience were contributing factors in choosing the purposive sample for this study (Patton, 1990). As Creswell & Creswell (2018) insisted it is required to get participants' engagement and willingness to share their lived experiences on crisis and how and which family governance structures are used to manage. Accordingly, we conducted four in-depth interviews; representing four family businesses. We also conducted three in-depth interviews with policymakers to triangulate our data and findings (Refer to table 2 for participant details). Adhering to the country's current health and safety procedures, we mainly used the online video conferencing application (Zoom) as our interview platform.

Interviews followed in open-ended nature and used a semi-structured protocol. When developing the protocol, the reliability of the study was guaranteed and protected objectivity. The protocol must comprise field procedures, and it should lead and facilitate the data reporting (Yin, 2003). The opening section of the protocol was designed as an unstructured narrative section, which allows participants to tell their stories on the floriculture business. The second section was guided to get an in-depth discussion on firms' performance during the crisis; challenges, the consequences of COVID-19; coping strategies (internal and external); future plans, and lessons learned.

In order to explore the given overarching research aims, we employed the Constructivist Grounded Theory Approach (CGTM) (Charmaz & Belgrave, 2019). CGTM helped to maintain an active interaction with the research participants and to interpret participants' views meaningfully. The research process was not linear; hence, a concurrent data analysis was executed throughout the data collection period, and constant reflections were used to enhance analytical thinking. The initial findings allowed the study to construct abstractions that was then used to develop theories (Charmaz & Belgrave, 2012). As an ongoing process, the study reviewed existing literature to understand survival and resilience strategies used by family businesses during this pandemic. Acknowledging the principles of CGTM, the study started with a detailed, nuanced analysis of one case and then moving to the careful analysis of subsequent cases. The recorded interviews were transcribed verbatim to provide the data for the analysis. The process of analysis initiated with reading and re-reading of the transcribed interview to gain an appreciation of the whole story (familiarization). Then, a free textual analysis was performed to highlight the potential significant points (sense making). The highlighted points were then grouped to form common clusters of meaning (categorization). The holistic reflective analysis of the clusters of meaning led to the emergence of themes that appeared to be salient to a particular interview (intra-case themes). After completing holistic reflective analysis of all interviewees, a meta-level analysis across the interviewees was performed (inter-case themes). To enable the reader to develop a detailed appreciation of the participants' experiences and to allow their voices to be heard, the analytical findings include direct quotations from the empirical material generated from the interviews. Finally, we integrated the elements derived from the empirical findings and developed a model that can be used to foster and thrive family businesses in similar contexts.

Table 2. Participant details. Interviewee's profile – exporters

Interview Number or Code	Interview was held with	Gender	Education	Year of foundation/ founders	Generation in the business	Business with	Export items	No. of employees
Family Business-1(FB1)	Chief Executive Officer (CEO)	Male	Degree	1999Husband and Wife	1st	Germany, Denmark, Holland, USA, Middle-East, Japan, Korea, Australia	Tissue culture and then move on with rooted cuttings and pot plants	50 (6 managers)
Family Business-2(FB2)	Chief Executive Officer (CEO)[1]	Male	Degree	2003Husband and Wife	1st	Denmark, Holland, USA, Japan, Australia	Indoor pot plants (Green and Mini)	100 (3 managers)
Family Business-3(FB3)	Managing Director (MD)	Female	Post-graduate Degree	1998Mother and daughters	2nd	Japan, Holland, USA, Australia	Cut foliage, pot plants	100 (7 managers)
Family Business-4(FB4)	Chief Executive Officer (CEO)	Male	Diploma in agriculture	Himself	1st	Netherlands, France, Holland, UAE, UK, Japan, Germany, Kuwait	Cut foliage	200[2]

The outcomes of the analytical process are developed as emergent themes presented in the following sections. The emergent themes based on the cohesion of participants' feedbacks were grouped into key themes and sub-themes (Clarke & Braun, 2017) to reflect the perceptions and understanding of the participants involved in the interviews. The inclusions of some quotes are demonstrated in following sections to reflect the wider data set and analysis undertaken (refer to annexure 2 - Data structure).

Table 3. Interviews profile – policy makers

Interview was held with	Position	Organization	Gender
Policy maker 1	Director	Government	Female
Policy maker 2	President	Floriculture association	Male
Policy maker 3	Coordinator	Small and Medium scale Floriculture growers association	Male

FINDINGS

Challenges Experienced During the Pandemic

In order to cope with the shock and the many changes caused by COVID-19, hard and brave decisions had to be made by family business owners (Le Breton-Miller & Miller 2022). As revealed from the data, most of the Sri Lankan exporters run as family businesses. Among other businesses, floriculture is one of the very important industries. As we noticed, in Sri Lanka, lots of suppliers are from rural sectors. If we take the floriculture export business, it has cut-foliage, rooted plants, cut-flowers and tissue culture. Out of which, Sri Lanka made a turnover of 16 to 17 million dollars in 2019. Out of which about 60 to 70 percent was from the cut-foliage. According to the Director from the state regulatory body, before Covid, *our exporters were doing very well. But during the pandemic, they had to face lots of problems (policy maker 1).*

When conducting the interviews, we were first interested in hearing participants' thoughts on the impact of the Covid-19 on their business. At the end of all seven thought-provoking interviews, we identified 6 major challenges experienced by family business owners during the pandemic.

Challenge one: Demand fluctuation

Out of the five family businesses, four businesses experienced an unexpected demand for floriculture products such as pot plants and tissue culture plants.

For example, CEO of the Family Business 1 mentioned that he had increased the laboratory facilities for his tissue culture products. Still, he is not in a position to cater to the increased demand.

The strange thing about this business is the overall demand for the plants increases tremendously. We actually can't meet the demand at the moment. We expanded the lab capacity by 40% this year. (CEO, FB1)

According to him, the reason for this high demand could be,

As I said most of our customers are from Europe and people are not travelling and have to stay at home. But the garden centres are opened and people have started home gardening, as it seems like that was the only thing that they could do. Because of that the demand for plants has really increased and it was estimated to increase between 25% to 30% during the pandemic. I would say we are in the lucky side of the business.

The CEO of FB 2 shared similar thoughts;

During Covid, I had to face the changes of both the local and foreign markets. I didn't have a clear picture at the beginning. Suddenly there was a huge demand for floriculture products. I would say, for us, the price was not the problem but it was to find a way to supply the increasing demand. (CEO, FB2)

I had a lot of orders from my buyers and due to high freight cost I faced some difficulties with exporting cut foliage. Luckily, the buyers agreed to bear the freight cost because the quality of our products is high. I have a growers' network to collect cut foliage. Due to that, I have supplied the buyers requirements and growers in our network also benefited in this crucial situation. (CEO, FB2)

However, the businesses focused on flowers did not receive such demand and had to pay off the staff salaries and other costs out of the savings, which made the owner very unhappy and frustrated.

I predicted that this would last only a couple of months, and we can get back to the normal conditions. But I was wrong. When things were getting worst, I felt terrible. I didn't see any light at the end of the tunnel. I am now maintaining my employees and the plants by using my own resources. No orders were received from many of my buyers. (CEO, FB 4)

Challenge Two: Increased Airfreight

Another challenge mentioned by the owners was the increase in airfreight. Because of the pandemic, the freight rates charges doubled, or some instances got tripled. Unfortunately, some of the companies who are dealing with bigger plants like rooted plants and cut foliage faced a lot of problems. Because their freight component of the cost went up; in some instances, the freight itself was more than their selling price, —this impacted on their export turnover. And a lot of companies suffered due to this problem.

Unfortunately, because of this pandemic situation, their freight cost was so high, they could not be sustained in the business because they could not get that proportional price increase from their customers. Pre-Covid, the fright charges were like 30% -35% from the selling price. But Post- Covid it is now increased to 70% – 80% from the selling price. It seems that there is no margin or sometimes incur a small loss. But a product like tissue culture plants need very minimal space; with one cubic foot we can send more than a thousand plants. Therefore, freight cost per plant is very low. Therefore, returns are high in tissue culture plants. So the freight cost hike did not very much effect tissue culture plant exporters. (CEO, FB1)

Challenge Three: Issues Relating to Labor

The next big challenge the floriculture industry faced was attracting and retaining the staff during the pandemic. The industry is mainly driven as labor-intensive, and most of the companies found it difficult to retain employees with the travel restrictions and fear of the pandemic. Also, staff wellbeing and health were major concerns during the pandemic.

FB1, FB2 and FB3 are highly concerned about their employees, and they provide separate transport for all workers, and all health guidelines were followed on their premises. Ayurvedic drinks that can develop immunity were given to all workers.

The FB2 informed that he had given bonuses to his workers in the year 2020 with this pandemic situation.

There were instances where sometimes the villagers complained to PHI (Public Health Inspector) when we commenced our operations. (CEO, FB2) But also appreciated our health concern.

Challenge Four: Unhealthy Competition

Another challenge mentioned by the business owners was the unnecessary competition among the members in the industry. There were instances where competitors compromise the price to sustain in the market.

There is a big competition among the suppliers. We expect the industry to grow fast. However, some of the exporters tend to stick with cut-foliage, and there was a lack of diversity. We prepared a strategic plan, but it is yet to be implemented. There are lots of exporters who export without any product differentiation. They just compromise by undercutting each other. They reduce the price to attract buyers. (Policymaker 1)

Challenge Five: Insufficient Support Given by the Government.

Participants complained about the lack of government support and lack of focus on the floriculture industry. The common perception was that "if the government had been involved, we would be doing much better" (CEO, FB 4).

If further elaborate;

There are no specific loan facilities for the sector. We borrow money based on the current rates. Banking procedures haven't changed You may need to show security and lots of other stuff. There are grants for some businesses. There are no special credit lines for us. However, we don't expect finical assistance as such. We know that government is also in a crisis. We do not ask for money. But we need the government to understand what this business is. (CEO, FB1)

I think the government has to move beyond their bureaucratic decisions and need to have a national focus. I really appreciate the support given by the Export Development Board. However, we have less scientific research on this business. It is required to have proper institutional support. No proper financial support schemes were found during the pandemic. (CEO, FB 2)

Challenge Six: Transferring of Leadership to the Next Generation

All four family businesses that we considered in our study explained that they are now thinking about the next level of ownership. This can be seen as a common issue in family businesses. But the Coivd -19 pandemic led the current owners to consider who is going to undertake the business next. However, FB 4 explained that;

My family blamed me for wasting my savings on plants and soil. I have to close the business soon, it seems. (CEO, FB 4)

Policymaker 1 also explained lot of exporters in the country are family businesses and their behaviors highly effects to the foreign exchange earnings to the country. Accordingly, government policies need to develop to maintain these family businesses.

This is a crucial issue in the country. Many poor employees depend on this type of family businesses and the closing of these businesses affects a number of families. This situation affects to social living status of the Sri Lankans. (Policymaker 1)

Survival Strategy of Covid-19 Pandemic

The results revealed that floriculture firms embrace significant trade achievements through Instinctive decision making and capacity of resource reallocation, prioritization and improvisation processes at individual, family group, inter-organizational levels and across these levels. Through synthesized coherence (Locke and Golden-Biddle, 2014) we developed the data structure (Refer Annexure 2). We, then proposed a model (as shown in Figure 1) of survival strategies in floriculture family businesses that depict how family businesses respond to the long-lasting crisis through macro, micro and meso levels of interactions.

Demand Fluctuation

Some of the family businesses handled the unexpended demand in a very effective way. According to some participants, the instinctive decision making and prediction ability helped them to face unexpected demands. Also, they have moved with lab expansion and capital-intensive systems.

In my case, my lab had the capacity of producing 1.2 million plants a year. Now I can produce 2 million plants a year. But now I doubt about 2022. I don't know what to do with that excess demand. The entire 2 million pants were sold out. I am still getting more demands. I have to look for a bigger lab facility. It's not easy as you say. For export, we need to maintain the quality and requirements. Now I'm looking for other possibilities to expand my business. (CEO, FB 1)

He also added the importance of focusing on the business and reflects on own mistakes to move forwards. From his view, we can realize that self-reflection and prediction are the most crucial factors during a crisis.

According to the CEO of FB1;

I did that. Any business makes mistakes. I took this as a good opportunity to look at my own business, say five to ten years and see how things went wrong. Now it is much more streamlined.

Similar thoughts were gathered from the interview with the MD at FB 3; according to her,

I believe in myself and my family, and my employees. We never want to stop. We look after employees and families. I always care for them. Basically, we have been dealing with many Covid 19 cases. I always have my staff to look after what we want. We always learned from my mistakes. We are not just jumping into opportunities. We, together with our staff, decide on our priorities.

On the other hand, diversification was another strategy they used to survive and sustain in the business.

We always change and do what the market want. We sell whatever we create. Diversification is key to our success. We didn't compromise on quality. We are always faithful to our buyers. That was the main reason as to why we survived during Covid. We never let them down. So during the pandemic, our customers never let us down. (MD, FB 3)

After Covid, we need to do more things to expand the industry. We need to move with different products varieties. It is essential do research and development. If we stagnate with a fewer variety, the risk is that when the buyer says no, we do not have anything to offer. We have a lack of infrastructure. (Policymaker1)

CEO FB2 shared a similar idea. He mentioned that diversification and value addition are the priorities in this industry. He used his instincts to move forward in the business.

The right use of technology is what we need the most. People were scared of investing in technology. However, being different, I always invest in technology and am never afraid of taking the risk. It is important to add value to our products. It takes time. But it is worth to spent capital and time for value addition to the products we have. I use my instincts and experience to do the feasibility support. (CEO, FB2)

Increased Airfreight

Some of the businesses moved to local markets and managed to balance their cash flow without much burden. Also, quality was the main concern in the industry, and they make sure to maintain the same quality and believing that buyers would bear the increased freight charges.

Freight charges increased, and for some products, some businesses bearded the portion of the freight cost, but we directly told them (customers) that we could not bear the freight cost. And we adjusted the selling price according to the freight charges. Because I was with the local market as well as in the foreign market, I was able to manage my cash flow without any problem. (CEO, FB2)

Else they save some of the money by cutting some of their nonessential expenditure.

When it (the Pandemic) was announced in Japan, the USA, and Holland, I was worried and panicked. We together with our finance department cut all our unnecessary commitments. We were so strict about what we were doing. (MD, FB 3)

Issues Relating to Labor

Almost all the companies undertook a humane approach to look after their employees. The employees were provided with all the necessary safety gear and health instructions. The company looked after both the employees and their families. The main human resource characteristics that owners used to sustain their employees were communication, listening, empathy, and trust.

Fortunately, I have a very well experienced staff just like the backbone of my company. We did struggle during the pandemic. We couldn't send the shipment. We had a problem with people coming to work. I didn't reduce their salaries. In fact this year I gave them a very good increase, as my business has been good. But I have told them that there could be occasions that we all have to carry the cost if we cannot ship the products. I communicated to them that I can't give you what I'm giving you now. They are very clear about that. I think commutation between CEO and the employees is the most important thing. (CEO, FB1)

He added how it is important to treat the employees as part of the family during a crisis situation.

I would say you have to be a good listener. That is very important. It's not about trying to push your way through and trying to give your opinions. I always I try to get people to gather and discuss the issue. And get their views. Then they feel they are part of the solution. That is extremely important.

...If an employee makes a mistake, I have to back the employee. If the mistake is a genuine one, you need to accept that as a human error. You have to do that to let people think innovatively. Otherwise, they think this is what I was told, and I should follow the rule. I have to talk to them, discuss with them and let them work on their own. Always support them. They will come up with new ideas. I have developed a very informal culture here in my business. My doors are opened all the time to discuss whatever problem they have. You have to build that situation. Then only you will get the best out of the people, especially during this trying time. They are part of the family. (CEO, FB1)

None of the companies had staff deduction. They treated that as an achievement and showed self-pride when exploring the fact. Most of the companies were able to pay bonuses/incentive? to their employees.

We didn't lose a single staff member. I'm worried about their wellbeing. Today I got all my staff vaccinated. We didn't stop production. Covid 19 is a health issue; if we use the proper precautionary, we would be safe. We gave all the protective gear, traditional medicine and let employees to steam during the work time. We build bio bubbles and we somehow managed it. (MD, FB 3)

Initially, I felt the risk. And things were uncertain. However, I didn't cut my staff. Although we were under a pandemic situation, I paid a bonus to my staff. (CEO, FB2)

Being different to others, the CEO of FB 2 also shared how he transformed from Labor intensive to capital intensive.

This industry is moreover run on labor. But I made a difference. I diversified the business with capital intensive technologies. I changed the systems. This was the main reason that I survived during the pandemic. There was a minimum impact to the business. We were under big pressure. We had to find a way to look after plants. Since we mechanized the system on some occasions, I managed the operation with only two individuals. And we used tables to place our plants, and that helped us to avoid growing weed. (CEO, FB2)

Unhealthy Competition

According to the policymakers, one reason that industry is not growing is due to unhealthy competition. The unexpected demand for floriculture products leads some of the companies to bypass the quality requirements.

However, according to CEO FB2, knowledge sharing is one of the best ways to move forward and stop unnecessary competition.

There is a big competition among the growers which I don't like. I would like to share my technical expertise with the competitors. I think that it's the best way for the growth of this industry. I build friendly relationships with others. (CEO, FB2)

This was seconded by policymaker 3, who represented a floriculture association. According to him,

Because of the unhealthy competition, we may lose our buyers. Therefore floriculture businesses need to work together and maintain the quality of the products. (Policymaker 3)

Government Support

Government support is very important. There should be firm government policies to attract investors. If there is no proper government support, there won't be any industry to talk about in the next five years. The decisions should consider the consequences.

Last year we decided that we want to make a strategic plan for the industry. There was a lot of support given by the government. The agencies in Sri Lanka had been very supportive throughout the time towards this industry. However, I'm not that satisfied with the support given by top regulatory bodies when it comes to planning and support. We are trying our best to get the expected government support. The sector needs support. If the government gives that support, there will be many more people who will be benefited, employment wise and economically. (CEO, FB 1)

He further clarified:

We need the high authorities to know about the requirements of the industry. They just think floriculture is just what you see around the road. They don't see beyond. We would like the government to understand the infrastructure required for the industry. We need to show our buyers, look, this is what we have in Sri Lanka, we need to show that the infrastructure we use in the industry has quality as any other place in the world.

Our plan was to have selected show them growers from different districts for different products and to make them grow plants for export market. We then how to grow plants, and then we buy products from them. Subsequently, out of these groups of people, at least some of them will be in a position in export on their own. They will be open to a wider market. We have to work on this matter. (CEO, FB 1)

We have to create a system to measure the quality of the product. We have to have a traceability system and establish the standards. Although there are some protests against our efforts, we need to have a good system to check the quality. (Policymaker 1)

Acknowledging the above facts, Policymaker 2 insists that post-crisis support from the government is required to cope with the new normal condition of local small growers.

If you take the local business in Sri Lanka in floriculture, there are lot of small nurseries and organizations spread all over Sri Lanka. There are associations (e.g. Suwahas Mal has 20000 – 25000 members) funded by the Sri Lankan government. Roughly I would say there are around 100000 people who are involved in this business. That segment of the business was also affected. Especially due to the current lockdown. When the country was opened after the lockdown, we saw the same trend in Sri Lanka; the local customers also started buying plants for their home gardens. Flower gardening is a stress releasing exercise; due to that in the lockdown period also local growers got a higher demand for their plants. But due to the lack of weddings and ceremonies, cut flower producers faced a lot of financial issues. However, during the third wave, now things have stopped. The local business mainly goes on provisional or district wise as they have exhibitions organized by associations. After the third-wave now, people have lost this market. No exhibitions, no fairs nothing...(Policymaker 2)

Transferring of Leadership to the Next Generation

Continuation of a family business is not only important for the family itself. It is crucial for the country's economy and employee security as well.

Policymaker 1 exclaimed that,

The second generation is not interested in the business. Fathers started the business with a very humble beginning but their daughters and sons with foreign education were not ready to continue the business. (Policymaker 1)

However, during the Coiv-19 pandemic, the owners were able to receive their family support, and there is a tendency that the second generation will join the business.

One of my daughters got interested in this business during the pandemic, and she felt sorry for me, and she started working with me. Now I have got her involved with quality assurance. I think she will be a good successor. Even my clients are asking me what will happen after me. Now I have hope. (CEO, FB 1)

As a different opinion, the CEO of FB 2 mentioned that he is willing to hand over the business to the staff:

I'm focusing on my second level staff to run the business. I do not depend on my children. They can monitor the business. But I always believe in my staff, and I feel they can run the business. I always give them the freedom to make decisions. (CEO, FB2)

A common theme recognized from the success stories;

You need to make sure how you are going to survive during a crisis. It may be different from business to business. (CEO, FB 1)

There should be a change in our attitudes. We have our own natural resources, which is a blessing, such as climate and soil. We need to use those to expand the industry. (Policymaker 1)

DISCUSSION

Based on the findings discussed above, we developed a framework to understand how family businesses survive during a crisis.

The model implies that a family business incorporates cohesion (Family support), flexibility (Instinctive decision making and Founder ideologies and capabilities) and communication (Humane approaches) (Olson, 2000), to increase its capacity to produce for the market, meet customer needs, earn better prices and attain profitable operations even in the pandemic situation. The study opines that the unique strength of family businesses lies in their ability to oblige as a resource improver and stress defense when disruption is encountered (Danes et al., 2002).

Figure 1. Model of survival, resilience and renewal strategies in floriculture family businesses

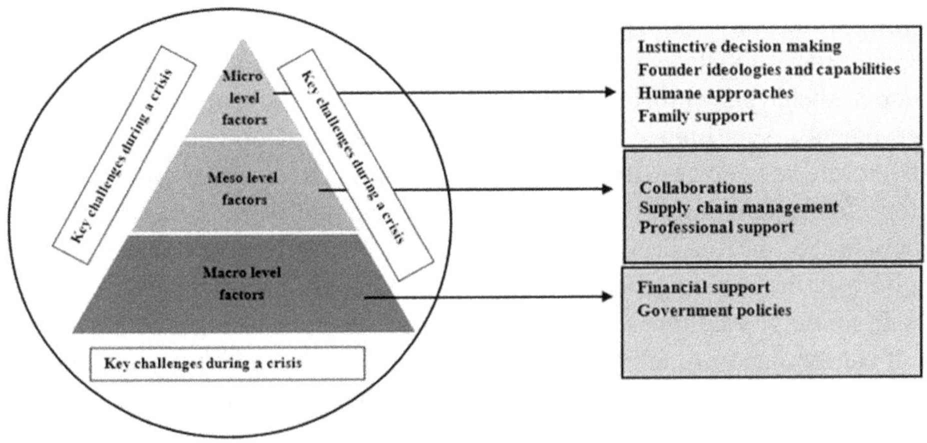

Family business literature mostly highlights that family firms rely heavily on family labor, specifically on management positions. Interestingly, the majority of the management positions in the selected cases of our study are convened by non-family labors. As we were informed, those employees are pertained as a part of the family and extends emotional responses to them. Undoubtedly, showing emotional responses on employees and their families is likely more effective when taking management priority to adjust to the new normal such as shifting workhours, following health instructions, salary adjustment and so on. The role of family and family business leaders during the crisis has been emphasized (Herbane, 2019) in the study. As Smith & Riley (2012) proposed, our cases revealed the key attributes for crisis leadership; powerful two-way interpersonal communication skills, the capacity to empathize with the feelings of others, the ability to quickly develop new ideas and solutions and turn problems into opportunities. At the micro level, the family firms show four survival strategies; collect the facts, build a contingency plan, be convincing and communicate to bring positive changes in the business and in turn enhance survival and growth of the business. Thus, founder's capabilities, such as sensing and seizing, continuous learning, succession planning, mobilizing resources and reconfiguration are essential for family business's survival and growth.

We agree that the institutional theory predicts organizational attributes, such as interpersonal relationships influence the way family businesses evolve and responses to environmental pressures or disruptions (Tindiwensi et al., 2020). The findings insist that the selected firms extract value from cooperation, contacts and networks with fellow firms, associations and professional bodies in obtaining information, enhancing product quality and expanding the production process. The firms that successfully face the crisis opined the importance of ample investment in research and development to develop new products with market requirements (sudden) and to enhance the firm's survival and growth (Belitski & Khalil, 2020).

Given the inconclusive debate, policy maker 3 denoted that family business owners are behaving with a lack of transparency, and they are envious on others' trade achievements. As he opined, only few firms dominate the floriculture export market and there are so many restrictions laid on newcomers. Accordingly, the floriculture sector's future remains at the hands of few people and there is no strong second layer of the sector. Kets de Vries (1993) claims that 70% of family businesses fail to survive over the second generation and the third-generation' failure recorded 90%. As said so, the floriculture sector could have the effects of losing a family business and it can be intensely felt by the business' stakeholders and the community. In here, the responder specifically emphasized that there is an urgent requirement to execute risk assessment and evaluation mechanism for the floriculture sector, like financial sector, to ensure the sustainability of the sector. This becomes a skeptical view and further examination is required to be considered.

Family business's philosophy is unique and comes from the family itself, and family governance structures accelerate or inhibit family power within family firms. However, the arrival of the Covid-19 pandemic has made things worse, feeding concerns about the future of the business and the role of family businesses. Given that concern, it is common to seek government assistance and facilities in terms of finance, policies, assurance and wellbeing. The majority of our respondents indicated that the government support was extended towards the loan repayment deferrals, low-interest loans, tax rebates, airfreight reliefs arrangements and providing curfew passes. However, national-level crisis management regulations and mechanisms were not properly formed to the sector. In line with that, in general, the respondents claimed that the government recognition of the floriculture sector is minimum, and authorities do not recognize the real economic contributions of the sector. They further argued that the absence of a specific authority for the sector becomes crucial since there is no common platform to discuss the issues that arise. Thus, direct government intervention on the floriculture sector is a must and there is a vital requirement to establish a so-called 'Floriculture Council'.

Our findings mainly propose that it does not look harmful that the floriculture family businesses do not having a methodical approach to manage crisis. Interestingly, an environment that is based on cohesion, flexibility, communication, collaboration and government support seems to be a good basis to deal with COVID-19 crisis. However, Mokhbar et al. (2017) indicate that family businesses mostly fail to survive beyond the first-generation family owners due to the lack of capability to plan its progression and transitioning phase of the business. Due to crisis like Covid, if there is no concern about the succession of the business, family business collapses easily. The failure of family business would not only influence the family but also the stakeholders such as employees, suppliers, creditors and so on and create a public scandal. Thus, in a dynamic environment, family business's strategic planning needs to be oriented to the long-term sustainability performance, analyze all investments and risk associated and focused on capital preservation and short-term drive actions. All these notes mean that family businesses should be evaluated to understand the future growth predictions, and it should be executed through a professional risk assessment and evaluation authority. Thus, government investigations need to protect family businesses to maintain continuous foreign exchange earnings and to protect employees' social wellbeing.

CONCLUSION

Our study aims to provide both theoretical and empirical contributions to the field of family business research and crisis management. The study contributes to the extant literature on what family businesses do to adapt to a rapidly changing business environment and appropriate responses to disruptions by offering an empirical basis for a currently unexplored research area in the most developing nations. In general, it is opined that especially in developing nations, a significant number of family businesses do not survive and grow for longer decades (Morgan et al., 2021). We further intend to contribute to the stream of literature by revealing the fact that not only business owner adjustment strategies but also simultaneous government and inter-organizational intervention on family business can be helpful in thriving the business during the pandemic.

What we evidence at current situation is reaction time is a key driver for success in any business. The difference between the verbs "to have" or "to lose" makes family businesses think twice about their investment decisions and causes them to deploy a detailed management analysis according to their set-up strategy (Cioca et al., 2020). Our findings mainly pointed that family business's philosophy is unique and comes from the family values, traditions, and beliefs that are spread throughout the business, finally encompassing the firm's strategy. The family business intends to analyze very carefully all investments and the risk associated. In this respect, family businesses intended to be risk averse, especially applicable for the floriculture business, where the competition is not at a height level.

The findings will be used either by a family business owner individually or by the whole sector to increase knowledge on the effect of survival strategies on the growth and development of the floriculture sector during the pandemic period. Based on the survival strategies in floriculture farms, the knowledge and application of crisis management theories will extend, and would lead to the progression of the sector, specifically in a developing context. The results will feature a satisfactory view of the floriculture farms' endeavor in the global pandemic situation. This will be transmitting the message that a family business must focus on specific strategies, micro, meso and macro, that could lead to the survival and sustainability of the sector, which in turn may act as a catalyst to gain competitive advantage and market success. All these notes will help in mapping out the survival strategies of floriculture growers in the family business system, which provides a direction to link individual, social and organizational levels environment to deploy resources in effective manner and to manage the crisis well in the future.

The study was conducted on family businesses in the floriculture export sector; hence results may/must be used cautiously in other sectors, and economies that are not fundamentally defined. However, the study depicts the floriculture sector as a lucrative area for family business research. Moreover, since the study's geographical focus on Western Province in Sri Lanka it may limit the transferability of our results to other countries. The institutional theory framework we used extends only one lens through which to examine macro, micro and meso levels of interactions in the seven cases studied. Despite these limitations, we open up several avenues for future research on how family businesses absorb from crisis experiences, succeed obstacles by learning, and/or integrate changes to their business to survive and reinforce the crisis. Moreover, there is a complex interplay between macro, micro and meso levels and the founder's capabilities on sensing and seizing, continuous learning, succession planning, mobilizing resources and reconfiguration needs further investigation.

REFERENCES

Afredo, D., Kotler, J., Chua, J. H., & Chrisman, J. J. (2014). Ability and willingness as sufficiency condition for family-oriented particularistic behaviour: Implication for theory and empirical studies. *Journal of Small Business Management*, *52*(2), 344–364. doi:10.1111/jsbm.12102

Belitski, M., & Khalil, S. (2020). Dynamic capabilities for firm performance under the information technology governance framework. *European Business Review*, *32*(2), 129–157. doi:10.1108/EBR-05-2018-0102

Bundy, J., Pfarrer, M. D., Short, C. E., & Coombs, W. T. (2017). Crises and crisis management: Integration, interpretation, and research development. *Journal of Management*, *43*(6), 1661–1692. doi:10.1177/0149206316680030

Central Bank Report. (2020). Annual Report Central Bank of Sri Lanka, Central Bank of Sri Lanka.

Charmaz, K., & Belgrave, L. (2012). Qualitative interviewing and grounded theory analysis. The SAGE handbook of interview research: The complexity of the craft, 2, 347-365. Sage.

Charmaz, K., & Belgrave, L. L. (2019). Thinking about data with grounded theory. *Qualitative Inquiry*, *25*(8), 743–753. doi:10.1177/1077800418809455

Cioca, A., Wehbe, K., Popescu, D., & Popescu, C. (2020). The main drivers for sustainable decisions in a family business that impact the company's performance. *Sustainability*, *12*(20), 8659. doi:10.3390u12208659

Clarke, V., & Braun, V. (2017). Thematic analysis. *The Journal of Positive Psychology*, *12*(3), 297–298. doi:10.1080/17439760.2016.1262613

Combs, J. G., Shanine, K. K., Burrows, S., Allen, J., & Pounds, T. (2020). What do we know about business families? Setting the stage for leveraging family science theories. *Family Business Review*, *33*(1), 38–63. doi:10.1177/0894486519863508

Creswell, J. (2013). *Qualitative Inquiry & Research Design – Choosing Among Five Approaches* (3rd ed.). Sage.

Creswell, J. W., & Creswell, J. D. (2018). *Research Design: Qualitative, Quantitative and Mixed Methods Approaches* (5th ed.). SAGE Publications, Inc.

Danes, S. M. (2006). Tensions within family business-owning couples over time. *Stress, Trauma and Crisis*, *9*(3–4), 227–246. doi:10.1080/15434610600854244

Danes, S. M., Haberman, H. R., & Mc Tavish, D. (2005). Gendered discourse about family business. *Family Relations*, *54*(1), 116–130. doi:10.1111/j.0197-6664.2005.00010.x

Danes, S. M., Loy, J. T., & Stafford, K. (2008). Management practices of small private firms within a quality framework. *Journal of Small Business Management*, *46*(3), 21–30. doi:10.1111/j.1540-627X.2008.00250.x

Danes, S. M., Rueter, M. A., Kwon, H. K., & Doherty, W. (2002). Family FIRO model: An application to family business. *Family Business Review*, *15*(1), 31–43. doi:10.1111/j.1741-6248.2002.00031.x

Danes, S. M., Stafford, K., & Loy, J. T. (2007). Family business performance: The effects of gender and management. *Journal of Business Research*, *60*(10), 1058–1069. doi:10.1016/j.jbusres.2006.12.013

De Massis, A., Audretsch, D., Uhlaner, L., & Kammerlander, N. (2018). Innovation with limited resources: Management lessons from the German Mittelstand. *Journal of Product Innovation Management*, *35*(1), 125–146. doi:10.1111/jpim.12373

Department of Census and Statistics. (2021). *Number and area of Agriculture holdings by all sectors and by district*. Statistics. http://www.statistics.gov.lk/Agriculture/StaticalInformation/CensusOfAgriculture/NumberAndAreaOfAgricultureHoldingsByAllSectorsAndbyDistrict

Dyer, W. G. (2010). *Cultural Change in Family Firms: Anticipating and Managing Business and Family Transitions*. Jossey-Bass.

EDB trade Analysis System. (2021). Export Development Board.

Food and Agriculture Organization, United Nations (UNFAO). (2020). *COVID-19: Our hungriest, most vulnerable communities face "a crisis within a crisis*. FAO. https://www.fao.org/news/story/en/item/1269721/icode/?utm_source=twitter&utm_medium=social+media&utm_campaign=fao (31.05.2021)

Friedland, R., & Alford, R. R. (1991). Bringing society back in: Symbols, practices, and institutional contradictions. In W. W. Powell & P. J. DiMaggio (Eds.), *The new institutionalism in organizational analysis* (pp. 232–263). University of Chicago Press.

Greenwood, R., & Hinings, C. R. (1996). Understanding radical change. *Academy of Management Review*, *21*, 1022–1054. doi:10.2307/259163

Habbershon, T. G., Mary, W., & MacMillan, I. C. (2006). A unified systems perspective of family firm performance. In P. Z. Poutziouris, K. X. Smyrnios, & S. B. Klein (Eds.), *Handbook of Research on Family Business* (pp. 67–79). Edward Elgar. doi:10.4337/9781847204394.00013

Hategan, C. D., Curea-Pitorac, R. I., & Hategan, V. P. (2019). The Romanian Family Businesses Philosophy for Performance and Sustainability. *Sustainability*, *11*(6), 1715. doi:10.3390u11061715

Herbane, B. (2019). Rethinking organizational resilience and strategic renewal in SMEs. *Entrepreneurship and Regional Development*, *31*(5–6), 476–495. doi:10.1080/08985626.2018.1541594

Jaskiewicz, P., Combs, J., & Bau, S. (2015). Entrepreneurial legacy: Towards a theory of how some family firms nurture transgenerational entrepreneurship. *Journal of Business Venturing*, *30*(1), 29–49. doi:10.1016/j.jbusvent.2014.07.001

Jaskiewicz, P., Neubaum, D. O., De Massis, A., Daniel, T., & Holt, D. T. (2020). The Adulthood of Family Business Research Through Inbound and Outbound Theorizing. *Family Business Review*, *33*(1), 10–17. doi:10.1177/0894486520904461

Kets de Vries, M. F. R. (1993). The dynamics of family controlled firms: The good and the bad news. *Organizational Dynamics*, *21*(3), 59–71. doi:10.1016/0090-2616(93)90071-8

Kraus, S., Clauss, T., Breier, M., Gast, J., Zardini, A., & Tiberius, V. (2020). The economics of COVID-19: Initial empirical evidence on how family firms in five European countries cope with the corona crisis. *International Journal of Entrepreneurial Behaviour & Research*, *26*(5), 1067–1092. doi:10.1108/IJEBR-04-2020-0214

Le Breton-Miller, I., & Miller, D. (2022). Family businesses under COVID-19: Inspiring models–Sometimes. *Journal of Family Business Strategy*, *13*(2), 100452. doi:10.1016/j.jfbs.2021.100452

Leaptrott, J. (2005). An institutional theory view of the family business. *Family Business Review*, *18*(3), 215–228. doi:10.1111/j.1741-6248.2005.00043.x

Locke, K., & Golden-Biddle, K. (2014). Constructing opportunities for contribution: Structuring intertextual coherence and 'problematization' on organizational studies. *Academy of Management Journal*, *40*(5), 1023–1062. doi:10.2307/256926

Miller, D., & Le Breton-Miller, I. (2006). Family Governance and Firm Performance: Agency, Stewardship, and Capabilities. *Family Business Review*, *19*(1), 73–87. doi:10.1111/j.1741-6248.2006.00063.x

Mokhbar, M., Gi Gi, T., Abdul Rasid, S. Z., Vakilbashi, A., Mohd Zamil, N., & Woon, S. Y. (2017). Succession planning and family business performance in SMEs. *Journal of Management Development*, *36*(3), 330–347. doi:10.1108/JMD-12-2015-0171

Morgan, M., Emmanuel, E. O., Christian, A., Winifred, E., & Anthony, O. (2021). Dynamic capabilities of family business: A catalyst for survival and growth. *Problems and Perspectives in Management*, *19*(1), 137–150. doi:10.21511/ppm.19(1).2021.12

Niehm, L. S., Tyner, K., Shelley, M. C., & Fitzgerald, M. A. (2010). Technology adoption in small family-owned businesses: Accessibility, perceived advantage, and information technology literacy. *Journal of Family and Economic Issues*, *31*(4), 498–515. doi:10.100710834-010-9197-0

Oliver, C. (1997). Sustainable competitive advantage: Combining institutional and resource-based views. *Strategic Management Journal*, *18*(9), 697–713. doi:10.1002/(SICI)1097-0266(199710)18:9<697::AID-SMJ909>3.0.CO;2-C

Olson, D. H. (2000). Circumplex model of marital and family systems. *Journal of Family Therapy*, *22*(2), 144–167. doi:10.1111/1467-6427.00144 PMID:6840263

Patton, M. Q. (1990). *Qualitative Evaluation and Research Methods*. Sage Publications.

Pramono, R., Suyantoko2, Purwanto, A., Kristiana, Y., Yuliantoro, N. and Asbari, M. (2020). Implementation Of Analysis of Talent Management in Family Business. *International Journal of Advanced Science and Technology*, *29*(6), 6124–6146.

Quansah, E., & Hartz, D. E. (2021). Strategic adaptation: Leadership lessons for small business survival and success. *American Journal of Business*, *36*(3/4), 190–207. doi:10.1108/AJB-07-2020-0096

Report, I. P. S. (2020). The Annual Sri Lanka State of the Economy Report, Institute of Policy Studies of Sri Lanka. IPS Publications Unit.

Saunders, B., Sim, J., Kingstone, T., Baker, S., Waterfield, J., Bartlam, B., & Jinks, C. (2017). Saturation in qualitative research: Exploring its conceptualization and operationalization. *Quality & Quantity*, *52*(4), 1893–1907. doi:10.100711135-017-0574-8 PMID:29937585

Selznick, P. (1996). Institutionalism "old" and "new.". *Administrative Science Quarterly*, *41*(2), 270–277. doi:10.2307/2393719

Shepherd, D. A. (2009). Grief recovery from the loss of a family business: A multi- and meso-level theory. *Journal of Business Venturing*, *24*(1), 81–97. doi:10.1016/j.jbusvent.2007.09.003

Smith, J. A., & Eatough, V. (2006). Interpretative phenomenological analysis. In G. M. Breakwell, S. Hammond, C. Fife-Schan, & J. A. Smith (Eds.), *Research Methods in Psychology*. Sage.

Smith, L., & Riley, D. (2012). School leadership in times of crisis. *School Leadership & Management*, *32*(1), 57–71. doi:10.1080/13632434.2011.614941

Sri Lanka Labour Force. (2019). *Survey Annual Report*. Department of Census and Statistics, Sri Lanka (http://www.statistics.gov.lk/LabourForce/StaticalInformation/AnnualReports/2019)

Stafford, K., Duncan, K. A., Danes, S. M., & Winter, M. (1999). A research model of sustainable family businesses. *Family Business Review*, *12*(3), 197–208. doi:10.1111/j.1741-6248.1999.00197.x

Tienda, M., & Raijman, R. (2004). Promoting Hispanic immigrant entrepreneurship in Chicago. *Journal of Developmental Entrepreneurship*, *9*(1), 1–21.

Tindiwensi, C.K., Abaho, E., Munene, J.C., Muhwezi, M. and Nkote, I.N. (2020), Entrepreneurial bricolage in smallholder commercial farming: a family business perspective. *Journal of Family Business Management*. doi:10.1108/JFBM-04-2020-0036

Winter, M., & Morris, E. (1998). Family resource management and family business: Coming together in theory and research. In The Entrepreneurial Family, RKZHeck (ed.). Needham, MA: Family Business Resources, Inc.

Wright, L. (2020). Annals of history: Crossroads. A scholar of the plague thinks that pandemics wreak havoc—and open minds. *The New Yorker*.

WTO. (2020a). *Trade set to plunge as COVID-19 Pandemic upends global economy. World* Trade Organisation Press Release. https://www.wto.org/english/news_e/pres20_e/pr855_e.htm#:~:text=World%20merchandise%20trade%20is%20set,effectiveness%20of%20the%20policy%20responses. (accessed 29.05.2021).

WTO. (2020b). *Methodology for the WTO trade forecast*. WTO. https://www.wto.org/english/news_e/pres20_e/methodpr855_e.pdf

Yin, R. K. (2003). *Case Study Research: Design and Methods*. Sage publications.

ADDITIONAL READINGS

Galappattige, A. (2020). COVID-19 and Food and Agriculture in Sri Lanka - Update on Impact of Lock down March 20, Agricultural Situation Agriculture in the News. *Global Agricultural Information Network, Voluntary Report, CE2020-0002*. https://www.fas.usda.gov/data/sri-lanka-covid-19-and-food-and-agriculture-sri-lanka-update-impact-lock-down-march-20

World Bank in Sri Lanka. (2021). *Overview*. World Bank. https://www.worldbank.org/en/country/srilanka/overview#1

ENDNOTES

1 Recipient of presidential award as the best exporter

2 Now reduced to 15 due to the pandemic situation

APPENDIX

Appendix A: Agriculture Export Data

(Sources: Export Development Board, Sri Lanka)

Figure 2. Analysis of Vegetable Export (Kg.)

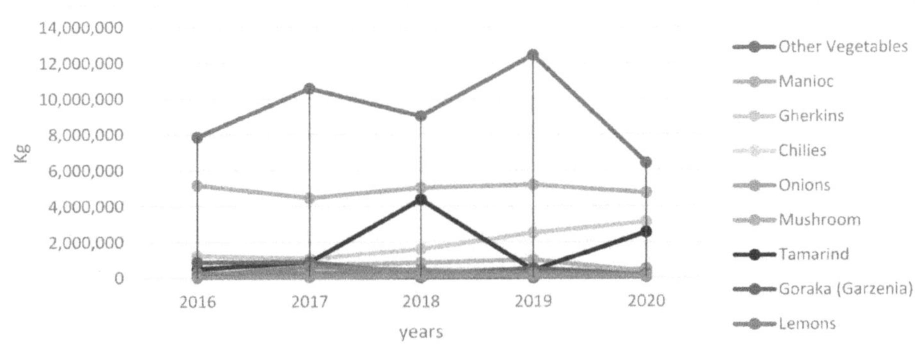

Figure 3. Analysis of Vegetable export (Value in US $ million)

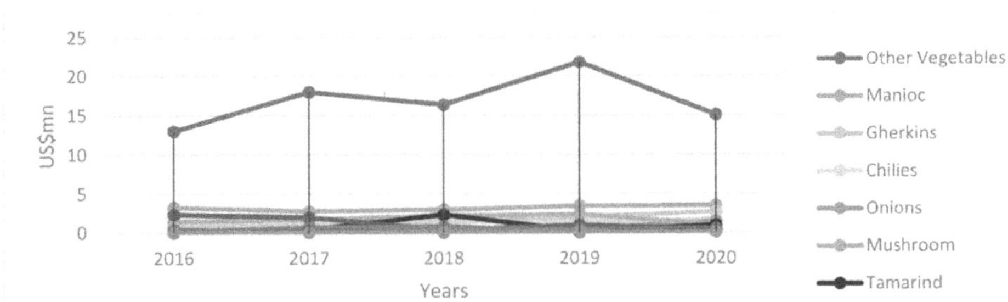

Figure 4. Analysis of Fruits Export (Kg.)

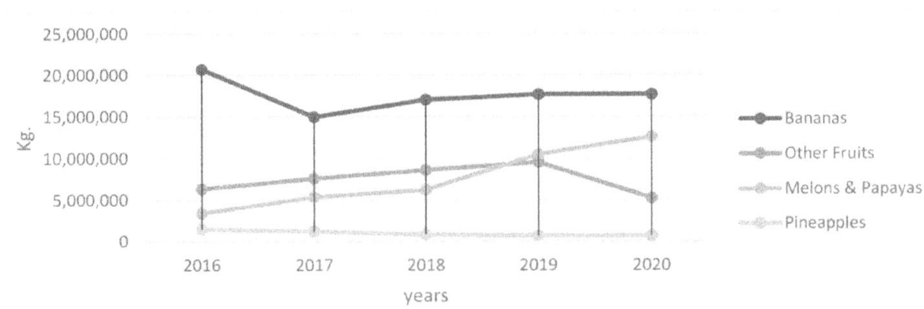

Figure 5. Analysis of Fruits Export (Value in US $ million)

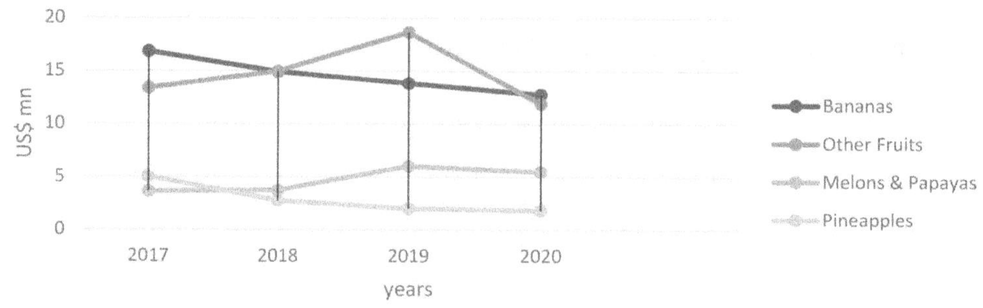

Figure 6. Analysis of Floriculture Export (Kg.)

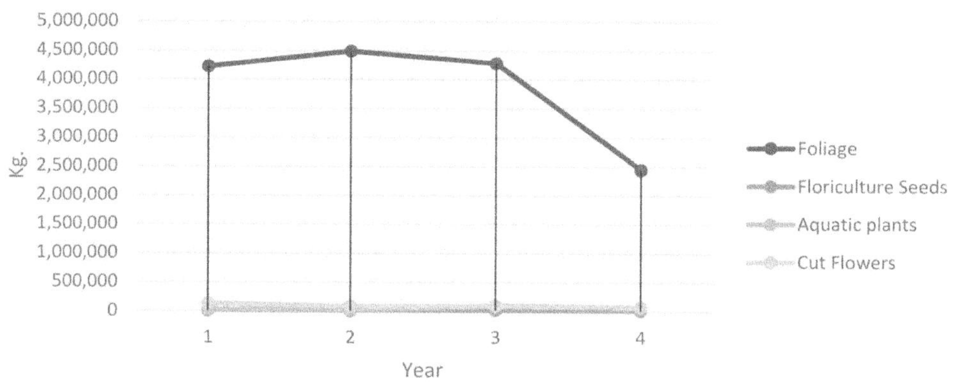

Figure 7. Analysis of Floriculture Export (Value in US $ million)
Sources: Export Development Board, Sri Lanka

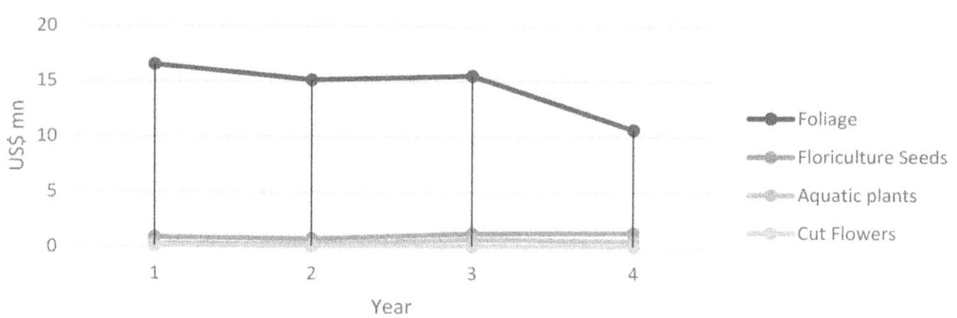

Appendix B

Table 3. Data structure (Authors original construction)

First Order Concepts	Second Order Themes	Aggregate Dimensions
Stay in alert	Instinctive decision making	Micro-level
Identifying the loss-making segments		
Dealing with customers		
Looking for competitive advantages		
Effective communication and gather information		
Overestimation about the situation		
New product development	Founder ideologies and capabilities	
Attitude and self-trust		
Openness to changes and seeking opportunities		
Approaching the local market		
Expand the international market		
Maintaining the product quality		
Employee training		
Having clear values towards employees and customers (honesty, credibility, industriousness)		
Having or showing compassion on employees	Humane approaches	
Situational understanding and provide leave facilities		
Caring and kindness towards employees		
Provide health and safety instructions		
Bear expenses for employee health and care		
Bonus and other financial support		
Looking after the business	Family support	
Financial support or business development		
Emotional support		
Idea generation		

continues on following page

Table 3. Continued

First Order Concepts	Second Order Themes	Aggregate Dimensions
Seeking new partnerships	Collaborations	Meso level
Developing a second layer of the ownership		
Coaching and mentoring the employees		
Work along with associations		
Meeting and collaborations with fellow business owners		
Lack of transparency and jealousy		
Engage with research and development	Seeking professional support	
Innovations		
Distribution of responsibilities and employee training		
Dealing with local market and distributers	Supply chain management	
Finding new suppliers		
Becoming more capital intensive		
Insurance	Financial support	Macro-level
Repayment deferrals and loan terms extended		
Airfreight		
Tax rebates		
	Government policies	
National level crisis management regulations		
Direct government intervention on the floriculture industry		
Risk assessments and evaluation procedure		

Chapter 12 A Picture of Family Businesses in Indonesia During the COVID-19 Pandemic

Hotniar Siringoringo
Gunadarma University, Indonesia

E. S. Margianti
Gunadarma University, Indonesia

Sudaryanto Sudaryanto
Gunadarma University, Indonesia

ABSTRACT

This chapter explores family business conditions during the COVID-19 pandemic. To fulfill this goal, data from Biro Pusat Statistik (Statistics Indonesia) and national/international mass media were used. More than 95% of business in Indonesia are family business. Family businesses based on scale vary from home industry, micro, small, medium, to the big corporations. Family businesses play an essential role in driving Indonesia's economy. Statistically, 80% of Indonesia's GNP is contributed by family businesses. In 2019 family businesses contributed to a GDP of 53.28%.

INTRODUCTION

Indonesia's economy is driven by family business as happens in countries across the world. This is indicated by the contribution of family businesses to Gross National Product (GNP) or Gross Domestic Product (GDP). GNP is different from GDP in terms of the economic agents and area. GNP is "the value of finished goods and

DOI: 10.4018/978-1-6684-7394-8.ch012

services produced by residents within a financial year". On the other hand, GDP is "the value of finished goods and services produced domestically within a financial year".

According to Hasbi (2015), 80% of Indonesia's GNP is contributed by family businesses. But based on PWC (2014) survey the contribution of the family business to GDP is only 25%. Referring to the input of GNP and GDP calculation, this statistic indicates that many Indonesian family businesses are operated overseas. Using the GDP as an indicator, the contribution of the family business to the Indonesian economy increase this last decade. According to the 2019 economic survey conducted by BPS, family businesses contribute to a GDP of 53.28%. The contribution increases by 28.28% in four years. The survey result also shows that family businesses permeate 85,416,493 laborers. This is equivalent to 96.18% of the entire workforce (Biro Pusat Statistik-Statistics Indonesia, 2020).

Many factors contribute to the good performance of a family business as well as the sustainability of the business. Researchers show the effect of entrepreneurial orientation on business profitability (Casillas et al., 2011), and on business performance (Aloulou, 2018; Akhtar et al., 2015). However, a contrary result was found by Rachmawati et al. (2022) in Indonesian family businesses. They found that "entrepreneurial orientation does not affect business performance".

Kellermanns et al. (2008) state that in the practice of family business in Indonesia, family members who own shares also participate in business management. Dyer (2006) in their study found a negative and significant influence between family involvements on business performance. Dyer result is also supported by Yudha and Singapurwoko (2017). They found that family members of the controlling shareholders who acted as directors negatively affected business performance in Indonesia.

FAMILY BUSINESS SCALE AND IMPACT OF COVID-19 PANDEMIC

According to PWC (2014), more than 95% of business in Indonesia is family business. These family businesses based on scale vary from home industry, micro, small, medium up to the big corporation. Table 1 shows the percentage of each scale in 2014 (PWC, 2014) based on yearly revenue (billions USD). They are doing business in manufacture (50%), transportation (13%), general (13%), construction (7%), and others (5%). We can conclude from the table that family businesses with yearly revenue less than 5 billion USD are 3%.

Table 1. Composition of the family business in Indonesia based on revenue in 2014

No	Revenue (USD)	Percentage	No	Revenue (USD)	Percentage
1	5-10 billion	27%	4	51-100 billion	20%
2	11-20 billion	7%	5	101-500 billion	23%
3	21-50 billion	3%	6	>500 billion	17%

Source: PWC (2014).

Five largest family businesses in Indonesia are "PT. HM. Sampoerna", "PT. Indofood Sukses Makmur Tbk.", "Djarum Group", Bakrie Group", and "Ciputra Group". These family businesses are also included in the biggest corporation in Indonesia. According to Wuisan (13 Sept 2021) Bank Central Asia (BCA), a unit business of Djarum Group is the largest company based on market capitalization.

"PT. H.M. Sampoerna" was founded by the Sampoerna family in the year 1913. It was the first company to produce cigarettes in Indonesia. Since May 2005, a majority share of "PT. H.M. Sampoerna" has been acquired by Philip Morris. Since then, "PT. H.M. Sampoerna" is no longer a family business. This company absorbs more than 63,000 employees, with more than 41,000 permanent employees. Its market share is 28.8%, with 79.5 billion unit volume, 92.4 trillion Rupiah net revenue, and 8.6 trillion Rupiah net profit (PT. HM. Sampoerna, 2020).

"PT. Indofood Sukses Mandiri Tbk" or simply "Indofood" was founded on 14 August 1990 as a family business. Its business core is food according to its name. Up to 2022, PT. Indofood Sukses Makmur Tbk. is still a family business type but its share is open to the public. In 2020 the corporation earned 81.73 trillion Rupiah net revenue and 6.46 trillion Rupiah net profit. PT Indofood Sukses Mandiri Tbk. is a corporation, comprised of many companies with various products and brands (Perwitasari, 23 March 2021).

"PT Djarum" is another cigarette business company in Indonesia, founded in 1951 as a family business. It remains as a family business although it has become a big corporation with 17 unit businesses and various business types. The owner, the second generation of the family is the richest man in Indonesia according to Ho and Karmali (2021). The corporation absorbs 75,000 employees.

The Bakrie group was founded in 1942 by the first generation of the Bakrie family. It is now led by the third generation of the family. Its business varies from mine to telecommunication and has 10 unit businesses. Similar to the above-mentioned family businesses, this corporation also sells shares to the public. The Bakrie group in 2020 earned net revenue of 2.455 trillion Rupiah.

The "Ciputra Group" is a family business type and was founded in 1981. It was started with the housing construction business and up to now, its core business is construction. Since 1990 the company has entered other businesses besides construction such as telecommunications, healthcare, brokerage, education, media, and e-commerce. It is now led by the second generation. The corporation has been listed on the stock market. According to Tari (2021) the "Ciputra Group" earned 8.07 trillion Rupiah net revenue in 2020.

Although many family businesses are corporations scale, most family businesses are on the micro, small, and medium scale, as can be seen in Table 1. In fact, many large companies started from micro industries, such as *PT. H.M. Sampoerna*, *PT. Djarum*, and others. As stated at the press conference of *Kementrian Koordinator Bidang Perekonomian* (Coordinating Ministry for Economic Affairs, 28 April 2021) of the 64.19 million MSMEs in Indonesia, 64.13 million are still micro and small enterprises (MSEs) and informal sector.

Micro and Small Enterprises (MSEs) are affected by the covid-19 pandemic. The impact of the covid-19 pandemic is very severe for MSEs operations. The 1998 economic crisis did not have this heavy impact on MSEs in Indonesia (*Direktorat Statistik Industri* - Directorate of Industrial Statistics, 2021). According to the Directorate of Industrial Statistics (2021), until the fourth quarter of 2020, 7.06% of MSEs were closed and 11.25% were temporarily out of production due to the covid-19 pandemic. Of those that closed the business and stopped production, the beverage industry was the most affected.

MSEs growth in the first quarter of 2020 declined sharply to negative, which was -13.02%. In the second quarter of 2020 MSEs growth was slightly better to -9.57%. However, in the third quarter, MSEs growth has improved and has reached a positive (3.33%). Although it declined again in the fourth quarter of 2020, which was 1.5%, but still in positive growth. The industries with the most temporary closures were the tobacco processing industry (52.8%), the electrical equipment industry (22.43%), and the other transportation equipment industry (19.84%).

The main factor causing temporary closure or closing due to bankruptcy is finance. Although Atmadja et al. (2018) showed micro company performance does not depend on microfinance. Several institutions (such as *Biro Pusat Statistik*-Statistic Indonesia, *Bappenas* - National Development Planning Agency, and the World Bank) surveyed the MSMEs. Their result showed that many MSMEs have difficulty paying off loans and paying electricity, gas, and employee salaries.

Due to government policy of mobility restriction, closure of public places, prohibition of gathering, and stop of non-essential activities, many businesses cannot operate. When there are no business activities, the business owner does not get income. As a consequence, they don't have enough money to pay off loans, electricity, gas, employee salaries, or to buy raw materials. This condition forces some of the business owners to lay off employees, and eventually, the business closed. Other constraints experienced by MSMEs include difficulty in obtaining raw materials, capital, declining customers, distribution, and production being hampered.

Shopping malls were closed during the first, second, and third quarters of 2020. Although shopping malls open after that period, the activity was still limited. Since mid of 2021, all citizens were encouraged to install "Peduli Lindungi" application on their smartphones. People were allowed enter the shopping malls by proving that they have been vaccinated first doze or second dose. People enter to the shopping mall by scanning the barcode provided in the front gate of the shopping mall through "Peduli Lindungi" application and clicking check-in. With this regulation, many people are reluctant to enter the shopping mall, not only the customer but also the seller.

GOVERNMENT SUPPORT

Realizing the high contribution of the family business to the economy, the government shows support through policy, regulation, and also funding and management. Researches show financial support influences the performance of family businesses, particularly microenterprise (Al Mamun & Hayat, 2019; Beck et al., 2015). In tackling the pandemic and its aftermath, the government provided several stimuli through loan restructuring policies, additional capital assistance, easing payment of electricity bills, and other financing support.

Since the announcement of WHO the world pandemic of covid-19 in 2020, the government has supported MSMEs by ordering the Financial Services Authority (OJK) to provide credit relaxation to MSMEs with assets under IDR 10 billion. In this policy, the relaxation was in the form of lowering interest rates and postponing instalments cost for a year, both from the banking and non-bank financial industries. In addition, a year-long instalment suspension was also applied to motorcycle taxis, taxi drivers, and fishermen who have vehicle instalments (Siringoringo & Kuruppuge, 2021). Up to 23 September 2021, the government continued to support the businesses to revive the national economy.

To implement additional capital assistance, the government established "PEN" (*Pemulihan Ekonomi Nasional*) program in early 2020. The PEN program is the main instrument used by the Government to conquer covid-19 and to recover the economy as a result of the pandemic in 2020 and 2021. The total budget allocation for the PEN Program in the national revenue and expenditure budget (APBN) is IDR 699.43 trillion in 2021, and IDR 695.2 trillion in 2020. As explained by Minister of Finance, Sri Mulyani, the largest component of the PEN budget in 2021 (IDR 395.93 trillion) was used in the health sector such as treatment for covid-19 patients, incentives for health workers, and procurement & implementation of vaccines (Tira, 23 Sep 2021).

As explained at the press conference conducted by the office of Coordinating Minister for Economic Affairs (*Kementrian Koordinator Bidang Perekonomian*) (28 April 2021) in recovering the economy, PEN program for Micro, Small, and Medium Enterprises (MSMEs) in 2020 is IDR 112.84 trillion. This financial assistance was distributed to more than 30 million MSMEs. For 2021 budgeting, PEN program allocated IDR 121.90 trillion to revitalized MSMEs. The PEN program in 2020 has been noted to successfully support the business, especially the informal sector and MSMEs to survive the impact of the pandemic. Apart from that, it is also noted to reduce the decline in the workforce. As reported from Biro Pusat Statistik (Indonesia Statistics) data as of August 2020, there was the creation of new job opportunities with the addition of 0.76 million people who started the businesses and an increase of 4.55 million informal workers.

Until September 23, 2021 disbursement realization of funding from PEN program has reached IDR 52.9 trillion to 27.39 million MSMEs. The PEN funds are channelled through several programs such as interest subsidies, placement of government funds to banks and partners to support the restructuring program and increase MSME working capital (Isma, 23 Sept 2021). Basically in this program, the government mainly pays attention to MSEs. According to Bahtiar (2021) percentage of MSE is 99.92% from all businesses in Indonesia (equal to 64.13 million businesses).

During the covid-19 pandemic, government supported to the family businesses in the scale of micro, small, and medium mostly on funding. As can be seen in the subsection above, at the beginning of the pandemic, MSEs were shocked and unprepared with the impact of social distancing, temporary cessation of operations except for primary ones, and disruption to the supply chain.

Apart from funding support, the government also pushed the MSMEs to go onboard to digital platforms. This support was formulated in the policy and issuing the "Program Gerakan Nasional Bangga Buatan Indonesia (Gernas BBI)." The application of information technology products (application and related products) that developed by Indonesian in MSMEs is the goal of this program. As a result of this "Gernas BBI", more than 3.8 million creative players and MSMEs has succeeded invited to onboard to e-commerce platforms to expand the market. This figure is higher than the target at 2 million MSMEs. Therefore, the total number of MSME units onboarding reached 11.4 million.

SURVIVAL STRATEGY

The resilience of family businesses toward crisis has been proved. The world economy has experienced crises several times, such as in 1929, 1998, 2008, and others. This economic crisis also had an impact on the Indonesian economy. Many researches show that family businesses especially the ones with micro, small, and medium sizes survive during the crisis (Van Essen et al., 2015). Family businesses can retain their employees during a crisis (Rivo-López, 2020).

Apart from the fact that the growth of micro, small, and medium industries has decreased, this type of business is the most enduring during the crisis. As mentioned in subsection above, in the first quarter of the year 2020 the growth of micro, small, and medium industries was down very sharp, but in the next quarter, the growth increased and again experienced positive growth in the third quarter. Many micros, small, and medium industries were bankrupt or closed temporary, but at the same time, many new businesses have emerged or diversified from businesses that went bankrupt or temporarily closed. Some MSMEs wait and see until the government announced the new normal in mid-2020. During the waiting, they stop the production activities. Some of them backed to usual business, or diversified the product, but some of them shifted to another business.

The most growing businesses during the covid-19 pandemic were delivery and e-commerce. When people's mobility was limited whilst their need for food and other primary needs were not reduced, delivery business and e-commerce gained consumers. The Indonesian Logistics Association (Asosiasi Logistik Indonesia - ALI) noted that the flow of goods shipments grew by 40% during the covid-19 pandemic. This increase was largely contributed by the pharmaceutical industry, medical devices, and consumer goods (Rabbi, 8 July 2021). The delivery service for goods with the highest growth is delivery within the city.

During the pandemic, marketplace function and delivery service attracted the most consumers. A few delivery businesses online-based emerging in Indonesia are "GoJek" and "Grab". Initially "Gojek" was founded by Indonesia, providing transportation services using motorcycles that can be ordered through phone calls. Since Jan 2015, Gojek introduced an online transportation service based on android and iOS. In subsequent developments, Gojek diversified its product into 14 varieties, such as "GoRide", "GoCar", "GoFood", "GoMed", "GoMart", "GoShop", GoSend", etc. Gojek is a local product but has been expanded abroad.

Grab is an imported product that initially provided transportation services using a car. Similar to Gojek, it is also expanded and diversified its product into 18 varieties. Grab products are more varied compared to Gojek. Aside from transportation, marketplace, and delivery services, Grab also operates as an insurance agent, clean and fix, and hotel reservation. In food delivery, Grab gain more customer than Gojek.

One of the MSME survival strategies is the adoption of information technology. During the pandemic (2020-2021) online marketplace arose. The use of the marketplace is increasingly in demand by sellers during the pandemic because it is not possible to open an offline store. Various marketplaces had indeed developed in Indonesia before the pandemic, such as Bukalapak, Bhineka, Tokopedia, Shopee, BliBli, Shoppingcom, JD.ID, Lazada, OLX, and Elevania. The marketplace is more desirable because consumers can view and compare many stores in the same web location, just like when they are doing shop offline at a shopping mall.

Many business people who were previously reluctant to use IT have changed. The mobility restriction triggers them to utilize the marketplace. Much informal business with a single employee who is the owner of the business, by utilizing the marketplace and delivery service gain profit.

CONCLUSION

MSEs were hit badly by the covid-19 pandemic, especially in the first quarter of 2020. Its growth was decline very sharp to -13.02%. However, its growth was increased in the third quarter of 2020 to 3.33%. But apart from the growth decline due to business closure, a new business arise.

Family businesses in Indonesia survive by diversifying the product, starting a new business, innovation, digitization, or wait and see. The role of the government in providing funding assistance through the PEN program is very helpful for MSMEs recovery. The support of Indonesian government also through the "Program Gerakan Nasional Bangga Buatan Indonesia (Gernas BBI)." Evidence showed the government policies supported not only the business of the MSMEs but also the family.

REFERENCES

Akhtar, C. S., Ismail, K., Hussain, J., & Rehman, M. U. (2015). Investigating the moderating effect of family on the relationship between Entrepreneurial orientation and success of enterprise: Case of Pakistani manufacturing SMEs. *International Journal of Entrepreneurship and Small Business*, *26*(2), 233–247. doi:10.1504/IJESB.2015.071825

Al Mamun, A., Adaikalam, J., & Mazumder, M. N. H. (2012). Examining the effect of Amanah Ikhtiar Malaysia's microcredit program on microenterprise assets in rural Malaysia. *Asian Social Science*, *8*(4), 272–280. doi:10.5539/ass.v8n4p272

Al Mamun, A., & Hayat, N. (2019). Microcredit and microenterprises performance in Malaysia. *International Journal of Applied Behavioral Economics*, *8*(2), 1–13. doi:10.4018/IJABE.2019040101

Aloulou, W. J. (2018). Examining entrepreneurial orientation's dimensions – performance relationship in Saudi family businesses: Contingency role of family involvement in management. *Journal of Family Business Management*, *8*(2), 126–145. doi:10.1108/JFBM-02-2018-0007

Atmadja, A., Sharma, P., & Su, J. (2018). Microfinance and microenterprise performance in Indonesia: An extended and updated survey. *International Journal of Social Economics*, *45*(6), 957–972. doi:10.1108/IJSE-02-2017-0031

Atmadja, A. S., Su, J. J., & Sharma, P. (2016). Examining the impact of microfinance on microenterprise performance (implications for women-owned microenterprises in Indonesia). *International Journal of Social Economics*, *43*(10), 962–981. doi:10.1108/IJSE-08-2014-0158

Bahtiar, R. A. (2021). Dampak pandemi covid-19 terhadap sektor usaha mikro, kecil, dan menengah serta solusinya. *Info Singkat: Kajian Singkat terhadap Isu Aktual dan Strategis, 13*(10), 19-24.

Beck, T., Lu, L., & Yang, R. (2015). Finance and growth for microenterprises: Evidence from rural China. *World Development*, *67*, 38–56. doi:10.1016/j.worlddev.2014.10.008

Biro Pusat Statistik. (2020). *Statistik Indonesia, Statistical Yearbook of Indonesia.* . doi:10.3389/fpsyg.2015.00002

Casillas, J. C., Moreno, A. M., & Barbero, J. L. (2011). Entrepreneurial orientation of family firms: Family and environmental dimensions. *Journal of Family Business Strategy*, *2*(2), 90–100. doi:10.1016/j.jfbs.2011.03.002

Direktorat Statistik Industri. (2021). *Industri Mikro dan Kecil di Masa Pandemi COVID-19, 2020*. Biro Pusat Statistik.

Hasbi, H. (2015). Islamic microfinance institution: The capital structure, growth, performance and value of firm in Indonesia. *Procedia: Social and Behavioral Sciences*, *211*(1), 1073–1080. doi:10.1016/j.sbspro.2015.11.143

Ho, J., & Karmali, N. (2021). *Indonesia's 50 Richest 2021: Combined Wealth Rises To Record $162 Billion*. https://www.forbes.com/sites/naazneenkarmali/2021/12/14/indonesias-50-richest-2021-combined-wealth-rises-to-record-162-billion/?sh=1f53a6e4687f

Isma. (2021). *Bantuan Pemerintah ke Sektor UMKM akan Terus Berlanjut*. https://infopublik.id/kategori/nasional-ekonomi-bisnis/566905/bantuan-pemerintah-ke-sektor-umkm-akan-terus-berlanjut#:~:text=Menteri%20Koordinator%20Bidang%20Perekonomian%2C%20Airlangga,terealisasi%20sebesar%20Rp52%2C9%20triliun

Kementrian Koordinator Bidang Perekonomian. (2021). *Dukungan Pemerintah Bagi UMKM Agar Pulih di Masa Pandemi*. https://www.ekon.go.id/publikasi/detail/2939/dukungan-pemerintah-bagi-umkm-agar-pulih-di-masa-pandemi

Perwitasari, A. S. (2021). *Wow, Pendapatan Indofood Sukses Mandiri (INDF) di 2020 Capai Rp. 81,73 trilliun rupiah*. https://stocksetup.kontan.co.id/news/wow-pendapatan-indofood-sukses-makmur-indf-di-2020-capai-rp-8173-triliun#:~:text=81%2C73%20triliun-,Wow%2C%20pendapatan%20Indofood%20Sukses%20Makmur%20(INDF)%20di%202020,capai%20Rp%2081%2C73%20triliun&text=KONTAN.CO.ID%20%2D%20JAKARTA,kinerja%20mantap%20di%20tahun%202020.&text=Berdasarkan%20laporan%20keuangan%20perusahaan%2C%20pendapatan,mencapai%20Rp%2081%2C73%20triliun

PT. HM. Sampoerna Tbk. (2020). *Laporan tahunan*. https://www.sampoerna.com/resources/docs/default-source/sampoerna-market-documents/annual-reports---en/annual-report-2020.pdf?sfvrsn=c0cf95b4_2

Rachmawati, E., Suliyanto, & Suroso, A. (2022). Direct and indirect effect of entrepreneurial orientation, family involvement and gender on family business performance. *Journal of Family Business Management*, *12*(2), 214–236. doi:10.1108/JFBM-07-2020-0064

Rivo-López, E., Villanueva-Villar, M., Vaquero-García, A., & Lago-Peñas, S. (2022). Do family firms contribute to job stability? Evidence from the great recession. *Journal of Family Business Management*, *12*(1), 152–169. doi:10.1108/JFBM-06-2020-0055

Santia, T. (2021). *Sudah Tersedot Rp 395,92 Triliun, Dana PEN untuk Apa Saja?* https://www.liputan6.com/bisnis/read/4666305/sudah-tersedot-rp-39592-triliun-dana-pen untuk-apasaja#:~:text=Program%20PEN%20merupakan%20instrumen%20utama,di%20tahun%202020%20maupun%202021.&text=Dana%20PEN%20sektor%20kesehatan%20juga,untuk%2029%2C29%20juta%20orang

Tahunan, L. (2020). *Annual report 2020*. https://bakrie-brothers.com/wp-content/uploads/2020/10/BNBR-Annual-Report-2020-INDO-web-2.pdf

Tari, D. N. (2021). *Kinerja 2020: Kebal Pandemi, Laba Ciputra (CTRA) Tumbuh Dua Digit*. https://market.bisnis.com/read/20210415/192/1381600/kinerja-2020-kebal-pandemi-laba-ciputra-ctra-tumbuh-dua-digit

Van Essen, M., Strike, V. M., Carney, M., & Sapp, S. (2015). The resilient family firm: Stakeholder outcomes and institutional effects. *Corporate Governance*, *23*(3), 167–183. doi:10.1111/corg.12087

Wuisan, P. A. (2021). *Keren! Ini Dia Daftar 10 Perusahaan Terbesar di Indonesia*. https://www.modalrakyat.id/blog/perusahaan-terbesar-di-indonesia

Compilation of References

(KPMG. (2021). *The Impact of Covid-19 on Family Businesses*. KPMG. https://home.kpmg/xx/en/home/insights/2021/03/the-impact-of-Covid-19-on-family-businesses.html.

Abadiea, A., & Gardeazabal, J. (2008). Terrorism and the world economy. *European Economic Review*, *52*(1), 1–27. doi:10.1016/j.euroecorev.2007.08.005

Afredo, D., Kotler, J., Chua, J. H., & Chrisman, J. J. (2014). Ability and willingness as sufficiency condition for family-oriented particularistic behaviour: Implication for theory and empirical studies. *Journal of Small Business Management*, *52*(2), 344–364. doi:10.1111/jsbm.12102

Aglozo, E. Y., Akotia, C. S., Osei-Tutu, A., & Annor, F. (2021). Spirituality and subjective well-being among Ghanaian older adults: Optimism and meaning in life as mediators. *Aging & Mental Health*, *25*(2), 306–315. doi:10.1080/13607863.2019.1697203 PMID:31814428

Ahn, H. (2008). Junzi as a tragic person: A self psychological interpretation of the Analects. *Pastoral Psychology*, *57*(1), 101–113. doi:10.100711089-008-0133-2

Ahrens, J. P., Uhlaner, L., Woywode, M., & Zybura, J. (2018). „Shadow Emperor" or "loyal Paladin"? The Janus Face of Previous Owner Involvement in Family Firm Successions. *Journal Of Family Business Strategy*, *9*(1), 73–90. doi:10.1016/j.jfbs.2017.11.003

Ahrens, J.-P., Calabrò, A., Huybrechts, J., & Woywode, M. (2019). The Enigma of the Family Successor–Firm Performance Relationship: A Methodological Reflection and Reconciliation Attempt. *Entrepreneurship Theory and Practice*, *43*(3), 437–474. doi:10.1177/1042258718816290

Akhtar, C. S., Ismail, K., Hussain, J., & Rehman, M. U. (2015). Investigating the moderating effect of family on the relationship between Entrepreneurial orientation and success of enterprise: Case of Pakistani manufacturing SMEs. *International Journal of Entrepreneurship and Small Business*, *26*(2), 233–247. doi:10.1504/IJESB.2015.071825

Al Mamun, A., Adaikalam, J., & Mazumder, M. N. H. (2012). Examining the effect of Amanah Ikhtiar Malaysia's microcredit program on microenterprise assets in rural Malaysia. *Asian Social Science*, *8*(4), 272–280. doi:10.5539/ass.v8n4p272

Al Mamun, A., & Hayat, N. (2019). Microcredit and microenterprises performance in Malaysia. *International Journal of Applied Behavioral Economics*, *8*(2), 1–13. doi:10.4018/IJABE.2019040101

Al Roya Press and Publishing House. (2019). *Entrepreneurship Research & Case Studies from Oman.* Al Roya Press and Publishing House. https://www.ibrict.edu.om/ieu/resources/Ent_resources/Entrepreneurship%20Research%20&%20Case%20Studies%20from%20Oman.pdf

Alderson, K., & Shane, S. (2018). *Understanding the Family Business Exploring the Differences Between Family and Nonfamily Businesses* (2nd ed.). Entrepreneurship and Small Business Management Collection.

Aleke, B., Ojiako, U., & Wainwright, D. (2011). ICT adoption in developing countries: Perspectives from small-scale agribusinesses. *Journal of Enterprise Information Management*, *24*(1), 68–84. doi:10.1108/17410391111097438ALkiyumi. B. (2017, July 18). Economic Impact of Family Business. *Oman Observer*. https://www.omanobserver.om/article/77433/Opinion/economic-impact-of-family-businesses

AlmeidaAron. (2021). Top Founder/Promoter Family Managed Companies in India! *Trade Brains*. https://tradebrains.in/promoter-family-managed-companies-india/

Aloulou, W. J. (2018). Examining entrepreneurial orientation's dimensions – performance relationship in Saudi family businesses: Contingency role of family involvement in management. *Journal of Family Business Management*, *8*(2), 126–145. doi:10.1108/JFBM-02-2018-0007

Alvarez & Marsal. (2021). *Family Business in India.* ICSG. https://www.alvarezandmarsal.com/sites/default/files/77597_tag_india_familybusinessreport_05_singles.pdf

Alves, A. A., & Moreira, J. M. (2013). *Business ethics in the school of Salamanca. Handbook of the philosophical foundations of business ethics*. Springer.

Amran, N. A., & Ahmad, A. C. (2011). Board Mechanisms and Malaysian Family Companies' Performance. *Asian Journal of Accounting and Governance*, 15-26.

Anderson, R. C., & Reeb, D. M. (2003). Founding-family ownership and firm performance: Evidence from the S&P 500. *The Journal of Finance*, *58*(3), 1301–1328. doi:10.1111/1540-6261.00567

Andrews, P. (2020). Globally Most Businesses Are Family Owned. *Family Business United.* https://familybusinessunited.com/2020/10/27/globally-most-businesses-are-family-owned/

Anh, M. (2021). *Commercial and service activities continue to be affected by the COVID-19 epidemic.* ChinhPhu. https://thanglong.chinhphu.vn/hoat-dong-thuong-mai-dich-vu-tiep-tuc-chiu-anh-huong-tu-dich-covid-19

Anteby, M., & Molnar, V. (2012). Collective memory meets organizational identity: Remembering to forget in a firm's rhetorical history. *Academy of Management Journal*, *55*(3), 515–540. doi:10.5465/amj.2010.0245

Arfa, A. (2021, July 8). *How Has MCO Affected The Malaysian Economy?* Taylors. https://university.taylors.edu.my/en/campus-life/news-and-events/news/how-has-mco-affected-the-malaysian-economy.html

Arshed, N., & Danson, M. (2016). Enterprise: Concepts and Issues. In J. Sanders (Ed.), *Family Business* (pp. 113–130). Goodfellow Publishers.

Ashok, R. (2021, July 04). Omani Women empowered to run family business. *Gulf News*. https://gulfnews.com/world/gulf/oman/omani-women-empowered-to-run-family-business-1.80424959

Asia, G. (2016, August). 100 top groups. *Globe Asia*, *10*(Special Issue), 42–79.

Astrachan, J. H., & Jaskiewicz, P. (2008). Emotional returns and emotional costs in privately held family businesses: Advancing traditional business valuation. *Family Business Review*, *21*(2), 139–149. doi:10.1111/j.1741-6248.2008.00115.x

Astrachan, J. H., & Shanker, M. C. (2003). Family businesses' contribution to the US economy: A closer look. *Family Business Review*, *16*(3), 211–219. doi:10.1177/08944865030160030601

Astrov, V., Ghodsi, M., Grieveson, R., Holzner, M., Kochnev, A., Landesmann, M., Pindyuk, O., Stehrer, R., Tverdostup, M., & Bykova, A. (2022). Russia's invasion of Ukraine: Assessment of the humanitarian, economic, and financial impact in the short and medium term. *International Economics and Economic Policy*, *19*(2), 331–381. doi:10.100710368-022-00546-5

Aswicahyono, H., Hill, H., & Narjoko, D. (2010). Industrialisation after a deep economic crisis: Indonesia. *The Journal of Development Studies*, *46*(6), 1084–1108. doi:10.1080/00220380903318087

Atmadja, A. S., Su, J. J., & Sharma, P. (2016). Examining the impact of microfinance on microenterprise performance (implications for women-owned microenterprises in Indonesia). *International Journal of Social Economics*, *43*(10), 962–981. doi:10.1108/IJSE-08-2014-0158

Atmadja, A., Sharma, P., & Su, J. (2018). Microfinance and microenterprise performance in Indonesia: An extended and updated survey. *International Journal of Social Economics*, *45*(6), 957–972. doi:10.1108/IJSE-02-2017-0031

Authority of Small and Medium Enterprises Development. (n.d.). Omanportal. https://omanportal.gov.om/wps/wcm/connect/en/site/home/gov/gov1/gov5governmentorganizations/raffd/raffd_1

Ayaa Technologies. (2020). *E-commerce development*. Ayaa Technologies. https://ayaatechnologies.com/ecommerce-development/

Back to the Future: The SBGH Story. (n.d.). Suhail Bahwan Group. https://www.suhailbahwangroup.com/corporate-profile/back-to-the-future

Backman, M. (2001). *Asian eclipse: Exposing the dark side of business in Asia*. John Wiley.

Badwe, A. (2021). Family Businesses SHOWED Resilience During COVID-19 Pandemic. *The Bridge Chronicle*. https://www.thebridgechronicle.com/business/family-businesses-showed-resilience-during-Covid-19-pandemic

Bahfein, S. (2021). *John Riady anggap pandemi COVID-19 berkah bagi Lippo*. Kompas.com. https://properti.kompas.com/read/2021/03/14/070000221/john-riady-anggap-pandemi-covid-19-berkah-bagi-lippo

Bahtiar, R. A. (2021). Dampak pandemi covid-19 terhadap sektor usaha mikro, kecil, dan menengah serta solusinya. *Info Singkat: Kajian Singkat terhadap Isu Aktual dan Strategis, 13*(10), 19-24.

Bai, C., Quayson, M., & Sarkis, J. (2021). COVID-19 pandemic digitization lessons for sustainable development of micro-and small-enterprises. *Sustainable production and consumption, 27*, 1989-2001.

Baker, S. R., Bloom, N., Davis, S. J., & Terry, S. J. (2020). Covid-induced economic uncertainty (No. w26983). National Bureau of Economic Research.

Bang, N. P., Ray, S., & Ramachandran, K. (2017). *Family businesses: The emerging landscape 1990-2015*. Thomas Schmidheiny Centre for Family Enterprise, Indian School of Business.

Bank Indonesia. (2021). *Laporan Tahunan Bank Indonesia 2020*. Bank Indonesia.

Bao, Q. (2021). *International visitors decrease by 1 billion, 2020 becomes the 'catastrophe' year of the tourism industry*. Vietnam National Administration of Tourism.

Baragde, D. B., & Jadhav, A. U. (2021). Impact of COVID-19 on Indian SMEs and Survival Strategies. In *Handbook of Research on Strategies and Interventions to Mitigate COVID-19 Impact on SMEs* (pp. 280–298). IGI Global. doi:10.4018/978-1-7998-7436-2.ch014

Barbalet, J. (2016). *Confucianism and the Chinese State: Reexamining Max Weber's China*. Palgrave Macmillan.

Bardwell, H., & Iqbal, M. (2020). The Economic Impact of Terrorism from 2000 to 2018. *Peace Economics, Peace. Science & Public Policy, 27*(2), 227–261.

Bauer, H. J., & Hallier, B. (1999). *Kultur und Geschichte des Handels* [*Culture and history of trade.*]. EHI-EuroHandelsinst.

Bazerman, M. H., & Moore, D. A. (2012). *Judgment in Managerial Decision Making*. John Wiley & Sons.

Beck, T., Lu, L., & Yang, R. (2015). Finance and growth for microenterprises: Evidence from rural China. *World Development, 67*, 38–56. doi:10.1016/j.worlddev.2014.10.008

Belitski, M., & Khalil, S. (2020). Dynamic capabilities for firm performance under the information technology governance framework. *European Business Review, 32*(2), 129–157. doi:10.1108/EBR-05-2018-0102

Benedictow, O. J. (2004). The Black Death 1346-1353: The Complete History. Boydell Press.

Berrone, P., Cruz, C. L., & Gómez-Mejía, R. (2012). Socioemotional wealth in family firms theoretical dimensions, assessment approaches, and agenda for future research. *Family Business Review, 25*(3), 258–279. doi:10.1177/0894486511435355

Besanko, D., Dranove, D., Shanley, M., & Schaefer, S. (2016). *Economics of Strategy* (7th ed.). Wiley.

Birchall, J. (1997). *The international co-operative movement.* Manchester University Press.

Biro Pusat Statistik. (2020). *Statistik Indonesia, Statistical Yearbook of Indonesia.*. doi:10.3389/fpsyg.2015.00002

Boshkoska, M., & Jankulovski, N. (2020). Coronavirus impact on global economy. Annals of the 'Constantin Brâncuşi" University of Târgu Jiu. *Economy Series, 4*, 18–23.

Botero, I. C., Cruz, C., Massis, A. D., & Nordqvist, M. (2015). Family business research in the European context. *European Journal of International Management, 9*(2), 139–159. doi:10.1504/EJIM.2015.067858

Bowen, G. A. (2009). Document analysis as a qualitative research method. *Qualitative Research Journal, 9*(2), 27–40. doi:10.3316/QRJ0902027

BPS. (2020a). *Analisis Isu Terkini 2020.* BPS RI.

BPS. (2020b). *Analisis Hasil Survei Dampak COVID-19 Terhadap Pelaku Usaha.* BPS RI.

BPS. (2020c). *Statistik E-Commerce 2020.* BPS RI.

BPS. (2021a). *Analisis Isu Terkini 2021.* BPS RI.BPS. (2021b). *PDB seri.* BPS RI. https://www.bps.go.id/indicator/11/65/3/-seri-2010-pdb-seri-2010.html

BPS. (2021c). *Analisis Hasil Survei Dampak COVID-19 Terhadap Pelaku Usaha Jilid 2.* BPS RI.

BPS. (2022). *Analisis Isu Terkini 2022.* BPS RI.

Breier, M., Kallmuenzer, A., Clauss, T., Gast, J., Kraus, S., & Tiberius, V. (2021). The role of business model innovation in the hospitality industry during the COVID-19 crisis. *International Journal of Hospitality Management, 92*, 102723. doi:10.1016/j.ijhm.2020.102723 PMID:36919038

Bridge, S., O'Neill, K., & Cromie, S. (2003). *Understanding Enterprise, Entrepreneurship and Small Business* (2nd ed.). Palgrave Macmillan, Basingstoke.

Bundy, J., Pfarrer, M. D., Short, C. E., & Coombs, W. T. (2017). Crises and crisis management: Integration, interpretation, and research development. *Journal of Management, 43*(6), 1661–1692. doi:10.1177/0149206316680030

Business Gateways. (2021). *Oman registers 14% increase in the number of SMEs in 2020.* Business Gateways. https://businessgateways.com/news/2021/02/09/Oman-registers-14-per-cent-number-SMEs-2020

C. P. P. R. (2020). Effects of Covid-19 On Transportation: What the Experts Say." Centre for Public Policy Research (CPPR), September 24, 2020. https://www.cppr.in/centre-for-urban-studies/effects-of-Covid-19-on-transportation-what-the-experts-say

Cabinet of the Hungarian Prime Minister. (2021). *Részt Veszünk Az Uniós Lőszerbeszerzésben, De Csakis A Magyar Katonák Kapnak Belőle Lőszert.* Hungarian Prime Minister. https://koronavirus.gov.hu/terkepek/fertozottek

Cadieux, L. (2007). Succession in Small and Medium-Sized Family Businesses: Toward a Typology of Predecessor Roles During and After Instatement of the Successor. *Family Business Review*, *20*(2), 95–109. doi:10.1111/j.1741-6248.2007.00089.x

Campopiano, G., De Massis, A. V., & Kotlar, J. (2019). Environmental jolts, family-centered non-economic goals and innovation: Toward a framework of family firm resilience. In E. Memili & C. Dibrell (Eds.), *The palgrave handbook of heterogeneity among family firms* (pp. 773–789). Palgrave Macmilan.

Cao, N. (2019). A Sinicized world religion?: Chinese christianity at the contemporary moment of globalization. *Religions*, *10*(8), 459. doi:10.3390/rel10080459

Carr, J. C., & Sequeira, J. M. (2007). Prior Family Business Exposure as Intergenerational Influence and Entrepreneurial Intent: A Theory of Planned Behavior Approach. *Journal of Business Research*, *60*(10), 1090–1098. doi:10.1016/j.jbusres.2006.12.016

Casalino, N., Żuchowski, I., Labrinos, N., Nieto, Á. L. M., & Martín-Jiménez, J. A. (2019). Digital strategies and organizational performances of SMEs in the age of Coronavirus: Balancing digital transformation with an effective business resilience. *Law and Economics Yearly Review*, *8*(2), 347–380. doi:10.2139srn.3563426

Casillas, J. C., Moreno, A. M., & Barbero, J. L. (2011). Entrepreneurial orientation of family firms: Family and environmental dimensions. *Journal of Family Business Strategy*, *2*(2), 90–100. doi:10.1016/j.jfbs.2011.03.002

Central Bank Report. (2020). Annual Report Central Bank of Sri Lanka, Central Bank of Sri Lanka.

Chafuen, A. A. (1986). *Christians for freedom: Late-scholastic economics*. Ignatius Press.

Charmaz, K., & Belgrave, L. (2012). Qualitative interviewing and grounded theory analysis. The SAGE handbook of interview research: The complexity of the craft, 2, 347-365. Sage.

Charmaz, K., & Belgrave, L. L. (2019). Thinking about data with grounded theory. *Qualitative Inquiry*, *25*(8), 743–753. doi:10.1177/1077800418809455

Chatterjee, S. R. (2001). Relevance of traditional value frameworks in contemporary chinese work organizations: Implications for managerial transition. *Journal of Human Values*, *7*(1), 21–32. doi:10.1177/097168580100700103

Cheema, M. A., Faff, F., & Szulczyk, K. R. (2022). The 2008 global financial crisis and COVID-19 pandemic: How safe are the safe haven assets? *International Review of Financial Analysis*, *83*, 102316. doi:10.1016/j.irfa.2022.102316 PMID:36536650

Cheng & Co. (2019, October 1). *Sustaining Family Businesses through Generations*. Cheng and Co. https://chengco.com.my/wp/2019/10/01/sustaining-family-businesses-through-generations/

Chen, M. S., & Eweje, G. (2019). Establishing ethical Guanxi (interpersonal relationships) through confucian virtues of Xinyong (trust), Lijie (empathy) and Ren (humanity). *Corporate Governance: The International Journal of Business in Society*, *20*(1), 1–15. doi:10.1108/CG-01-2019-0015

Chittoor, R., & Das, R. (2007). Professionalization of Management and Succession Performance—A Vital Linkage. *Family Business Review*, *20*(1), 65–79. doi:10.1111/j.1741-6248.2007.00084.x

Cho, J., Miller, D., & Lee, J. (2018). Too much of a good thing: Family involvement and the survival of listed Korean firms. *Journal of Family Business Strategy*, *9*(4), 223–237. doi:10.1016/j.jfbs.2018.10.001

Chriscaden, K. (2020). Impact of COVID-19 on people's livelihoods, their health, and our food systems. World Health Organization.

Christian Today. (2009). The Christian billionaire's approach to the financial crisis. *Christian Today*. https://www.christiantoday.com/article/the.christian.billionaires.approach.to.the.financial.crisis/22926.htm

Chua, E. (2009, March 26). *Billionaire: Remember purpose of life amid recession*. The Christian Post. https://www.christianpost.com/news/billionaire-remember-purpose-of-life-amid-recession.html

Chua, C. (2004). Defining Indonesian Chineseness under the new order. *Journal of Contemporary Asia*, *34*(4), 465–479. doi:10.1080/00472330480000221

Chua, J. H., Chrisman, J. J., & Bergiel, E. B. (2009). An agency theoretic analysis of the professionalized family firm. *Entrepreneurship Theory and Practice*, *33*(2), 355–372. doi:10.1111/j.1540-6520.2009.00294.x

Chua, J. H., Chrisman, J. J., & Sharma, P. (1999). Defining the family business by behavior. *Entrepreneurship Theory and Practice*, *23*(4), 19–39. doi:10.1177/104225879902300402

Cicek, A., Kelleci, R., & Vandekerkhof, P. (2021). Determinants of family meetings in private family businesses. *Journal of Family Business Management*. . doi:10.1108/JFBM-11-2020-0110

CII. (2021). *Family Business*. CII. https://www.cii.in/sectors.aspx?enc=prvePUj2bdMtgTmvPwvisYH+ 5EnGjyGXO9hLECvTuNt8Yt8MGwm3xV7pjS9tGblw

Cioca, A., Wehbe, K., Popescu, D., & Popescu, C. (2020). The main drivers for sustainable decisions in a family business that impact the company's performance. *Sustainability*, *12*(20), 8659. doi:10.3390u12208659

Ciotti, M., Ciccozzi, M., Terrinoni, A., Jiang, W. C., Wang, C. B., & Bernardini, S. (2020). The COVID-19 pandemic. *Critical Reviews in Clinical Laboratory Sciences*, *57*(6), 365–388. doi:10.1080/10408363.2020.1783198 PMID:32645276

Clark, C., Davila, A., Regis, M., & Kraus, S. (2020). Predictors of COVID-19 voluntary compliance behaviors: An international investigation. *Global Transitions*, *2*, 76–82. doi:10.1016/j.glt.2020.06.003 PMID:32835202

Clarke, V., & Braun, V. (2017). Thematic analysis. *The Journal of Positive Psychology*, *12*(3), 297–298. doi:10.1080/17439760.2016.1262613

Clauss, T., Breier, M., Kraus, S., Durst, S., & Mahto, R. V. (2022). Temporary business model innovation–SMEs' innovation response to the Covid-19 crisis. *R & D Management*, *52*(2), 294–312. doi:10.1111/radm.12498

Clement, P. (2010). The term "macroprudential": Origins and evolution. *BIS Quarterly Review*, (March), 59–67.

Combs, J. G., Shanine, K. K., Burrows, S., Allen, J., & Pounds, T. (2020). What do we know about business families? Setting the stage for leveraging family science theories. *Family Business Review*, *33*(1), 38–63. doi:10.1177/0894486519863508

Conza, E., Lamb, P. W., & De Massis, A. (2020). Practicing resilience in family firms: An investigation through T phenomenography. *Journal of Family Business Strategy*, *11*(2), 100355. doi:10.1016/j.jfbs.2020.100355

Correspondent, S. (2021). Govt. Unveils ₹6.28 Lakh Cr STIMULUS Post Second Covid Wave. *The Hindu*. https://www.thehindu.com/business/Economy/nirmala-sitharaman-unveils-new-covid-recovery-package-expands-credit-relief/article35020572.ece

Creswell, J. (2013). *Qualitative Inquiry & Research Design – Choosing Among Five Approaches* (3rd ed.). Sage.

Creswell, J. W., & Creswell, J. D. (2018). *Research Design: Qualitative, Quantitative and Mixed Methods Approaches* (5th ed.). SAGE Publications, Inc.

Danes, S. M. (2006). Tensions within family business-owning couples over time. *Stress, Trauma and Crisis*, *9*(3–4), 227–246. doi:10.1080/15434610600854244

Danes, S. M., Haberman, H. R., & Mc Tavish, D. (2005). Gendered discourse about family business. *Family Relations*, *54*(1), 116–130. doi:10.1111/j.0197-6664.2005.00010.x

Danes, S. M., Loy, J. T., & Stafford, K. (2008). Management practices of small private firms within a quality framework. *Journal of Small Business Management*, *46*(3), 21–30. doi:10.1111/j.1540-627X.2008.00250.x

Danes, S. M., Rueter, M. A., Kwon, H. K., & Doherty, W. (2002). Family FIRO model: An application to family business. *Family Business Review*, *15*(1), 31–43. doi:10.1111/j.1741-6248.2002.00031.x

Danes, S. M., Stafford, K., & Loy, J. T. (2007). Family business performance: The effects of gender and management. *Journal of Business Research*, *60*(10), 1058–1069. doi:10.1016/j.jbusres.2006.12.013

Dat, H. (2021). Looking back at the impact of the Covid-19 epidemic on Vietnam's tourism and development trends in 2021. *Figures & Event review of the GSO*. https://consosukien.vn/nhin-lai-tac-dong-cua-dich-covid-19-doi-voi-du-lich-viet-nam-va-xu-huong-phat-trien-nam-2021.htm

Dave, S. (2021). *Oman government's support to SMEs*. Ooredoo. https://www.ooredoo.om/Showcasepage/OmanSupportSmes.aspx

Davis, F. D., Bagozzi, R. P., & Warshaw, P. R. (1989). User Acceptance of Computer Technology: A Comparison of Two Theoretical Models. *Management Science*, *35*(8), 982–1003. Retrieved 2021, from https://www.jstor.org/stable/2632151v. doi:10.1287/mnsc.35.8.982

De Massis, A., Audretsch, D., Uhlaner, L., & Kammerlander, N. (2018). Innovation with limited resources: Management lessons from the German Mittelstand. *Journal of Product Innovation Management*, *35*(1), 125–146. doi:10.1111/jpim.12373

De Massis, A., Chua, J., & Chrisman, J. J. (2008). Factors Preventing Intra-Family Succession. *Family Business Review*, *21*(2), 183–199. doi:10.1111/j.1741-6248.2008.00118.x

De Massis, A., Frattini, F., Majocchi, A., & Piscitello, L. (2018). Family firms in the global economy: Toward a deeper understanding of internationalization determinants, processes, and outcomes. *Global Strategy Journal*, *8*(1), 3–21. doi:10.1002/gsj.1199

De Massis, A., Sieger, P., Chua, J. H., & Vismara, S. (2016). 'Incumbents' Attitudes towards Intrafamily Succession: An Investigation of its Antecedents,'. *Family Business Review*, *29*(3), 278–300. doi:10.1177/0894486516656276

Dean, K. (2020). Religion and the Chinese diaspora in Southeast Asia. *Review of Religion and Chinese Society*, *7*(2), 220–249. doi:10.1163/22143955-00702005

Dede, N. P., & Ayranci, E. (2014). Exploring the connections among spiritual leadership, altruism, and trust in family businesses. *Quality & Quantity*, *48*(6), 3373–3400. doi:10.100711135-013-9962-x

Denrell, J., & March, J. G. (2001). Adaptation as information restriction: The hot stove effect. *Organization Science*, *12*(5), 523–538. doi:10.1287/orsc.12.5.523.10092

Department of Census and Statistics. (2021). *Number and area of Agriculture holdings by all sectors and by district*. Statistics. http://www.statistics.gov.lk/Agriculture/StaticalInformation/CensusOfAgriculture/NumberAndAreaOfAgricultureHoldingsByAllSectorsAndbyDistrict

Dev, S. M., & Sengupta, R. (2020). Covid-19: Impact on the Indian economy. *Indira Gandhi Institute of Development Research, Mumbai April.*

Direktorat Statistik Industri. (2021). *Industri Mikro dan Kecil di Masa Pandemi COVID-19, 2020*. Biro Pusat Statistik.

Djono, A. L. (2020). *Mendidik anak papua dengan hati*. Berita Satu. https://www.beritasatu.com/archive/652931/mendidik-anak-papua-dengan-hati

Doebele, J. (2005). Southeast Asia's 40 richest. *Forbes*. https://www.forbes.com/2005/09/078/southeast-asia -richest-cz_05seal

Dun & Bradstreet: Over 82% of Smes Had Negative Impact During Covid-19. (2021, April 22). The Economic Times. https://economictimes.indiatimes.com/small-biz/sme-sector/dun-bradstreet-over-82-of-smes-had-negative-impact-during-Covid-19/articleshow/82197779.cms?from=mdr

Duong, T., & Truong, X. (2021). *Tax policy to support SMEs during the pandemic in Vietnam compared to some countries*. Phaply. https://phaply.net.vn/chinh-sach-thue-ho-tro-doanh-nghiep-vua-va-nho-trong-dai-dich-cua-viet-nam-so-voi-mot-so-nuoc-a250797.html

Dyer, W. G. (2010). *Cultural Change in Family Firms: Anticipating and Managing Business and Family Transitions*. Jossey-Bass.

Edamadaka, P., & Seike, I. (2019). *Digitalization in Indonesia*. Singapore: SBayCurrent Consulting.

EDB trade Analysis System. (2021). Export Development Board.

EHI. (1994). Scannersysteme – Neue Impulse für Organisation und Marketing. [Scanner systems – New impulses for organization and marketing.] Köln.

EHI. (1999). Factory Outlet Center.

Englisch, P., & Ambrosini, F. (2020). Family Businesses and COVID-19: Our support and recommendations.

Ernst & Young. (2020). *Economic impact of COVID-19: A Malaysian context*. Earnest and Young. eiscentre.perkeso.gov.my: https://eiscentre.perkeso.gov.my/wp-content/uploads/2020/04/COVID-19-Economic-Impact_Malaysia_080420.pdf

Esgate, A., & Groome, D. (2005). *An Introduction to Applied Cognitive Psychology*. Psychology Press.

Evatt, C. (2010). *Brain biases*. Brain Shortcuts. http://brainshortcuts.blogspot.com/2010/11/optimism-bias.html

Fang, C., Lee, J., & Schilling, M. A. (2009). Balancing Exploration and Exploitation Through Structural Design: The Isolation of Subgroups and Organizational Learning. *Organization Science*, *21*(3), 625–642. doi:10.1287/orsc.1090.0468

Fashion TodayKW 27/2022

Fauci, A. S., Lane, H. C., & Redfield, R. R. (2020). Covid-19—Navigating the uncharted. *The New England Journal of Medicine*, *382*(13), 1268–1269. doi:10.1056/NEJMe2002387 PMID:32109011

Ferrari F. (2021). The postponed succession: an investigation of the obstacles hindering business transmission planning in family firms. *Journal of Family Business Management*. doi:10.1108/JFBM-09-2020-0088

Ferrari, F. (2019a), The Daughters' Career in Family Firms: A Reflection on the Cultural/Contextual Aspects, Pereira E.T. and Paoloni P.(Eds), Global Perspectives on Women in Management and the Labor Markets, IGI Global Publishing.

Ferrari, F. (2019b), Investigating Inner Dynamics in Family Firms. A Multilevel Model of Analysis, Camisón C. and González T. (eds), Competitiveness, Organizational Management, and Governance in Family Firms, IGI Global Publishing.

Ferrari, F. (2020). Exploring the side effects of Socio-Emotional Wealth. A multilevel analysis approach to the dysfunctional dynamics in family business succession. International Journal of Entrepreneurship and Small Business, 40(1), 128-146. doi:10.1504/IJESB.2020.106943

Ferrari, F. (2017). 'The tragedy of having a daughter. Construction and reproduction of gender stereotypes in Italian family SMEs', *Reti. Italian Juournal of Cognitive Sciences, 01*, 133–151.

Ferrari, F. (2019). In the mother's shadow: Exploring power dynamics in family business succession. *Gender in Management, 34*(22), 121–139. doi:10.1108/GM-07-2017-0091

Ferrari, F. (2021a). The Eluded Succession: Readiness to Change and Resistance to Retirement among Elderly Family Business Founders and Owners. *Change Management: An International Journal, 21*(2), 1–19. doi:10.18848/2327-798X/CGP/v21i02/1-19

Ferrell, O. C., & Hartline, M. D. (2014). *Marketing Strategy: Text and Cases* (6th ed.). Cengage Learning.

Food and Agriculture Organization, United Nations (UNFAO). (2020). *COVID-19: Our hungriest, most vulnerable communities face "a crisis within a crisis*. FAO. https://www.fao.org/news/story/en/item/1269721/icode/?utm_source=twitter&utm_medium=social+media&utm_campaign=fao (31.05.2021)

Forbes. (n.d.). Top 100 Arab Family Businesses In The Middle East 2020. *Forbes Middle East*. https://www.forbesmiddleeast.com/list/top-100-arab-family-businesses-in-the-middle-east-2020-1

Friedland, R., & Alford, R. R. (1991). Bringing society back in: Symbols, practices, and institutional contradictions. In W. W. Powell & P. J. DiMaggio (Eds.), *The new institutionalism in organizational analysis* (pp. 232–263). University of Chicago Press.

General statistics office. (2021). *Tourism in 2020 suffering because of COVID-19*. Hanoi General statistics office. https://www.gso.gov.vn/du-lieu-va-so-lieu-thong-ke/2021/01/du-lich-nam-2020-lao-dao-vi-covid-19/

General statistics office. (2021). *Vietnam economy 2020: A year of charges of growth*. Hanoi General statistics office.

Gersick, K. E., Lansberg, I., Desjardins, M., & Dunn, B. (1999). Stages and transitions: Managing change in the family business. *Family Business Review, 12*(4), 287–297. doi:10.1111/j.1741-6248.1999.00287.x

Giang, H. (2021). *Vietnam national Union of Bank workers*. VNUBW. http://vnubw.org.vn/tin-tuc/t6927/ngan-hang-tang-cuong-ho-tro-doanh-nghiep-nho-va-vua-vuot-kho.html

Giménez, E., & Novo, J. A. (2020). A Theory of Succession in Family Firms. *Journal of Family and Economic Issues*, *41*(1), 96–120. doi:10.100710834-019-09646-y

Glatter, K. A., & Finkelman, P. (2021). History of the Plague: An Ancient Pandemic for the Age of COVID-19. *The American Journal of Medicine*, *134*(2), 176–181. doi:10.1016/j.amjmed.2020.08.019 PMID:32979306

Gomez, E. T. (2007). Family firms, generational change and identity formation: The Chinese in Britain and Malaysia. *East Asia: An International Quarterly*, *24*(2), 153–172. doi:10.100712140-007-9012-1

Gomez-Mejia, L. R., Haynes, K. T., Nunez-Nickel, M., Jacobson, K. J. L., & Moyano-Fuentes, J. (2007). Socioemotional wealth and business risks in family-controlled firms: Evidence from Spanish olive oil mills. *Administrative Science Quarterly*, *52*(1), 106–137. doi:10.2189/asqu.52.1.106

Greenwood, R., & Hinings, C. R. (1996). Understanding radical change. *Academy of Management Review*, *21*, 1022–1054. doi:10.2307/259163

Grunebaum, D. (2020). *In Malaysia, Businesses Adapt to Survive COVID*. VOA News. https://www.voanews.com/a/east-asia-pacific_malaysia-businesses-adapt-survive-covid/6198371.html

Gupta, M. S. (2021). *What is Digitization, Digitalization, and Digital Transformation?* Arc Web. https://www.arcweb.com

Ha, L. (2020). Some solutions to promote industrial and commercial development; remove difficulties in production and business. *Department of industry and trade - Lang Son province, 1*. https://soct.langson.gov.vn/vi/mot-so-giai-phap-day-manh-phat-trien-cong-nghiep-thuong-mai-thao-go-kho-khan-trong-san-xuat-kinh

Habbershon, T. G., Mary, W., & MacMillan, I. C. (2006). A unified systems perspective of family firm performance. In P. Z. Poutziouris, K. X. Smyrnios, & S. B. Klein (Eds.), *Handbook of Research on Family Business* (pp. 67–79). Edward Elgar. doi:10.4337/9781847204394.00013

Habbershon, T. G., & Williams, M. L. (1999). A resource-based framework for assessing the strategic advantages of family firms. *Family Business Review*, *12*(1), 1–25. doi:10.1111/j.1741-6248.1999.00001.x

Habbershon, T. G., Williams, M., & MacMillan, I. C. (2003). A unified system perspective of family firm performance. *Journal of Business Venturing*, *18*(4), 451–465. doi:10.1016/S0883-9026(03)00053-3

Hahn, H. W. (1984). *Geschichte des Deutschen Zollvereins: Kleine Vandenhoeck-Reihe*.

Hai, C. T. (2019). Vietnam Social Sciences. *Vietnam Journals Online*. https://vjol.info.vn/index.php/khxhvn/issue/view/4236

Hallier, B. (1995). Der Handel auf dem Weg zur Marketingführerschaft. [Retail on the way to marketing leadership.] *Absatzwirtschaft, A*.

Hallier, B. (1999d). Wird ECR zum Club der Grossen? [Will ECR become a club of the big ones?] In: von der Heydt (ed.) *A: Handbuch Efficient Consume Response–Konzepte, Erfahrungen, Herasuforderungen, S*, 55-61.

Hallier, B. (2011a). *Von der Krise zur Kompetenz. [From crisis to competence.*]

Hallier, B. (2011b). Smart Phones and QR-Codes. In: Pantano, E. & Timmermans, H. (eds.), Advanced Technology Management for Retailing: Frame works and Cases. IGI Global.

Hallier, B. (2011c). The Evolution Tornado Retail. In Advanced Technologies Management for Retailing: Frameworks and Cases (pp. 26-40). IGI Global. doi:10.4018/978-1-60960-738-8.ch002

Hallier, B. (2022a). 50 Years Perspective.

Hallier, B. (2022b). Promoting Life-Style.

Hallier, B. (2022c). Empowered Logistics.

Hallier, B. (2022d). Darwinism in the Textile Sector.

Hallier, B. (2022e). Accelleration by Disruption.

Hallier, B. (1987). Sich ins Regal hineinrechnen. [Count yourself on the shelf.]. *Absatzwirtschaft, 10*, 87.

Hallier, B. (1999b). EHI – Factory Outlet Center.

Hallier, B. (2002). *Sammler, Stifter und Mäzene des Handels* [*Collector, benefactor and patron of the trade.*]. EHI.

Hasbi, H. (2015). Islamic microfinance institution: The capital structure, growth, performance and value of firm in Indonesia. *Procedia: Social and Behavioral Sciences, 211*(1), 1073–1080. doi:10.1016/j.sbspro.2015.11.143

Hategan, C. D., Curea-Pitorac, R. I., & Hategan, V. P. (2019). The Romanian Family Businesses Philosophy for Performance and Sustainability. *Sustainability, 11*(6), 1715. doi:10.3390u11061715

Hau, M. (2020). *Ministry of Planning and Investment.* MPI. https://www.mpi.gov.vn/Pages/tinbai.aspx?idTin=47732&idcm=188

Hauptmann, G. (1943). *Die Weber* [[*The weavers]*]. Vol. 2). Suhrkamp.

Havrancsik, I., & Havrancsik, D. (2021). Summary on the answers of family-owned business to the challenges of the pandemic by Szinergia Ltd. *Europea*. https://ec.europa.eu/eurostat https://www.ksh.hu/?lang=hu

Hayward, A., & Evennett, T. (2021). *Six things family business owners should be thinking about now*. EY. https://www.ey.com/en_uk/unlocking-ambitions-of-private-businesses-and-their-owners/six-things-family-business-owners-should-be-thinking-about-now

Hayward, A., & Evennett, T. (2021). *Six things family business owners should be thinking about now.* EY. www.ey.com: https://www.ey.com/en_uk/unlocking-ambitions-of-private-businesses-and-their-owners/six-things-family-business-owners-should-be-thinking-about-now

Heck, R. K. Z., & Trent, E. (1999). The prevalence of family business from a household sample. *Family Business Review*, *12*(3), 209–224. doi:10.1111/j.1741-6248.1999.00209.x

Hefner, R. W. (2021). Islam and institutional religious freedom in Indonesia. *Religions*, *12*(6), 415. doi:10.3390/rel12060415

Heidel, B. (2013). *Scannerdaten im Einzelhandelsmarketing* (Vol. 68). Springer-Verlag. [*Scanner data in retail marketing* (Vol. 68).]

Henkel, L. A., & Mather, M. (2007). Memory attributions for choices: How beliefs shape our memories. *Journal of Memory and Language*, *57*(2), 163–176. doi:10.1016/j.jml.2006.08.012

Herbane, B. (2019). Rethinking organizational resilience and strategic renewal in SMEs. *Entrepreneurship and Regional Development*, *31*(5–6), 476–495. doi:10.1080/08985626.2018.1541594

Hermanto, Y. P. (2020). True response to COVID-19 plague reviewed from the perspective of Christian faith. *IOSR Journal of Humanities and Social Science*, *25*, 33–36.

Hindustan Times. (2019). The Global Variations in Family Business Structures. *Hindustan Times*. https://www.hindustantimes.com/analysis/the-global-variations-in-family-business-structures/story-NrikbnqLCGQUVlw0VEwTcO.html

Ho, J., & Karmali, N. (2021). *Indonesia's 50 Richest 2021: Combined Wealth Rises To Record $162 Billion*. https://www.forbes.com/sites/naazneenkarmali/2021/12/14/indonesias-50-richest-2021-combined-wealth-rises-to-record-162-billion/?sh=1f53a6e4687f

Hoffmann-Holland, K. (2009). *Ethics and human rights in a globalized world: An interdisciplinary and international approach*. Mohr Siebeck.

Holland, J. (1992). Genetic algorithms. *Scientific American*, *267*(1), 66–72. doi:10.1038scientificamerican0792-66

Hooker, J. (2003). *Working Across Cultures*. Stanford University Press. https://dailysocial.id/post/lippo-groups-john-riady-takes-on-the-conglomerate-investment-in-the-technology-landscape

Huong, D. (2021). The Government of the socialist republic of Vietnam. *Baochinhphu*. https://baochinhphu.vn/Kinh-te/Gia-tri-xuat-khau-nong-lam-thuy-san-tang-manh-bat-chap-dich-COVID19/436310.vgp

Huynh, T. L. D. (2020). The COVID-19 risk perception: A survey on socio-economics and media attention. *Economic Bulletin*, *40*(1), 758–764.

IBEF. (2021). *Brand India*. IBEF. https://www.ibef.org/industry/services.aspx

IBN. (2021). *India's COVID Stimulus MEASURES: Indirect Relief, Short-Term Goals*. India Briefing News. https://www.india-briefing.com/news/india-covid-stimulus-indirect-relief-credit-guarantee-loans-compliance-relaxations-22588.html/

Ibrahim, N. A., & Angelidis, J. P. (2005). The long-term performance of small businesses: Are there differences between "Christian-based" companies and their secular counterparts? *Journal of Business Ethics*, *58*(1), 187–193. doi:10.100710551-005-1413-8

Ibrahim, N. A., Rue, L. W., McDougall, P. P., & Greene, G. R. (1991). Characteristics and practices of "Christian-based" companies. *Journal of Business Ethics*, *10*(2), 123–132. doi:10.1007/BF00383615

IMF. (2021). *Policy Responses to covid19*. IMF. https://www.imf.org/en/Topics/imf-and-covid19/Policy-Responses-to-COVID-19

In Charts: State Of Covid-Hit Indian Economy . (2021, July 16.) Times of India. https://timesofindia.indiatimes.com/business/india-business/indian-economy-in-explained-10-charts/articleshow/84465093.cms

Indian Express. (2020). Explained: How Covid-19 Has Affected the Global Economy. *The Indian Express*. https://indianexpress.com/article/explained/explained-how-has-Covid-19-affected-the-global-economy-6410494/

International Finance Corporation. (2018). *Family business governance handbook*. IFC. https://www.ifc.org/wps/wcm/connect/2c93b2cb-dec6-4819-9ffb60335069cbac/Family_Business_Governance_Handbook.pdf?MOD=AJ PERES&CVID=mskqtDE.

I-scoop. (2021). *Digitization, digitalization, digital and transformation disruption*. I-Scoop. https://www.i-scoop.eu/digital-transformation/digitization-digitalization-digital-transformation-disruption/

Isma. (2021). *Bantuan Pemerintah ke Sektor UMKM akan Terus Berlanjut*. https://infopublik.id/kategori/nasional-ekonomi-bisnis/566905/bantuan-pemerintah-ke-sektor-umkm-akan-terus-berlanjut#:~:text=Menteri%20Koordinator%20Bidang%20Perekonomian%2C%20Airlangga,terealisasi%20sebesar%20Rp52%2C9%20triliun

Iswara, M. A. (2020, July 31, 2020). Indonesia ranks among most religious countries in Pew study. *The Jakarta Post*. https://www.thejakartapost.com/news/2020/07/30/indonesia-ranks-among-most-religious-countries-in-pew-study.html

Izraeli, D. (1973). The three wheels of retailing: A theoretical note. *European Journal of Marketing*, *7*(1), 70–74. doi:10.1108/EUM0000000005101

Jaskiewicz, P., Combs, J., & Bau, S. (2015). Entrepreneurial legacy: Towards a theory of how some family firms nurture transgenerational entrepreneurship. *Journal of Business Venturing*, *30*(1), 29–49. doi:10.1016/j.jbusvent.2014.07.001

Jaskiewicz, P., Neubaum, D. O., De Massis, A., Daniel, T., & Holt, D. T. (2020). The Adulthood of Family Business Research Through Inbound and Outbound Theorizing. *Family Business Review, 33*(1), 10–17. doi:10.1177/0894486520904461

Jayatilaka, T. (2020). *Tatler in Culture & Travel: "Post-Covid-19 era: Is working in the office still relevant?"* Tatler. https://www.tatlerasia.com/culture/travel/sg-how-relevant-is-the-office-in-the-post-covid-era-ytl-land-development-zalora-malaysia?tool=addthis#.Yx2SSasAnBY.link

Jesudason, J. V. (1989). *Ethnicity and the economy: The state, Chinese business, and multinationals in Malaysia*. Oxford University Press.

Jobel, K. (2021). *Reduced Inequalities-The Start of SMEs in Oman.* Sustainable Oman. https://sustainableoman.com/reduced-inequalities-the-start-of-smes-in-oman/

Johnson, J., & Powell, P. (1994). Decision making, risk and gender: Are managers different? *British Journal of Management, 5*(2), 123–138. doi:10.1111/j.1467-8551.1994.tb00073.x

Jones, L., Palumbo, D., & Brown, D. (2021, January 24). *Coronavirus: How the Pandemic Has Changed the World Economy*. BBC News. https://www.bbc.com/news/business-51706225

Jones, E., & Nisbett, R. (1971). *The actor and the observer: Divergent perceptions of the causes of behavior*. General Learning Press.

Juergensen, J., Guimón, J., & Narula, R. (2020). European SMEs amidst the COVID-19 crisis: Assessing impact and policy responses. *Economia e Politica Industriale, 47*(3), 499–510. doi:10.100740812-020-00169-4

Juhro, S. M., Prabheesh, K. P., & Lubis, A. (2021). The Effectiveness of Trilemma Policy Choice in the Presence of Macroprudential Policies: Evidence from Emerging Economies. *The Singapore Economic Review, 66*(3), 1–45. doi:10.1142/S0217590821410058

Kahneman, D., Knetsch, J., & Thaler, R. (1991). Anomalies: The Endowment Effect, Aversion, and Status Quo Bias. *The Journal of Economic Perspectives, 5*(1), 193–206. doi:10.1257/jep.5.1.193

Kao, H. S. R., & Sek-Hong, N. (1995). Chinese values in work organization: An alternative approach to change and development. *Journal of Human Values, 1*(2), 173–189. doi:10.1177/097168589500100203

Karmali, N. (2018). Indonesia's Richest 2018: Mochtar Riady's Lippo Group Faces Fresh Challenge. *Forbes*. https://www.forbes.com/sites/naazneenkarmali/2018/12/12/indonesias-richest-2018-driven-to-diversify/?sh=67890b571962

Kása, R., Radácsi, L., and Csákné, F.J. (2019). Családi vállalkozások definíciós operacionalizálása és hazai arányuk becslése a kkv-szektoron belül. [Definitional operationalization of family businesses and estimation of their domestic share within the SME sector.] *Statisztikai szemle, 97*, 146-174 doi:10.20311/stat2019.2.hu0146

Katadata. (2021a). *Kontribusi UMKM Terhadap Ekonomi Terus Meningkat*. Katadata. https://databoks.katadata.co.id/datapublish/2021/08/13/kontribusi-umkm-terhadap-ekonomi-terus-meningkat

Katadata. (2021b). *Jumlah Pelaku UMKM di Tokopedia Meningkat Selama Pandemi COVID-19*. Katadata. https://databoks.katadata.co.id/datapublish/2021/03/25/jumlah-pelaku-umkm-di-tokopedia-meningkat-selama-pandemi-COVID-19

Katadata. (2021c). *Lewat Market Place 77 UMKM Terbantu Pasarkan Produk Saat Pandemi COVID-19*. Katadata. https://databoks.katadata.co.id/datapublish/2021/05/05/lewat-marketplace-77-umkm-terbantu-pasarkan-produk-saat-pandemi-COVID-19

Katadata. (2021d). *QRIS*. Katadata. https://databoks.katadata.co.id/search/cse/qris

Katadata. (2021e). *Internet Terjangkau Bantuan Paling Dibutuhkan UMKM Saat Pandemi*. Retrieved September 11, 2021, from https://databoks.katadata.co.id/datapublish/2021/03/24/internet-terjangkau-bantuan-paling-dibutuhkan-umkm-saat-pandemi

Kelly, E., & Marchese, K. (2015). Supply chains and value webs. In M. Canning & E. Kelly (Eds.), *Business ecosystems come of age* (pp. 55–62). Deloitte University Press.

Kementerian Komunikasi dan Informatika Republik Indonesia. (2021). *Peraturan Menteri Komunikasi dan Informatika tentang Perubahan Ketiga atas Peraturan Menteri Komunikasi dan Informatika Nomor 13 Tahun 2019 tentang Penyelenggaraan Jasa Telekomunikasi*. Informatika Republik Indonesia. https://peraturan.bpk.go.id/Home/Details/203125/permenkominfo-no-14-tahun-2021

Kementrian Koordinator Bidang Perekonomian. (2021). *Dukungan Pemerintah Bagi UMKM Agar Pulih di Masa Pandemi*. https://www.ekon.go.id/publikasi/detail/2939/dukungan-pemerintah-bagi-umkm-agar-pulih-di-masa-pandemi

Kenton, W. (2020). Succession Planning. *Investopedia*. https://www.investopedia.com/terms/s/succession-planning.asp

Kets de Vries, M. F. R. (1993). The dynamics of family controlled firms: The good and the bad news. *Organizational Dynamics*, *21*(3), 59–71. doi:10.1016/0090-2616(93)90071-8

Klynn, B. (2021). Cognitive bias: What it is and how to overcome it. *BetterUp*. https://www.betterup.com/blog/cognitive-bias.

Knowledge at Wharton Staff. (2009). *Lippo Group CEO James Riady: 'Money and power are a blessing and a curse'*. Wharton. https://knowledge.wharton.upenn.edu/article/lippo-group-ceo-james-riady-money-and-power-are-a-blessing-and-a-curse/

Kondratieff, N. D. (1926). Die langen wellen der konjunktur. [The long waves of the economy.]. *Archiv für Sozialwissenschaft und Sozialpolitik*, *56*(3), 573–609.

Kosała, M., & Wach, K. (2014). Linking Regional Knowledge Laboratory and Growth of SMEs – Empirical Investigation in Southern Region of Poland. *Research Gate*. https://www.researchgate.net/publication/274374372_Linking_Regional_Knowledge_Laboratory_and_Growth_of_smes_-_Empirical_Investigation_in_Southern_Region_of_Poland

Kotlar, J., Signori, A., De Massis, A., & Vismara, S. (2018). Financial wealth, socioemotional wealth, and IPO underpricing in family firms: A two-stage gamble model. *Academy of Management Journal*, *61*(3), 1073–1099. doi:10.5465/amj.2016.0256

Kraus, S., Clauss, T., Breier, M., Gast, J., Zardini, A., & Tiberius, V. (2020). The economics of COVID-19: Initial empirical evidence on how family firms in five European countries cope with the corona crisis. *International Journal of Entrepreneurial Behaviour & Research*, *26*(5), 1067–1092. doi:10.1108/IJEBR-04-2020-0214

Krishnan, R. (2020). Importance Of Succession Planning For Business Families. *Business World*. https://www.businessworld.in/article/Importance-Of-Succession-Planning-For-Business-Families-/03-10-2020-326948/

Kuhn, P. (2008). *Chinese among Others: Emigration in Modern Times*. National University of Singapore Press.

Kumar, M., & Ayedee, D. (2021). Technology Adoption: A Solution for SMEs to overcome problems during COVID-19. *Forthcoming. Academy of Marketing Studies Journal*, *25*(1).

Kurma S. (2020, June 11). A case study on entrepreneurship and small family business in indian tourism industry. *London Journal of Research in Management and Business.*

Kusnandar, V. B. (2021). Sebanyak 86,88% Penduduk Indonesia Beragama Islam. *Katadata Media Networks*. https://databoks.katadata.co.id/datapublish/2021/09/30/sebanyak-8688-penduduk-indonesia-beragama-islam

Kusuma, B. (2017, July 22). Papua Education, The Key to Overcome Separatism. *Republika.co.id*. https://www.republika.co.id /berita/oth7t2413/papua-education-the-key-to-overcome-separatism

Lai, P. (2017). The Literature Review of Technology Adoption Models and Theories for the Novelty Technology. *JISTEM -. Journal of Information Systems and Technology Management*, *14*(1). doi:10.4301/S1807-17752017000100002

Landers, R. (2012). Unfolding the IKEA Effect: Why We Love the Things We Build. *Journal of Consumer Psychology*, *22*(3), 453–460. doi:10.1016/j.jcps.2011.08.002

Langer, E. J. (1975). The Illusion of Control. *Journal of Personality and Social Psychology*, *32*(2), 311–328. doi:10.1037/0022-3514.32.2.311

Laudon, K. C., & Laudon, J. P. (2014). *Management Information Systems: Managing the Digital Firm* (13th ed.). Pearson.

Lawton, G. (2022). Plague: Black death bacteria persists and could cause a pandemic. Wilson, E. (ed.). New Scientist. London.

Le Breton-Miller, I., & Miller, D. (2018). Beyond the firm: Business families as entrepreneurs. *Entrepreneurship Theory and Practice*, *42*(4), 527–536. doi:10.1177/1042258717739004

Le Breton-Miller, I., Miller, D., & Steier, L. P. (2004). Towards an Integrative Model of Effective FOB Succession. *Entrepreneurship Theory and Practice*, *28*(4), 305–328. doi:10.1111/j.1540-6520.2004.00047.x

Le Bretton-Miller, I., & Miller, D. (2022). Family businesses under COVID-19: Inspiring models – Sometimes. *Journal of Family Business Strategy*, *13*(100452), 100452. doi:10.1016/j.jfbs.2021.100452

Leaders in Drilling & Oilfield Services. (2021). MB Holding Co. http://www.mbholdingco.com

Leaptrott, J. (2005). An institutional theory view of the family business. *Family Business Review*, *18*(3), 215–228. doi:10.1111/j.1741-6248.2005.00043.x

Lee, J. K. Y. (2021). Still a Chinese Family Business? *Journal of Chinese Overseas*, *17*(2), 399–418. doi:10.1163/17932548-12341450

Lee, J. K. Y., & Gomez, E. T. (2014). Advancing tacit knowledge: Malaysian family SMEs in Manufacturing. *Asian Economic Papers*, *13*(2), 1–24. doi:10.1162/ASEP_a_00275

Lee, J. K. Y., & Tan, J. D. (2022). Adapting to local markets and political changes: Chinese businesses in Malaysia and Indonesia. *South East Asia Research*, *30*(4), 452–471. doi:10.1080/0967828X.2022.2145989

Lee, J. K. Y., & Xavier, J. A. (2022). Strategizing family business with a Chandlerian perspective on 3Ms: A case study of London Biscuits Berhad in Malaysia. *Journal of Asia Business Studies*, *16*(1), 181–199. doi:10.1108/JABS-10-2019-0302

Leung, T. K. P., Lai, K. H., Chan, R. Y., & Wong, Y. H. (2005). The roles of xinyong and guanxi in Chinese relationship marketing. *European Journal of Marketing*, *39*(5/6), 528–559. doi:10.1108/03090560510590700

Lifestyle Magazine, K. L. (2012). Tan Sri Francis Yeoh – Steering YTL with vision. *KL Lifestyle Magazine*. https://www.ytlcommunity.com/shownews.asp?newsID=1197

Lim, J. (2020). Family Business: A second look at the next generation of family business owners. *The Edge Markets*. https://www.theedgemarkets.com/article/family-business-second-look-next-generation-family-business-owners

Lin, F. M. (2020). *Developing the Owner Strategy for Family Businesses*. PWC. https://www.pwc.com/my/en/perspective/epb/200721-developing-the-owner-strategy-for-family-businesses.html

Lincoln, A. T. (2020). Reading Hebrews in a Time of Pandemic: Heroism and Hope in the Face of Fear. *The Expository Times*, *131*(11), 471–479. doi:10.1177/0014524620946689

Lind, M., Visentini, M., Mäntylä, T., & Del Missier, F. (2017). Choice-Supportive Misremembering: A New Taxonomy and Review. *Frontiers in Psychology*, *8*, 2062. doi:10.3389/fpsyg.2017.02062 PMID:29255436

Linh, K. (2021). *How does Covid-19 affect Vietnamese businesses?* Baokiem to annhanuoc. http://baokiemtoannhanuoc.vn/kiem-toan-trong-nuoc/covid-19-tac-dong-den-cac-doanh-nghiep-viet-nam-nhu-the-nao-147152

Lin, K. W., & Huang, K. P. (2014). Moral judgment and ethical leadership in Chinese management: The role of Confucianism and collectivism. *Quality & Quantity*, *48*(1), 37–47. doi:10.100711135-012-9747-7

Locke, K., & Golden-Biddle, K. (2014). Constructing opportunities for contribution: Structuring intertextual coherence and 'problematization' on organizational studies. *Academy of Management Journal*, *40*(5), 1023–1062. doi:10.2307/256926

Loo, D. (2008, June 23). *Lippo to invest $10 billion in Asia in 5 yrs*. Reuters. https://www.reuters.com/article/us-property-summit-lippo-idUKSP7151220080623

Luhmann, N. (1979). *Trust and Power*. Wiley.

Lu, Y., Wu, J., Peng, J., & Lu, L. (2020). The perceived impact of the Covid-19 epidemic: Evidence from a sample of 4807 SMEs in Sichuan Province, China. *Environmental Hazards*, *19*(4), 323–340. doi:10.1080/17477891.2020.1763902

Lynn, M., Naughton, M., & VanderVeen, S. (2009). Faith at work scale (FWS): Justification, development, and validation of a measure of Judeo-Christian religion in the workplace. *Journal of Business Ethics*, *85*(2), 227–243. doi:10.100710551-008-9767-3

Malaysian Department of Statistics. (2021). *Demographic Statistics First Quarter 2021, Malaysia*. Malaysian Department of Statistics. https://www.dosm.gov.my/v1/index.php?r=column/pdfPrev&id=aVlJRDAvbjhWWEhQa1YvSWhsSjF3QT09

Manikutty, S. (2000). Family Business Groups in India: A Resource-Based View of the Emerging Trends. *Family Business Review*, *13*(4), 279–292. doi:10.1111/j.1741-6248.2000.00299.x

March, J. G. (1991). Exploration and exploitation in organizational learning. *Organization Science*, *2*(1), 71–87. doi:10.1287/orsc.2.1.71Martínez-Romero, M., & Rojo Ramírez, A. (2016, January-June). SEW: Looking for a definition and controversial issues. *European Journal of Family Business*, *6*(1), 1–9. doi:10.1016/j.ejfb.2015.09.001

Marquis, C., & Tilcsik, A. (2013). Imprinting: Toward a Multilevel Theory. *The Academy of Management Annals*, *7*(1), 195–245. doi:10.5465/19416520.2013.766076

Mather, M., & Johnson, M. K. (2000). Choice-supportive source monitoring: Do our decisions seem better to us as we age? *Psychology and Aging*, *15*(4), 596–606. doi:10.1037/0882-7974.15.4.596 PMID:11144319

Mathews, T., & Blumentritt, T. (2015). A sequential choice model of family business succession. *Small Business Economics, 45*(1), 15–37. doi:10.100711187-015-9628-2

Miller, D., & Le Breton-Miller, I. (2006). Family Governance and Firm Performance: Agency, Stewardship, and Capabilities. *Family Business Review, 19*(1), 73–87. doi:10.1111/j.1741-6248.2006.00063.x

Minh, A. (2021). *Vietnam government portal.* Bao Chin Phu. https://baochinhphu.vn/Kinh-te/Doanh-nghiep-danh-gia-cao-muc-do-huu-ich-cua-cac-chinh-sach-ho-tro/440223.vgp

Minh, V. (2021). *Website of the Vietnamese Party Committee.* HCMCPV. https://hcmcpv.org.vn/tin-tuc/nganh-du-lich-tang-cuong-cac-bien-phap-phong-chong-dich-covid-19-1491878889

Ministry of Finance. (2020). *Fiscal and Monetary Policies to Deal with Slowdown Due to Covid-19.* Press Information Bureau. https://pib.gov.in/PressReleasePage.aspx?PRID=1656925

Ministry of health portal. 2021. *COVID-19 epidemic bulletin of the Ministry of Health on the evening of July 31: An additional 4,564 cases of COVID-19, bringing the total number of cases of the day to 8,624.* Hanoi Ministry of health portal. https://moh.gov.vn/tin-lien-quan/-/asset_publisher/vjYyM7O9aWnX/content/ban-tin-dich-covid-19-cua-bo-y-te-toi-31-7-them-4-564-ca-mac-covid-19-nang-tong-so-mac-trong-ngay-len-8-624-ca

Ministry of Planning and Investment. (2019). *Vietnam Enterprise White Paper 2019.* Hanoi Ministry of Planning and Investment.

Ministry of Planning and Investment. (2021). *Socio-economic targets in 2020.* Ministry of Planning and Investment.

Miroshnychenko, I., De Massis, A., Miller, D., & Barontini, R. (2021). Family Business Growth Around the World. *Entrepreneurship Theory and Practice, 45*(4), 682–708. doi:10.1177/1042258720913028

Mitchell, M. (1996). *An Introduction to Genetic Algorithms.* MIT Press.

Mitchell, T., & Thompson, L. (1994). A theory of temporal adjustments of the evaluation of events: Rosy Prospection & Rosy Retrospection. In C. Stubbart, J. Porac, & J. Meindl (Eds.), *Advances in managerial cognition and organizational information-processing* (Vol. 5, pp. 85–114). JAI press.

Mode ohne schlechtes Gewissen [Fashion without a guilty conscience] . (2022, August 12). Kölner Stadt-Anzeiger.

Mohamed, Z., Abd Kadir, Z., & Raof, N. A. A. (2018). Malaysia Industrial Master Plans (IMPs) and the focus on the nation technology and innovation development. *Journal of Science. Technology and Innovation Policy, 4*(2), 11–19.

Mohsin Haider Darwish. (2020). NH Doman. https://www.mhdoman.com/

Mokhbar, M., Gi Gi, T., Abdul Rasid, S. Z., Vakilbashi, A., Mohd Zamil, N., & Woon, S. Y. (2017). Succession planning and family business performance in SMEs. *Journal of Management Development*, *36*(3), 330–347. doi:10.1108/JMD-12-2015-0171

Monitor, G. E. (2020). *National Report 2019 -2020.* Unizwa. https://www.unizwa.edu.om/Final%20Oman%20GEM%20National%20report2019_2020_Oct%2020.pdf

Moody's Analytics. (2021). *India - Industrial Production.* Moody's Analytics. https://www.economy.com/india/industrial-production

Morewedge, C. K., & Giblin, C. E. (2015). Explanations of the endowment effect: An integrative review. *Trends in Cognitive Sciences*, *19*(6), 339–348. doi:10.1016/j.tics.2015.04.004 PMID:25939336

Morgan, M., Emmanuel, E. O., Christian, A., Winifred, E., & Anthony, O. (2021). Dynamic capabilities of family business: A catalyst for survival and growth. *Problems and Perspectives in Management*, *19*(1), 137–150. doi:10.21511/ppm.19(1).2021.12

Morris, M., & Schindebutte, M. (2005). Entrepreneurial values and the ethnic entrepreneur: An examination of six sub-cultures. *Journal of Small Business Management*, *43*(4), 453–479. doi:10.1111/j.1540-627X.2005.00147.x

Muskita, P. (2019). Ovo confirms unicorn status. *Tech in Asia.* https://www.techinasia.com/ovo-confirms-unicorn-status

Nasseri, Z. A. (2020, June 14). Al Raffd Funds R.O. 99m among 2,563 SMEs. *Oman Observer.* https://www.omanobserver.om/article/12628/Main/al-raffd-funds-ro-99m-among-2563-smes

Neckebrouck, J., Schulze, W., & Zellweger, T. (2018). Are family firms good employers? *Academy of Management Journal*, *61*(2), 553–585. doi:10.5465/amj.2016.0765

Nexdigm Private Limited. (2021). Impact of Covid-19 on the Manufacturing Sector In India - Coronavirus (COVID-19) - India. *Welcome to Mondaq.* Nexdigm Private Limited. https://www.mondaq.com/india/operational-impacts-and-strategy/1086172/impact-of-Covid-19-on-the-manufacturing-sector-in-india

Ngui, C. (2002). *Asian family businesses: From riches to rags.* Malaysian Business.

Niehm, L. S., Tyner, K., Shelley, M. C., & Fitzgerald, M. A. (2010). Technology adoption in small family-owned businesses: Accessibility, perceived advantage, and information technology literacy. *Journal of Family and Economic Issues*, *31*(4), 498–515. doi:10.100710834-010-9197-0

Nishida, J. M., & Redding, S. G. (1992). Firm development and diversification strategies as products of economic cultures: the Japanese and Hong Kong cotton textile. *European Business Systems: Firms and Markets in Their National Contexts*, 241.

Oliver, C. (1997). Sustainable competitive advantage: Combining institutional and resource-based views. *Strategic Management Journal*, *18*(9), 697–713. doi:10.1002/(SICI)1097-0266(199710)18:9<697::AID-SMJ909>3.0.CO;2-C

Olson, D. H. (2000). Circumplex model of marital and family systems. *Journal of Family Therapy*, *22*(2), 144–167. doi:10.1111/1467-6427.00144 PMID:6840263

Oman Budget. (2021). Ministry of Finance. https://mof.gov.om/Portals/1/documents/Financial-reports/The-state-budget/2021/2021(Eng).pdf

Oman Development Bank - Annual Report (2020). Oman Development Bank. https://odb.om/public/uploads/docs/ODB_AR20_eng.pdf

Oman focuses on diversification and infrastructure investment. (2018). Oxford Business Group. https://oxfordbusinessgroup.com/overview/strong-and-stable-sultanate-continues-evolve-focus-diversification-and-infrastructure-investment

Oman's Leading Business Clans. (2020). Muscat Daily. https://www.muscatdaily.com/2020/06/29/omans-leading-business-clans/

ONA. (2021). Oman registers over 20% increase in SMEs. *Times of Oman.* https://timesofoman.com/article/103300-oman-registers-over-20-increase-in-smes

ONA. (2021). Over 56,000 SMEs registered in Oman till August 2021. *Times of Oman*https://timesofoman.com/article/108177-over-56000-smes-registered-in-oman-till-august-2021

ONA. (2021, June 08). SMEs in Oman come to the fore during the COVID pandemic. *Times of Oman.* https://timesofoman.com/article/102336-smes-in-oman-come-to-the-fore-during-covid-pandemic

ONA.(2021). Over 50,000 SMEs registered in Oman till June 2021. *Times of Oman.* https://timesofoman.com/article/105418-over-50000-smes-registered-in-oman-till-june-2021

Online, F. E. "Coronavirus Latest Highlights: Kerala May See up to 5 Lakh Cases till August 20, Central Team Raises Alarm over Onam Festivities." The Financial Express, August 10, 2021. https://www.financialexpress.com/lifestyle/health/coronavirus-in-india-latest-update-live-ahead-of-Covid-19-third-wave-indias-weekly-cases-decline-several-states-reopen-schools-for-offline-classes/2306949

Online, F. E. "Impact on Indian Economy after the Covid-19 Second Wave." The Financial Express. The Financial Express, June 21, 2021. https://www.financialexpress.com/economy/impact-on-indian-economy-after-the-Covid-19-second-wave/2275353/

Opten. (2020). *A hazai cégek 40 százaléka családi jellegű vállalkozás.* [40 percent of domestic companies are family businesses.] Opten. https://www.opten.hu/kozlemenyek/a-hazai-cegek-40-szazaleka-csaladi-jellegu-vallalkozas

Overbecke, K. K., Bilimoria, D., & Perelli, S. (2013). The dearth of daughter successors in family businesses: Gendered norms, blindness to possibility, and invisibility. *Journal of Family Business Strategy*, *4*(3), 201–212. doi:10.1016/j.jfbs.2013.07.002

Ozili, P. K., & Arun, T. 2020. Spillover of COVID-19: Impact on the Global Economy. SSRN *Electronic Journal.* doi:10.2139/ssrn.3562570

Pantano, E., & Timmermans, H. J. (2011). *Advanced technologies management for retailing: frameworks and cases*. Business Science Reference. doi:10.4018/978-1-60960-738-8

Parviainen, P., Kääriäinen, J., Tihinen, M., & Teppola, S. (2017). Tackling the digitalization challenge: How to benefit from digitalization in practice. *International Journal of Information Systems and Project Management*, *5*(1), 63–77. doi:10.12821/ijispm050104

Patton, M. Q. (1990). *Qualitative Evaluation and Research Methods*. Sage Publications.

Paul, M. (2021). Oman unveils new tourism campaign to promote art and culture. *Travel Daily Media*. https://www.traveldailymedia.com/oman-unveils-new-tourism-campaign-to-promote-art-and-culture/

Pemerintah Republik Indonesia. (2022). *Peraturan Pemerintah Pengganti Undang-Undang (Perpu) tentang Cipta Kerja*. Peraturan. https://peraturan.bpk.go.id/Home/Details/234926/perpu-no-2-tahun-2022

Permatasari, S., & Amin, H. (2022, May 29). *Lippo tycoon eyes hospitals, schools for Jokowi's new capital*. BNN Bloomberg. https://www.bnnbloomberg.ca/lippo-tycoon-eyes-hospitals-schools-for-jokowi-s-new-capital-1.1772150

Perry, R. D., & Fetherston, J. D. (1997, January). Perry, Robert d. and Fetherston, Jacqueline D. Yersinia pestis—Etiologic Agent of Plague. *Clinical Microbiology Reviews*, *10*(1), 35–66. doi:10.1128/CMR.10.1.35

Perwitasari, A. S. (2021). *Wow, Pendapatan Indofood Sukses Mandiri (INDF) di 2020 Capai Rp. 81,73 trilliun rupiah*. https://stocksetup.kontan.co.id/news/wow-pendapatan-indofood-sukses-makmur-indf-di-2020-capai-rp-8173-triliun#:~:text=81%2C73%20triliun-,Wow%2C%20pendapatan%20Indofood%20Sukses%20Makmur%20(INDF)%20di%202020,capai%20Rp%2081%2C73%20triliun&text=KONTAN.CO.ID%20%2D%20JAKARTA,kinerja%20mantap%20di%20tahun%202020.&text=Berdasarkan%20laporan%20keuangan%20perusahaan%2C%20pendapatan,mencapai%20Rp%2081%2C73%20triliun

Phaniharan, V. R. C. (2021, April 4). "Resilient Mindset of Family Business Helped Sail through Pandemic." The Hans India. The Hans India. Retrieved from https://www.thehansindia.com/news/cities/hyderabad/resilient-mindset-of-family-business-helped-sail-through-pandemic-680086

Piac és profit. (2019). Nem mindegy, mit nevezünk családi vállalkozásnak. *Piac és profit*. https://piacesprofit.hu/kkv_cegblog/nem-mindegy-mit-nevezunk-csaladi-vallalkozasnak/3/

Piantoni, G. (1990). *La successione familiare in azienda. Continuità dell'impresa e ricambio generazionale*. EtasLibri.

Picone, P. M., De Massis, A., Tang, Y., & Piccolo, R. F. (2021). The Psychological Foundations of Management in Family Firms: Values, Biases, and Heuristics. *Family Business Review*, *34*(1), 12–32. Advance online publication. doi:10.1177/0894486520985630

Pinker, S. (2011). *The Better Angels of our Nature*. Viking.

Pipatanantakurn, K., & Ractham, V. V. (2016). Knowledge creation aiding family business succession plan. *International Journal of Business and Management Science*, *6*(1), 63–84.

Pohl, R. F. (2017). *Cognitive illusions: Intriguing phenomena in thinking, judgment, and memory*. Routledge.

Porfírio, J. A., Felício, J. A., & Carrilho, T. (2020). Family business succession: Analysis of the drivers of success based on entrepreneurship theory. *Journal of Business Research*, *115*, 250–257. doi:10.1016/j.jbusres.2019.11.054

Portfolio. (2020). There is a sector that has not been harmed by the coronavirus - Modernization of agriculture can accelerate. *Portfolio*. https://www.portfolio.hu/bank/20201117/van-olyan-szektor-aminek-nem-artott-a-koronavirus-felgyorsulhat-a-mezogazdasag-modernizacioja-457322

Powell, M., & Ansic, D. (1997). Gender differences in risk behavior in financial decisionmaking: An experimental analysis. *Journal of Economic Psychology*, *18*(6), 605–628. doi:10.1016/S0167-4870(97)00026-3

Poza, E. J., & Daugherty, M. S. (2014). *Family Business* (4th ed.). Cengage Learning.

Pramono, R., Suyantoko2, Purwanto, A., Kristiana, Y., Yuliantoro, N. and Asbari, M. (2020). Implementation Of Analysis of Talent Management in Family Business. *International Journal of Advanced Science and Technology*, *29*(6), 6124–6146.

Press Information Bureau. (2021). *Fiscal and Monetary Policies to Deal with Slowdown Due to Covid-19*. Press Information Bureau. https://pib.gov.in/PressReleasePage.aspx?PRID=1656925

Presson, P. K., & Benassi, V. A. (1996). Illusion of control: A meta-analytic review. *Journal of Social Behavior and Personality*, *11*(3), 493–510.

PricewaterhouseCoopers. (2020). *Agents of change: Earning your licence to operate: PwC's NextGen Survey 2019 - Malaysia Report*. PWC. www.pwc.com/my: https://www.pwc.com/my/en/publications/2020/nextgen-survey.html

PricewaterhouseCoopers. (2021). Family Business Survey 2021. Vietnam: PricewaterhouseCoopers.
.

PricewaterhouseCoopers. (2021). *Family Business Survey 2021: The Malaysia Chapter*. PWC. www.pwc.com/my: https://www.pwc.com/my/en/assets/publications/2021/pwc-family-business-survey-2021-malaysia.pdf

Pronin, E., Lin, D. Y., & Ross, L. (2002). The Bias Blind Spot: Perceptions of Bias in Self Versus Others. In Personality and Social Psychology Bulletin, 28, 369–381, Doi:10.1177/0146167202286008

PT. HM. Sampoerna Tbk. (2020). *Laporan tahunan*. https://www.sampoerna.com/resources/docs/default-source/sampoerna-market-documents/annual-reports---en/annual-report-2020.pdf?sfvrsn=c0cf95b4_2

PwC. (2014). *Survey Bisnis Keluarga 2014: Indonesia*. PWC. https://www.pwc.com/id/en/publications/assets/indonesia-report-family-business-survey-2014.pdf

QRIS. (2021). *Satu QR Code untuk semua payment*. QRIS. https://qris.id/homepage/

Quansah, E., & Hartz, D. E. (2021). Strategic adaptation: Leadership lessons for small business survival and success. *American Journal of Business*, *36*(3/4), 190–207. doi:10.1108/AJB-07-2020-0096

Quynh, N. (2021). *Drive retail growth with digital transformation*. Bao Ninh Binh. https://baoninhbinh.org.vn/thuc-day-tang-truong-nganh-ban-le-bang-viec-chuyen-doi-so/d2021070808254637.htm

Rachmawati, E., Suliyanto, & Suroso, A. (2022). Direct and indirect effect of entrepreneurial orientation, family involvement and gender on family business performance. *Journal of Family Business Management*, *12*(2), 214–236. doi:10.1108/JFBM-07-2020-0064

Raju, G. & Sivakumar, N. V. (2019). *PwC India Family Business Survey 2019*. PWC.

Randerson, K., Bettinelli, C., Fayolle, A., & Anderson, A. (2015). Family entrepreneurship as a field of research: Exploring its contours and contents. *Journal of Family Business Strategy*, *6*(3), 143–154. doi:10.1016/j.jfbs.2015.08.002

Rashid, S., & Ratten, V. (2020). A dynamic capabilities approach for the survival of Pakistani family-owned business in the digital world. *Journal of Family Business Management*, *10*(4), 373–387. doi:10.1108/JFBM-12-2019-0082

Rathbun, B. C. (2012). From vicious to virtuous circle: Moralistic trust, diffuse reciprocity, and the American security commitment to Europe. *European Journal of International Relations*, *18*(2), 323–344. doi:10.1177/1354066110391308

Report, I. P. S. (2020). The Annual Sri Lanka State of the Economy Report, Institute of Policy Studies of Sri Lanka. IPS Publications Unit.

Reserve bank of India. (2021). *Annual report*. Reserve Bank of India. https://rbi.org.in/scripts/AnnualReportPublications.aspx?Id=1327

Riady, M. (2016). *Manusia Ide*. PT Kompas Media Nusantara.

Richter, P. (2014). Invitation to Indonesia. *The Geospel Coalition*. https://www.thegospelcoalition.org/article/indonesia-invitation/

Riedel, S. (2005). Plague: From natural disease to bioterrorism. *Proceedings - Baylor University. Medical Center*, *18*(2), 116–124. doi:10.1080/08998280.2005.11928049 PMID:16200159

Rivo-López, E., Villanueva-Villar, M., Vaquero-García, A., & Lago-Peñas, S. (2021). Do family firms contribute to job stability? Evidence from the great recession. *Journal of Family Business Management*, *12*(1), 152–169. doi:10.1108/JFBM-06-2020-0055

Rosenblatt, P., de Mik, L., Anderson, R., & Johnson, P. (1985). *The family in business: Understanding and dealing with the challenges entrepreneurial families face*. Jossey-Bass.

Ross, L., Greene, D., & House, P. (1977). The false consensus effect: An egocentric bias in social perception and attribution processes. *Journal of Experimental Social Psychology, 13*(3), 279–301. doi:10.1016/0022-1031(77)90049-X

Ross, L., & Ward, A. (1996). Naive realism in everyday life: Implications for social conflict and misunderstanding. In T. Brown, E. S. Reed, & E. Turiel (Eds.), *Values and Knowledge* (pp. 103–135). Erlbaum.

Rotter, J. B. (1990). Internal versus external control of reinforcement: A case history of a variable. *The American Psychologist, 45*(4), 489–493. doi:10.1037/0003-066X.45.4.489

Rovnick, N. (2009, January 23). *Interview: Francis Yeoh explains YTL's divine performance*. Global Capital Asia. https://www.globalcapital.com/asia/article/28mvfg22uqekr0unx7x1c/emerging-markets/interview-francis-yeoh-explains-ytls-divine-performance

Saigal, M., Mehrotra, S., & Mukadam, S. (2018). *Family Businesses In India*. Alvarez and Marsal. https://www.alvarezandmarsal.com/sites/default/files/77597_tag_india_familybusinessreport_05_singles.pdf

Saleem, I., Siddique, I., & Ahmed, A. (2020). An extension of the socioemotional wealth perspective Insights from an Asian sample. *Journal of Family Business Management, 10*(4), 293–312. doi:10.1108/JFBM-04-2019-0022

Sankhe, R. (2020). Managing Family Businesses during Covid-19. Fortune India: Business News, Strategy, Finance and Corporate Insight. *Fortune India*. https://www.fortuneindia.com/opinion/managing-family-businesses-during-Covid-19/104733

Santia, T. (2021). *Sudah Tersedot Rp 395,92 Triliun, Dana PEN untuk Apa Saja?* https://www.liputan6.com/bisnis/read/4666305/sudah-tersedot-rp-39592-triliun-dana-pen untuk-apasaja#:~:text=Program%20PEN%20merupakan%20instrumen%20utama,di%20tahun%20 2020%20maupun%202021.&text=Dana%20PEN%20sektor%20kesehatan%20juga,untuk%20 29%2C29%20juta%20orang

Saragih, H. S., & Tan, J. D. (2018). Co-innovation: A review and conceptual framework. *International Journal of Business Innovation and Research, 17*(3), 361–377. doi:10.1504/IJBIR.2018.095542

Sarbah, A., & Xiao, W. (2015). Good corporate governance structures: A must for family businesses. *Journal of Business and Management, 3*, 40–57.

Saud Bahwan Group. (2021). *About.* Saud Bahwan Group. https://saudbahwangroup.com/

Saunders, B., Sim, J., Kingstone, T., Baker, S., Waterfield, J., Bartlam, B., & Jinks, C. (2017). Saturation in qualitative research: Exploring its conceptualization and operationalization. *Quality & Quantity, 52*(4), 1893–1907. doi:10.100711135-017-0574-8 PMID:29937585

Schumpeter, J. A. (1961). Konjunkturzyklen. *Eine theoretische, historische und statistische Analyse des kapitalistischen.* Prozesses Bd. I.

Selznick, P. (1996). Institutionalism "old" and "new.". *Administrative Science Quarterly, 41*(2), 270–277. doi:10.2307/2393719

Shahbaz, M. (2013). Linkages between inflation, economic growth and terrorism in Pakistan. *Economic Modelling, 32*, 496–506. doi:10.1016/j.econmod.2013.02.014

Shanfari Group of Companies. (2016). *About.* Shanfari Group of Companies. https://www.shanfari.com/about.php

Sharma, P., Chrisman, J. J., & Chua, J. H. (1997). Strategic Management of the Family Business: Past Research and Future Challenges. *Family Business Review, 10*(1), 1–35. doi:10.1111/j.1741-6248.1997.00001.x

Sharma, P., Chrisman, J. J., & Chua, J. H. (2003). Predictors of Satisfaction with the Succession Process in Family Firms. *Journal of Business Venturing, 18*(5), 667–687. doi:10.1016/S0883-9026(03)00015-6

Sharma, P., Chrisman, J. J., Pablo, A. L., & Chua, J. H. (2001). Determinants of initial satisfaction with the succession process in family firms: A conceptual model. *Entrepreneurship Theory and Practice, 25*(3), 17–35. doi:10.1177/104225870102500302

Sharma, P., Chua, J. H., & Chrisman, J. J. (2000). Perceptions about the extent of succession planning in Canadian family firms. *Canadian Journal of Administrative Sciences, 17*(3), 233–244. doi:10.1111/j.1936-4490.2000.tb00223.x

Sharot, T. (2011). *The Optimism Bias: A Tour of The Irrationally Positive Brain.* Pantheon. doi:10.1016/j.cub.2011.10.030

Sharot, T., Riccardi, A. M., Raio, M. C., & Phelp, E. A. (2007). *Neural Mechanism Mediating Optimism Bias*. Nature Publisching Group. doi:10.1038/nature06280

Shaw, W. (2009). Marxism, business ethics, and corporate social responsibility. *Journal of Business Ethics, 84*(4), 565–575. doi:10.100710551-008-9725-0

Shepherd, D. A. (2009). Grief recovery from the loss of a family business: A multi- and meso-level theory. *Journal of Business Venturing, 24*(1), 81–97. doi:10.1016/j.jbusvent.2007.09.003

Shepperd, B. H., Hartwick, J., & Warshaw, P. R. (1988). The theory of reasoned action: A meta-analysis of past research with recommendations for modifications and future research. *The Journal of Consumer Research, 15*(3), 325–343. doi:10.1086/209170

Shibata, I. (2021). The distributional impact of recessions: The global financial crisis and the COVID-19 pandemic recession. *Journal of Economics and Business, 115*, 105971. doi:10.1016/j.jeconbus.2020.105971 PMID:35702646

Shukaili, A. A., Kassim, N. M., Al Suleimani, B., Ahmed, Z., Mondal, S., & Kausar, Y. (2020). *Global Entrepreneurship Monitor: Oman National Report 2019*. Authority for Small and Medium Enterprise Development. Global Entrepreneurship. https://www.unizwa.edu.om/Final%20Oman%20GEM%20National%20report2019_2020_Oct%2020.pdf

Siagian, K. (2022). *Lippo Group's John Riady takes on the conglomerate investment in the technology landscape*. Daily Social.

Siakas, K., Naaranoja, M., Vlachakis, S., & Siakas, E. (2014). Family businesses in the new economy: How to survive and develops in times of financial crisis. *Procedia Economics and Finance*, *9*, 331–341. doi:10.1016/S2212-5671(14)00034-3

Simarasl, N., Jiang, D. S., Kellermanns, F. W., & Debicki, B. J. (2020). Unmasking the social ghost in the machine: How the need to belong and family business potency affect family firm performance. *Family Business Review*, *33*(4), 351–371. doi:10.1177/0894486520948992

Siringoringo, H., & Kuruppuge, R. H. (2021). Government Policies During Pandemic: Indonesian vs Sri Lankan Perspective. In V. Kumar & G. Gupta (Eds.), *Strategic Management during a Pandemic*. Routledge. doi:10.4324/9781003125648-8

Smith, A. (2010). *The wealth of nations: An inquiry into the nature and causes of the wealth of nations*. Harriman House Limited.

Smith, J. A., & Eatough, V. (2006). Interpretative phenomenological analysis. In G. M. Breakwell, S. Hammond, C. Fife-Schan, & J. A. Smith (Eds.), *Research Methods in Psychology*. Sage.

Smith, L., & Riley, D. (2012). School leadership in times of crisis. *School Leadership & Management*, *32*(1), 57–71. doi:10.1080/13632434.2011.614941

Soll, J. B., Milkman, K. L., & Payne, J. W. (2015). Outsmart Your Own Biases. *Harvard Business Review*, pp.64–71. https://hbr.org/2015/05/outsmart-your-own-biases

Songini, L., & Gnan, L. (2015). Family involvement and agency cost control mechanisms in family small and medium-sized enterprises. *Journal of Small Business Management*, *53*(3), 748–779. doi:10.1111/jsbm.12085

Sri Lanka Labour Force. (2019). *Survey Annual Report*. Department of Census and Statistics, Sri Lanka (http://www.statistics.gov.lk/LabourForce/StaticalInformation/AnnualReports/2019)

Stafford, K., Duncan, K. A., Danes, S. M., & Winter, M. (1999). A research model of sustainable family businesses. *Family Business Review*, *12*(3), 197–208. doi:10.1111/j.1741-6248.1999.00197.x

Staw, B. M. (1997). The escalation of commitment: An update and appraisal. In Shapira, Zur (ed.). Organizational Decision Making. Cambridge University Press.

Sudan, T., & Taggar, R. (2021). Recovering supply chain disruptions in post-COVID-19 pandemic through transport intelligence and logistics systems: India's experiences and policy options. *Frontiers in Future Transportation*, *2*, 660116. doi:10.3389/ffutr.2021.660116

Suddaby, R., & Jaskiewicz, P. (2020). Managing traditions: A critical capability for family business success. *Family Business Review*, *33*(3), 234–243. doi:10.1177/0894486520942611

Suhartono, H., & Baigorri, M. (2022, August 25). *Lippo Karawaci Mulls Buying CVC's Siloam Hospitals Stake*. Bloomberg. https://www.bloomberg.com/news/articles/2022-08-25/lippo-karawaci-said-to-mull-buying-cvc-s-siloam-hospitals-stake

Suzuki, J. (2018). *Lippo tycoon looks to young-gun grandson to build digital empire*. Asia Nikkei. https://asia.nikkei.com/Spotlight/Asian-Family-Conglomerates/Lippo-tycoon-looks-to-young-gun-grandson-to-build-digital-empire

Tahunan, L. (2020). *Annual report 2020*. https://bakrie-brothers.com/wp-content/uploads/2020/10/BNBR-Annual-Report-2020-INDO-web-2.pdf

Tan, M. M., Musa, A. F., & Su, T. T. (2022). The role of religion in mitigating the COVID-19 pandemic: the Malaysian multi-faith perspectives. *Health Promotion International*, *37*(1), daab041.

Tan, C.-B. (1995). The study of Chinese religions in Southeast Asia. In L. Suryadinata (Ed.), *Southeast Asian Chinese: The Socio-Cultural Dimension*. Times Academic Press.

Tan, J. D. (2021). *The panorama of succession: nurturing transgenerational entrepreneurship in family business (parent-child dyad)*. Penerbit Andi.

Tan, J. D., Supratikno, H., Pramono, R., Purba, J. T., & Bernarto, I. (2019). Nurturing transgenerational entrepreneurship in ethnic Chinese family SMEs: Exploring Indonesia. *Journal of Asia Business Studies*, *13*(2), 294–325. doi:10.1108/JABS-04-2018-0132

Tari, D. N. (2021). *Kinerja 2020: Kebal Pandemi, Laba Ciputra (CTRA) Tumbuh Dua Digit*. https://market.bisnis.com/read/20210415/192/1381600/kinerja-2020-kebal-pandemi-laba-ciputra-ctra-tumbuh-dua-digit

The Business Times. (2019, September 13). Riady scion takes action to revive Lippo flagship. *The Business Times*. https://www.businesstimes.com.sg/real-estate/riady-scion-takes-action-to-revive-lippo-flagship

The Government of Malaysia. (2020). *Economic Stimulus Package 2020 "Bolstering Confidence, Stimulating Growth, Protecting Jobs."* MOF. https://www.mof.gov.my/pdf/pre2020/Booklet_2020_Economic_Stimulus_Package.pdf

The Impact of Covid-19 on India's Manufacturing Sector. (2021). The Wire. https://thewire.in/economy/the-impact-of-Covid-19-on-indias-manufacturing-sector

The Resilient Family Enterprise. (2021, June 2). Deloitte. https://www2.deloitte.com/global/en/pages/about-deloitte/articles/Covid-19/the-resilient-family-enterprise.htm

The Zubair Corporation. (2021). *About.* The Zubair Corporation. https://zubaircorp.com/en/about/the-zubair-story

Tienda, M., & Raijman, R. (2004). Promoting Hispanic immigrant entrepreneurship in Chicago. *Journal of Developmental Entrepreneurship*, *9*(1), 1–21.

Times Now News. (2021). From Ambanis To Wadias: Here Are 10 Richest Families of India. *Business News.* https://www.timesnownews.com/business-economy/companies/article/from-ambani-to-wadia-here-are-10-richest-families-of-india/592759

Times of India. (2021). First vs Second Wave of COVID-19 in India: Things You Need to Know. *The Times of India*. https://timesofindia.indiatimes.com/india/first-vs-second-wave-of-Covid-19-in-india-things-you-need-to-know/articleshow/82143427.cms

Times of Oman. (2021). Zubair SEC signed an agreement with the Ministry of Social Development. *Times of Oman*. https://timesofoman.com/article/106693-zubair-sec-signs-agreement-with-the-ministry-of-social-development

Tindiwensi, C.K., Abaho, E., Munene, J.C., Muhwezi, M. and Nkote, I.N. (2020), Entrepreneurial bricolage in smallholder commercial farming: a family business perspective. *Journal of Family Business Management*. doi:10.1108/JFBM-04-2020-0036

Tognazzo, A., & Neubaum, D. O. (2020). Family business leaders' metaphors and firm performance: Exploring the "roots" and "shoots" of symbolic meanings. *Family Business Review*, *33*(2), 130–151. doi:10.1177/0894486520910874

Tong, C. K. (1996). Centripetal authority, differentiated networks: The social organisation of Chinese firms in Singapore. In Gary Hamilton (Ed.), Asian Business Networks (pp. 133–56). de Gruyter.

Tooch, D. E. (2015). *Effective Accounting for Small Business: A Guide to Business and Personal Financial Success*. Cognella Academic Publishing.

Trang, L. (2021). *Nhan Dan (The People)*. 3 1. Accessed 6 9, 2021. https://nhandan.vn/dien-dan-dulich/du-lich-viet-nam-2020-phat-huy-noi-luc-trong-bao-covid-19-630469/

Trang, T. 2021. *News.* 12 3. Accessed 5 25, 2021. https://baotintuc.vn/kinh-te/gan-90-doanh-nghiep-tai-viet-nam-bi-anh-huong-boi-dich-benh-covid19-20210312100553768.htm

Tripathi, S., & Al Shahri, M. (2016). Omani Community in Digital Age: A Study of Omani Women Using Back Channel Media to Empower Themselves for Frontline Entrepreneurship. *International Journal of Information and Communication Engineering*, *10*(6).

Truong Thu Huong, Do Van Chuc. (2021). Solutions for small and medium-sized businesses to survive the Covid-19 pandemic. *Financial magazine,* 72.

United Nations. (2015). *Fund for Development of Youth Projects*. United Nations: Economic and Social Commission for Western Asia. https://archive.unescwa.org/fund-development-youth-projects

Uslaner, E. M. (2002). *The Moral Foundations of Trust*. Cambridge University Press.

van der Merwe, P., Saayman, A., & Jacobs, C. (2021). Assessing the economic impact of COVID-19 on the private wildlife industry of South Africa. *Global Ecology and Conservation, 28*, e01633. doi:10.1016/j.gecco.2021.e01633 PMID:34541259

van der Pligt, J., & Eiser, J. R. (1983). Actors and observers attributions, self-serving bias and positivity bias. *European Journal of Social Psychology, 13*(1), 95–104. doi:10.1002/ejsp.2420130107

Van Essen, M., Strike, V. M., Carney, M., & Sapp, S. (2015). The resilient family firm: Stakeholder outcomes and institutional effects. *Corporate Governance, 23*(3), 167–183. doi:10.1111/corg.12087

Vatsa, S. (2020.) A Study On The Impact Of Covid-19 On Businesses In Indian Economy.

Velavan, T. P., & Meyer, C. G. (2020). The COVID-19 epidemic. *Tropical Medicine & International Health, 25*(3), 278–280. doi:10.1111/tmi.13383 PMID:32052514

Venkatesh, V., & Bala, H. (2008). Technology Acceptance Model 3 and a Research Agenda on Interventions. Decision Science. *Decision Sciences, 39*(2), 273–315. doi:10.1111/j.1540-5915.2008.00192.x

Venkatesh, V., & Davis, F. D. (2000). A Theoretical Extension of the Technology Acceptance Model: Four Longitudinal Field Studies. *Management Science, 46*(2), 186–204. doi:10.1287/mnsc.46.2.186.11926

Venter, E., Boshoff, C., & Maas, G. (2005). The influence of successor-related factors on the succession process in small and medium-sized family businesses. *Family Business Review, 18*(4), 283–303. doi:10.1111/j.1741-6248.2005.00049.x

Vietnam Association of Seafood Exporters and Producers Seafood. (2021). *Export of agricultural, forestry and fishery products: Quality of growth is a measure*. Vietnam Association of Seafood Exporters and Producers Seafood.

Világgazdaság. (2021). A családi vállalkozások lehetnek a járvány nagy nyertesei. [Family businesses can be the big winners of the epidemic.] *Világgazdaság*. https://www.vg.hu/cegvilag/2021/05/a-csaladi-vallalkozasok-lehetnek-a-jarvany-nagy-nyertesei

Vinh, B. T. (2021). Factors affecting the access of small and medium-sized enterprises to loan provided by Vietinbank - Tay Tien Giang branch. *Industry and trade magazine*. https://tapchicongthuong.vn/bai-viet/cac-yeu-to-anh-huong-den-doanh-nghiep-vua-va-nho-vay-von-tai-ngan-hang-vietinbank-tay-tien-giang-79930.htm

Wahidin, D., Akimov, A., & Roca, E. (2021). The impact of bond market development on economic growth before and after the global financial crisis: Evidence from developed and developing countries. *International Review of Financial Analysis, 77*, 101865. doi:10.1016/j.irfa.2021.101865

Wah, S. S. (2001). Chinese cultural values and their implication to Chinese management. *Singapore Management Review, 23*(2), 75–83.

Wallau, F., & Kayser, G. (2001). In the federation of German industries (Ed.), Das industrielle Familienunternehmen—Kontinuität im Wandel. Berlin: Bundesverband der Deutschen Industrie (BDI e.V) and Ernst & Young.

Wang, X., Li, F., & Sun, Q. (2018). Confucian ethics, moral foundations, and shareholder value perspectives: An exploratory study. *Business Ethics (Oxford, England)*, *27*(3), 260–271. doi:10.1111/beer.12186

Weber, M. (1964). The religion of China: Confucianism and Taoism, (trans. Hans H. Gerth). New York: Free Press.

Weber, M. (1947b). The protestant sects and the spirit of capitalism. In *From Max Weber* (H. H. Gerth & C. W. Mills, Trans.). Oxford University Press.

Weick, K. E., & Sutcliffe, K. M. (2005). *Managing the unexpected. Resilient performance in an age of uncertainty*. Wiley.

Weick, K. E., Sutcliffe, K. M., & Obstfeld, D. (1999). Organizing for high reliability: processes for collective mindfulness. In B. Staw & R. Sutton (Eds.), *Research in Organizational Behavior* (pp. 81–124). JAI Press.

Wielsma, A. J., & Brunninge, O. (2019). 'Who am I? Who are we?' Understanding the impact of family business identity on the development of individual and family identity in business families. *Journal of Family Business Strategy*, *10*(1), 38–48. doi:10.1016/j.jfbs.2019.01.006

Wikipedia. (2021). *QR code*. Wikipedia. https://en.wikipedia.org/wiki/QR_code

Williams, D., Zorn, M. L., Crook, T. R., & Combs, J. G. (2013). Passing the Torch: Factors Influencing Transgenerational Intent in Family Firms. *Family Relations*, *62*(3), 415–428. doi:10.1111/fare.12016

Wilson, S. L. (2015). *Antecedents to business succession planning in small relationship- dependent service businesses*. [Unpublished PhD Thesis, Graduate College of the Oklahoma State University] https://hdl.handle.net/11244/45386

Winter, M., & Morris, E. (1998). Family resource management and family business: Coming together in theory and research. In The Entrepreneurial Family, RKZHeck (ed.). Needham, MA: Family Business Resources, Inc.

Wong-McDonald, A., & Gorsuch, R. L. (2000). Surrender to God: An additional coping style? *Journal of Psychology and Theology*, *28*(2), 149–161. doi:10.1177/009164710002800207

Wong, S. (1988). *Emigrant entrepreneurs: Shanghai industrialists in Hong Kong*. Hong Kong: Oxford University Press: Wong, Y. H., & Tam, J. L. (2000). Mapping relationships in China: Guanxi dynamic approach. *Journal of Business and Industrial Marketing*, *15*(1), 57–70. doi:10.1108/08858620010311557

Wong, S. L. (1993). The Chinese family firm: A model. *Family Business Review*, *6*(3), 327–340. doi:10.1111/j.1741-6248.1993.00327.x

Woods, J. A., Dalziel, T., & Barton, S. L. (2012). Escalation of commitment in private family businesses: The influence of outside board members. *Journal of Family Business Strategy*, *3*(1), 18–27. doi:10.1016/j.jfbs.2012.01.002

World Bank. (2021). *The world Bank in Vietnam.* World Bank. https://www.worldbank.org/en/country/vietnam/overview

World Bank. (2022). *Global Growth to Slow through 2023, Adding to Risk of 'Hard Landing' in Developing Economies.* World Bank. https://www.worldbank.org/en/news/press-release/2022/01/11/global-recovery-economics-debt-commodity-inequality

World Health Organization. (2021). Impact of Covid-19 on People's Livelihoods, Their Health and Our Food Systems. World Health Organization. https://www.who.int/news/item/13-10-2020-impact-of-Covid-19-on-people's-livelihoods-their-health-and-our-food-systems

World health Organization. (2021). *WHO Viet Nam situation reports by date.* World health Organization.

Wright, L. (2020). Annals of history: Crossroads. A scholar of the plague thinks that pandemics wreak havoc—and open minds. *The New Yorker.*

Wright, M., & Kellermanns, F. W. (2011). What can family firm research learn from management and entrepreneurship? *Journal of Family Business Strategy*, *2*(4), 187–198. doi:10.1016/j.jfbs.2011.10.002

WTO. (2020a). *Trade set to plunge as COVID-19 Pandemic upends global economy. World* Trade Organisation Press Release. https://www.wto.org/english/news_e/pres20_e/pr855_e.htm#:~:text=World%20merchandise%20trade%20is%20set,effectiveness%20of%20the%20policy%20responses. (accessed 29.05.2021).

WTO. (2020b). *Methodology for the WTO trade forecast.* WTO. https://www.wto.org/english/news_e/pres20_e/methodpr855_e.pdf

Wuisan, P. A. (2021). *Keren! Ini Dia Daftar 10 Perusahaan Terbesar di Indonesia.* https://www.modalrakyat.id/blog/perusahaan-terbesar-di-indonesia

Yang, F. (1999). *Chinese Christians in America: Conversion, assimilation, and adhesive identities.* The Pennsylvania State University Press.

Yap, A. (n.d.). *Family and Business: Planning for the Future.* RHB Group. www.crowehorwath.com.my: https://www.rhbgroup.com/files/business/business-solution/sme-knowledge-center/Crowe%20Horwath%20Newsletter%20Succession%20Planning.pdf

Yasin, N., & Khansari, Z. (2022). The Context for Business in Oman. In L.-P. Dana, A. Salamzadeh, V. Ramadani, & R. Palalić, Understanding Contexts of Business in Western Asia (pp. 43–58). World Scientific Publishing Company. doi:10.1142/9789811229695_0003

Yin, E., & Mahrous, A. (2022). Covid-19 global pandemic, workplace spirituality and the rise of spirituality-driven organisations in the post-digital era. *Journal of Humanities and Applied Social Sciences.*

Yin, R. K. (2003). *Case Study Research: Design and Methods.* Sage publications.

Your Article Library. (2014). *Family Business in India: A Historical Perspective (with Example).* Your Article Library. https://www.yourarticlelibrary.com/essay/family-business-in-india-a-historical-perspective-with-example/41128

Yousaf, I., Beljid, M., Chaibi, A., & Ajlouni, A. A. L. (2022). Do volatility spillover and hedging among GCC stock markets and global factors vary from normal to turbulent periods? Evidence from the global financial crisis and Covid-19 pandemic crisis. *Pacific-Basin Finance Journal, 73*, 101764. doi:10.1016/j.pacfin.2022.101764

Yusof, A. (2021). Timeline: How the COVID-19 pandemic has unfolded in Malaysia since January 2020. *Channel News Asia.* https://www.channelnewsasia.com/asia/timeline-how-covid-19-pandemic-has-unfolded-malaysia-january-2020-2082081

Zawawi Group . (2021). *Leading Business Group in the Sultanate of Oman.* Zawawi Group. https://www.zawawigroup.com/

Zellweger, T. M., & Astrachan, J. H. (2008). On the emotional value of owning a firm. *Family Business Review, 21*(4), 347–363. doi:10.1177/08944865080210040106

Zhu, Y., & Warner, M. (2004). Changing patterns of human resource management in contemporary China: WTO accession and enterprise responses. *Industrial Relations Journal, 35*(4), 311–328. doi:10.1111/j.1468-2338.2004.00316.x

Zimbardo, P., & Sword, R. K. M. (2017). Living and Loving Better with Time Perspective Therapy: Healing from the Past, Embracing the Present, Creating an Ideal Future. MCFarland & Company, Inc.

Zola, E. (2004). *Paradies der Damen* [*[Ladies' paradise*]].

About the Contributors

Hotniar Siringoringo is a professor at Gunadarma University, Jakarta Indonesia. She teaches undergraduate students in the Industrial Engineering and Management Program, postgraduate in the Information System Management program, and in the Economics program. She advises students' thesis of master program in Information System Management and doctoral program in economics. She also taught abroad as visiting professor at the West Pomeranian University of Technology in Szczecin, Poland, and to the Slovak University of Agriculture in Nitra, Slovak. She visited Ecuador as visiting researcher in Ministerio de Telecomunicaciones y Sociedad de la Informaci6n, Quito, Ecuador on Prometeo project April-July 2014. She published papers in international journals published by reputed publishers such as Inderscience and Emerald.

Ravindra Hewa Kuruppuge is a professor in Operations Management Department, Faculty of Management, University of Peradeniya, Sri Lanka. He completed B.Com Degree from University of Peradeniya and MBA Degree from University of Colombo, Sri Lanka. He received his PhD from the Department of Management and Marketing, Tomas Bata University in Zlin, Czech Republic. He is an author or co-author of more than 30 articles in scientific journals and presenter of several research conferences. His areas of research are Operations Management, Human Capital, Knowledge Management, Family Businesses and Tourism Management. He is currently teaching subjects Operations Management, Research Methodology, and Tourism Management.

* * *

Muna Said AL-Shahri has been an assistant lecturer at the University of Technology and Applied Sciences, Salalah, Oman, since 2013. She has a Master's degree in International Communication and Development from Swansea University, U.K. She is involved in research in media impact-related areas such as communication, tourism, new media, women empowerment, and new media. In addition, she has conducted workshops for local institutions in aspects such as I.P. skills and stress management. Recently, she has co-authored a research project titled "Advance Communication Role in Creating Consensus and Acceptability for Innovative Tourism to Support Diversified Economy Drive in The Sultanate" that was approved by Ministry of Higher Education, Research and Innovation, Oman.

Alam Tonmoy specialized in International Business Management minored in Transportation and Logistics Management. He is graduated from Universiti Utara Malaysia (UUM). He is actively involved in many leadership programs at university and regional level. His research area is international business and logistic management.

Oanh Kieu Le Dao is a lecturer in finance, Banking University of Ho Chi Minh City, Vietnam.

Jacob Donald Tan, B.B.A., M.B.A. (Business Management and Entrepreneurship), is a tenured professor in the Faculty of Economics and Business, Universitas Pelita Harapan in Indonesia. His specialization is in Chinese family business in the scope of succession strategies emphasizing on cultural values, as well as nurturing trust and entrepreneurial spirit to next generations. Recently, he published a book on the panorama of succession. His article, 'Nurturing transgenerational entrepreneurship in ethnic Chinese family SMEs: Exploring Indonesia' was published in the Journal of Asia Business Studies 13(2), 294-325 (2019).

Garima Madaan Dua was awarded Ph.D. in 2017 and held a Master's degree in Management with a specialization in Finance. She has a work experience of over 14 years, including three years of experience in the corporate sector. Dr. Garima has a keen interest in Investment Management, Security Analysis, Management of Financial Services, Financial Reporting and Analysis, Financial Accounting, and Management Accounting. Earlier, she worked with the School of Business Studies, Sharda University, as an Assistant Professor. Currently, she is working in administrative role in Denmark Technical University, Denmark.

Filippo Ferrari holds a Bachelor degree in Work and Organizational Psychology and a Master's degree in Adult Training and Education. He currently serves as a Lecturer at Bologna University, School of Economics, Management and Statistics, where he teaches Organizational Behaviour and Design and Human Resources Management. His fields of interests are International Human Resources Management, Organizational Reliability, Change Management, Adult Training.

Kanhiya Garg is a Graduate Student at CHRIST (Deemed to be University) - Delhi, NCR. The idea of Indian family businesses has always fascinated him and he's all in for taking a deep dive into the Indian markets!

Gaurav Gupta is currently Assistant Professor in Marketing at Amity University, Uttar Pradesh, India. He earned his Doctorate and Masters in Business Administration degree with a concentration in Marketing from Punjabi University, Patiala. He also studied marketing at the prestigious Wilkes University, Pennsylvania, USA, and is a recipient of Erasmus+, IIM-Bangalore Fellowship(s).

Bernd Hallier, born at July 28th 1947 in Hamburg/Germany, studied at Hamburg University and graduated with a MA-degree in Economics. He then worked in distribution where he became assistant to the Board and Key-account-manager of an international cigarette company. During that time additionally as a part-time student he wrote his PhD-thesis about the response to high-tech-innovation in wholesale/retail versus the relationship between trade and consumer-products industry. His analysis of cigarette-sales via vending machines (included in his thesis) could be seen as a first ECR-project applied already between 1979 and 1982 (Hallier, B., Organisation und Marktstrategie im Tabakwarenfachgroßhandel, Göttingen, 1983). In 1985 he became head of the Institute for Self-Service (ISB) in Cologne/Germany which he first transformed into the German Trade Institute (DHI) and then in 1993 into the European Trade Institute (EHI) today labeled as EHI Retail Institute. Already during his studies he gained international experience due to traineeships in Turkey, Israel, South Africa, Japan, China. Later he traveled and lectured in all continents of the world. He was honored in the Czech Republic by the the University of Economics in Prague (VSE) in 1994 for his help of transition; getting the Alois Rasin-Medal in 2000; getting the 50 years-jubilee-Medal in 2003. honored by a Dr.h.c in 2011 Beside his activities in Prague he had also supported Budweis University as a visiting professor from 2006-2009. In 2021 he became one of the founding members of the International Advisory Board of the Faculty of Economics of the University of South Bohemia in Ceske Budejuvice. In Russia he became in 2003 "Professor honoris causa" at the Moscow academy of business at the Government of Moscow; in 2007 doctor honoris causa at the Ural State University of Economics. In 2006 Hallier was appointed in China from the School of International Relations of Economics and Trade of the Harbin Institute of Technology as a commissioner in its consulting committee. In Kazakhstan in 2010 B.Hallier was appointed as a member of the Association of the Eurasian Economic Club of Scientists. This organization was established in 2008 by the president of Kazakhstan N. Nazarbayev and is backing the annual Astana Economic Forum in Kazakhstan. Among its speakers in 2010 had been three Nobel Prize Winners of Economics: Prof. Dr. R. A. Mundell (1999),

Prof. Dr. F. E. Kydland (2004) and Prof. Dr. R.Y. Aumann (2005) and additionally in 2011 the Nobel Laureats John Nash (1994), Sir James A. Mirrless (1996) and as a Nobel Laureat for Chemistry Roger D. Kornberg (2006) In 2011 B.Hallier was awarded with the "Star of Eurasia" and the title "Honorary Ambassador of Peace" by the Eurasian Economic Youth Forum. In 2012 it was labelled at the Astana Conference into the I World Economic Youth Forum - being attended by the Nobel Laureates Prof.Dr. Aumann and Prof. Dr. Maskin. In 2018 he cooperated with G-Global to start in Astana the Silk Road Mayors' Club. In Romania he got in 2011 the following awards: from Romanian American University: Special Academic Merit; Laudatio by Rector Prof.Dr.Ovidiu Folcut/Dean of the Faculty of European Economic Studies and Faculty of Management-MarketingProf.Dr.Alexandru Ionescu University MF Carol Davila: Diploma of Excellence; Laudatio by Rector Prof. Dr. Florian Popa The Senate of Romanian Scientific Management Society: Honorary Member; Laudatio by President Prof. Dr. Constantin Rosca Romanian Distribution Committee: Honorary Member; Laudatio by President Prof.Dr. Theodor Purcarea In 2012 within the framework of the International Year of Cooperatives declared by the General Assembly of the UN - the Republic of Moldova awarded Prof.Dr.Hallier the title "Honorary Member of the Moldavian Academic Cooperative Community". In 2013 Hallier became Adjunct Professor at Vitez University in Bosnia-Herzogewina. Together with Circle International he is establishing double diploma via Distance Learning. In 2016 he got awarded in Mumbai/India by the Retail Leadership Award for India and Africa. In 2017 he helped to organize the First African Congress against Food Losses and Food Waste in Nairobi / Kenya His publications cover themes of macro-economics as well a micro-economics especially in trade, but he also covers the intertwine between commerce and culture. His book "Culture and History of Commerce" is published in the German, Korean, and Russian tongue. The Chinese version is under preparation. His book "EuroShop" (German/English) became an international standard for shopfitting and was translated into Russian with the title "Modern stores. A history of technical development".

Yuhilza Hanum is the Assistant to the Director of Postgraduate program of Social and Cultural Magister, Gunadarma University, Indonesia. Her research interest includes industrial economics, small and medium enterprises, and e-government. Her undergraduate and graduate studies in Applied Physics and Computer Science is the reason behind her research methods. Email: yuhilza@staff.gunadarma.ac.id.

Divya Jain graduated from Sharda University and currently pursuing MBA from the same university. She has two months working experience in Blinkit company in CRM department. She has also done B.com. from school of open learning, Delhi University.

Narentheren Kaliappen is a Senior Lecturer at the School of International Studies, College of Law, Government International Studies, Universiti Utara Malaysia (UUM). He holds a PhD, MBA and BBA from UUM. He was conferred Distinguish Doctoral Dissertation Award by Academy for Global Business Advancement (based in the United States at AGBA conference 2015 for PhD thesis. He also published quite a number of WoS and Scopus indexed journals, including Emerald, Inderscience and Sage publications in the field of business management in addition to presenting several papers at local and international conferences. "Match Your Strategies for Brilliant Performance" and "Strategy Execution for Performance Excellence" are the latest books of the author. Notably, he received 2016 Emerald Literati Awards for Excellence for the paper entitled "Innovation strategies and performance are they truly linked". He received Best Teacher Award and Young Faculty Award in 2019. He has been constantly invited to deliver speeches in Vietnam, Singapore, Bahrain, Tunisia and conduct workshops in Malaysia, Thailand, India and Australia.

Lee Kean Yew was born in Kuala Lumpur, Malaysia. Prior to completing his PhD in Economics and Administration at Asia-Europe Institute, University Malaya, he is a academic director of Centre for Malaysia Chinese Studies undertakes scholarly work on Malaysia with special focus on the Chinese community and publishes its findings in books, conference proceedings or its bilingual journal. At the same time, he has been promoted as one of the associate researchers and associate members at both Department of Chinese Studies and Malaysian Chinese Research Centre (MCRC), University of Malaya by focusing in the research of overseas Chinese business and cultural studies. One of his job tasks is to promote mutual understanding and communication to tap the potential for cooperation between Malaysian Chinese and overseas companies. His research interests include entrepreneurial economics, innovation management, Chinese business studies, Asian ethnicity and development studies. His aim is to promote the interactions between Malaysian firms and governments, foster closer links among Malaysian and international business, thus contributing to the overall development of Malaysian-European or Malaysian-China economic and trade relations. He joined the International Council of Small Business (ICSB) since last year to promote the growth and development of small businesses in Malaysia. He has published more than 50 articles in the high impact ISI/SSCI/AHCI/SCOPUS indexing journal such as Asian Economic Papers, China Report, Journal of Asia Pacific Economy, Journal of Asian Business Studies, Journal of Contemporary Asia and South East Asia Journal. One of his masterpiece entitled: "Tacit knowledge innovation and enterprise development in Chinese family SMEs of Malaysia: Longitudinal case studies on plastic production across generational change" has won the best thesis award recognised by Taiwan Management Institute.

Trang Ngoc Thuy Le is PhD student in finance, Tomas Bata University, Czech Republic.

E. S. Margianti is a professor in Economy of Gunadarma University, Jakarta Indonesia. She is a senior lecturer and researcher in economics and management. She is the rector of Gunadarma University. Along with her duty as a rector to a big private university, she also advises doctoral program students. She publishes papers on business, information systems, marketing, and consumer behaviour topics in a reputed international journal.

Misdiyono is an associate professor in Economy. He riches with teaching experience in economy subjects for undergraduate since 1994, graduate since 2008, and postgraduate students since 2008. He supervises master student in economy field and co-supervise doctoral students in economy field. His research interests are financial, stock exchange, banking, and other financial related.

Sri Murtiasih is an assistant professor in Economy. She teaches and supervises undergraduate and graduate students since 1994 in economy field. Her research interests are consumer behavior, marketing, and brand equity.

Henrietta Nagy is a professor of Milton Friedman University, Hungary. She has been working in higher education for over 20 years. Her main research fields are regional policy, rural development, local economic development, HR aspects of territorial development. She has over 240 publications, including 70 journal articles in high ranked journals. She has 20 publications in Scopus and has over 950 citations.

Violena Hubenova Nencheva, Ph.D. studied my bachelor degree in Finance in Sofia, Bulgaria, in the University of National and World Economy. After that, she studied a master degree in International Business in the University of Dauphine, Paris, France. She returned to Bulgaria to study a second master and a PhD in Business economy and Marketing in the University of National and World Economy. Now, she is working as teaching professor in the Autonomous University of Queretaro, Mexico.

Suu Duy Nguyen is a lecturer in TDTU My research focus on banking and corporate finance.

Izabella Oláh, MATE, is an associate professor, economic consultant and agricultural entrepreneur. She obtained a scientific degree in the field of regional sciences, by examining small villages, hamlets and pigmy villages and their local economic development opportunities. As a research and innovation manager, economic agricultural engineer and German translator, she began to familiar with the issues of agile managers in the digital age. In her current research topics examine the role and value creation of family businesses in the local economy, the complex challenges related to generational change, as well as the solution options and long-term directions for the current challenges of digital agriculture.

Chandra Padmini is a senior scientist in Sri Lanka Council for Agricultural Research Policy, Sri Lanka.

Vilani Sachitra is a senior lecturer attached to the Department of Commerce, University of Sri Jayewardenepura, Sri Lanka. She obtained Ph.D. in the area of Business Management at the Management Science University, Malaysia. International finance, research methodology and operation research are the main teaching areas. Her research interest is mainly on international competitiveness, agribusiness, small and family business and capability approach. Currently, she has published fifty indexed journal articles, forty-two conference papers, two books, three text books and three book chapters. She has already awarded three research awards for her publications and outstanding reviewer award 2020 from Emerald Publishing.

Sudaryanto is an associate professor at Gunadarma University. He is a senior lecture and researcher in economics and management. His research interest is in industrial management and others management. He publishes papers in national and international repute journals.

Sangeeta Tripathi is an Assistant Professor of Mass Communication at the University of Technology and Applied Sciences, Oman, previously associated with the Institute of Management Studies, Noida, India. She has completed her education at Banaras Hindu University. She attended Oxford Summer Policy School, in London, in 2019. She was awarded UN Gold Ambassador Award in March 2022 for her cooperation with UN SDG-05. Recently she has been working on two funded projects approved by Ministry of Higher Education, Research and Innovation, Oman. The project titles are “Advance Communication Role in Creating Consensus and Acceptability for Innovative Tourism to Support Diversified Economy Drive in The Sultanate” and “Digital Citizenship among Young Omani Students: Towards Developing a New Digital Citizenship Framework.”

Kanchana Wijayawardena is a passionate and ambitious academic with a commendable teaching track record and a solid research background. During her 14 years of teaching at leading higher education institutes in Sri Lanka and Australia, she has built up a wealth of academic expertise in the fields of Human Resources Management and Personal and Professional Growth and Empowerment.

Index

R

S

T

W

X

Ensure Quality Research is Introduced to the Academic Community

Become an Evaluator for IGI Global Authored Book Projects

The overall success of an authored book project is dependent on quality and timely manuscript evaluations.

Applications and Inquiries may be sent to:
development@igi-global.com

Applicants must have a doctorate (or equivalent degree) as well as publishing, research, and reviewing experience. Authored Book Evaluators are appointed for one-year terms and are expected to complete at least three evaluations per term. Upon successful completion of this term, evaluators can be considered for an additional term.

If you have a colleague that may be interested in this opportunity, we encourage you to share this information with them.

www.ingramcontent.com/pod-product-compliance
Lightning Source LLC
LaVergne TN
LVHW081340300926
849161LV00008B/2027
9781668473948